NORTHERN CARTOGRAPHIC'S

VERMONT CROSS-COUNTRY SKI ATLAS

A Guide to the State's Ski Touring Centers

Edited and Compiled By: STEVE BUSHEY

northern Cartographic

Northern Cartographic, Inc., located in Burlington, Vermont, specializes in contract thematic mapping. In addition to providing custom cartographic service, the company also publishes a variety of products focused on New England, which are available for purchase by the public. Direct all inquiries to:

Northern Cartographic, Inc.
P.O. Box 133
Burlington, Vermont 05402
Phone: (802) 862-0074

Permission to reproduce, in any form, any part of the material in this publication requires prior written approval of the publisher.

Library of Congress Card Catalog Number 83-062994

ISBN 0-9606738-5-7

Copyright © 1983 by Northern Cartographic, Inc.

Printed by Villanti and Sons, South Burlington, Vt.

Cover photo by George A. Robinson, Jericho, Vt.

Acknowledgments

The producers of this Atlas wish to acknowledge the generous cooperation of the ski touring operators whose centers are featured in the pages which follow. In addition we would like to express our gratitude to Carol McAdam and Kerry Duame for their help in the text composition; Alex and Phyllis Rose for their encouragement of our work; Roy Feldman for his special support; and Loretta Bushey for her assistance with our transportation needs. We are grateful for the cooperation of the Vermont Travel Division through the person of Gregory Gerdel. Finally, we owe a special word of thanks to John Wiggins, John Tidd and Rob Center of VSTOA for their cogent suggestions and enthusiastic support of our research efforts.

                Steve Bushey
                Edward Antczak
                Peter Shea

                            Cartographic Assistants
                            Steven Farrow
                            Christie Most

Table of Contents

Introduction 7

Vermont Major Routes (Map) 12

Vermont Ski Touring Centers (Map) 13

Legend 14

Northern Vermont 15

Central Vermont 51

Southern Vermont 83

Additional Skiing Information 106

Epilogue 108

Bibliography 109

Index 110

Introduction

Before being transplanted to North America in the nineteenth century cross-country skiing had enjoyed more than a 4,000 year history. Originating in Scandinavia, skiing was less a sport and more a means of accomplishing utilitarian ends in Northern Europe's winter snowbound countries. During long months of snow cover, skis were often the most practical means of travelling village to village, a deadly tool for hunters and a decisive device for rapidly deploying military troops in winter time.

Skis started appearing in North America along with the Scandinavian immigrants in the nineteenth century. "Snowshoe" Thompson began mail runs in 1856 on skis over the Sierra Nevada between Plaurville, California and Carson Valley, Nevada, travelling 90 miles between towns. By 1900, Montreal, Ottawa, and Toronto had become important centers of skiing in Canada. In Montreal, at dusk, skiers could be seen telemarking down the slopes of Mont Royal, gliding home along snow-packed streets, passing sleighs and dodging horse droppings.

Since the turn of the century, skiing in Vermont had a distinguished history. Before the development and rapid spread of mechanical liftlines for alpine skiing in the 1930's, Vermont's quiet snow-covered villages had become havens for the city worn, who were drawn to the hills by the charm of sleigh filled streets and the healthy recreation of "ski running," skating and other winter sports.

The rage of downhill skiing overshadowed cross-country skiing before and after World War II. It was not until the 1960's that cross-country skiing came of age in the Green Mountain State. Many people began to recognize what a few had known—that touring near historic villages, skiing through valleys beside swelling hills and along the shores of ice-locked ponds was a recreation nonpareil. An outburst of interest in the sport saw the opening of Vermont's, indeed North America's, first ski touring centers. Presently the Vermont Travel Division lists sixty* ski touring centers in the state. Even by the most conservative of estimates (which would include our own) there are more than forty active centers.

Not only is Vermont "the snowplace of New England," but it is the "skiplace" as well. To understand the Green Mountain State's significance in the Alpine and Nordic skiing world one must appreciate its climatic and topographic endowment. Sandwiched between Vermont's borders, from the broad expanses of Lake Champlain in the west to the Connecticut River Valley in the east, is a succession of rolling hills, piedmont and mountain range. Except in the river valleys there are few flat spots. The main range of the Green Mountains rises to 4,000 feet

*see page 106 for further information.

and intercepts the storm systems which routinely track through the state. The result is heavy snowfalls.

With winter's bounty and its expansive area of highland topography, Vermont has achieved a standard of Nordic and Alpine skiing far out of proportion to its modest size and population. The University of Vermont and Middlebury College are annual competitors for the N.C.A.A. Championships. The state fosters internationally ranked skiers who have contributed significantly in America's quest for Olympic ski medals. In 1976, Bill Koch of Guilford stunned the Nordic Ski world with his Olympic silver medal victory.

In keeping with what is a Vermont tradition of excellence, the state's ski touring centers have come to provide the highest levels of quality to the consumer. While skiing "out one's back door" is enjoyable and the experience of a wilderness trek may be personally enriching, the modern Vermont touring center offers the skier a number of competitive advantages. The foundation and pride of a ski touring center is its trail system, a thoughtfully planned network designed for the pleasure and safety of the skier. Field and woodland trails are routinely maintained minimizing the hazards of overgrown brush, allowing the skier greater speed and distance.

Trail management has become a winter art at Vermont centers where trails are mechanically set with a track sled and snow machine. Many Vermont centers use trail grooming equipment that cost in the tens of thousands of dollars to compact, grade, condition, powder and retrack trails that offer less than optimal skiing conditions.

In some cases intensive snow management can extend the ski season. One central Vermont touring center has been blowing snow with guns now for several years to start the season a bit earlier. Some centers actually plow snow off a frozen pond, relocate it along the pond's edge, then pack and track it, competing for the prestige of early season skiing.

Of course, one of the best things about many Vermont centers is that when you are done skiing, the day does not have to end. These areas offer a wide range of services from dining and drinking to steaming hot tubs that only serve to enhance the day's pleasures.

This Atlas represents a contemporary sampling of more than forty ski touring centers in Vermont. It is hoped it will be used as a matchmaker between the prospective skier and some of the finest ski touring centers in the country. The Atlas has been designed to provide critical information about each ski area in the belief that it will reduce the sometime frustrating process of mailing and awaiting additional information concerning trails and facilities. The work has been based on the understanding that every skier is different in ability and desires, and th

knowledge that every ski area in Vermont will offer something exceptionally unique.
  The ski touring centers presented in this edition were found to fulfill certain minimum criteria. The selection process was governed by the desire to present the public with a catalogue of areas that make it their business to bring you good skiing. The featured ski centers which follow will be able to provide the skier with:
  1) A well cared for trail network, with a cumulative total of 20 or more kilometers of track.
  2) A staff in attendance during the area's operating hours to attend to your skiing needs.
  3) A varied mix of services that might include on premises: lodging, dining, a sales shop, ski rentals, etc.
  4) A central, sizable, heated room or ski lodge reserved or allocated for friendly skier congregations.
  The trail maps were compiled from a variety of sources. In every case the single most important source was the center's own trail map. Such eclectic origins have resulted in variation in the information portrayed from map to map. The reader is also cautioned to be aware of radical changes in scale which may occur from page to page and to view each map independently. The featured centers of this Atlas unanimously produce maps, most of which are more detailed, for use *on trail.* Our own maps are intended less for trail use than to present an overview of a center's network and to convey something of the character of an area. After some futile experimentation, the trail ratings (easy, more difficult, most difficult) were arrived at by a "self-report method" with each center providing its own estimation of trail difficulty.
  The critical reader may note that we have taken some liberty in varying the units on the map scales. The purpose of the regional locator maps is to guide the traveler along the highways. The scale in these maps is expressed in *miles* to allow corroboration with most car odometers and most Vermonters—who, contrary to the "you can't get there from here" myth, are more than happy to be of friendly assistance to anyone who asks. In those trail maps that are drawn to a scale, it is expressed in *kilometers.* The use of metric distances in cross-country skiing has become commonplace. For the benefit of the newcomer, a kilometer is a little over a half (.62) mile.
  Also for the benefit of the newcomer we will risk repeating a number of rules that are followed by all skiers. These rules are largely common sense and courtesy, but will be restated hoping that they will further protect the environment, that they will minimize trail conflicts between skiers and that they will preserve the integrity of private property over

which many trails are routed. Observance of these rules contributes to a better skiing experience for all.

1) *Do not litter.* Some people even have the energy to carry out other peoples trash if they stray upon it.
2) *Leave dogs at home.* Dogs place holes in the ski trail, harass skiers, urinate on trails. They may also chase deer through the woods for miles; under similar circumstances dogs have been shot in Vermont.
3) *Skiers pass each other by yelling "Track."* Upon hearing this command, the slower skier, the one in front, is expected to temporarily ski off the trail until the other passes.
4) When a *fall* occurs, the skier is expected to remove himself from the track as soon as possible to prevent any other collisions and promptly *fill in* his *sitzmark* or hole.
5) In the case of a multi-tracked trail, skiers are expected to ski on the track right of center.
6) When on a single tracked trail, when two skiers meet, the uphill skier must step off the track and allow the downhill skier the right-of-way.
7) *Do not walk on trails.* Footprints harden into icy holes which destroy good skiing.
8) *Respect all property you ski over.* Whether it is public or private do not strip bark from trees, start fires, trespass onto other's posted land, etc. Many trails exist for your skiing pleasure through the generosity of private land owners.
9) *Ski trails listed on ski center maps are for skiing only,* unless otherwise noted or permission is obtained from the appropriate source for alternative use. This expressly means *no* summer hiking, bike riding, etc., unless noted otherwise.
10) *Respect the judgment of the ski center professionals.* They are the foremost experts on weather and trail conditions. They are most capable of verifying any information concerning their area.
11) *Pay your trail fee.* Good trails demand a lot of human attention, from pre-season brushcutting to snowseason tracksetting late at night. This is expensive. In Vermont, failure to pay legally constitutes theft of services.

Good skiing to all.

TRAIL RATINGS

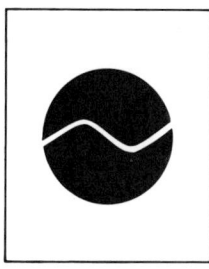 EASIER

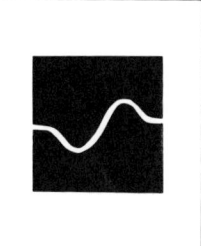 MORE DIFFICULT

 MOST DIFFICULT

Vermont Major Routes

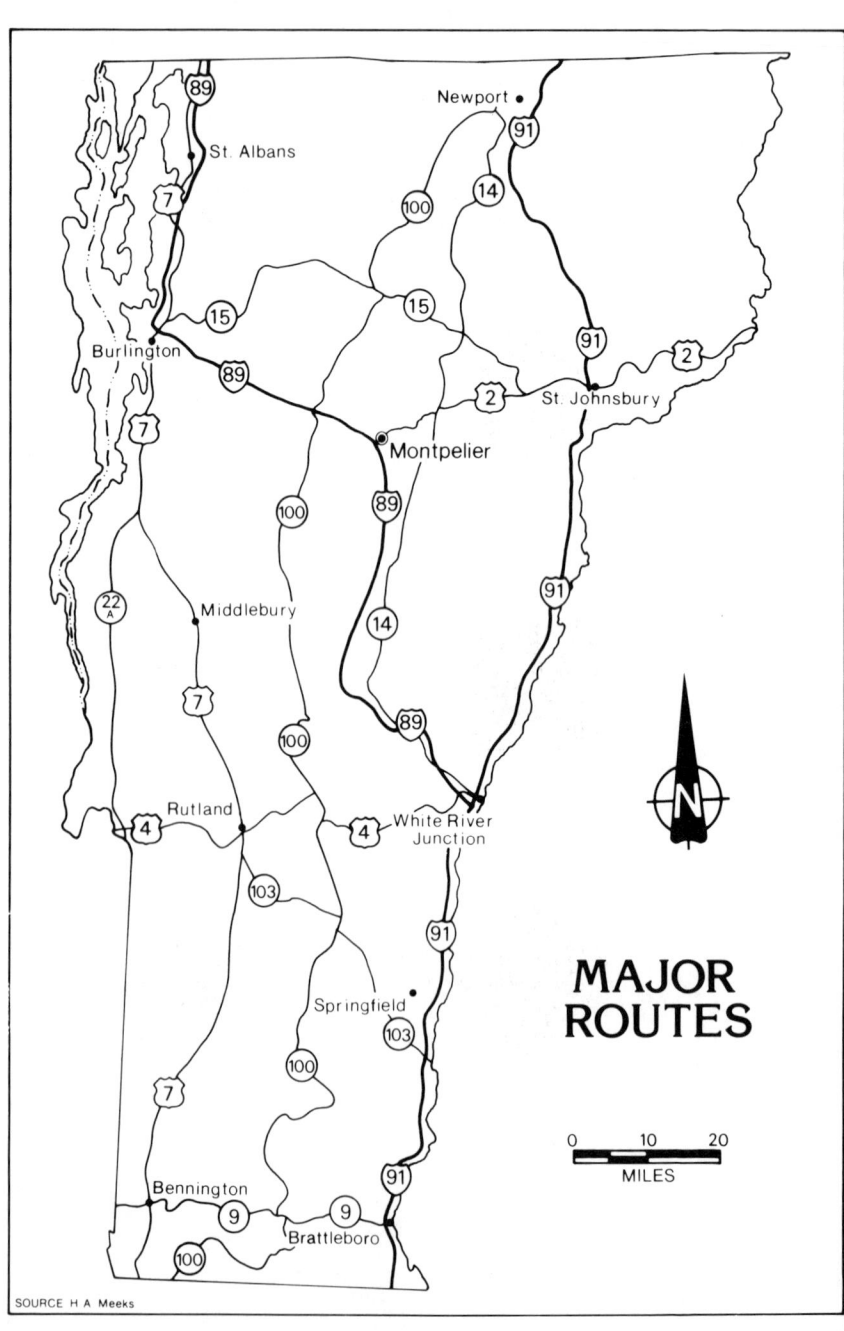

Vermont Ski Touring Centers 13

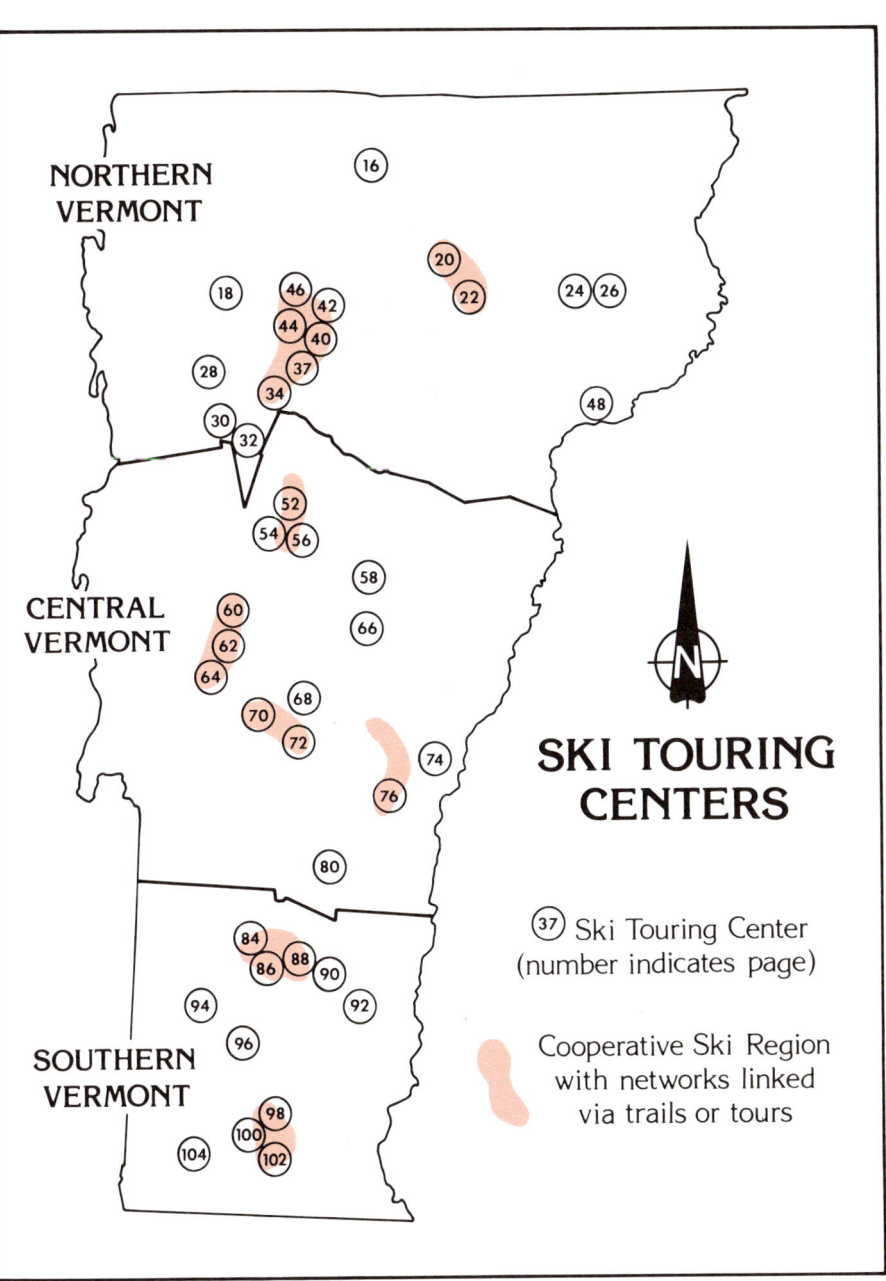

Legend

★ - Ski Touring Center

⎯⎯⎯ - Ski Trail

⎯³⎯ - Number Corresponds to Ski Trail Name List

⎯⎯⎯ - Roads

▪ ▟ - Structures

P, Ⓟ - Parking

〜 - Stream or River

 - Water Body

◌₈₆₂ - Prominent Hill or Mountain (elevations in feet)

TRAIL RATINGS
● Easier
■ More Difficult
◆ Most Difficult

1 km = .62 miles

NORTHERN VERMONT

Hazen's Notch
Ski Touring Center

Montgomery Center, Vt. 05471
Tel. 802-326-4708

Trail Network: 42 km.
Machine Groomed Trail: 30 km.
Hours of Operation: daily, 9:00 a.m. - 4:00 p.m.
Base Elevation: 1,000 ft.
High Trail: 1,680 ft.
Low Trail: 900 ft.

The Hazen's Notch Ski Touring Center is located high above the cozy, Mountain village of Montgomery Center. It sits at the base of the Jay Mountains, which sweep up abruptly from surrounding lowlands, precipitating heavy snows throughout the winter.

An extensive local network of trails allow the adventurous skier the opportunity to ski into and between the rugged walls of Hazen's Notch, or into the village of Montgomery Center. When the day's skiing is over, you can retreat into the warmth of the Ski House and luxuriate beside the Franklin fireplace with a bowl of homemade soup or goulash.

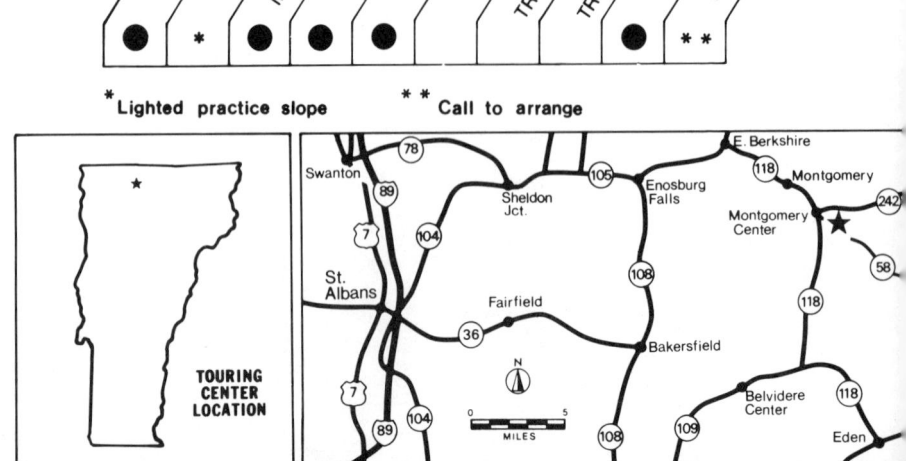

* Lighted practice slope
** Call to arrange

TOURING CENTER LOCATION

Northern Vermont 17

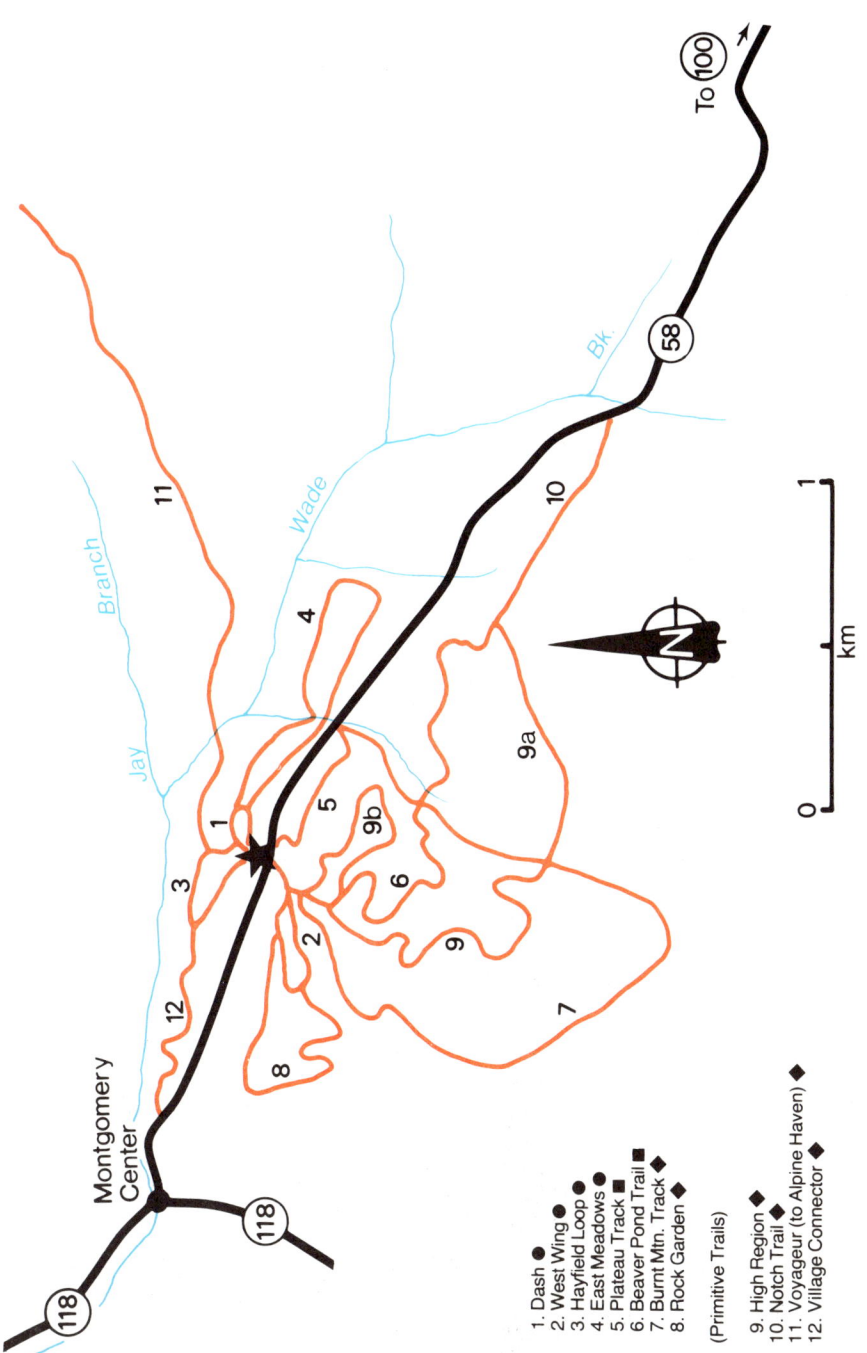

Stark Farm
Ski Touring Center

Route 128
Westford, Vt. 05494
Tel. 802-878-2282

Trail Network: **24** km.
Machine Groomed Trail: **12** km.
Hours of Operation: Sat. & Sun., **9:00** a.m. - **4:00** p.m.
Base Elevation: **500** ft.
High Trail: **700** ft.
Low Trail: **470** ft.

The Stark Farm Ski Touring Center offers versatile terrain for all levels of skiing. You can glide through the open and wooded meadows, almost to the small village of Westford, or strike out for the wooded hills and visit the waterfall and the beaver dams.

Hot spiced cider, hot doughnuts, homemade soup, and bagels are the specialties offered at the refreshment counter. Night touring with Miners' headlamps is available to groups.

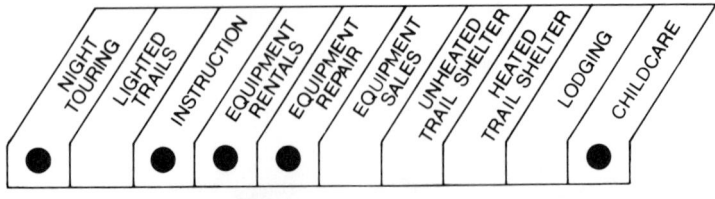

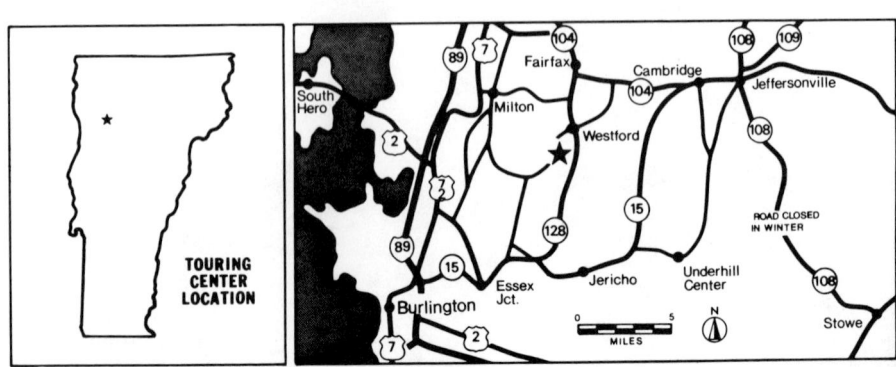

Northern Vermont 19

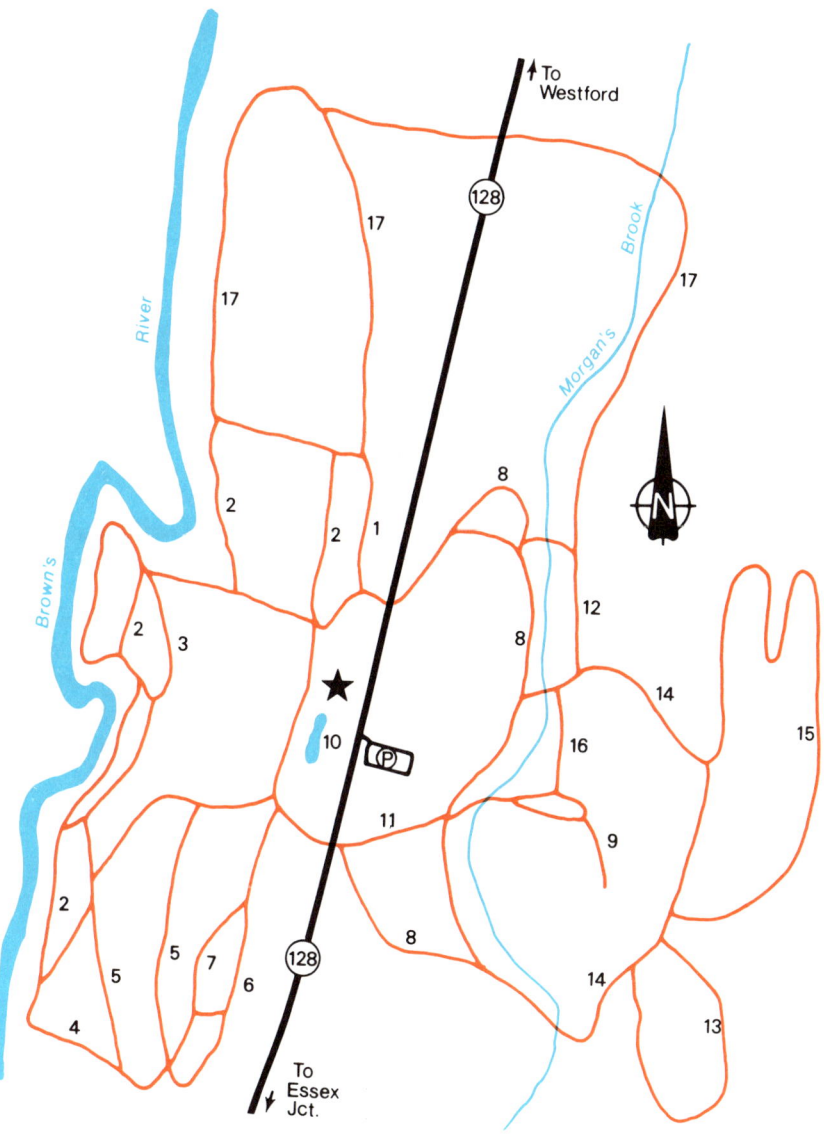

1. Beginner's Haven ●
2. Brown's River Run ●
3. Hogwash Dip ■
4. The Widowmaker ◆
5. Molly Stark Trail ■
6. Hissing Gooseneck ●
7. Night Pasture Trail ●
8. Morgan's Brook Trail ●
9. The Falls ◆
10. Farm Pond ●
11. Beaver Pond Trail ●
12. Little Meadows Trail ●
13. The Challenge ◆
14. Logging Road ■◆
15. Wilderness Trail ■
16. The Chute ■
17. Emily's Empire ●

**Schematic Representation
Map Is Not Drawn To Scale**

Craftsbury Nordic Ski Center

Box 31
Craftsbury Common, Vt. 05827
Tel. 802-586-2514

Trail Network: 50 km.
Machine Groomed Trail: 20 km.
Hours of Operation: daily, 9:00 a.m. - 5:00 p.m.
Base Elevation: 1,100 ft.
High Trail: 1,200 ft
Low Trail: 950 ft.

The Craftsbury Nordic Ski Center maintains its reputation for providing early season skiing by their snow management and collection practices. Once frozen Great Hosmer Pond acts as a giant collection surface. The first snowfalls send the snow collectors and plows into action, pushing even a slight dusting of snow from the center of the pond, outward into large banks by the shore, which are packed and mechanically track set.

The effort expended in creating early skiing allows the Nordic Center the opportunity to specialize in racing instruction, holding several clinics in the Thanksgiving to New Years interval. Anywhere from 6-8 races per winter are open to the "citizen" racer.

The ski tourist will find everything needed at the center, including a well stocked rental shop, lessons, guided tours, sauna, inexpensive accommodations, and meals.

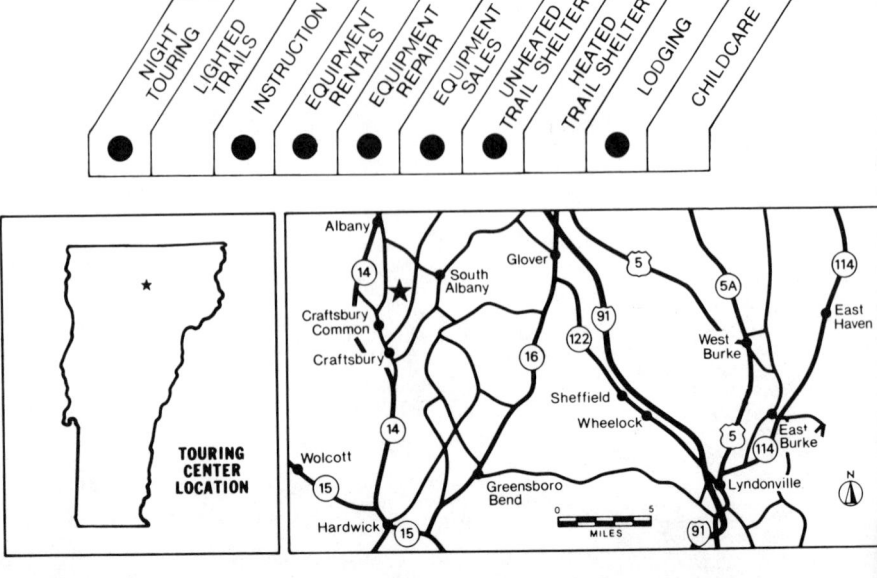

Northern Vermont 21

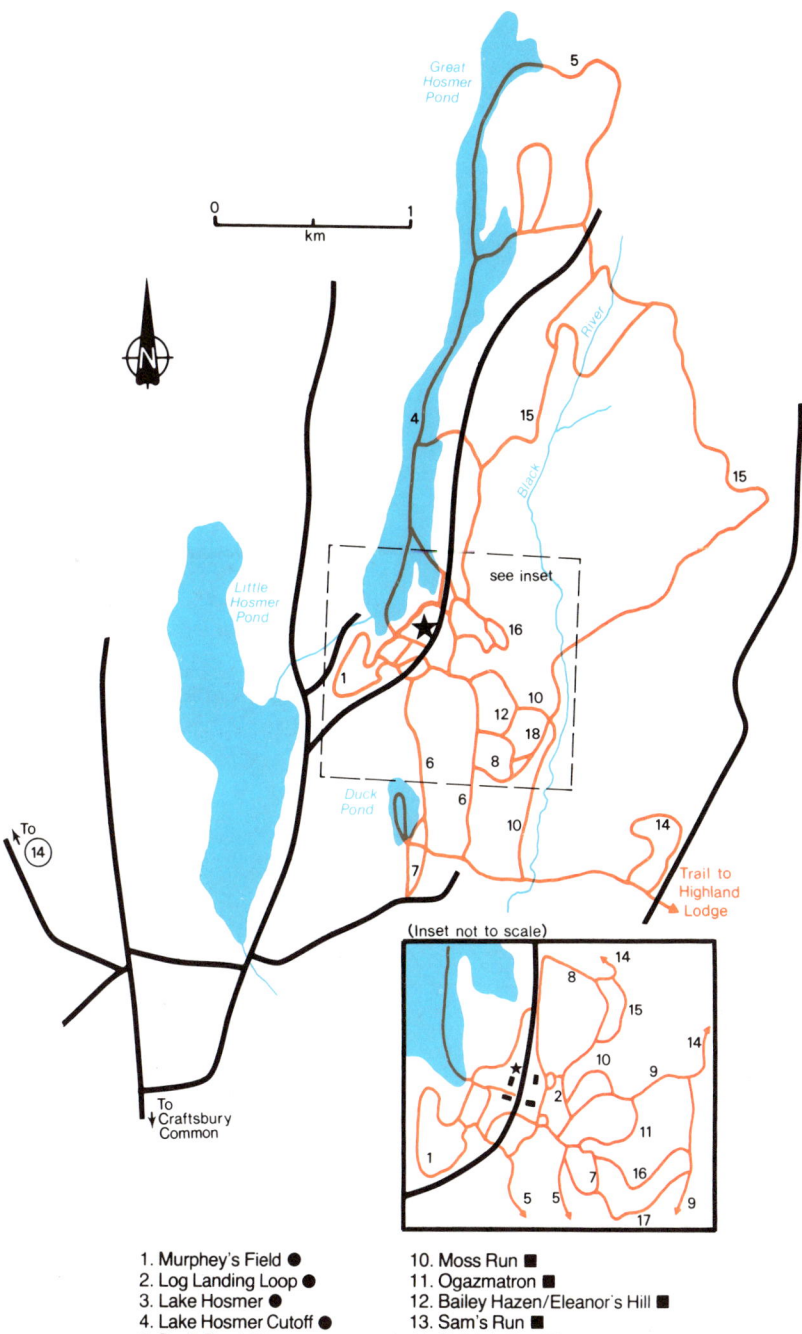

1. Murphey's Field ●
2. Log Landing Loop ●
3. Lake Hosmer ●
4. Lake Hosmer Cutoff ●
5. Duck Pond ■
6. Duck Pond Annex ■
7. Sugarbush ■
8. P.B. & J ■
9. Bailey Hazen Up! ■
10. Moss Run ■
11. Ogazmatron ■
12. Bailey Hazen/Eleanor's Hill ■
13. Sam's Run ■
14. Ruthie's Run ■
15. Screamin Meemie ◆
16. No Sweat ◆
17. World Cup ◆

Highland Lodge

Greensboro, Vt. 05841
Tel. 802-533-2647

Trail Network: 40 km.
Machine Groomed Trail: 30 km.
Hours of Operation: daily, 8:00 a.m. - 5:00 p.m.
Base Elevation: 1,500 ft.
High Trail: 2,120 ft.
Low Trail: 1,500 ft.

The Highland Lodge overlooks the snow covered depths of Caspian Lake, on a hill with a commanding panoramic view. The Lodge is noted for its fine dining and recreation opportunities. For the ultimate in recreation, dining, and drinking pleasures, contact the Lodge about guided inn to inn ski tours that run between the Craftsbury Center for Nordic Skiing, the Inn on the Common in Craftsbury, and the Highland Lodge. The hills, homes and history of the Craftsbury-Greensboro region are the stuff of pleasant dreams.

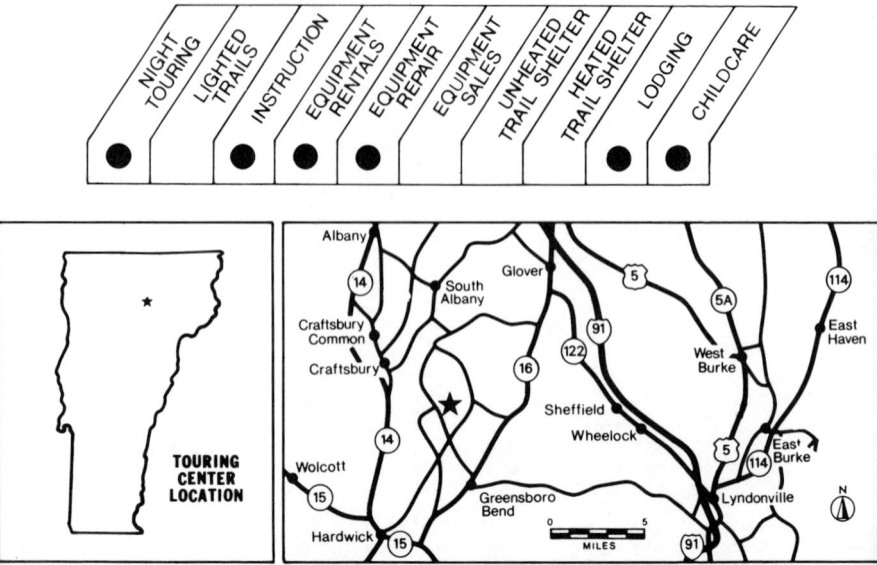

Northern Vermont 23

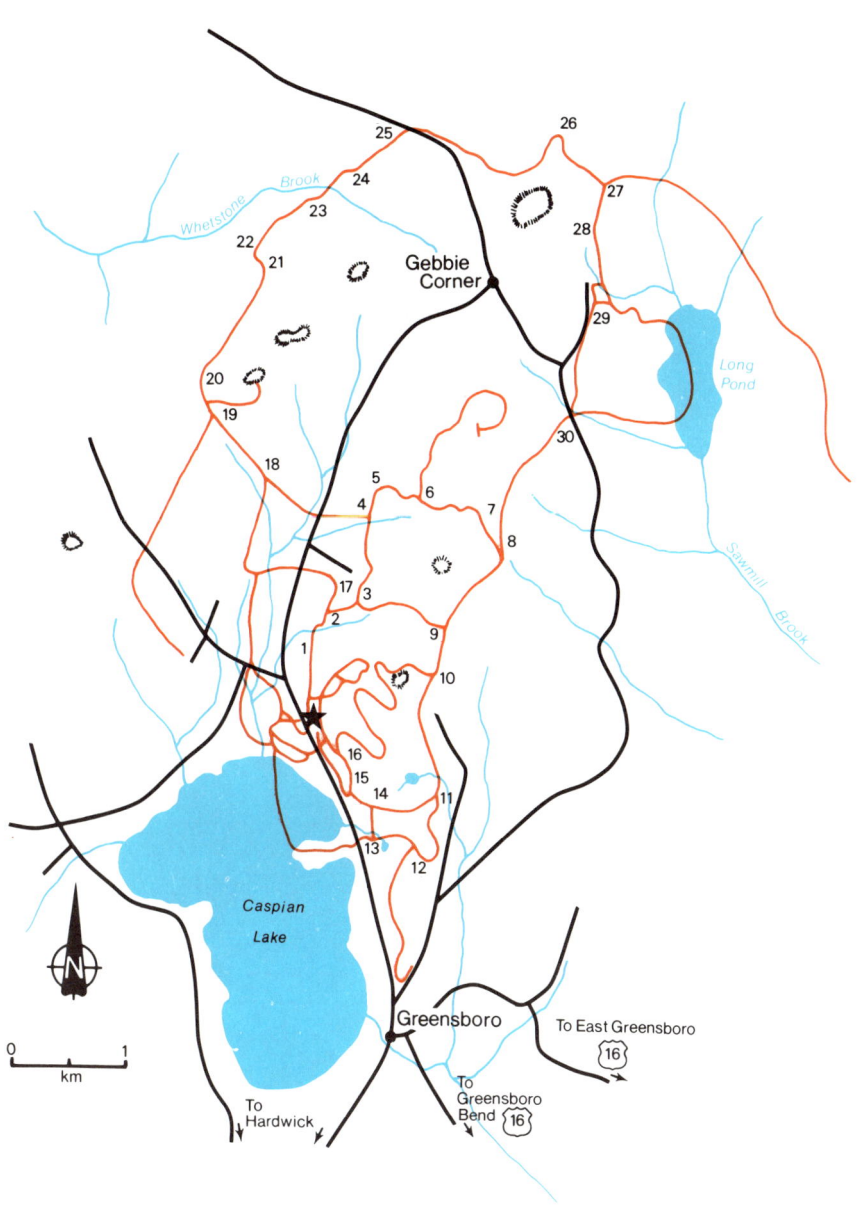

Numbers correspond to signposts

Darion
Ski Touring Center

Box 101
East Burke, Vt. 05832
Tel. 802-626-5914

Trail Network: 40 km.
Machine Groomed Trail: 40 km.
Hours of Operation: daily, 8:00 a.m. - 4:00 p.m.
Base Elevation: 1,100 ft.
High Trail: 1,100 ft.
Low Trail: 800 ft.

It is a well kept secret that some of the finest skiing in New England can be found in the Northeast Kingdom town of East Burke at Darion Ski Touring Center. The trails are expertly groomed and maintained, a trademark of the center. The trails run along the top of Bemis Hill through open meadow and pasture where one is startled at times by the ragged mountains in the distance and the patchwork symmetry of snow covered fields.

The Darion Inn itself is an old manor with many rooms, a restaurant, and tavern. A bunkhouse, converted from a barn, offers spacious suites for groups at reasonable rates.

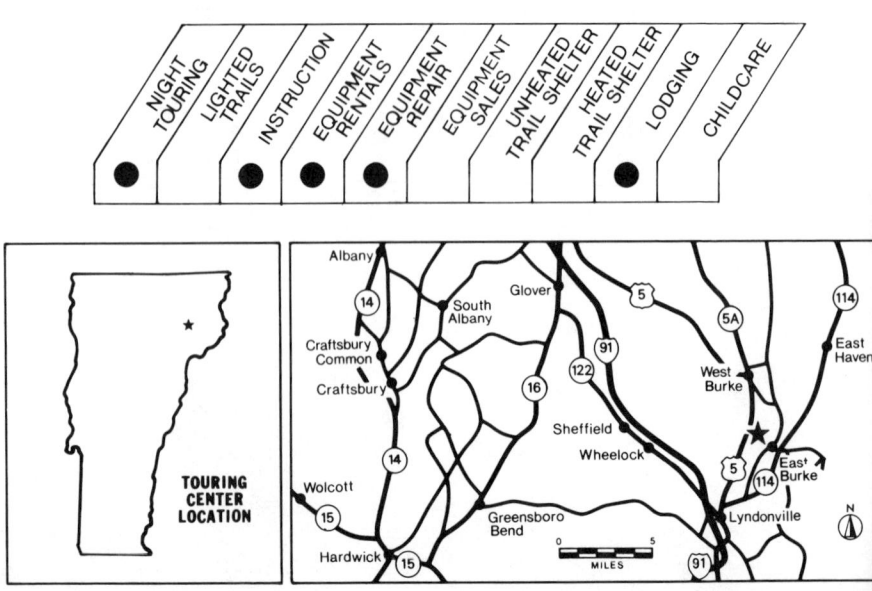

Northern Vermont 25

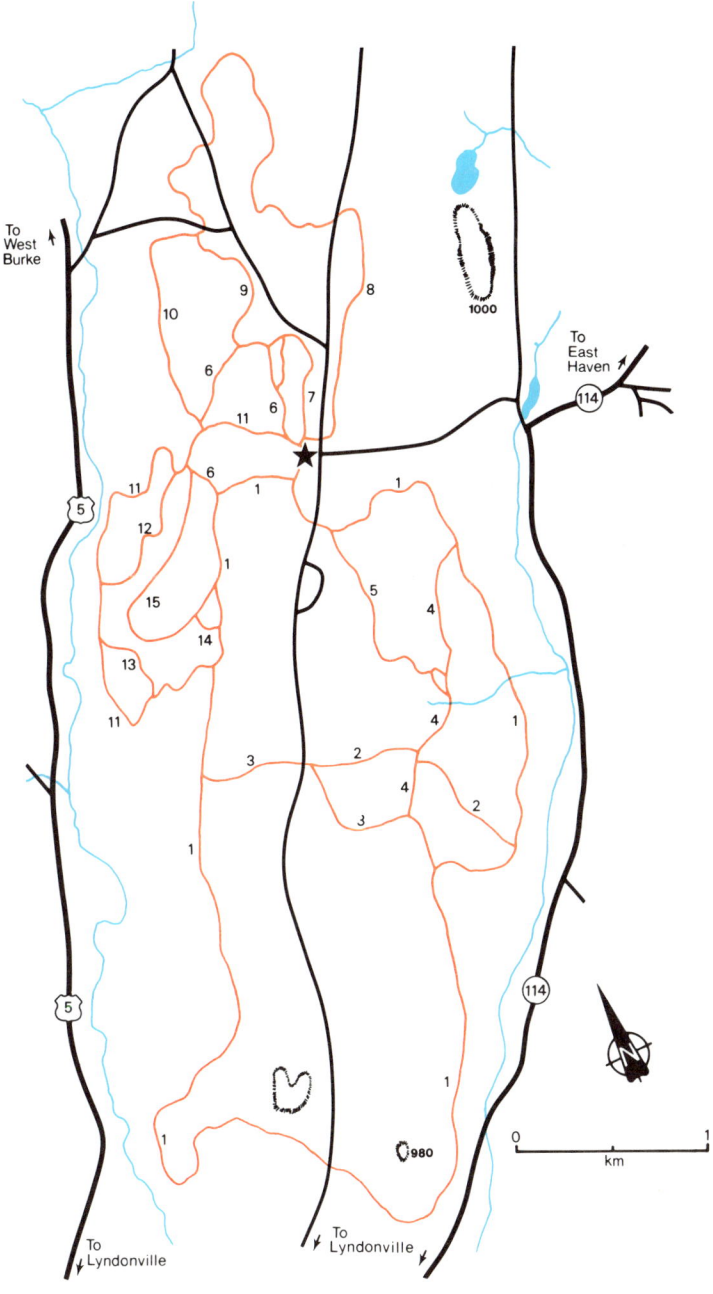

1. Bemis Ridge
2. Connector
3. Fox Run
4. Sugar Woods
5. William West
6. Loop
7. Pandora
8. Willoughby
9. Coronary
10. Bog Meadow
11. River Run
12. Chute
13. Bent's Lane
14. Vixin Loop
15. Penelope

Burke Mountain Ski Touring Center

East Burke, Vt. 05832
Tel. 802-626-8838

Trail Network: 35 km.
Machine Groomed Trail: 15 km.
Hours of Operation: daily. 8:00 a.m. - 4:00 p.m.
Base Elevation: 1,500 ft.
High Trail: 2,100 ft.
Low Trail: 1,400 ft.

The Burke Mt. Touring Center is a small touring center offering the skier a variety of trails with views of the Northeast Kingdom's rugged mountains. Trails twist through an interesting mix of hardwood and softwood forests, along Beaver dams, and through sugarbush. The tracks of wildlife are plentiful and birds abound.

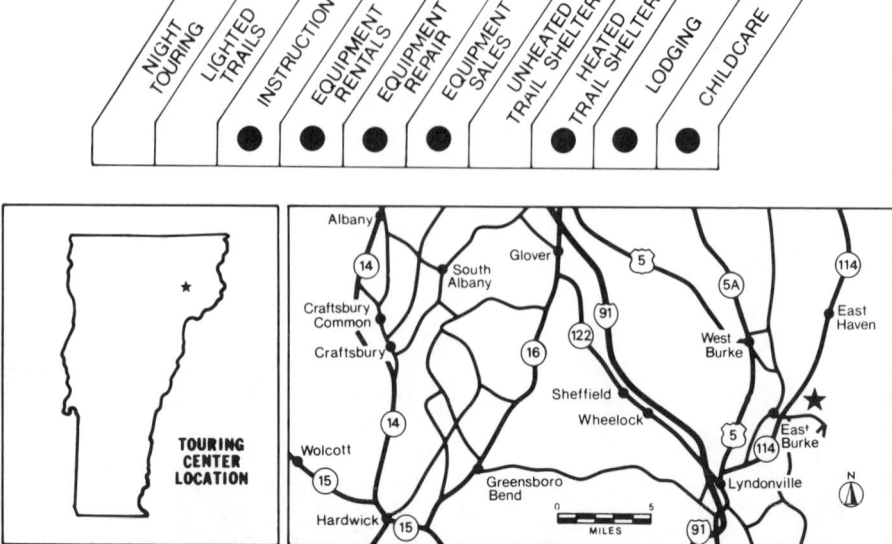

Northern Vermont

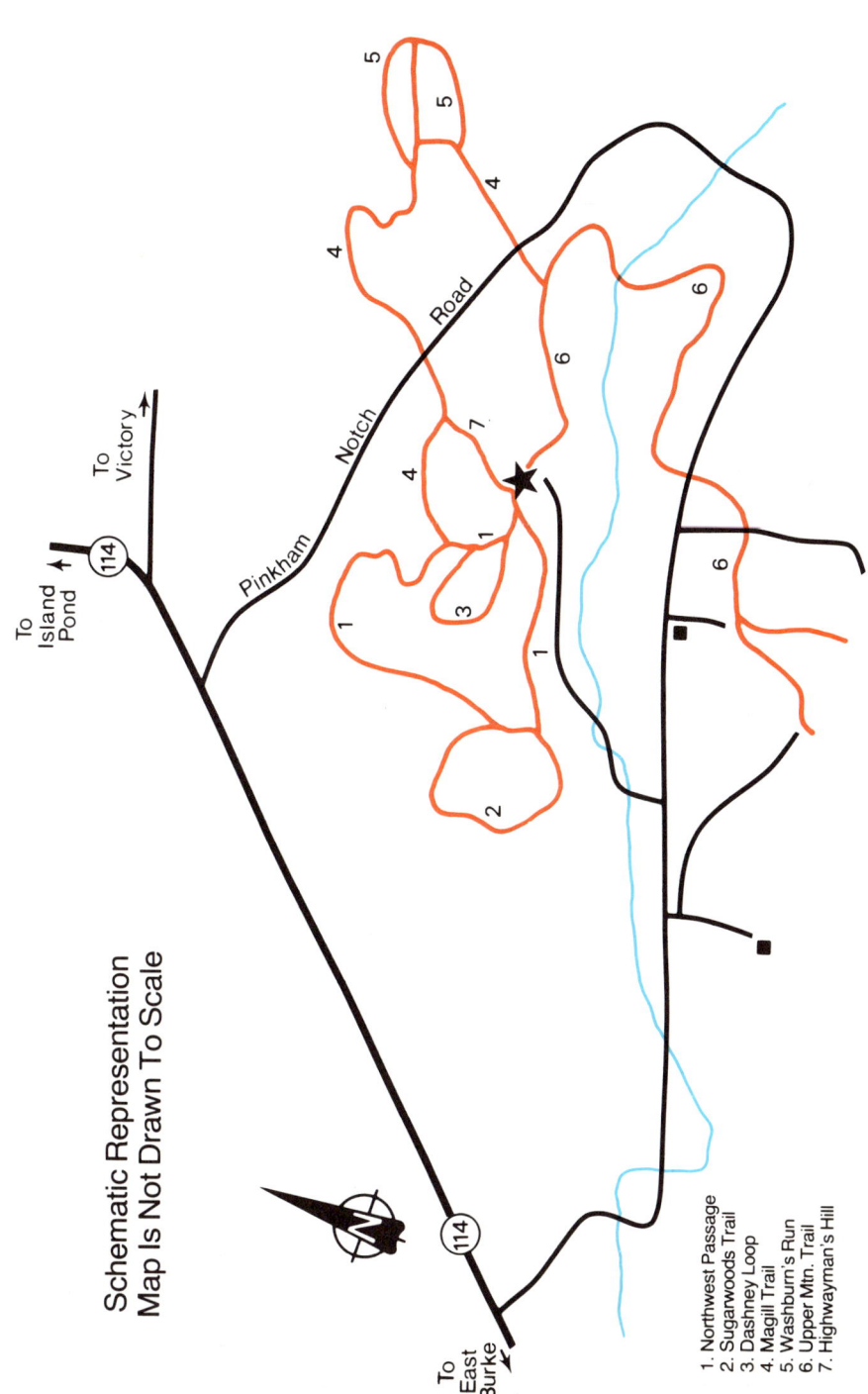

Catamount
Family Center

372 Gov. Chittenden Road
Williston, Vt. 05495
Tel. 802-879-6001

Trail Network: 25 km.
Machine Groomed Trail: 20 km.
Hours of Operation: Sun.-Tues., **9:00** a.m.-**dusk** / Wed.-Sat., **9:00** a.m.-**9:00** p.m.
Base Elevation: 620 ft.
High Trail: 700 ft.
Low Trail: 400 ft.

The Catamount Family Center is situated in the Champlain Valley, a short drive from Burlington. Its trails roll through fields, woods and over hills with fine views of Mt. Mansfield and Camel's Hump in the distance. The Catamount Tavern, located in a large log cabin, is a fine place to relax by the roaring fire after night skiing on Catamount's lit trail. The restaurant adjoining the tavern serves fine home cooking in a very cozy atmosphere.

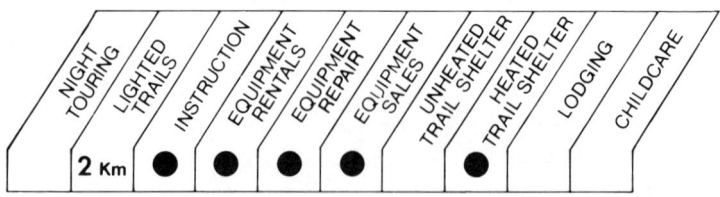

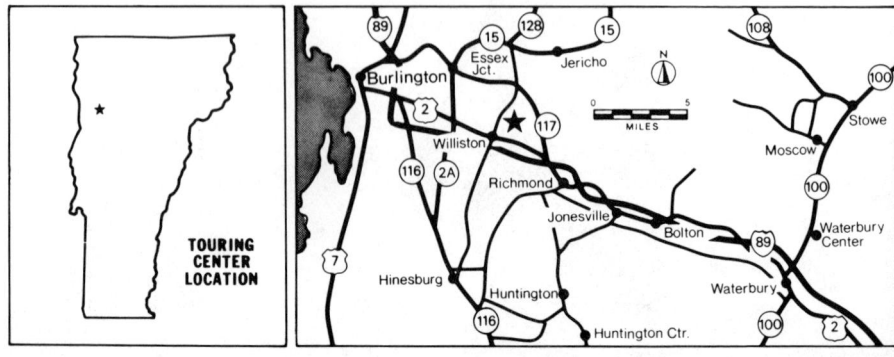

Northern Vermont

29

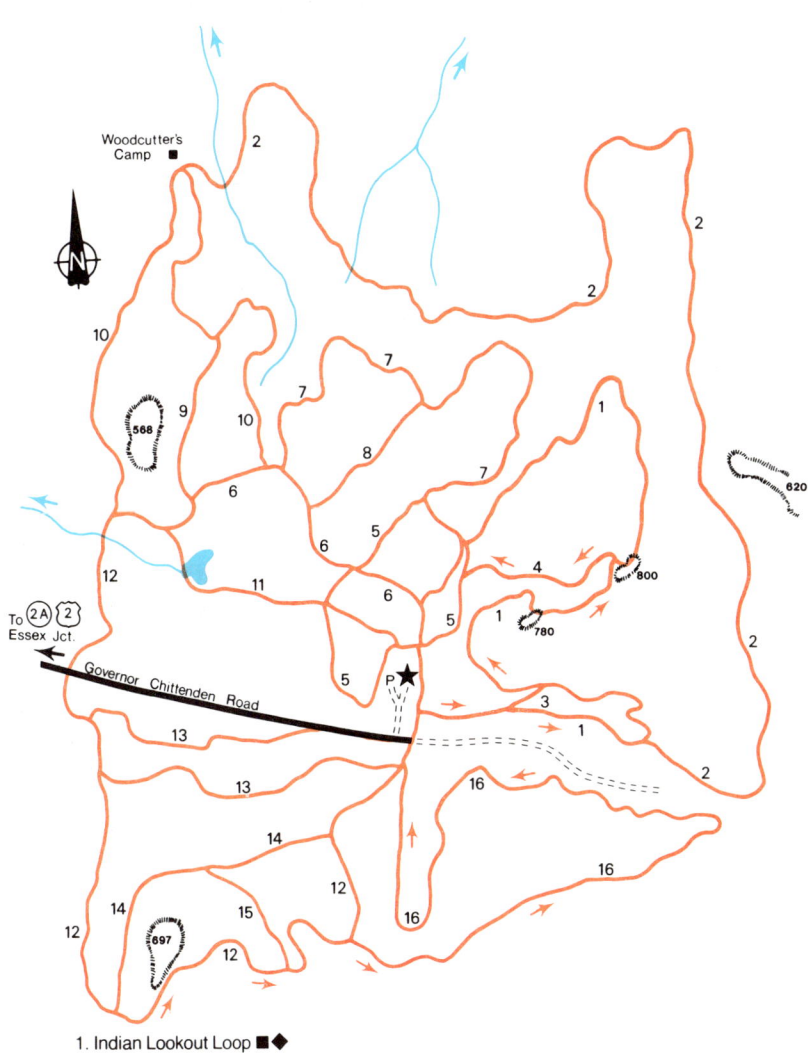

1. Indian Lookout Loop ■◆
2. Northwest Passage ◆
3. Cut OFF ■◆
4. Skidway ◆
5. Nite Trail ■
6. Woods Trace ●
7. 3 Rivers Loop ●
8. Lost Trail ●
9. Ridge Run ◆
10. Sandman's Track ●
11. Beaver Pond Bypass ●
12. Goose Hill Loop ●◆
13. Koch League Trail ●
14. Short Cut ■
15. Ramway ■
16. Race Trail ◆

Schematic Representation
Map Is Not Drawn To Scale

Sherman Hollow

Box 175, RR 1
Richmond, Vt. 05477
Tel. 802-434-2057

Trail Network: 40 km.
Machine Groomed Trail: 40 km.
Hours of Operation: daily, 9:00 a.m. -10:00 p.m.
Base Elevation: 1,000 ft.
High Trail: 1,467 ft.
Low Trail: 900 ft.

Many consider Sherman Hollow the pacesetter in cross-country skiing, with its racing and training programs, and 40 km of impeccably groomed and trackset trail. Their lit 3.5 km night ski trail is a superb example of lighting engineering, reducing glares and dark spots.

Not all is on the fast track at Sherman Hollow. Take a leisurely tour to heated Butternut Lodge with it's majestic views of Camel's Hump, one of Vermont's most photographed mountains. After your ski day is over, take an outdoor hot tub at the Main Lodge, which is serviced by lockers and showers. If your thirst has overcome you, try the Eight Pointer Lounge.

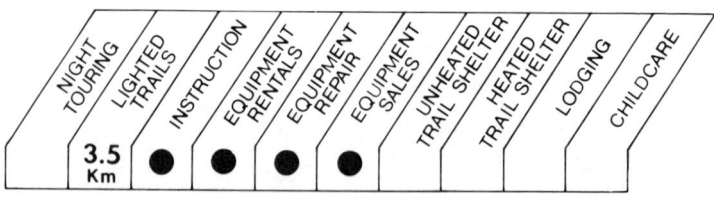

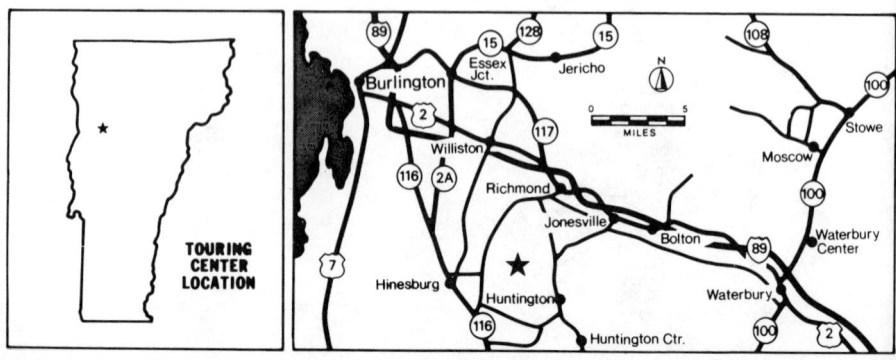

Northern Vermont 31

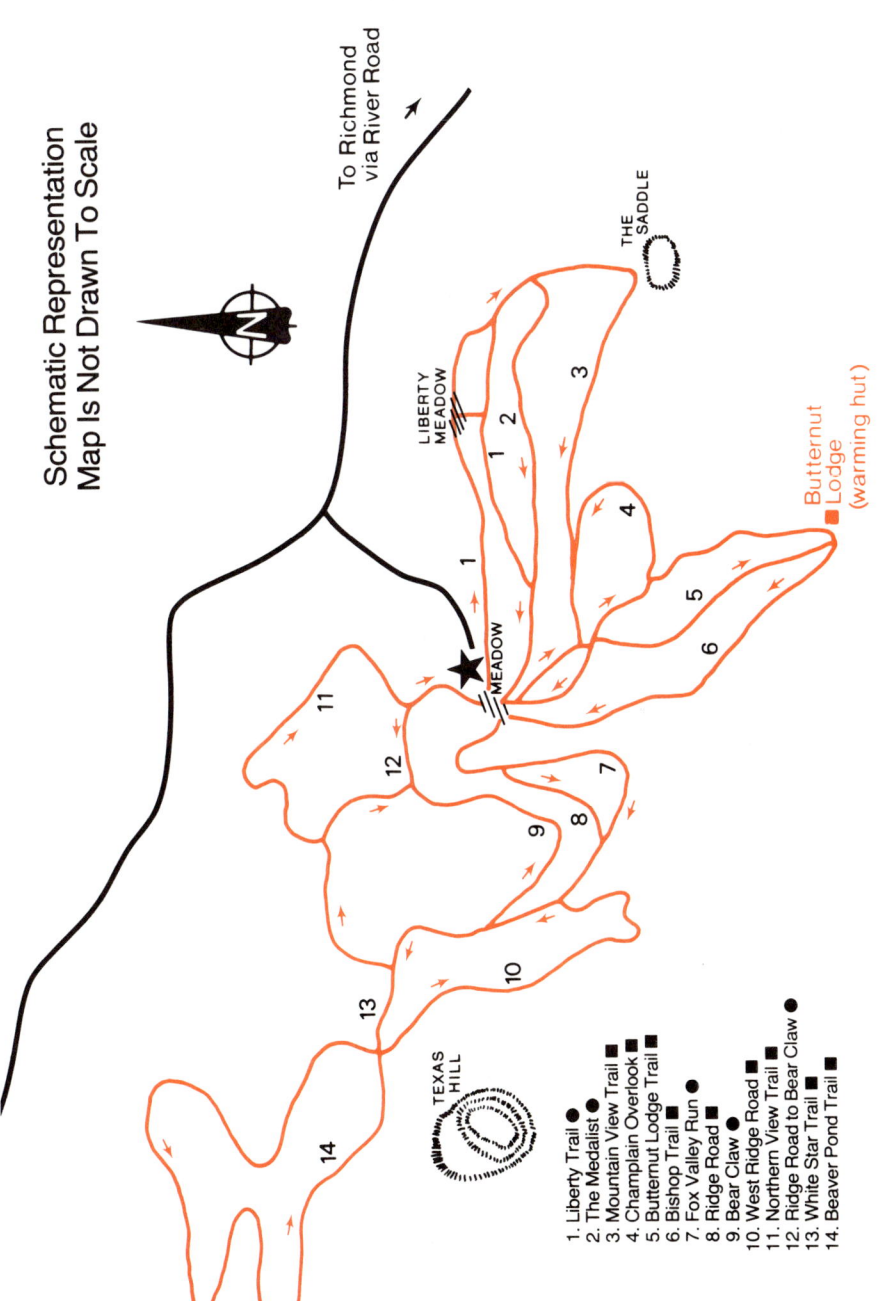

Camel's Hump Nordic Ski Center

Box 99, RD 1
Huntington, Vt. 05462
Tel. 802-434-2704

Trail Network: 50 km.
Machine Groomed Trail: 30 km.
Hours of Operation: Sat., Sun. & holiday weeks, 9:00 a.m. - 5:00 p.m.
Base Elevation: 1,350 ft.
High Trail: 2,300 ft.
Low Trail: 1,100 ft.

Camel's Hump Nordic Ski Center is located at road's end, high in the foothills, on the western slope of its namesake, a dramatic undeveloped 4000 foot peak. The views are breathtaking and the skiing is high alpine. The facilities at Camel's Hump are rustic and modest, including a small ski shop and a warming hut in the barn, which the whole family can enjoy.

For a real downhill thrill, try the Honey Hollow Ski Trail, which climbs to 1900 feet, then drops 1500 feet over 9 km to the Winooski River in Bolton. In the future, look for a network of trail huts for overnight skiers and a cross-country ski route from the Winooski River South, ultimately, to Breadloaf and Blueberry Hill.

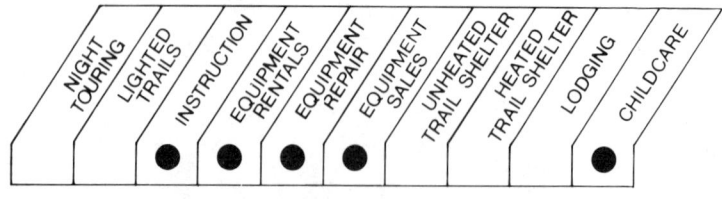

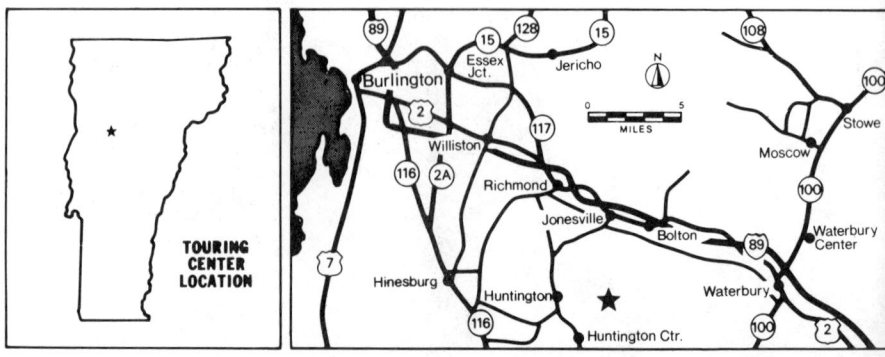

Northern Vermont 33

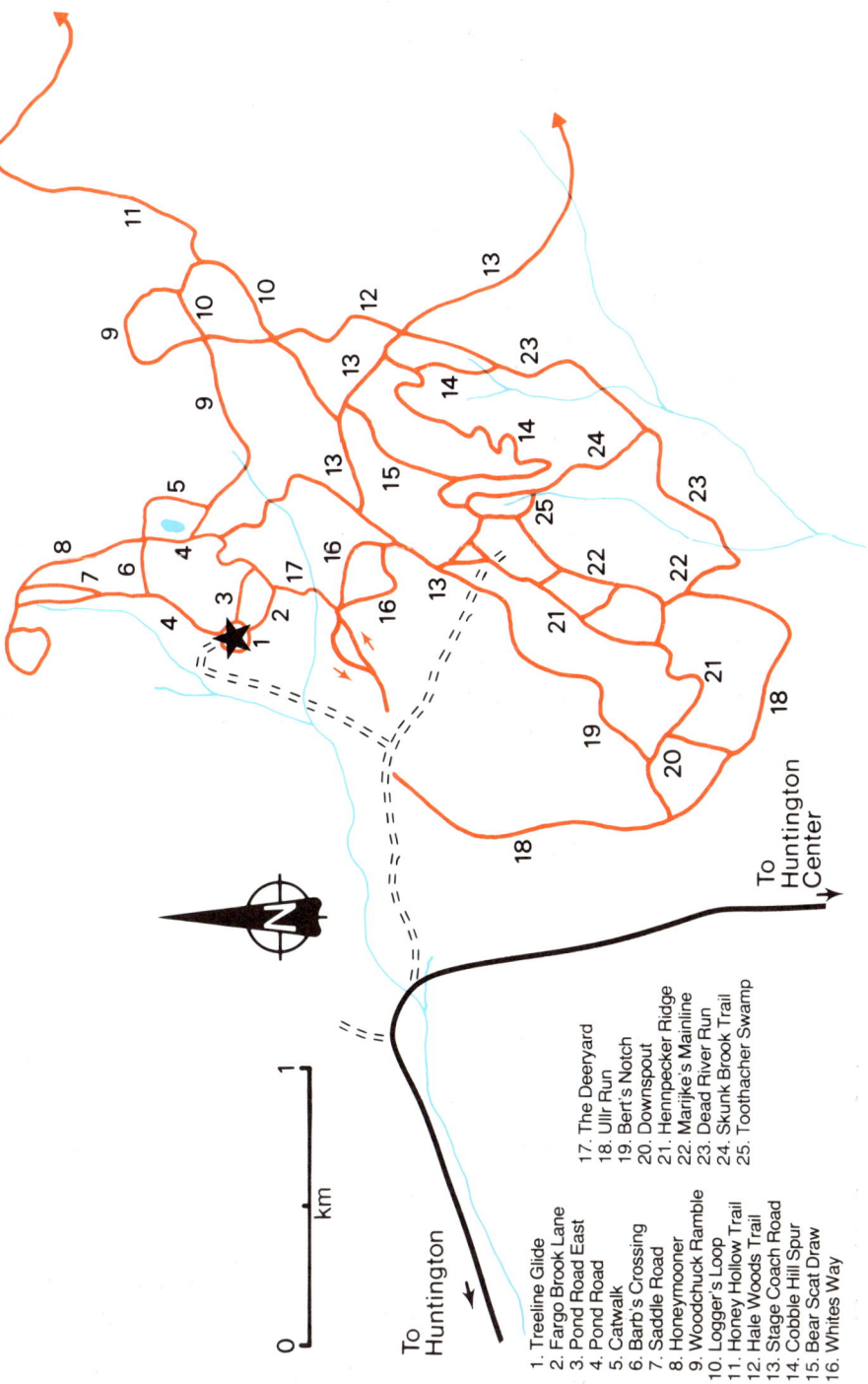

1. Treeline Glide
2. Fargo Brook Lane
3. Pond Road East
4. Pond Road
5. Catwalk
6. Barb's Crossing
7. Saddle Road
8. Honeymooner
9. Woodchuck Ramble
10. Logger's Loop
11. Honey Hollow Trail
12. Hale Woods Trail
13. Stage Coach Road
14. Bear Scat Draw
15. Cobble Hill Spur
16. Whites Way
17. The Deeryard
18. Ullr Run
19. Bert's Notch
20. Downspout
21. Hennpecker Ridge
22. Marijke's Mainline
23. Dead River Run
24. Skunk Brook Trail
25. Toothacher Swamp

Bolton Valley
Cross-Country Center

Bolton, Valley, Vt. 05477
Tel. 802-434-2131

Trail Network: 100 km.
Machine Groomed Trail: 32 km.
Hours of Operation: daily. 8:30 a.m. - 5:00 p.m.
Base Elevation: 2,000 ft.
High Trail: 3,500 ft
Low Trail: 2,000 ft.

Perched at 2,000 feet, between mountains rising upwards of 3,000 feet, the Bolton Valley Ski Touring Center has little flat terrain. Its high elevation results in increased snowpack and an extended ski season. The big operation in the valley is the Alpine Ski Area which allows cross country and Telemark skiers the use of lift lines. Bolton Valley is friendly and small, and an ideal place for "mixed family skiing". A 14 mile wilderness ski trail from Bolton to Trapp Family Ski Touring Center, in Stowe, leads the wilderness skier over high mountains and through quiet forests, a novelty that only experienced skiers should attempt.

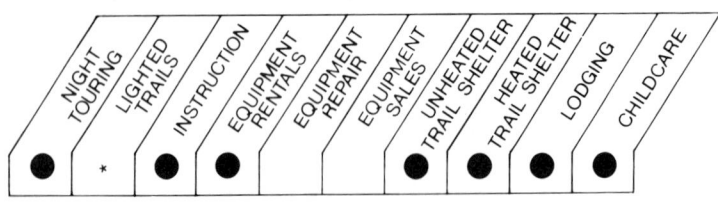

* Telemark on downhill trails

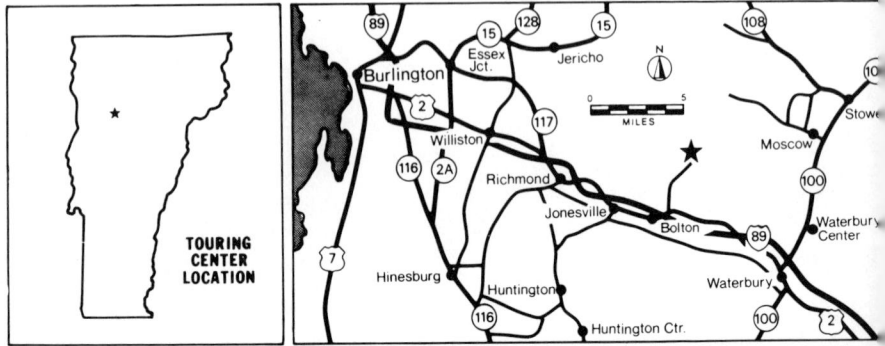

Northern Vermont 35

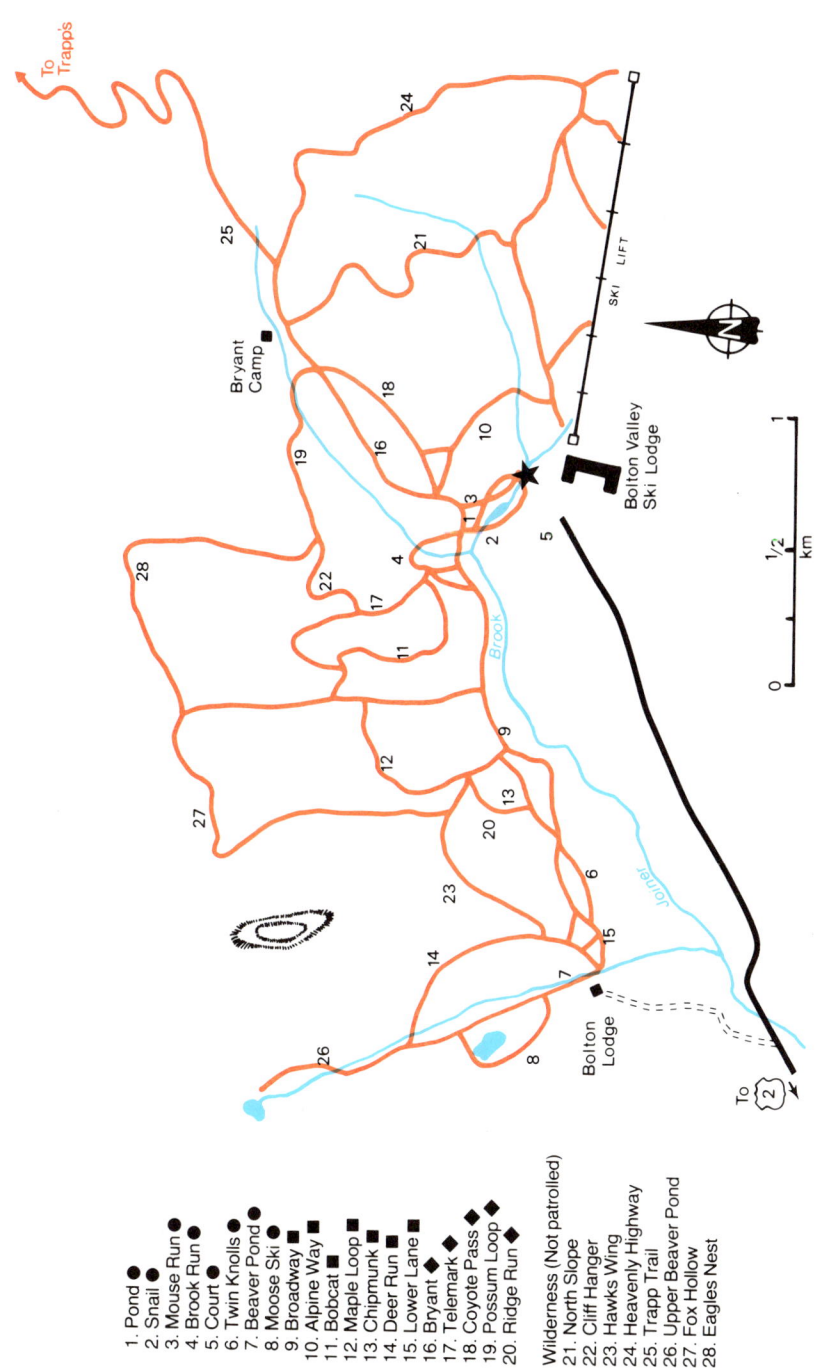

WIND CHILL CHART

Northern Vermont

WIND SPEED		ACTUAL THERMOMETER READING (°F)											
ENVIRONMENTAL CONDITIONS	M.P.H.	40	35	30	25	20	15	10	5	0	-5	-10	-15	-20	-25	-30	-35	-40	-45	-50	-55	-60

M.P.H.	40	35	30	25	20	15	10	5	0	-5	-10	-15	-20	-25	-30	-35	-40	-45	-50	-55	-60
0									EQUIVALENT CHILL TEMPERATURE												
5	35	30	25	20	15	10	5	0	-5	-10	-15	-20	-25	-30	-35	-40	-45	-50	-55	-65	-70
10	30	20	15	10	5	0	-10	-15	-20	-25	-35	-40	-45	-50	-60	-65	-70	-75	-80	-90	-95
15	25	15	10	0	-5	-10	-20	-25	-30	-40	-45	-50	-60	-65	-70	-80	-85	-90	-100	-105	-110
20	20	10	5	0	-10	-15	-25	-30	-35	-45	-50	-60	-65	-75	-80	-85	-95	-100	-110	-115	-120
25	15	10	0	-5	-15	-20	-30	-35	-45	-50	-60	-65	-75	-80	-90	-95	-105	-110	-120	-125	-135
30	10	5	0	-10	-20	-25	-30	-40	-50	-55	-65	-70	-80	-85	-95	-100	-110	-115	-125	-130	-140
35	10	5	-5	-10	-20	-30	-35	-40	-50	-60	-65	-75	-80	-90	-100	-105	-115	-120	-130	-135	-145
40	10	0	-5	-15	-20	-30	-35	-45	-55	-60	-70	-75	-85	-95	-100	-110	-115	-125	-130	-140	-150

Environmental Conditions	Danger Zones
Smoke rises vertically.	
Smoke shows direction of wind.	LITTLE DANGER
Leaves rustle, wind felt on face.	
Twigs in constant motion; light flags wave.	
Small branches sway.	INCREASING DANGER (Flesh may freeze within 1 minute)
Small trees begin to sway.	
Large branches sway; whistling heard in wires.	
Trees sway; difficult to walk against wind.	GREAT DANGER (Flesh may freeze within 30 seconds)
Twigs broken from trees; walking impeded.	
WINDS ABOVE 40 HAVE LITTLE ADDITIONAL EFFECT	

SOURCE: U.S. MILITARY

Trapp Family Lodge

Luce Hill
Stowe, Vt. 05672
Tel. 802-253-8511

Trail Network: 100 km.
Machine Groomed Trail: 60 km.
Hours of Operation: daily, 9:00 a.m. - 5:00 p.m.
Base Elevation: 1,350 ft.
High Trail: ft.
Low Trail: ft.

The most famous cross-country touring center in the United States, Trapp Family first opened for the 1968/69 winter season. This touring center has enjoyed immense popularity with its outstanding 100 km of tracked and wilderness trails. The trails vary in terrain and composition from high mountain meadows, to tall stands of hardwood and spruce, to old farm roads.

A favorite stop for skiers, the Slayton Pasture Cabin, 5 km from the Touring Center, serves soup and sandwiches, as does the Austrian Tea Room.

From Trapps via interconnected trails, it is possible to ski as far south as Bolton Valley Ski Touring Center by way of a rugged wilderness trail, or north to Sugarhouse Ski Touring Center via spectacular Smuggler's Notch. Like Stowe, Trapps has it all.

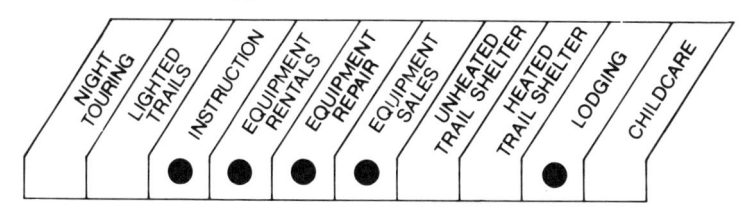

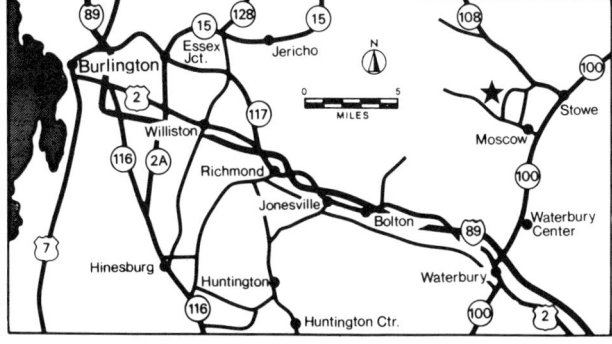

Northern Vermont

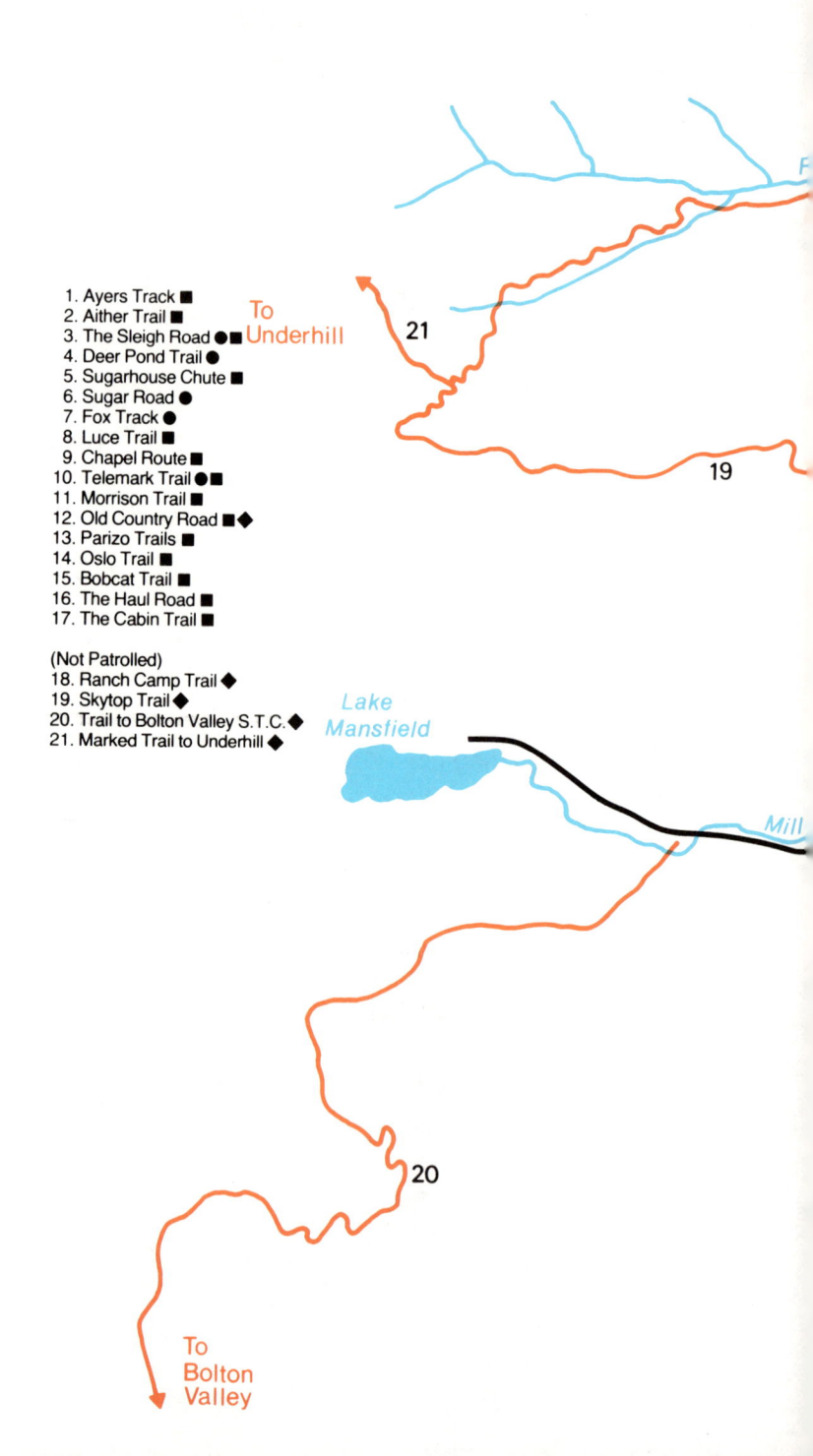

1. Ayers Track ■
2. Aither Trail ■
3. The Sleigh Road ● ■
4. Deer Pond Trail ●
5. Sugarhouse Chute ■
6. Sugar Road ●
7. Fox Track ●
8. Luce Trail ■
9. Chapel Route ■
10. Telemark Trail ● ■
11. Morrison Trail ■
12. Old Country Road ■ ◆
13. Parizo Trails ■
14. Oslo Trail ■
15. Bobcat Trail ■
16. The Haul Road ■
17. The Cabin Trail ■

(Not Patrolled)
18. Ranch Camp Trail ◆
19. Skytop Trail ◆
20. Trail to Bolton Valley S.T.C. ◆
21. Marked Trail to Underhill ◆

Northern Vermont

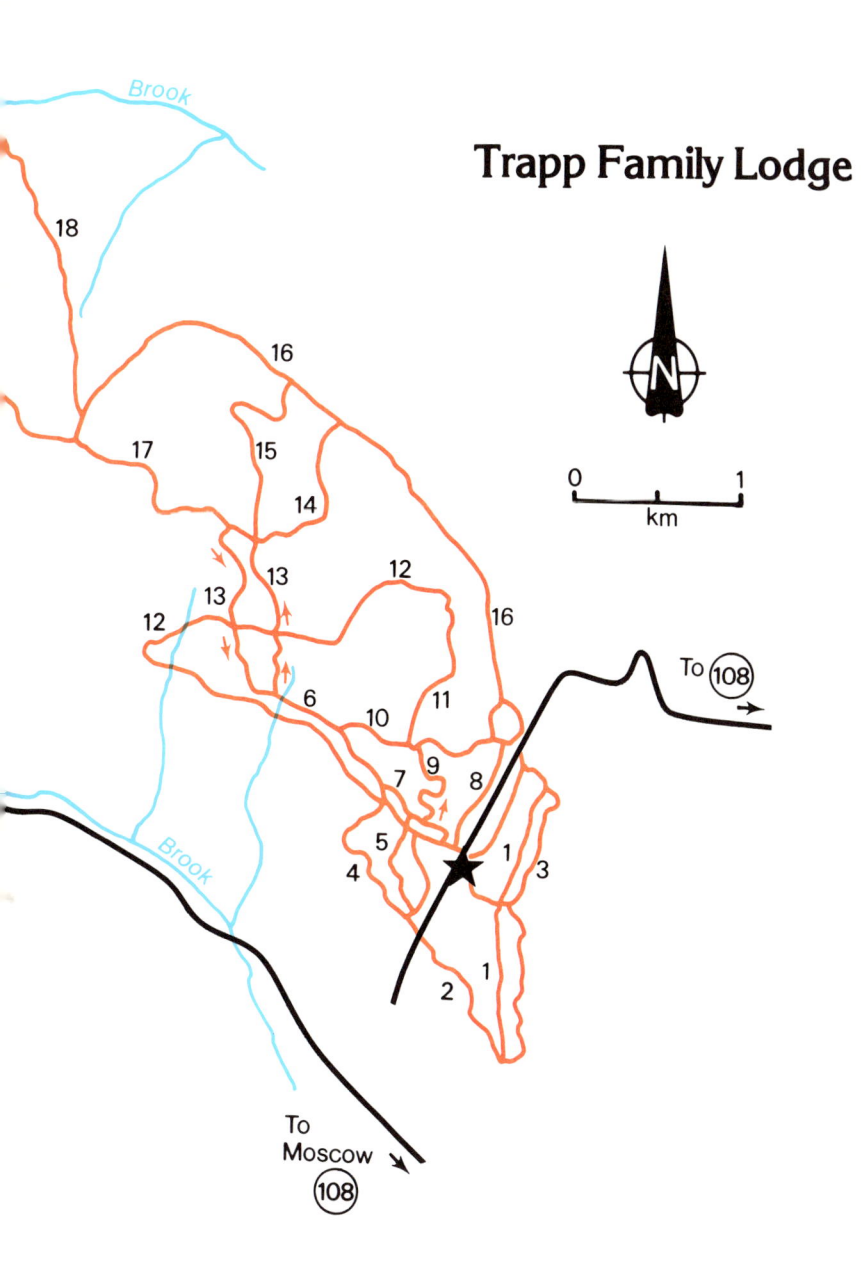

Trapp Family Lodge

Topnotch Touring Center

Mountain Road
Stowe, Vt. 05672
Tel. 802-253-8585

Trail Network: km.
Machine Groomed Trail: 20 km.
Hours of Operation: daily, 9:00 a.m. - 5:00 p.m.
Base Elevation: 950 ft.
High Trail: 1,150 ft
Low Trail: 875 ft.

Topnotch in Stowe sits by the Mountain Road. The Inn offers luxurious quarters and fine dining. The trails are largely beginner and intermediate with good connections to Stowe's other three touring centers.

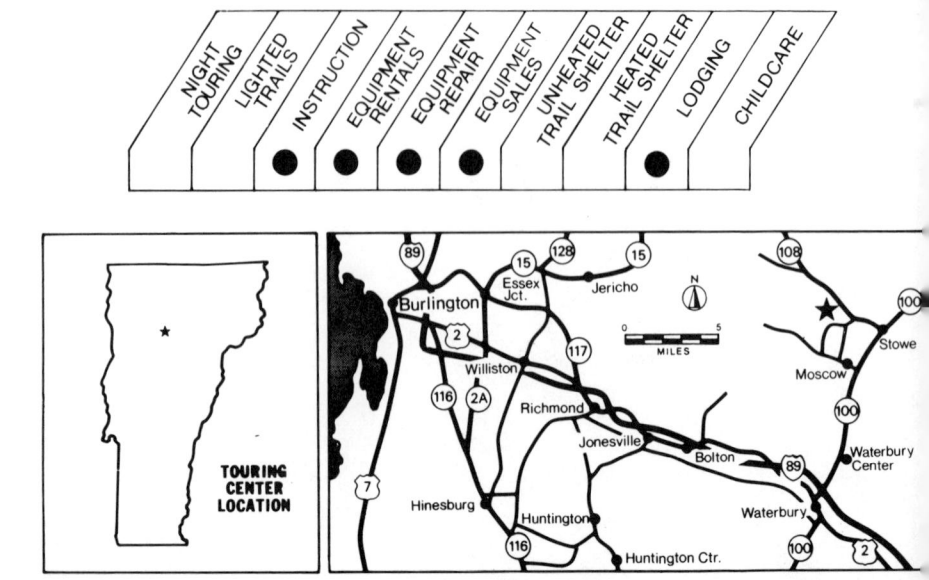

Northern Vermont 41

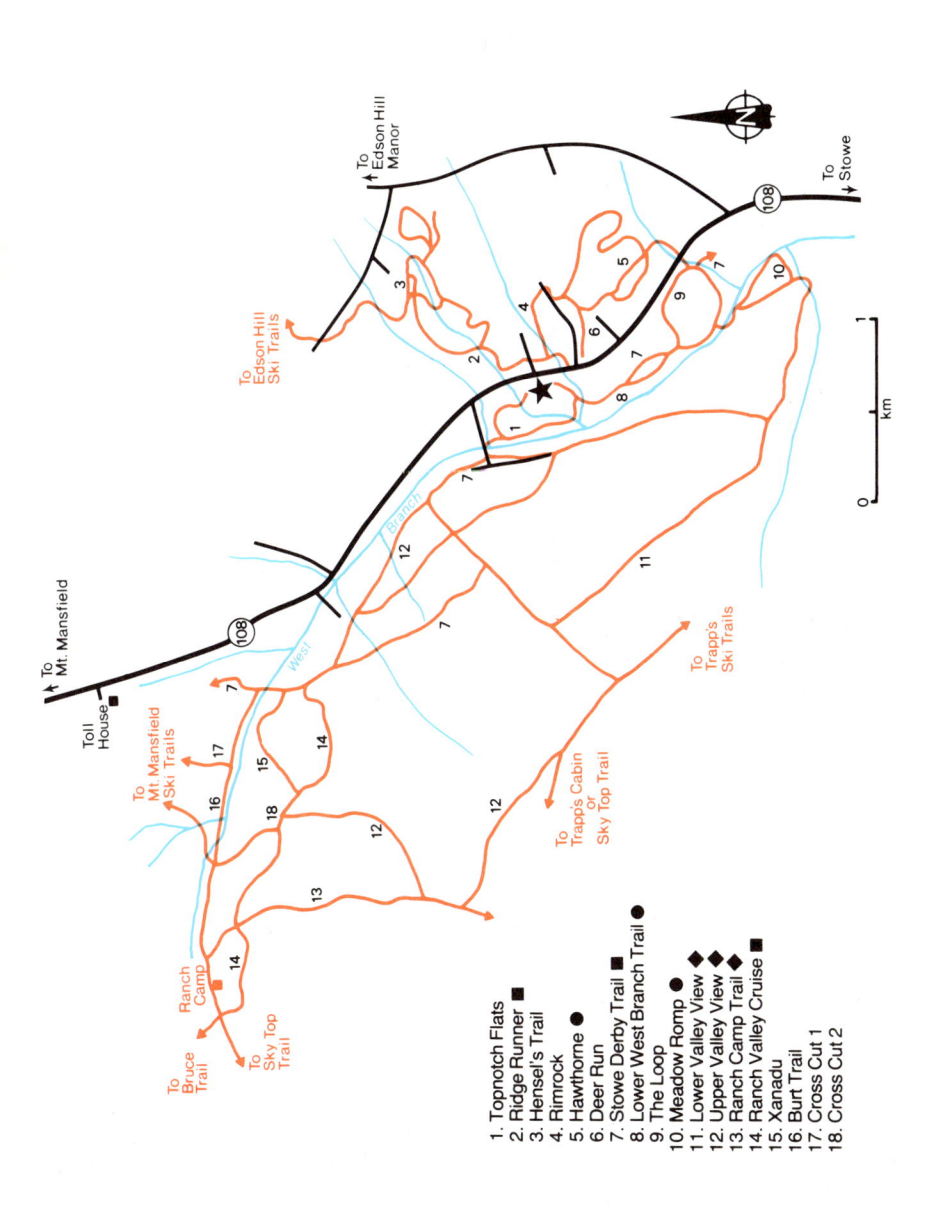

1. Topnotch Flats
2. Ridge Runner
3. Hensel's Trail
4. Rimrock
5. Hawthorne
6. Deer Run
7. Stowe Derby Trail
8. Lower West Branch Trail
9. The Loop
10. Meadow Romp
11. Lower Valley View
12. Upper Valley View
13. Ranch Camp Trail
14. Ranch Valley Cruise
15. Xanadu
16. Burt Trail
17. Cross Cut 1
18. Cross Cut 2

Edson Hill
Ski Touring Center

Edson Hill Manor
Stowe, Vt. 05672
Tel. 802-253-8954

Trail Network: 40 km.
Machine Groomed Trail: 25 km.
Hours of Operation: daily. 9:00 a.m. - 5:00 p.m.
Base Elevation: 1,300 ft.
High Trail: 2,100 ft.
Low Trail: 1,100 ft.

This touring center is situated on a beautiful estate, Edson Hill. Skiing at the center has an interesting history; nearly every trail name and junction has a story behind it. The views of Mt. Mansfield from the vicinity of Edson Hill are magnificent. It is possible, by using various trails, to ski to any or all of Stowe's other three ski touring centers. The manor itself is tasteful luxury and a fine place to stay after a day of skiing.

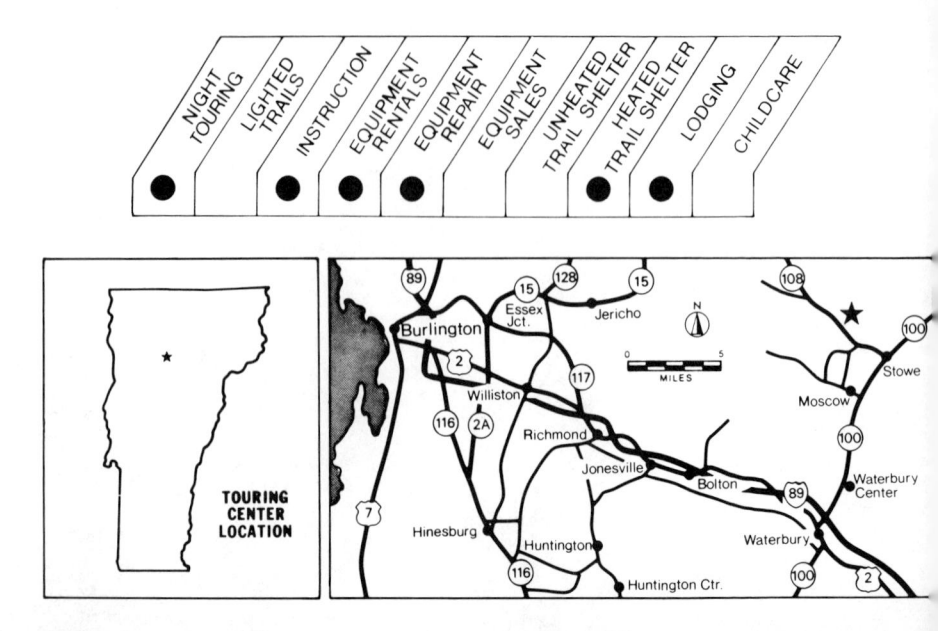

Northern Vermont 43

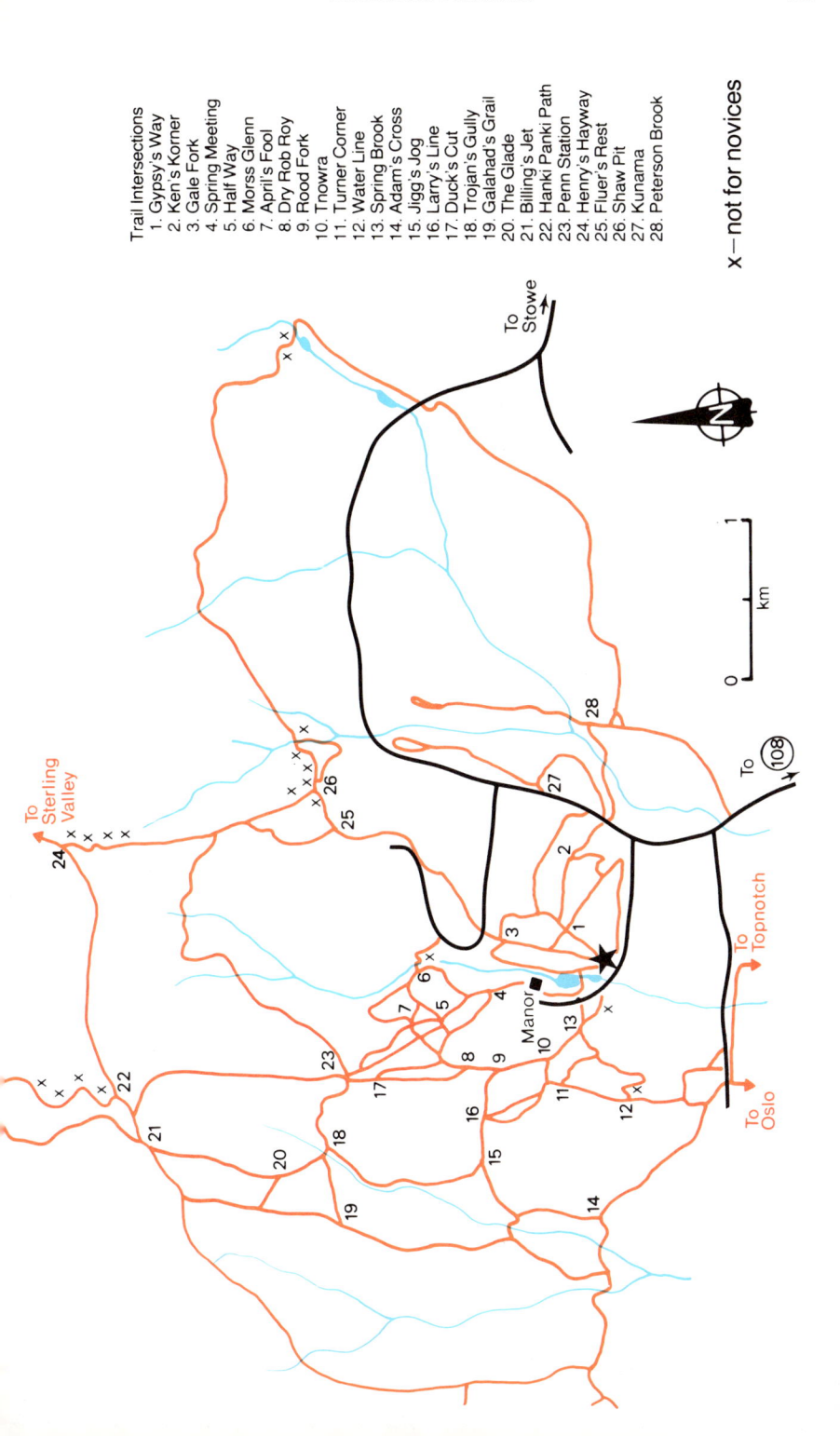

Trail Intersections
1. Gypsy's Way
2. Ken's Korner
3. Gale Fork
4. Spring Meeting
5. Half Way
6. Morss Glenn
7. April's Fool
8. Dry Rob Roy
9. Rood Fork
10. Tnowra
11. Turner Corner
12. Water Line
13. Spring Brook
14. Adam's Cross
15. Jigg's Jog
16. Larry's Line
17. Duck's Cut
18. Trojan's Gully
19. Galahad's Grail
20. The Glade
21. Billing's Jet
22. Hanki Panki Path
23. Penn Station
24. Henry's Hayway
25. Fluer's Rest
26. Shaw Pit
27. Kunama
28. Peterson Brook

x — not for novices

Mount Mansfield
Ski Touring Center

Mt. Mansfield Co.
Rt. 108
Stowe, Vt. 05672
Tel. 802-253-7311

Trail Network: 50 km.
Machine Groomed Trail: 25 km.
Hours of Operation: daily, 8:30 a.m. - 4:00 p.m.
Base Elevation: 1,200 ft.
High Trail: 1,800 ft.
Low Trail: 1,200 ft.

The Mt. Mansfield Touring Center trails strike into the heart of Ranch Valley, under Vermont's highest peak, Mt. Mansfield (4,393'). The Touring Center's trails connect with Stowe's other three ski touring centers, offering some of the best ski touring in the east. Cross-country and Norpine ski opportunities are available at Spruce Peak with the purchase of an Alpine lift ticket.

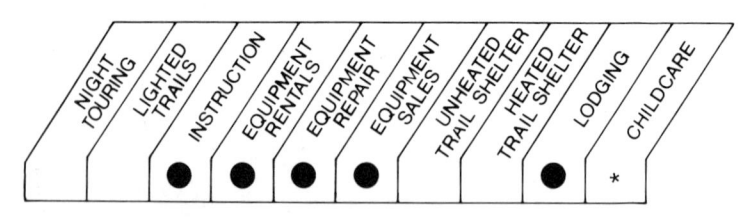

NIGHT TOURING	LIGHTED TRAILS	INSTRUCTION	EQUIPMENT RENTALS	EQUIPMENT REPAIR	EQUIPMENT SALES	UNHEATED TRAIL SHELTER	HEATED TRAIL SHELTER	LODGING	CHILDCARE
	●	●	●	●			●	*	

*At Spruce Peak

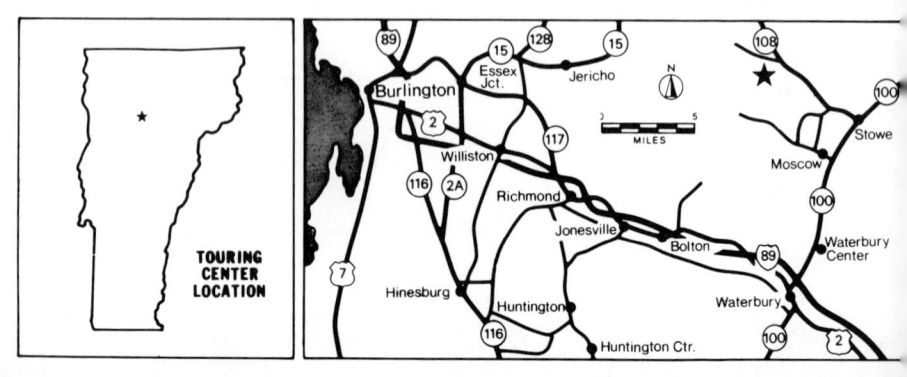

Northern Vermont

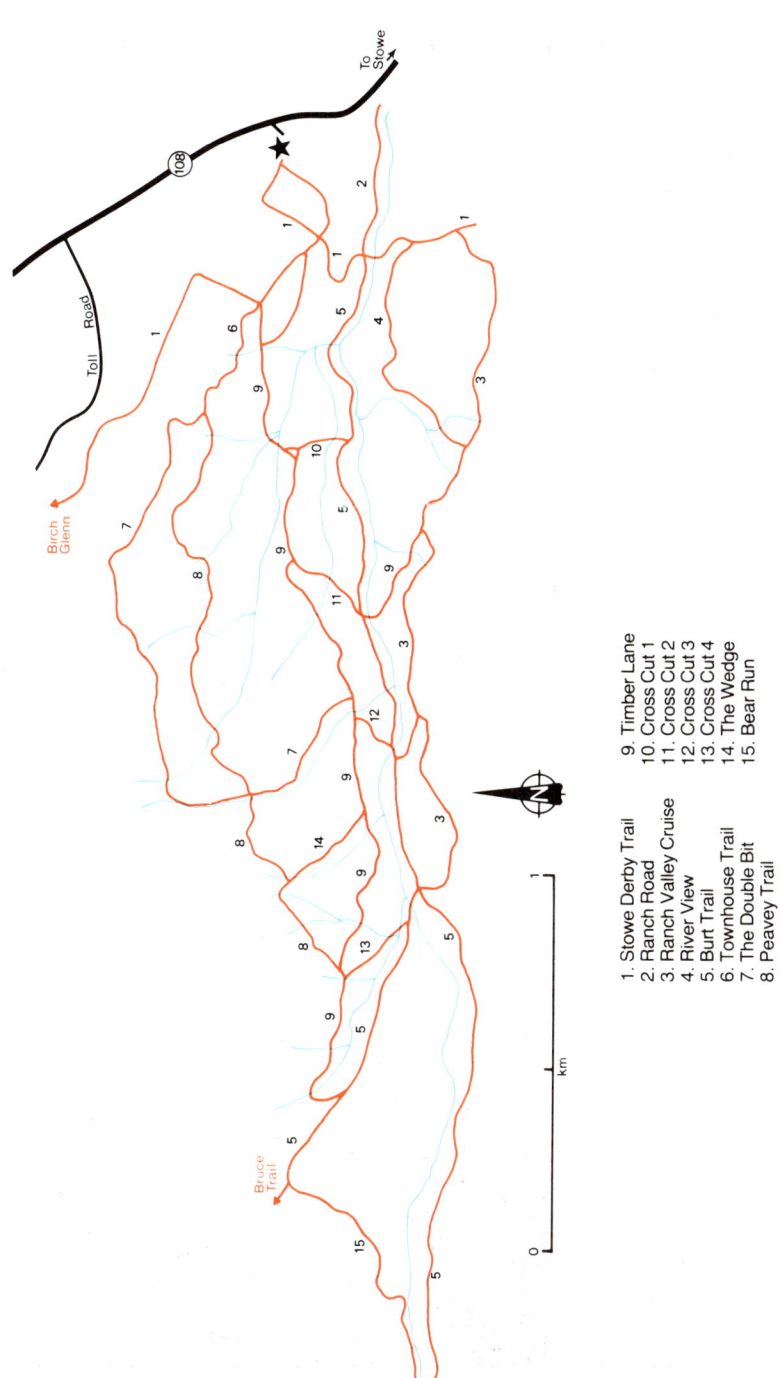

1. Stowe Derby Trail
2. Ranch Road
3. Ranch Valley Cruise
4. River View
5. Burt Trail
6. Townhouse Trail
7. The Double Bit
8. Peavey Trail
9. Timber Lane
10. Cross Cut 1
11. Cross Cut 2
12. Cross Cut 3
13. Cross Cut 4
14. The Wedge
15. Bear Run

Sugar House Nordic Center

The Village at Smuggler's Notch, Vt. 05464
Tel. 802-644-8851

Trail Network: 35 km.
Machine Groomed Trail: 35 km.
Hours of Operation: daily, 9:00 a.m. - 4:00 p.m.
Base Elevation: 1,000 ft.
High Trail: 1,800 ft.
Low Trail: 1,000 ft.

The Sugar House Nordic Center at Smuggler's Notch is a touring center in a complete mountain village resort. The village and center present the skier with a range and diversity of trails, services, and activities. Smuggler's is the site of some of the best Alpine skiing in the east. It offers luxurious lodging, restaurants, a scandinavian spa, and a lighted ice skating rink. For an exciting tour available in the area, inquire about skiing through Smuggler's Notch, between towering iced cliffs, and over to the Stowe side of the mountain.

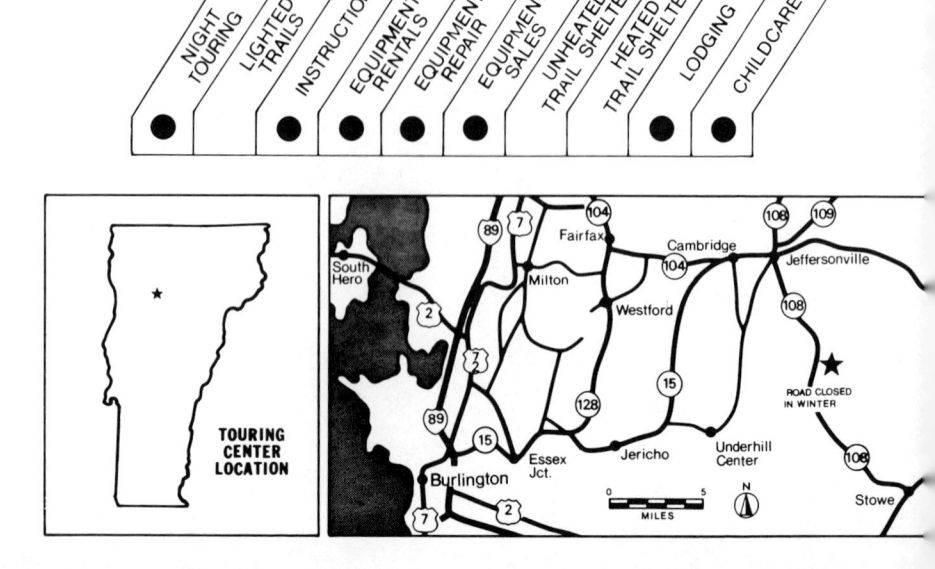

Northern Vermont 47

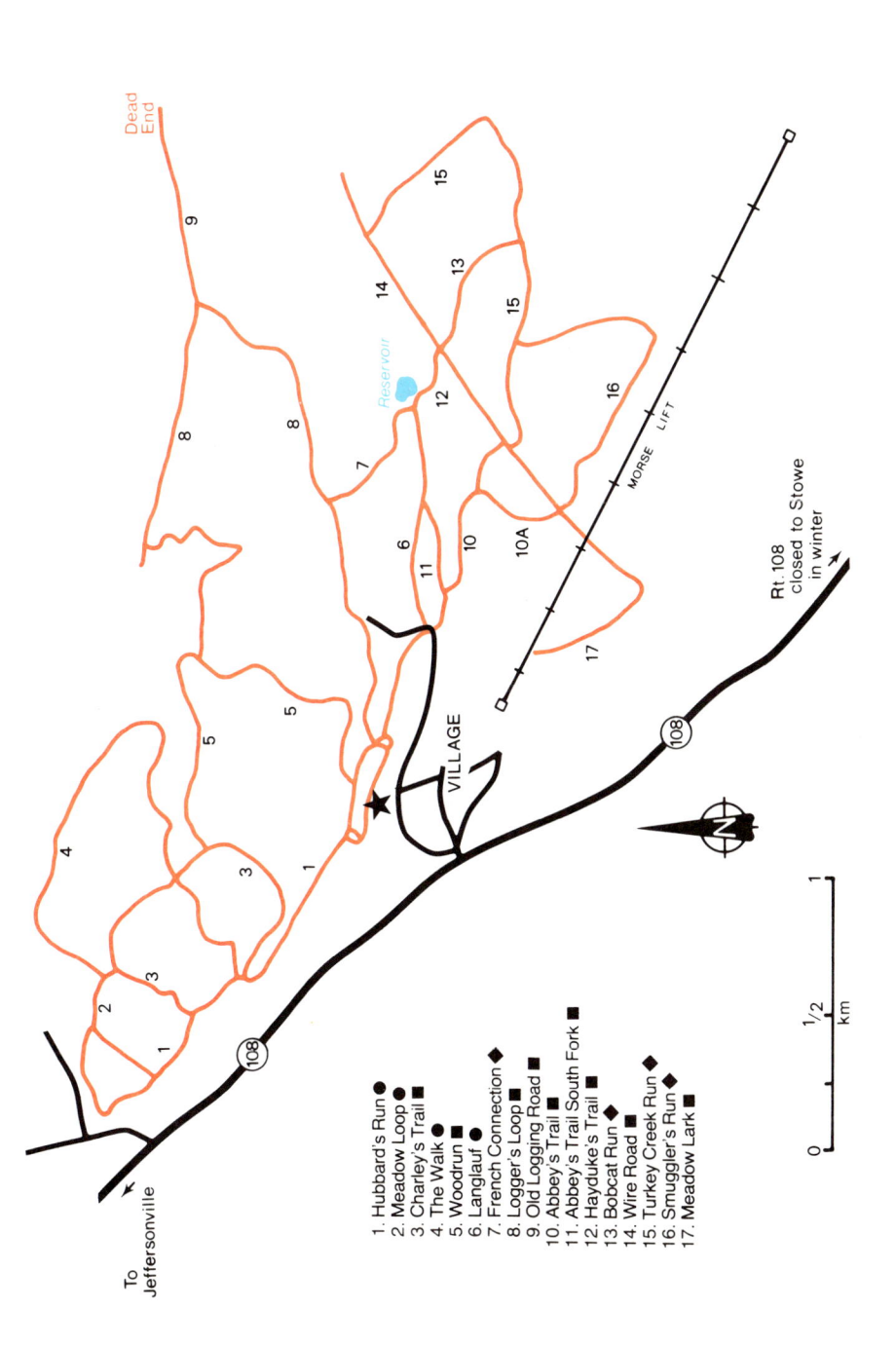

1. Hubbard's Run ●
2. Meadow Loop ●
3. Charley's Trail ■
4. The Walk ●
5. Woodrun ■
6. Langlauf ●
7. French Connection ◆
8. Logger's Loop ■
9. Old Logging Road ■
10. Abbey's Trail ■
11. Abbey's Trail South Fork ■
12. Hayduke's Trail ■
13. Bobcat Run ◆
14. Wire Road ■
15. Turkey Creek Run ◆
16. Smuggler's Run ◆
17. Meadow Lark ■

Rabbit Hill Inn

Route 18
Lower Waterford, Vt. 05848
Tel. 802-748-5168

Trail Network: 27 km.
Machine Groomed Trail: km.
Hours of Operation: daily. 8:00 a.m. - 5:00 p.m.
Base Elevation: 900 ft.
High Trail: 1,700 ft.
Low Trail: 650 ft.

The Rabbit Hill Inn Cross-Country Ski Center is situated a short distance from the banks of the Connecticut River. The trails, offering occasional imposing views of New Hampshire's White Mountains, range from challenging high hills behind the Inn, to the serene and snow covered river route that takes you beside one of America's most historic waterways locked in its winter sleep.

The Inn itself was constructed in 1825 and first opened as an inn in 1834. The village around it, although small, was built during the same age and is one of Vermont's most charming.

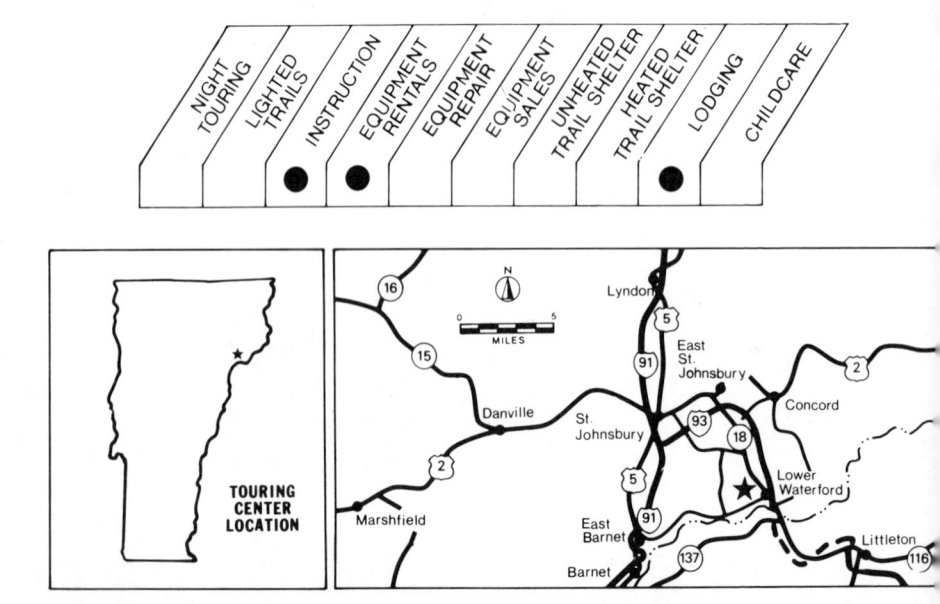

Northern Vermont 49

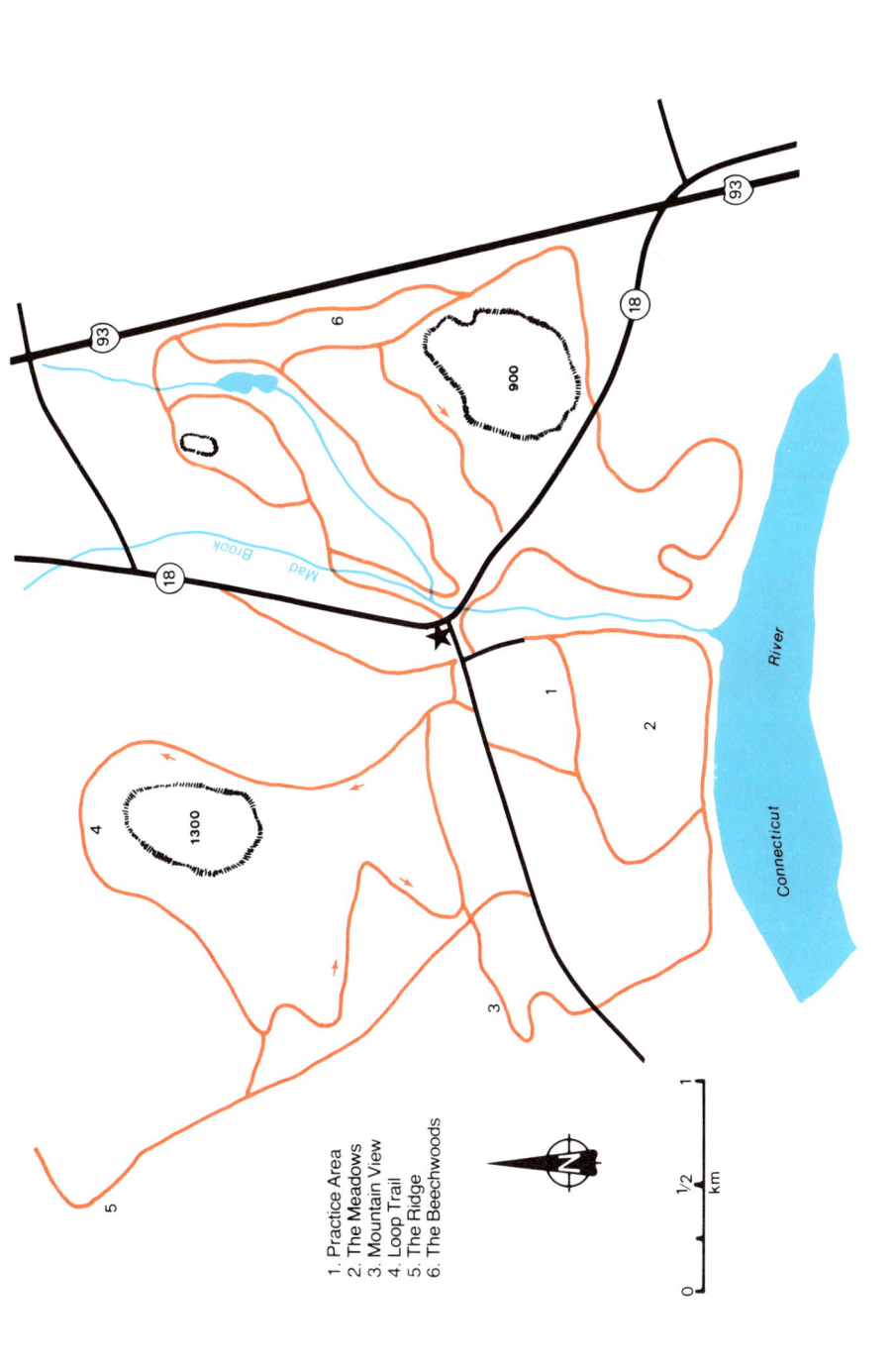

1. Practice Area
2. The Meadows
3. Mountain View
4. Loop Trail
5. The Ridge
6. The Beechwoods

CENTRAL VERMONT

Tucker Hill
Mad River Glen
Nordic Ski Centers

Box 146, RD 1
Waitsfield, Vt. 05673
Tel. 802-496-5851

Trail Network: 60 km.
Machine Groomed Trail: 40 km.
Hours of Operation: daily, 8:30 a.m. - 5:00 p.m.
Base Elevation: 1,100 ft.
High Trail: 2,000 ft.
Low Trail: 1,100 ft.

Above Tucker Hill Ski Touring Center stands the guardian of the Mad River Valley's prosperity and charm, the Lincoln Ridge with its four thousand foot peaks.

The Tucker Hill Ski Touring Center, Mad River Glen Nordic Center, and the Sugarbush Inn have a series of well integrated trail networks that allow the skier the opportunity to ski from inn to inn. The trails roam to the heights of high hills, wind through serene meadows and along streams locked in ice. Tucker Hill offers both cross-country and telemark instruction. The Inn itself offers warm hospitality and dining to match the area's skiing reputation.

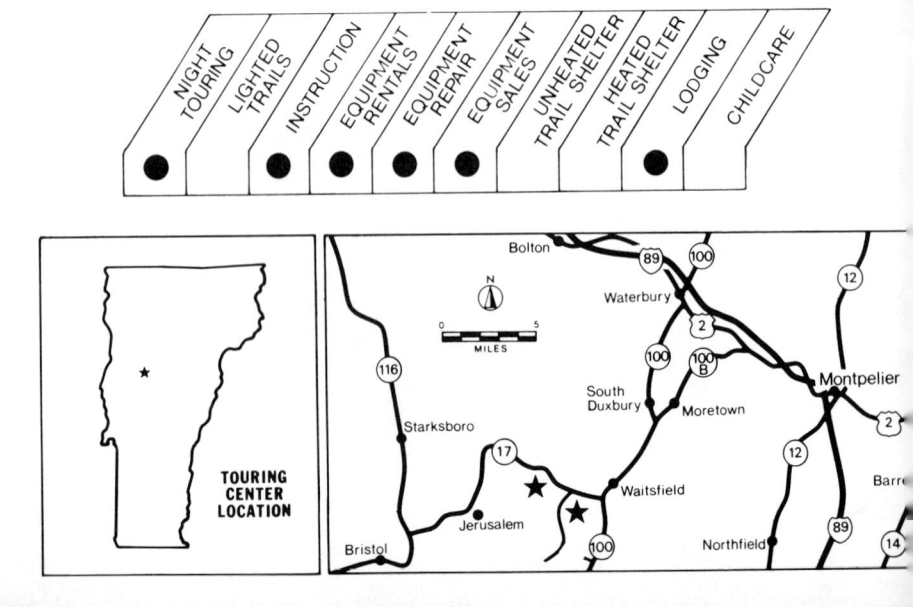

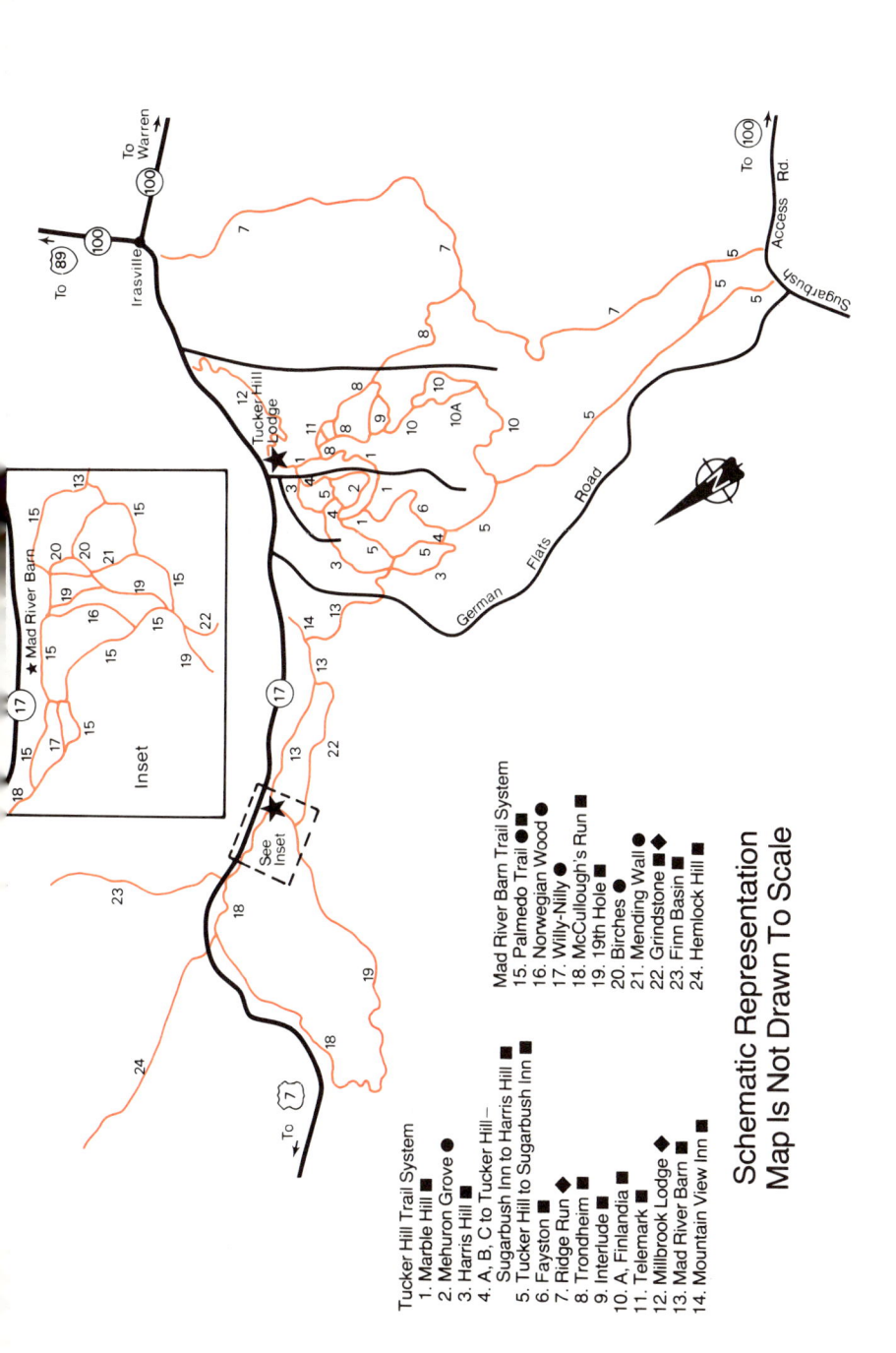

Central Vermont

Tucker Hill Trail System
1. Marble Hill ■
2. Mehuron Grove ●
3. Harris Hill ■
4. A, B, C to Tucker Hill—Sugarbush Inn to Harris Hill ■
5. Tucker Hill to Sugarbush Inn ■
6. Fayston ■
7. Ridge Run ◆
8. Trondheim ■
9. Interlude ■
10. A, Finlandia ■
11. Telemark ■
12. Millbrook Lodge ◆
13. Mad River Barn ■
14. Mountain View Inn ■

Mad River Barn Trail System
15. Palmedo Trail ●■
16. Norwegian Wood ●
17. Willy-Nilly ●
18. McCullough's Run ■
19. 19th Hole ■
20. Birches ●
21. Mending Wall ●
22. Grindstone ■◆
23. Finn Basin ■
24. Hemlock Hill ■

Schematic Representation
Map Is Not Drawn To Scale

Sugarbush Inn
Ski Touring Center

Warren, Vt. 05673
Tel. 802-583-2301

Trail Network: 50 km.
Machine Groomed Trail: 50 km.
Hours of Operation: daily, 9:00 a.m. - 6:00 p.m.
Base Elevation: 1,500 ft.
High Trail: 1,800 ft.
Low Trail: 1,100 ft.

The Sugarbush Inn in Warren offers a wide variety of touring terrain from golf course trails for easier skiing, to mountainous terrain underneath the 4000 foot peaks of Mount Abraham and Mt. Ellen. For the long distance or destination skier, one can choose from a mix of trails running north to the Tucker Hill Inn ski trails. Skiers staying at the Inn may take full advantage of an indoor heated pool, jacuzzi, and saunas after the skis are off. The "Valley" itself also has some of the finest Alpine and Telemark skiing in Vermont.

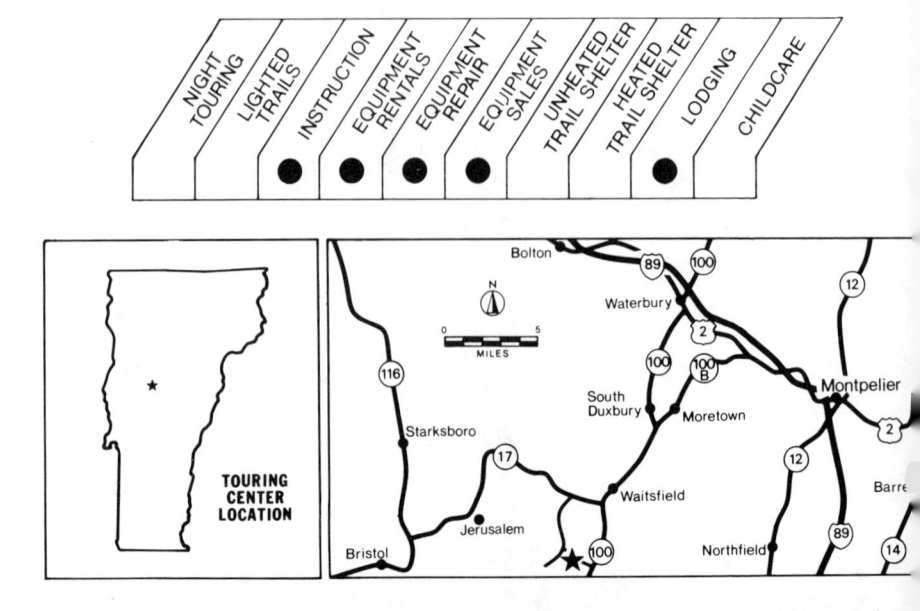

Central Vermont

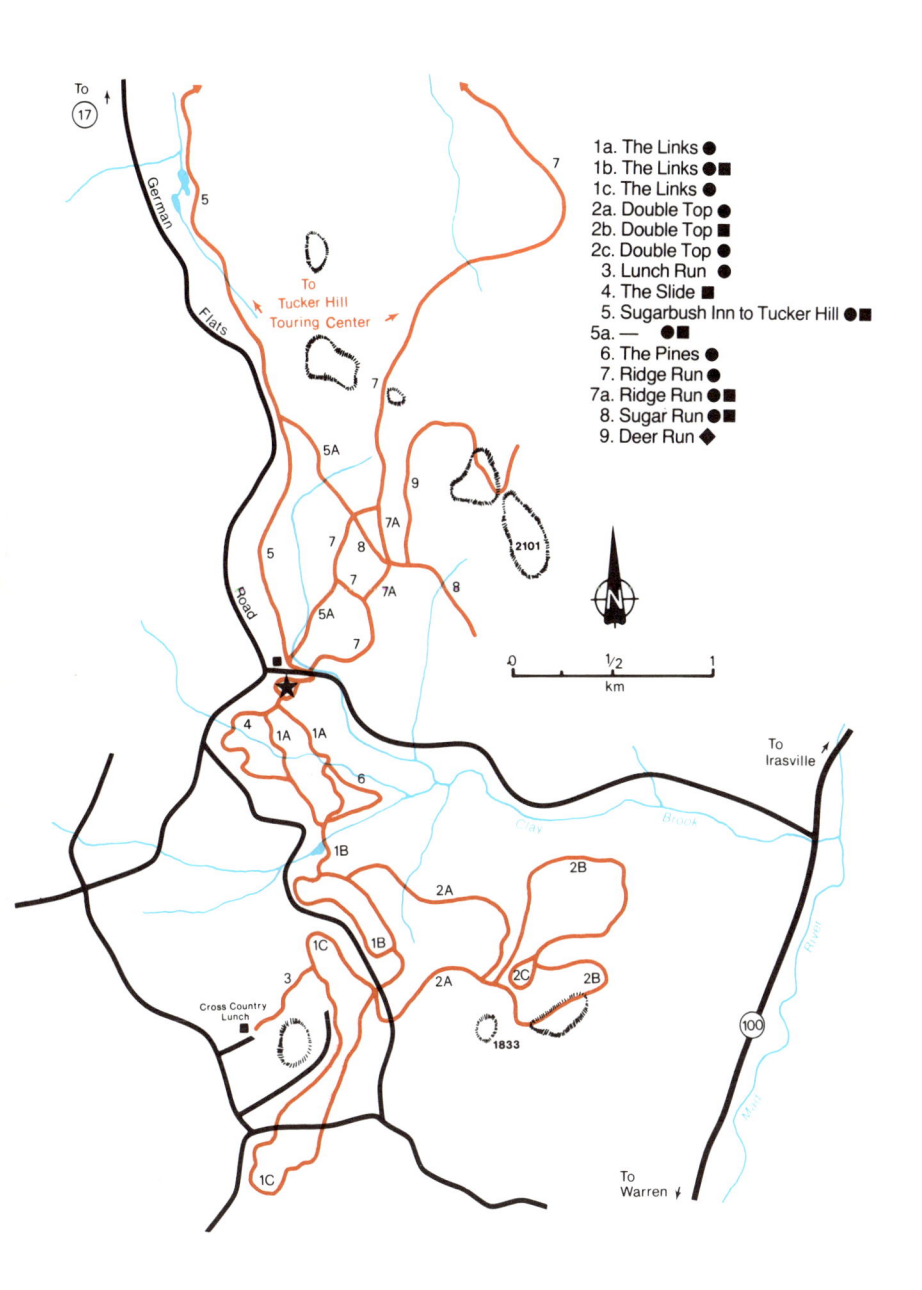

1a. The Links ●
1b. The Links ●■
1c. The Links ●
2a. Double Top ●
2b. Double Top ■
2c. Double Top ●
3. Lunch Run ●
4. The Slide ■
5. Sugarbush Inn to Tucker Hill ●■
5a. — ●■
6. The Pines ●
7. Ridge Run ●
7a. Ridge Run ●■
8. Sugar Run ●■
9. Deer Run ◆

Ole's
Cross-Country Ski Center

Warren Sugarbush Airport
Warren, Vt. 05674
Tel. 802-496-3430

Trail Network: 40 km.
Machine Groomed Trail: 40 km.
Hours of Operation: daily. 8:00 a.m. - 5:00 p.m.
Base Elevation: 1,250 ft.
High Trail: 2,100 ft.
Low Trail: 800 ft.

Ole Mosesen is a salmon fishing guide in his native Norway during the summer months and has been operating a ski touring center in Warren since 1971. The terrain immediately surrounding the center is gradual and rolling through both fields and woodlands. The center itself is in the tower of the Warren-Sugarbush Airport (closed for winter.)

Ole is renowned for his Norwegian sixth sense about snow which he applies successfully to both ski waxing and track-setting. Visitors will frequently find top racers from area schools and colleges, and occasionally the U.S. Team, training at Ole's.

Cafe Ole provides hot soup and snacks from noon through the afternoon. The Cold Spring Farm Inn is an alternative lunch stop; advanced phone reservation is suggested.

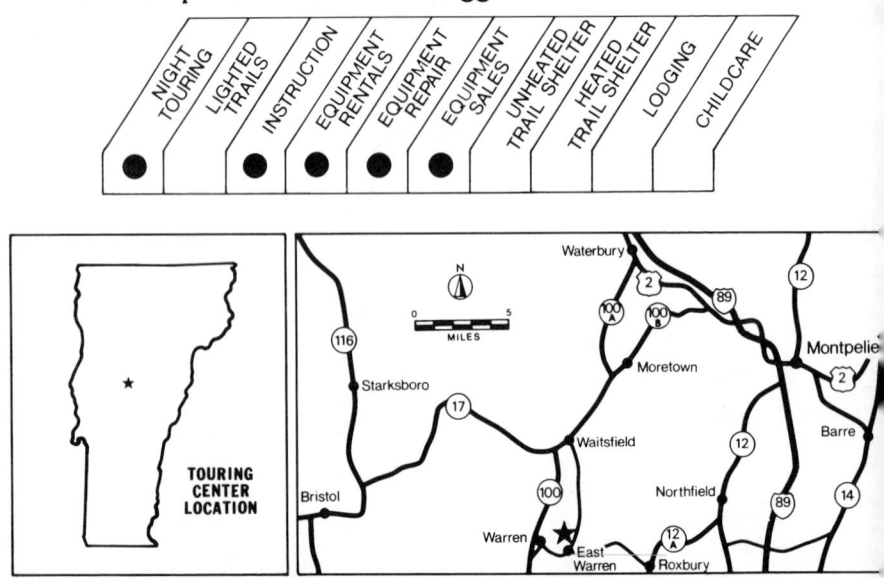

Central Vermont

All trails beginner to intermediate difficulty

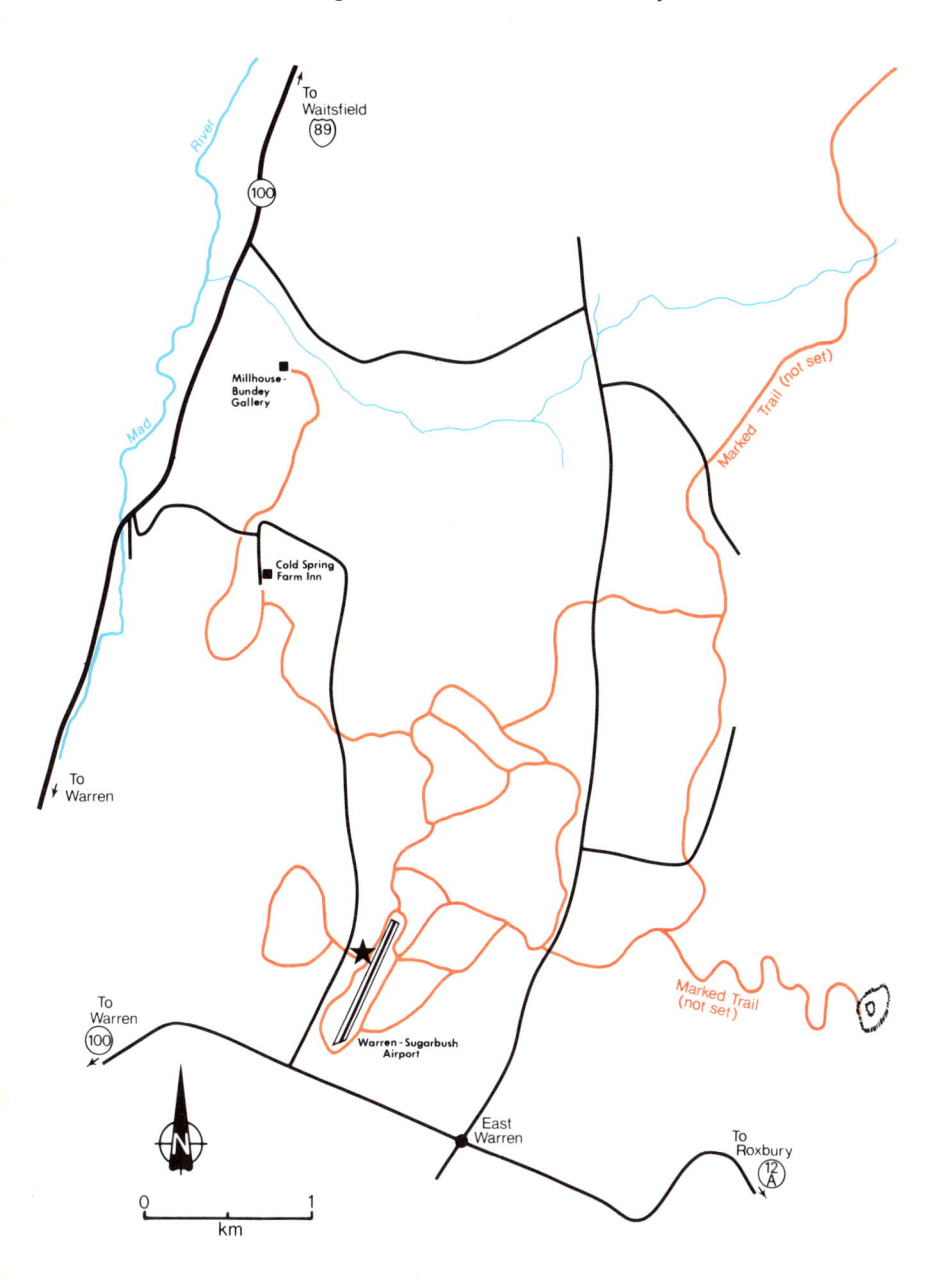

Green Trails
Touring Center

Pond Village
Brookfield, Vt. 05036
Tel. 802-276-3412

Trail Network: 40 km.
Machine Groomed Trail: km.
Hours of Operation: daily, 9:00 a.m. - 4:00 p.m.
Base Elevation: 1,250 ft.
High Trail: 1,800 ft.
Low Trail: 1,200 ft.

The Green Trails Inn and Ski Touring Center is tucked away in the quiet historic village of Brookfield whose novel floating bridge spans a narrow pond west of the Inn. In addition to ski touring through rolling hills and wide meadows, one can skate on the pond next to the floating bridge, or enjoy a horse drawn sleigh ride upon arrangement with the Inn.

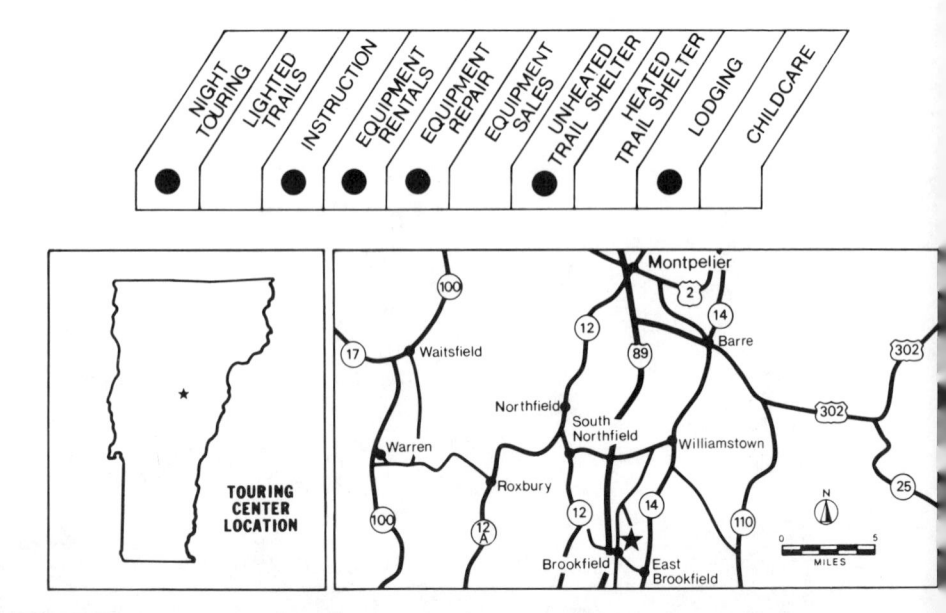

Central Vermont 59

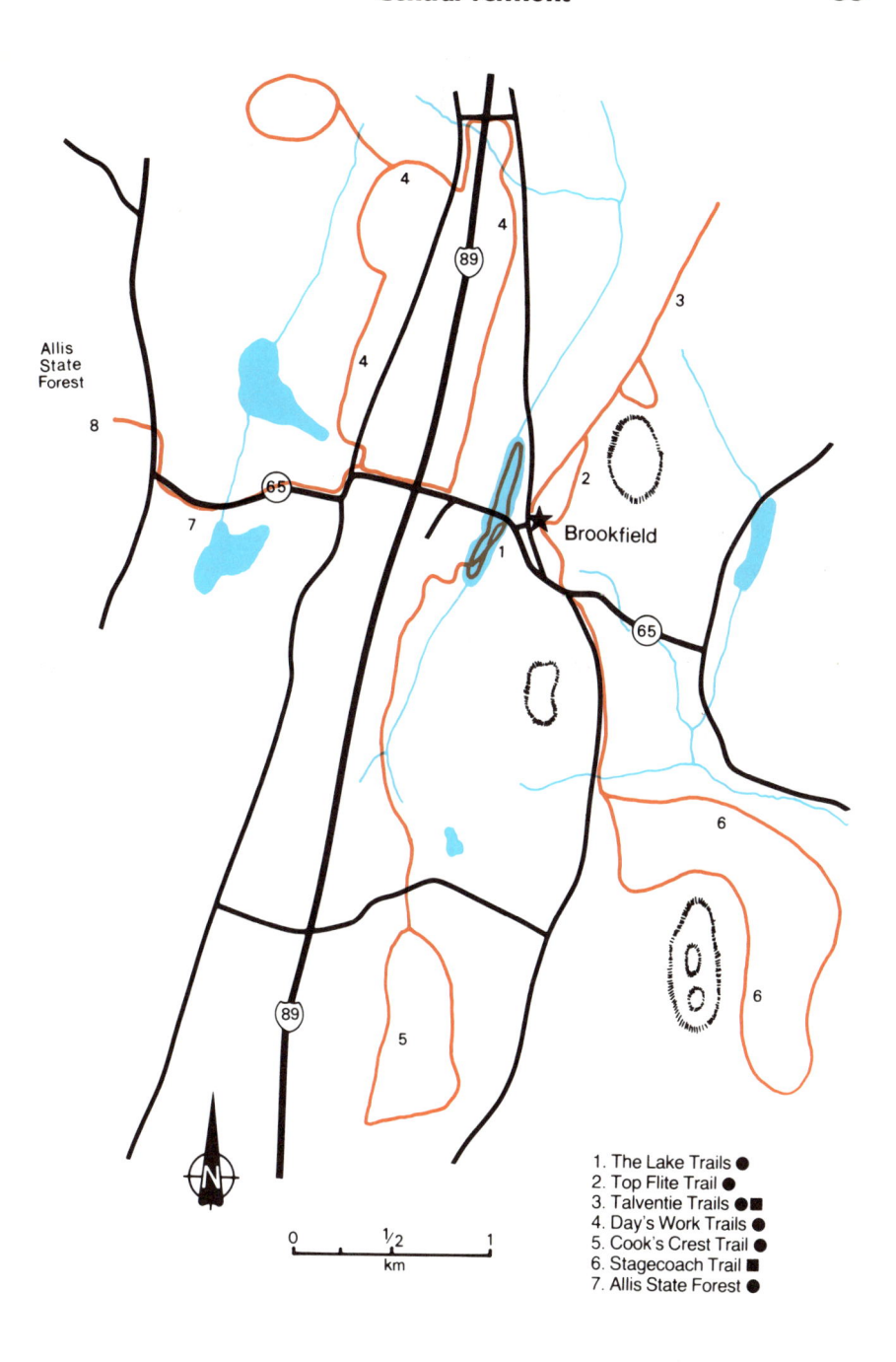

1. The Lake Trails ●
2. Top Flite Trail ●
3. Talventie Trails ●■
4. Day's Work Trails ●
5. Cook's Crest Trail ●
6. Stagecoach Trail ■
7. Allis State Forest ●

Carroll and Jane Rikert Ski Touring Center "Breadloaf Campus"

c/o Middlebury College
Service Building
Middlebury, Vt. 05753

Trail Network: 30 km.
Machine Groomed Trail: 30 km.
Hours of Operation: daily, 9:00 a.m. - 4:00 p.m.
Base Elevation: 1,400 ft.
High Trail: 1,700 ft.
Low Trail: 1,400 ft.

Middlebury College offers a quality cross-country skiing experience at two locations. The first is at the Breadloaf campus near the Middlebury Snowbowl where the Main Touring Center is located with ski trails linking south into the Blueberry Hill trail system.

The 3.5 kilometer John "Red" Kelly ('31) trail is located on the golf course on campus, and it is lit with floodlights for night skiing every night until 10 p.m.

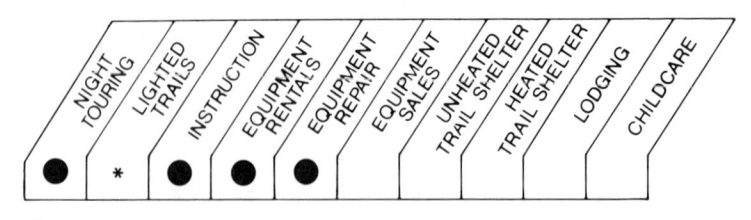

* At golf course

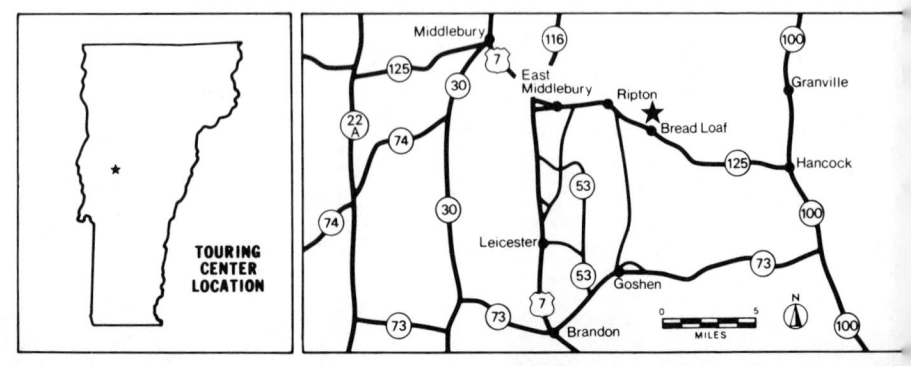

Central Vermont 61

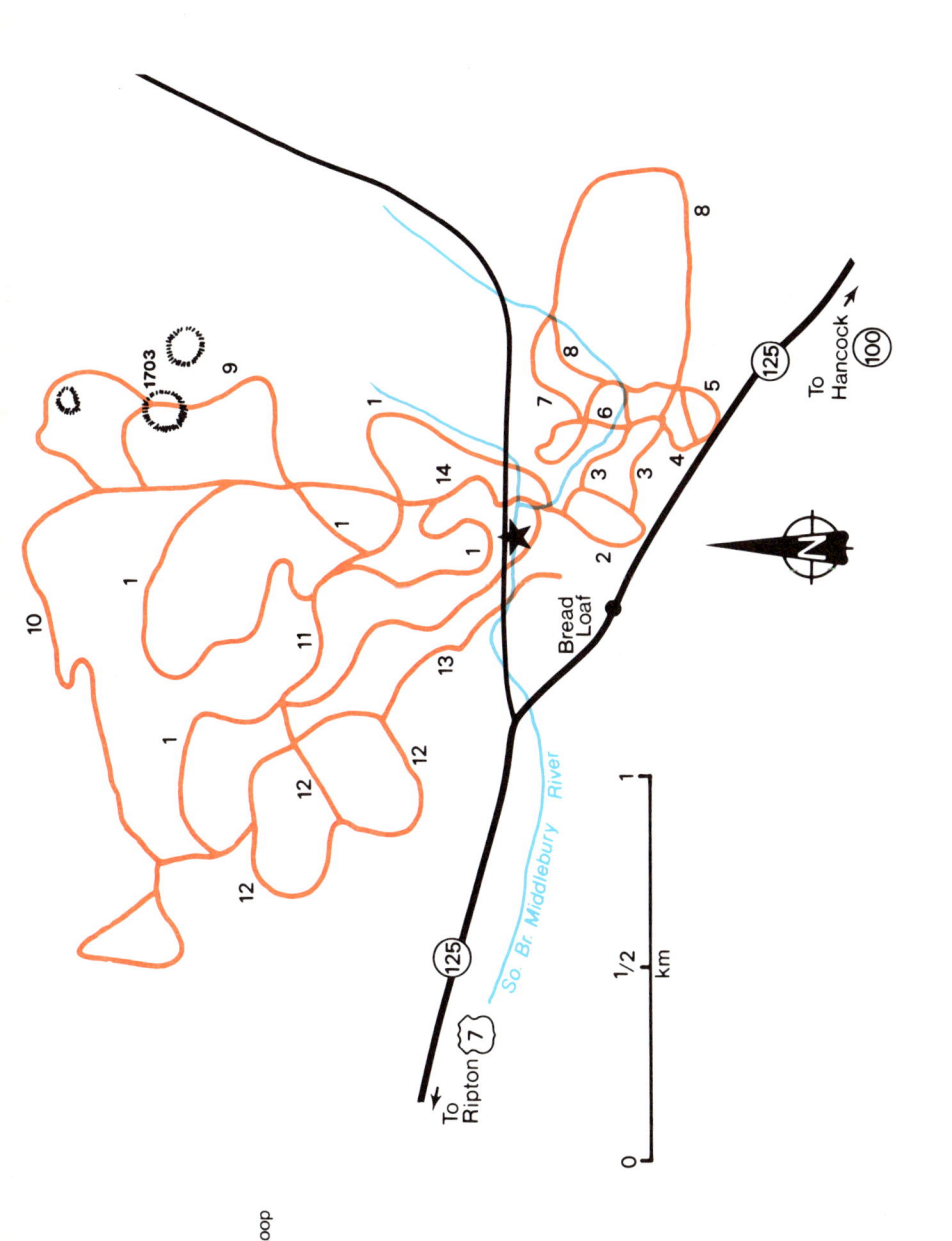

1. Collegiate Racing Loop
2. Practice Loop
3. Turkey Trot
4. Moose Hill
5. Deer Run
6. Porcupine Path
7. Snow Snake
8. River Run
9. Logging Loop
10. Timberline
11. Cross-over
12. The Figure Eight
13. "Way" Home
14. Myhre's Hill

Blueberry Hill

Goshen, Vt. 05733
Tel. 802-247-6535 or 247-6735

Trail Network: 80 km.
Machine Groomed Trail: 50 km.
Hours of Operation: daily, 9:00 a.m. - 5:00 p.m.
Base Elevation: 1,800 ft.
High Trail: 3,200 ft.
Low Trail: 700 ft.

Blueberry Hill is a very active touring center, with a unique charm, many special events, and a well connected, far-reaching, trail network. The noted American Ski Marathon and Pig Race are held annually in February and March. Blueberry Hills' new trails range as far north as the Middlebury College cross-country trails on the Breadloaf campus to the Churchill House trails to the south. Inn to inn skiing is thriving in this region.

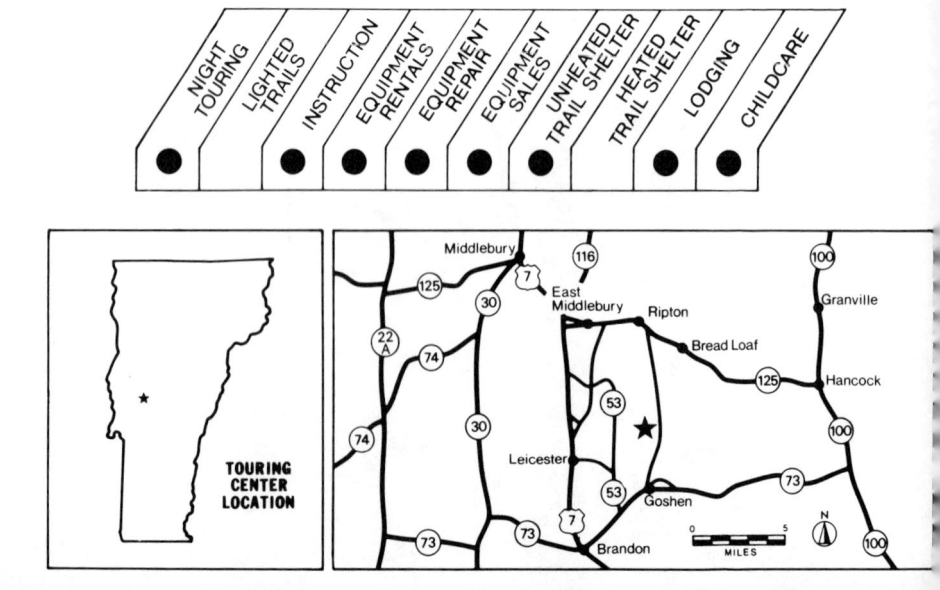

Central Vermont

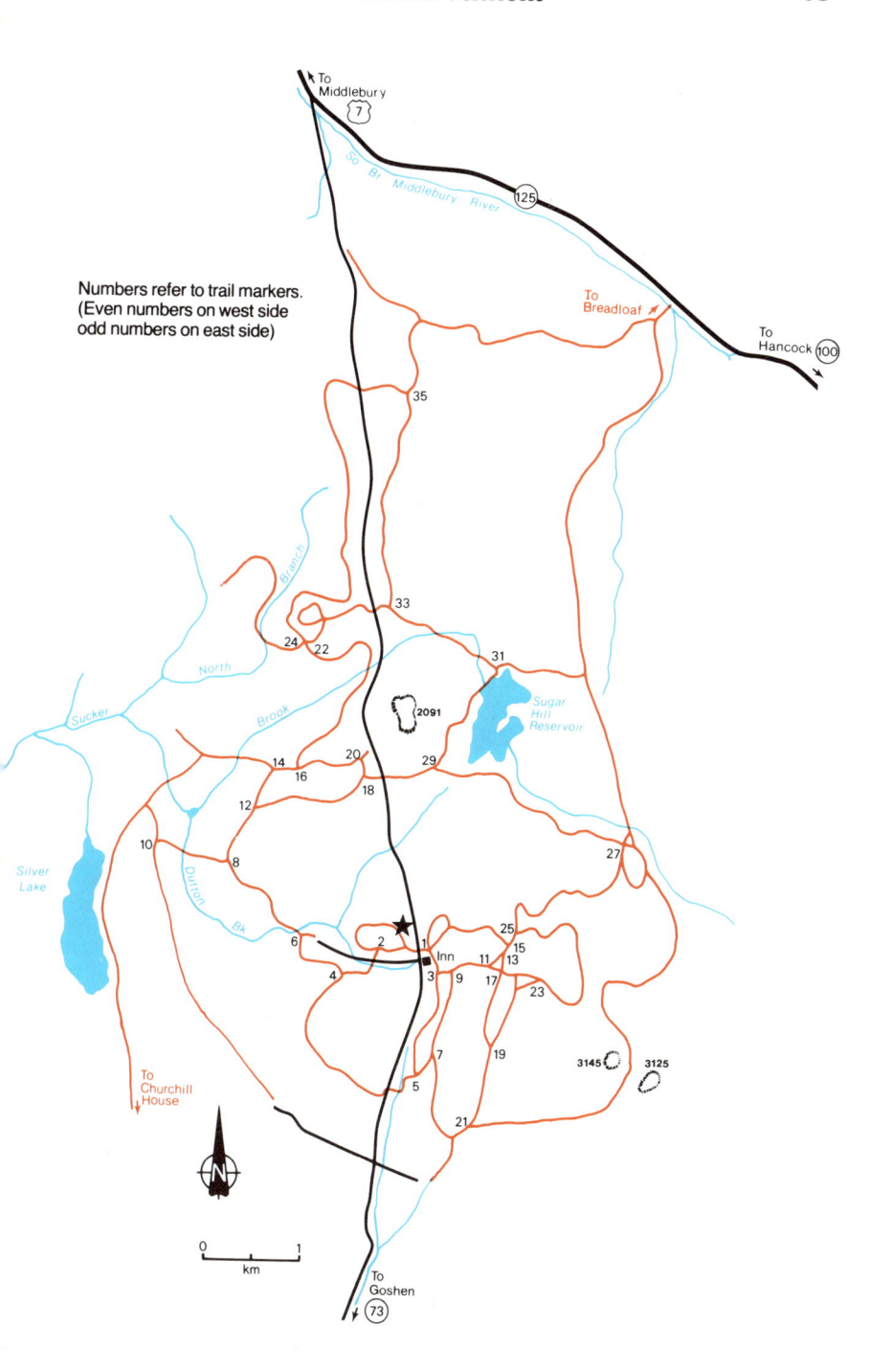

63

Churchill House

RD 3
Brandon, Vt. 05733
Tel. 802-247-3300

Trail Network: 24 km.
Machine Groomed Trail: 16 km.
Hours of Operation: daily, 9:00 a.m. - 4:30 p.m.
Base Elevation: 770 ft.
High Trail: 1,700 ft.
Low Trail: 770 ft.

Churchill House is an inn northeast of the town of Brandon. It has its own small network of trails and access to the greater network of trails at Blueberry Hill Ski Touring Center.

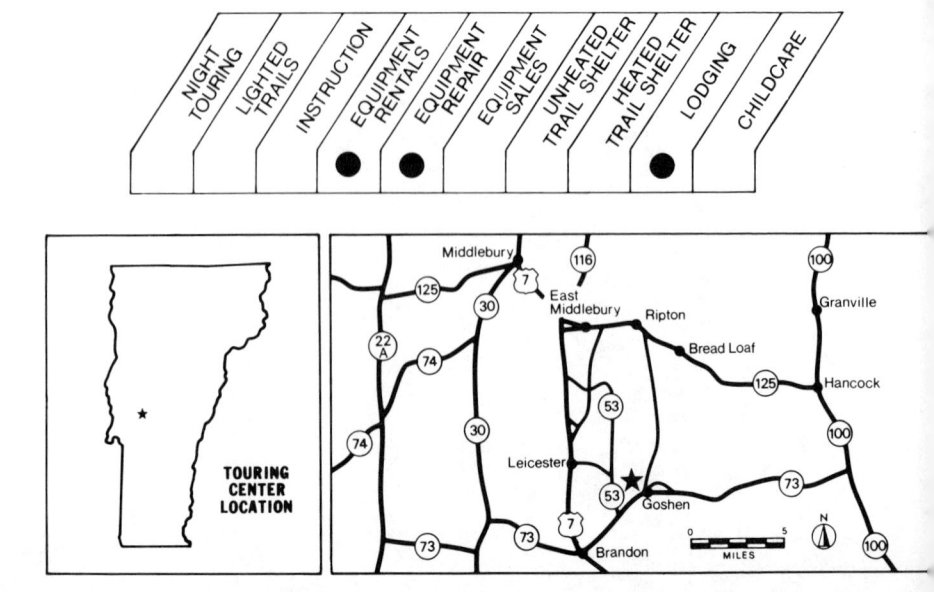

Central Vermont

To Blueberry Hill

To (125)

Goshen

To (100)

73

To (7)

0 — 1 km

N

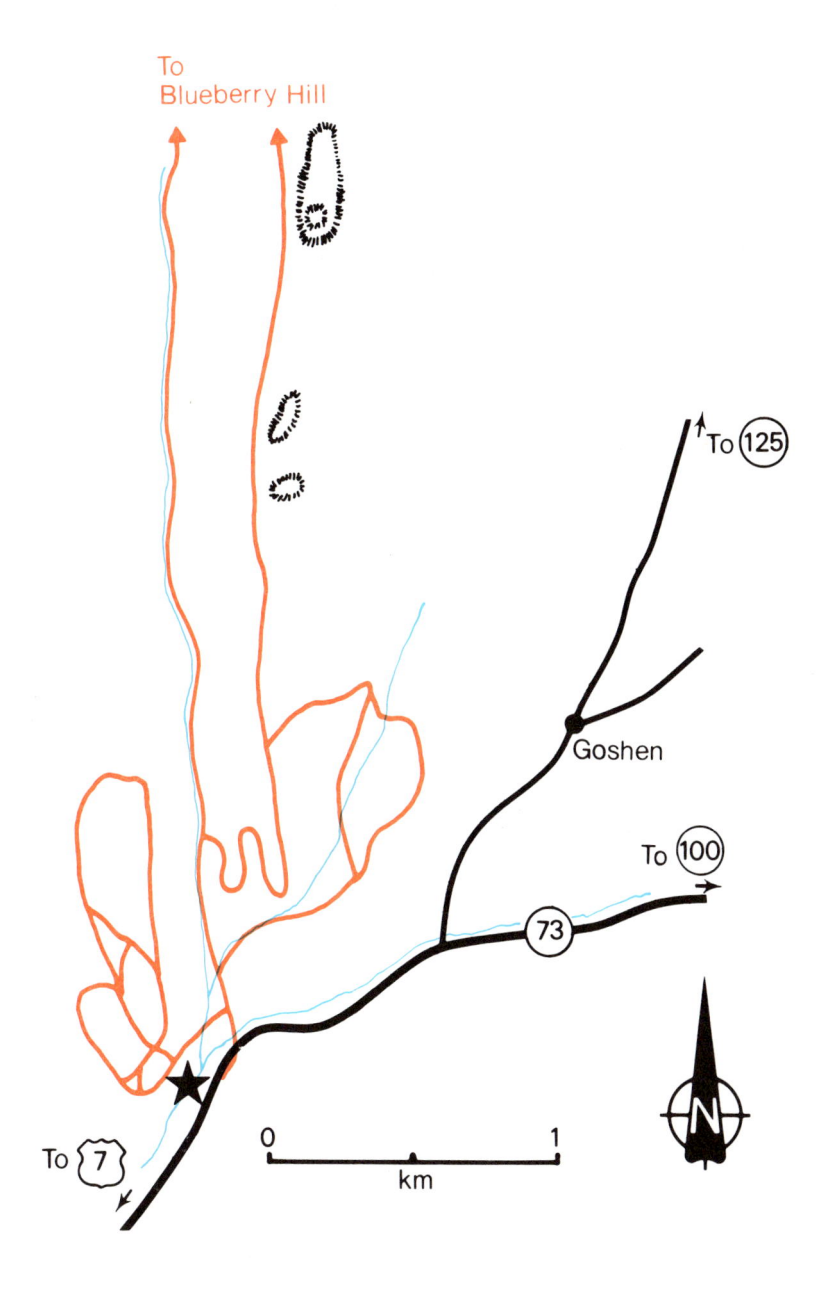

All trails beginner to intermediate difficulty

Green Mountain Touring Center

RD 2
Stockfarm Road
Randolph, Vt. 05060
Tel. 802-728-5575

Trail Network: 45 km.
Machine Groomed Trail: 35 km.
Hours of Operation: daily. Sunrise to sunset
Base Elevation: 800 ft.
High Trail: 1,350 ft.
Low Trail: 800 ft.

Associated with the Three Stallion Inn and located on a 1500 acre parcel of land, the Green Mountain Ski Touring Center offers the skier a varied terrain and trails which track through fields and woodlands. Some trails parallel the Third Branch of the White River. After skiing the visitor can enjoy a wood-fired Finnish sauna, home-cooked meals, fireplace, and the newly added cocktail lounge.

In the past special events have included a 40 kilometer marathon race in February. Trail network is undergoing a significant expansion as of this writing.

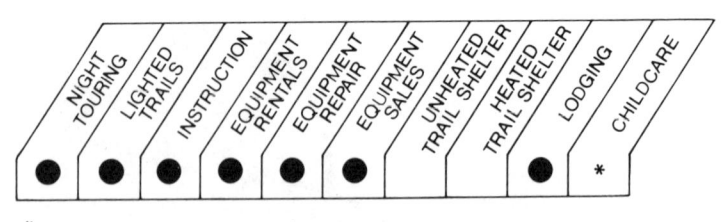

*By arrangement

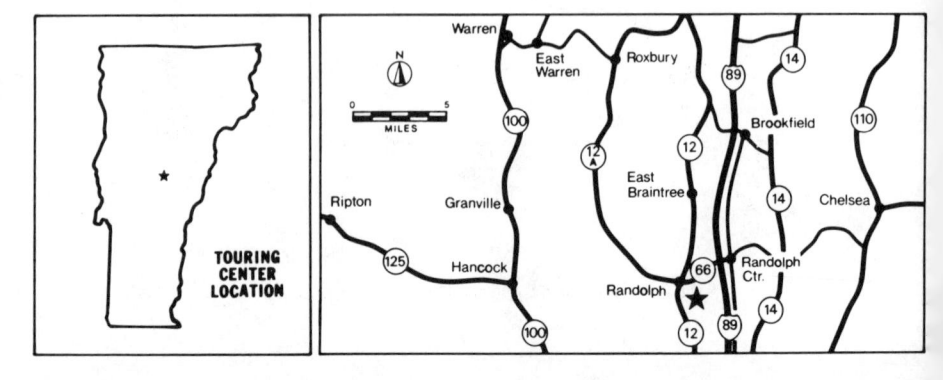

Central Vermont 67

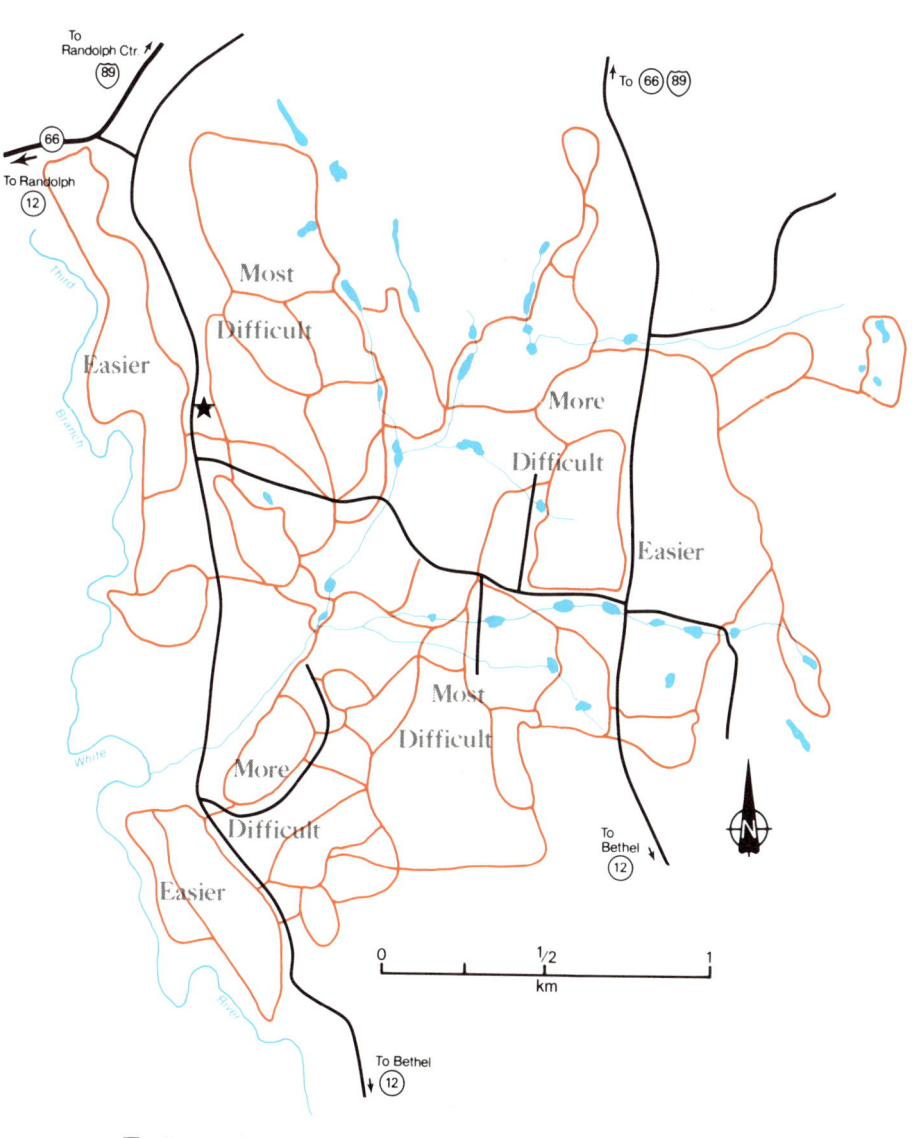

Trail network to be expanded and trail difficulties rated during the 1984 season

Trail Head
Ski Touring Center

Box 37, Route 100
Stockbridge, Vt. 05772
Tel. 802-746-8038

Trail Network: 30 km.
Machine Groomed Trail: 15 km.
Hours of Operation: daily, 9:00 a.m. - dusk
Base Elevation: 800 ft.
High Trail: 2,000 ft.
Low Trail: 800 ft.

The Trail Head Ski Touring Center is located on Route 100, next to the village of Stockbridge. A variety of skiable terrain from lowland river meadows, to the hills that swell out of the river plains offer pleasant skiing and good views. In addition to cross-country ski lessons, Norpine ski lessons are available.

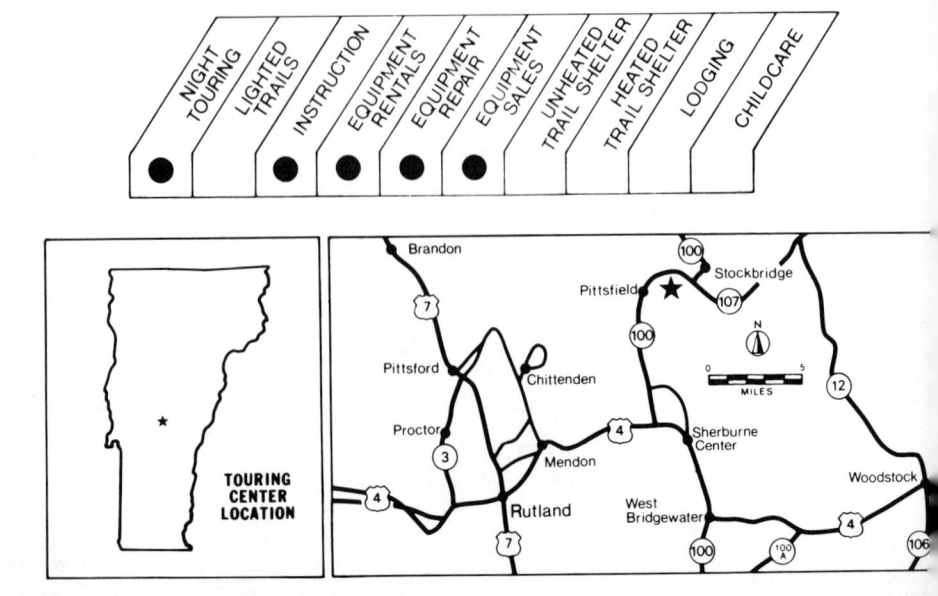

Central Vermont

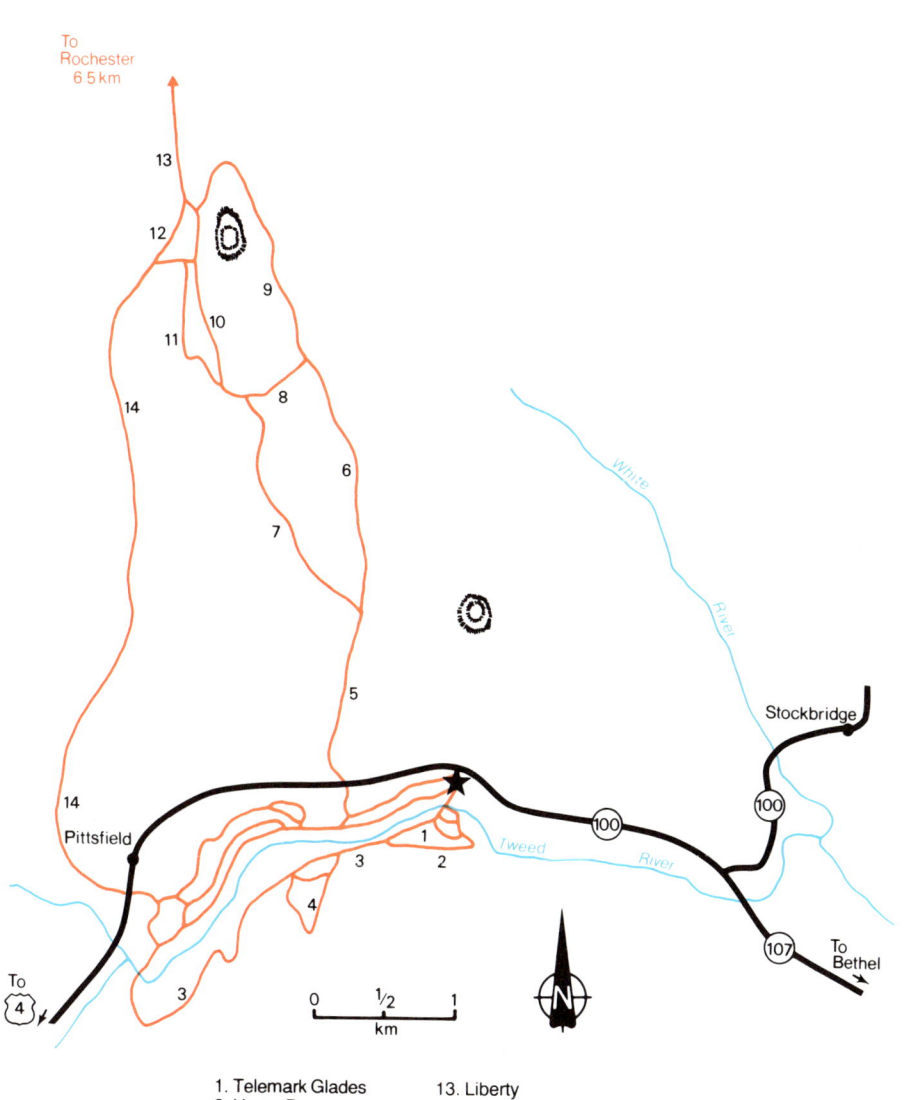

1. Telemark Glades
2. Upper Doe
3. Buck Dancer
4. Dancer Loop
5. Mayo Meadow Hill
6. South Contest Trail
7. Clipper's Chase
8. Pine Plummet
9. North Contest Trail
10. Hill Road
11. Rabbit Run
12. Guernsey Brook Road
13. Liberty
14. Guided Tours Only

Mountain Top
Ski Touring Center

Mountain Top Road
Chittenden, Vt. 05737

Trail Network: 90 km.
Machine Groomed Trail: 35 km.
Hours of Operation: daily, 9:00 a.m. - 5:00 p.m.
Base Elevation: 1,800 ft.
High Trail: 2,100 ft.
Low Trail: 1,500 ft.

Located 10 miles northwest of Rutland at an elevation of 2,000 feet is the Mountain Top Ski Touring Center. As the leaves fall from the trees in the autumn and the temperature slides below freezing, the snow guns stand ready to provide the anxious skier with some early season touring. While the snowmaking coverage is not extensive, Mother Nature usually provides a generous blanket of snow early in the season for one of the state's largest ski touring networks.

Mountain Top Inn and Ski Touring Center offers a complete winter experience with horsedrawn sleigh rides, ice skating, tobogganing, and sledding. The Inn offers dramatic views of the Green Mountains soaring over Chittenden Reservoir.

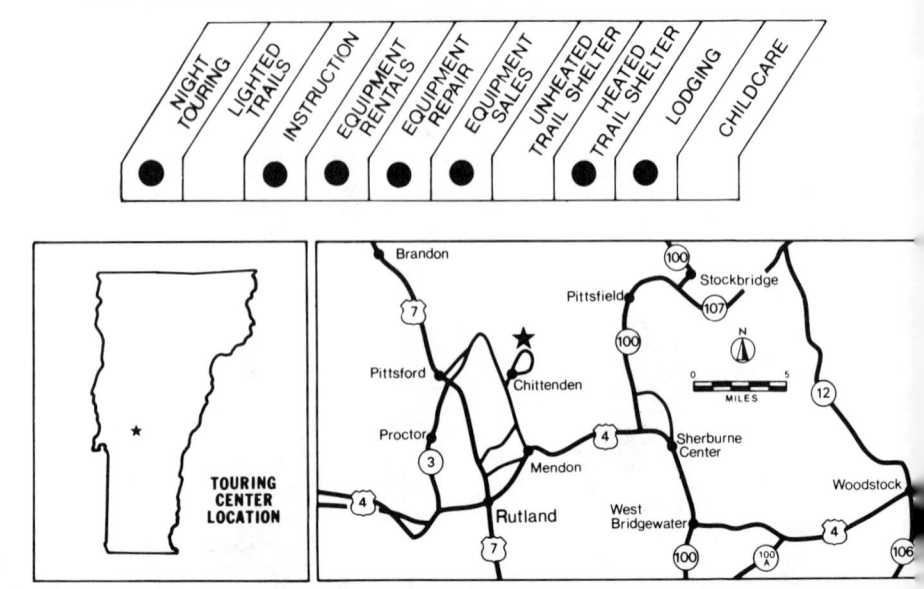

Central Vermont

71

Chittenden Reservoir

keep off ice

Chittenden

To ⑦ ④

N

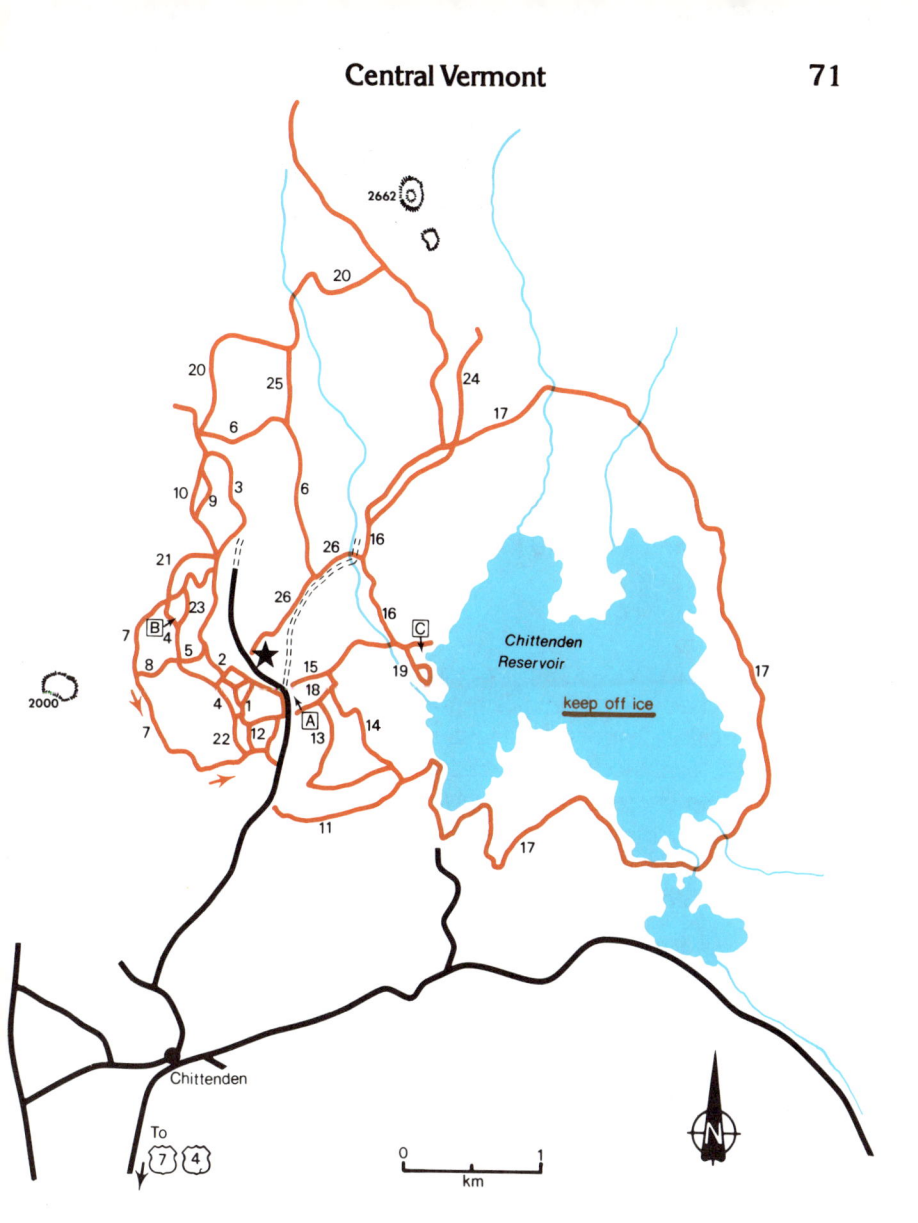

0 ——— 1
km

1. Turkey Trak 1km ●
2. Interfield 2km ■◆
3. Sugar House Run 2km ●■
4. Logger Head 2km ●■
5. Black Out .2km ◆
6. Deer Run 4km ●■
7. Challenger 2km ◆
8. Blue Side Winder 1km ■
9. Orange Dive 1km ◆
10. Red Alert 1km ■
11. Wolves Rendezvous 2km ●
12. Looper 1km ●
13. The El 1.5km ●
14. Reservoir Run 1km ■
15. Zipper 1km ◆
16. Boondocks 3km ■◆
17. Round Robin 20km ●■◆
18. Bounder 1.2km ●
19. Snow Goose 1km ●
20. Lost Horizon 12km ◆
21. Randall's Run 1km ■
22. Herbie's Run .25km ◆
23. Ridge Run 1km ■
24. Red Camp 1km ●
25. De Bonis Cutback .5km ●
26. Hewitt Brook Trail .5km ●■
A. Mtn. Top Inn
B. Log Cabin
C. Chalet

Mountain Meadows
Ski Touring Center

Route 4
Killington, Vt. 05751
Tel. 802-775-7077

Trail Network: 40 km.
Machine Groomed Trail: 25 km.
Hours of Operation: daily, 9:00 a.m. - 5:00 p.m.
Base Elevation: 1,600 ft.
High Trail: 1,700 ft
Low Trail: 1,400 ft.

Mountain Meadows Ski Touring Center is nestled in a high mountain valley, just five miles from Killington Ski Area. The ski center is located at the Mountain Meadows Lodge, a century-old converted farmhouse and barn, which can accommodate seventy guests.

From the center, the trail network spreads out over Kent Pond and throughout the surrounding hills, with a wilderness spur that snakes down the valley. Trails are carefully machine groomed with V-type dual track setters, making easy, smooth skiing for all levels of ability.

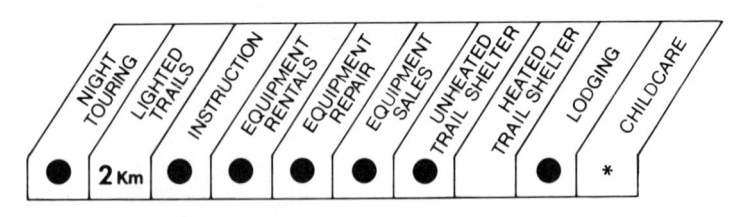

NIGHT TOURING	LIGHTED TRAILS	INSTRUCTION	EQUIPMENT RENTALS	EQUIPMENT REPAIR	EQUIPMENT SALES	UNHEATED TRAIL SHELTER	HEATED TRAIL SHELTER	LODGING	CHILDCARE
● 2 Km	●	●	●	●	●		●	*	

* By arrangement

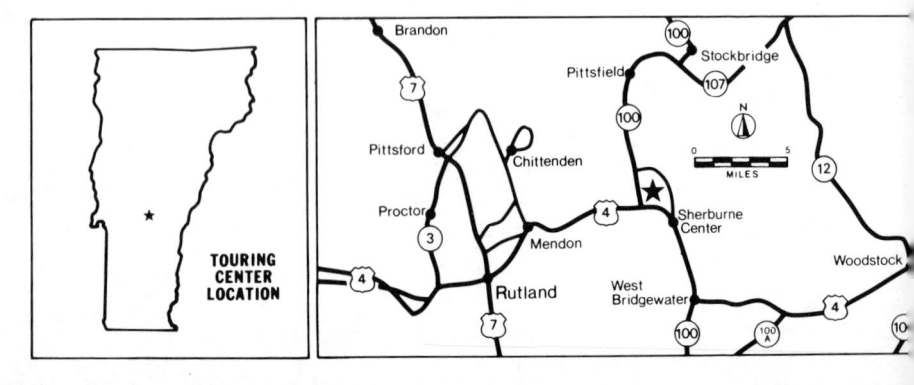

Central Vermont 73

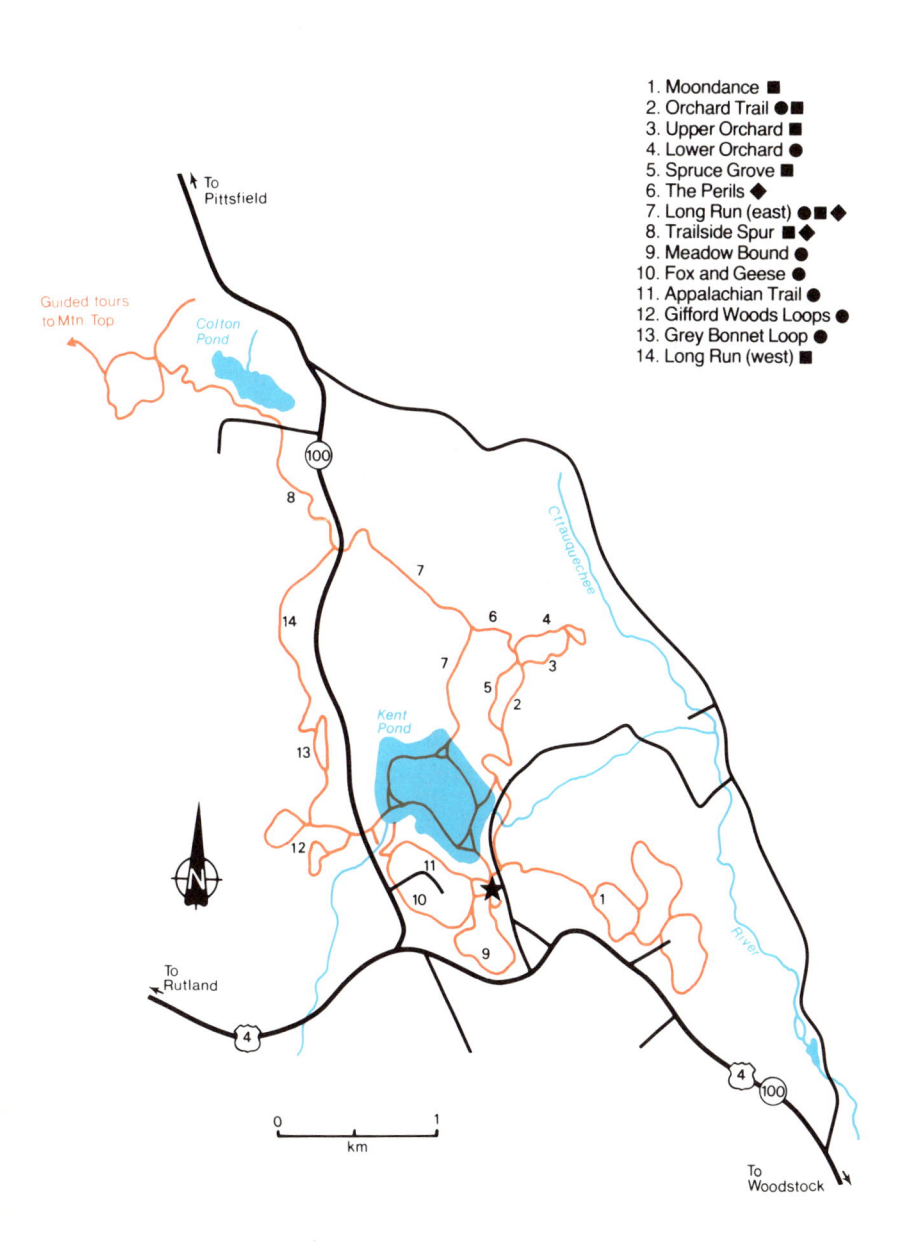

1. Moondance ■
2. Orchard Trail ●■
3. Upper Orchard ■
4. Lower Orchard ●
5. Spruce Grove ■
6. The Perils ◆
7. Long Run (east) ●■◆
8. Trailside Spur ■◆
9. Meadow Bound ●
10. Fox and Geese ●
11. Appalachian Trail ●
12. Gifford Woods Loops ●
13. Grey Bonnet Loop ●
14. Long Run (west) ■

Wilderness Trails
Nordic Ski School
and Touring Center

Quechee Inn
Clubhouse Road
Quechee, Vt. 05059
Tel. 802-295-7620

Trail Network:　　　km.
Machine Groomed Trail:　　km.
Hours of Operation: daily, 8:00 a.m. - dark
Base Elevation:　600 ft.
High Trail:　1,000 ft.
Low Trail:　500 ft.

Ski touring at Wilderness Trails in Quechee offers one the unique opportunity of skiing into one of Vermont's most photographed spots, the Quechee River Gorge. At the head of the Gorge trail rushes an immense waterfall, which when frozen, creates a magnificent ice formation.

Wilderness Trails also offers a drink-of-your-choice ticket at the Red Pines Restaurant for anyone using the trail system. The restaurant is just off the trail and makes a perfect rest stop.

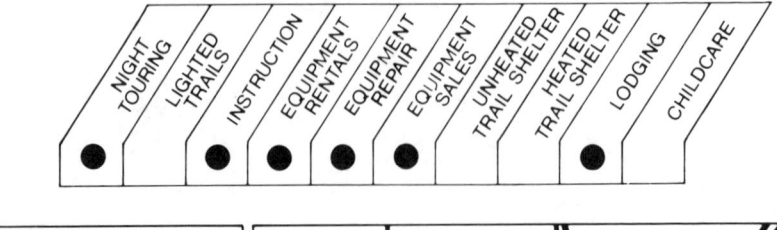

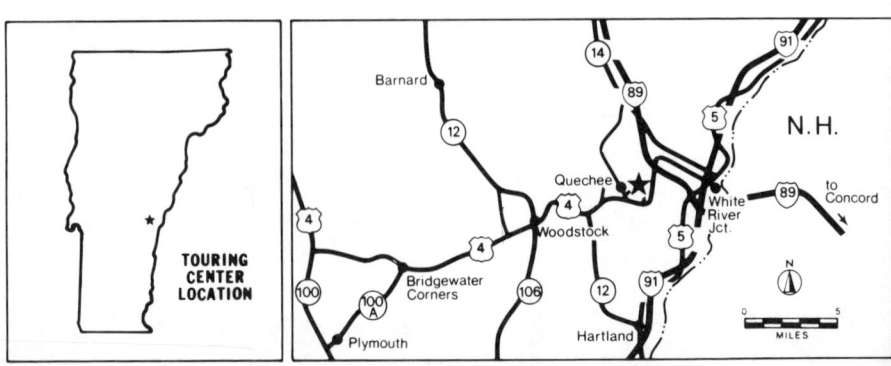

Central Vermont

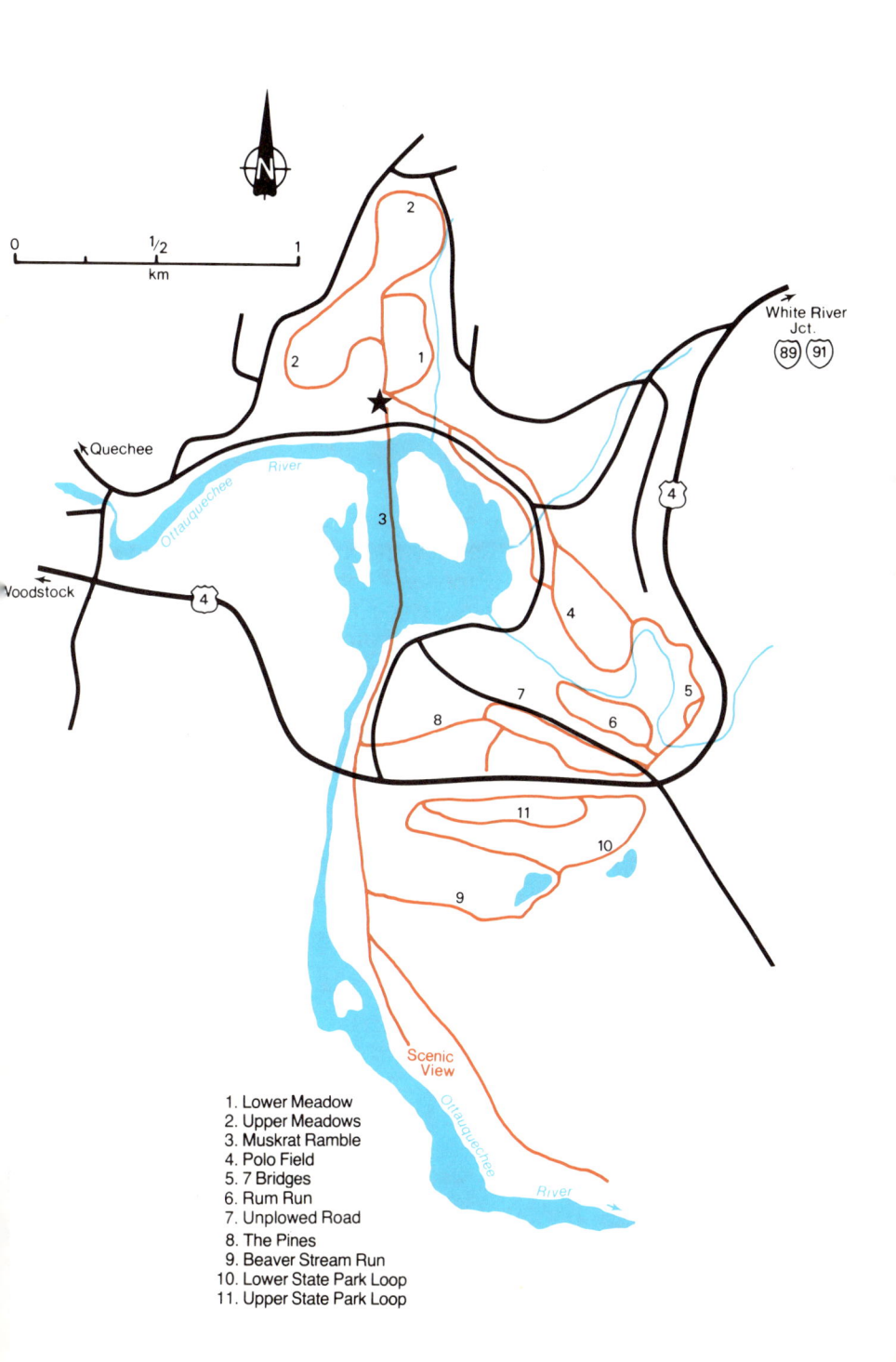

1. Lower Meadow
2. Upper Meadows
3. Muskrat Ramble
4. Polo Field
5. 7 Bridges
6. Rum Run
7. Unplowed Road
8. The Pines
9. Beaver Stream Run
10. Lower State Park Loop
11. Upper State Park Loop

Woodstock
Ski Touring Center

Route 106
Woodstock, Vt. 05091
Tel. 802-457-2114

Trail Network: 75 km.
Machine Groomed Trail: 35 km.
Hours of Operation: daily, 9:00 a.m. - dusk
Base Elevation: 700 ft.
High Trail: 1,800 ft.
Low Trail: 700 ft.

The Woodstock Ski Touring Center, housed in the luxurious clubhouse of the Woodstock Country Club, is one of the most complete touring operations in North America. It consists of two large touring areas in addition to the ungroomed Skyline Trail. The Mt. Tom trail network utilizes carriage roads first cut on the baronial estate of Frederick Billings in the 1880s. It is also the first tree farm in the state of Vermont. The trail networks in this part of Vermont are very well integrated, and it is impossible to ski from the Kedron Valley Inn in South Woodstock north on a multi-night, multi-inn tour to the small town of East Barnard.

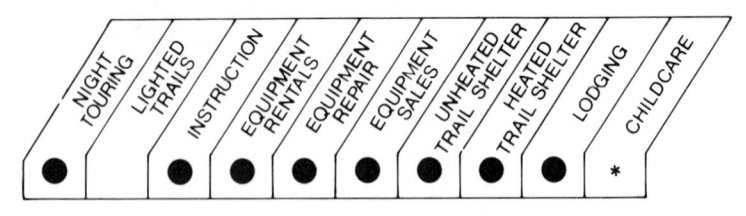

NIGHT TOURING	LIGHTED TRAILS	INSTRUCTION	EQUIPMENT RENTALS	EQUIPMENT REPAIR	EQUIPMENT SALES	UNHEATED TRAIL SHELTER	HEATED TRAIL SHELTER	LODGING	CHILDCARE
●	●	●	●	●	●	●	●	*	

*Call for information

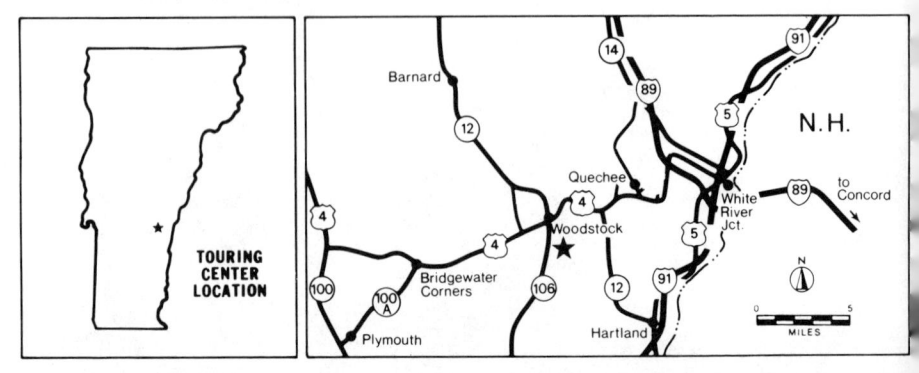

Central Vermont

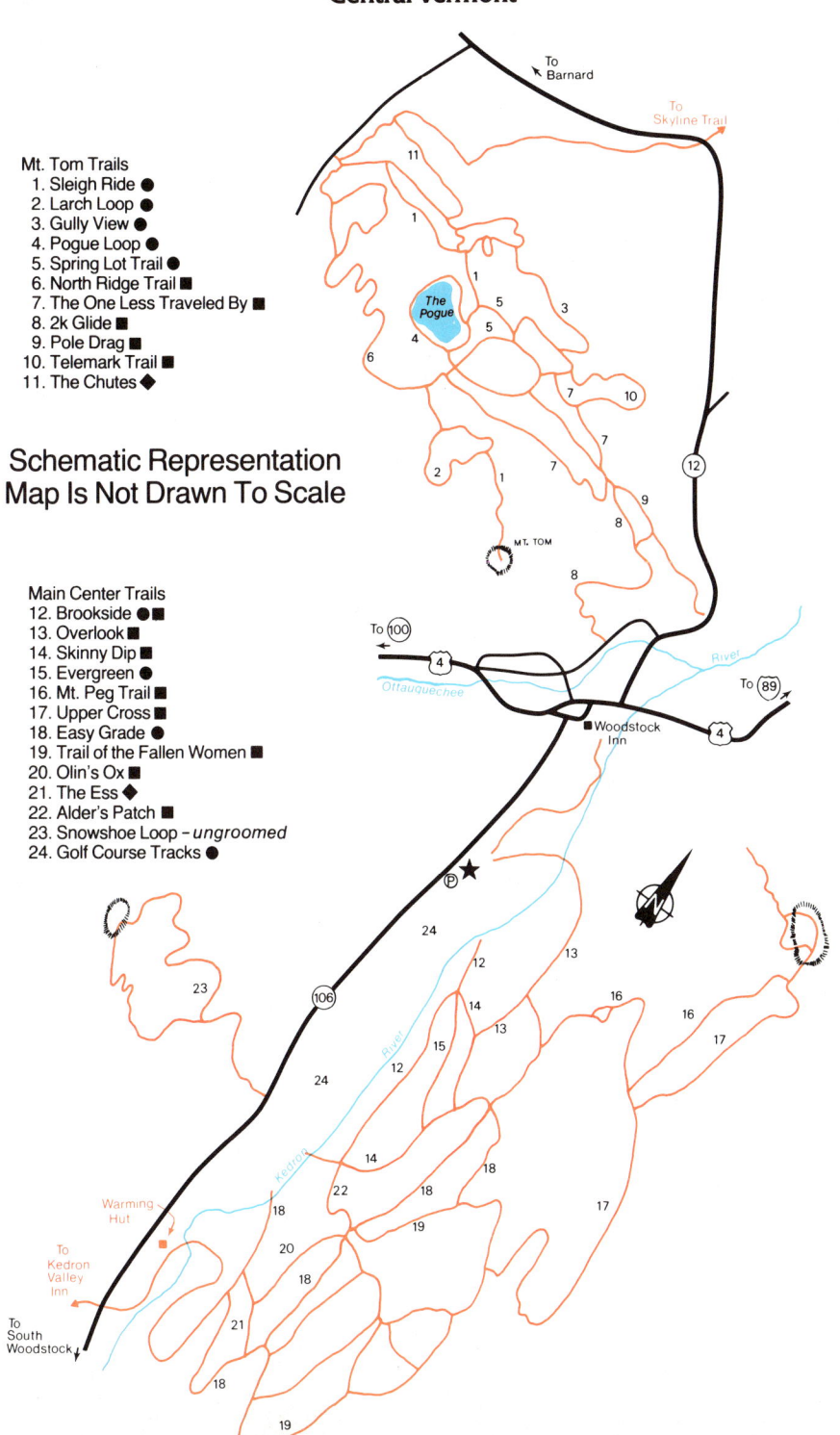

Mt. Tom Trails
1. Sleigh Ride ●
2. Larch Loop ●
3. Gully View ●
4. Pogue Loop ●
5. Spring Lot Trail ●
6. North Ridge Trail ■
7. The One Less Traveled By ■
8. 2k Glide ■
9. Pole Drag ■
10. Telemark Trail ■
11. The Chutes ◆

Schematic Representation
Map Is Not Drawn To Scale

Main Center Trails
12. Brookside ● ■
13. Overlook ■
14. Skinny Dip ■
15. Evergreen ●
16. Mt. Peg Trail ■
17. Upper Cross ■
18. Easy Grade ●
19. Trail of the Fallen Women ■
20. Olin's Ox ■
21. The Ess ◆
22. Alder's Patch ■
23. Snowshoe Loop – *ungroomed*
24. Golf Course Tracks ●

Central Vermont

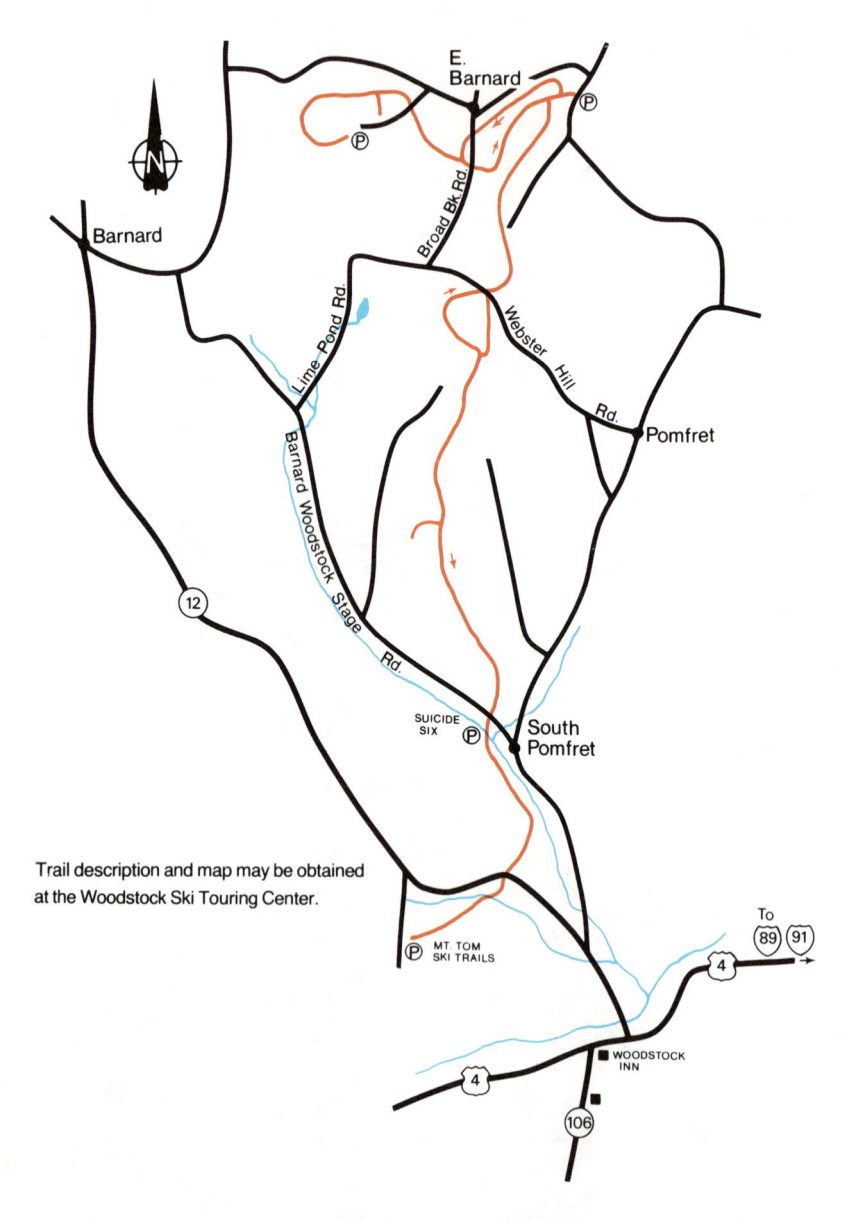

Trail description and map may be obtained at the Woodstock Ski Touring Center.

**Schematic Representation
Map Is Not Drawn To Scale**

WAXING GUIDE

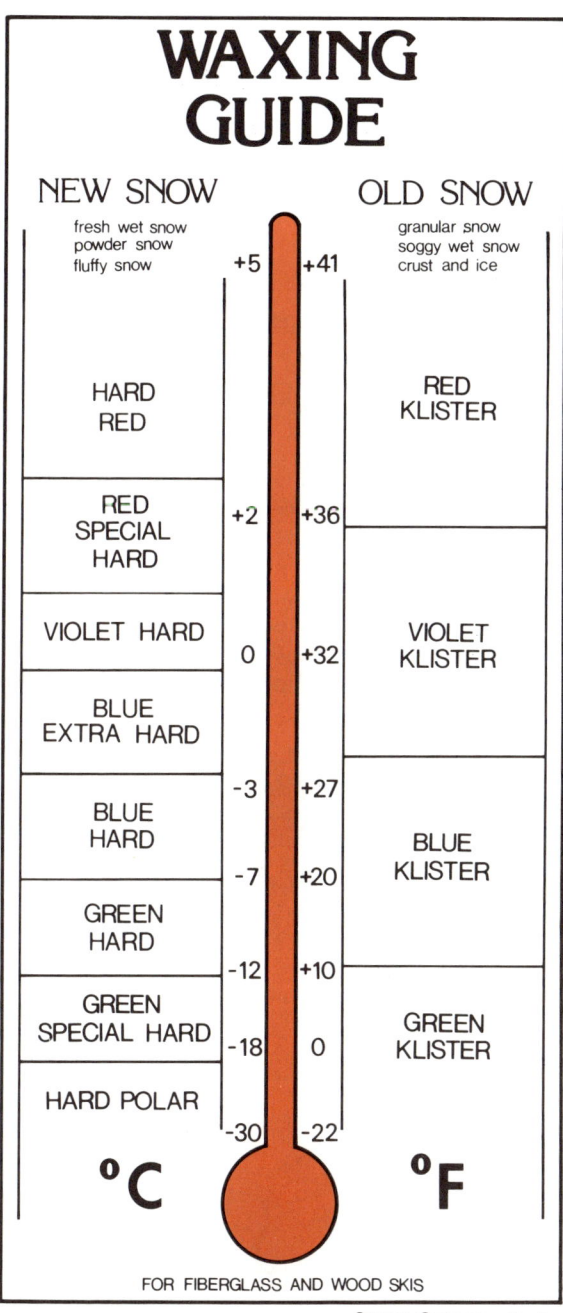

NEW SNOW			OLD SNOW
fresh wet snow powder snow fluffy snow	+5	+41	granular snow soggy wet snow crust and ice
HARD RED			RED KLISTER
RED SPECIAL HARD	+2	+36	
VIOLET HARD	0	+32	VIOLET KLISTER
BLUE EXTRA HARD			
BLUE HARD	-3	+27	BLUE KLISTER
GREEN HARD	-7	+20	
GREEN SPECIAL HARD	-12	+10	GREEN KLISTER
HARD POLAR	-18	0	
	-30	-22	
°C			°F

FOR FIBERGLASS AND WOOD SKIS

Source: Swix wax chart

Fox Run
Ski Touring Center

Fox Lane
Ludlow, Vt. 05149
Tel. 802-228-8871

Trail Network: 25 km.
Machine Groomed Trail: 25 km.
Hours of Operation: daily, 7:00 a.m. - 4:00 p.m.
Base Elevation: 1,000 ft.
High Trail: 1,200 ft.
Low Trail: 800 ft.

Fox Run is a small touring center located on golf course lands, next door to Okemo Mountain. More than half-a-dozen Alpine ski areas are within an hour's drive of Fox Run.

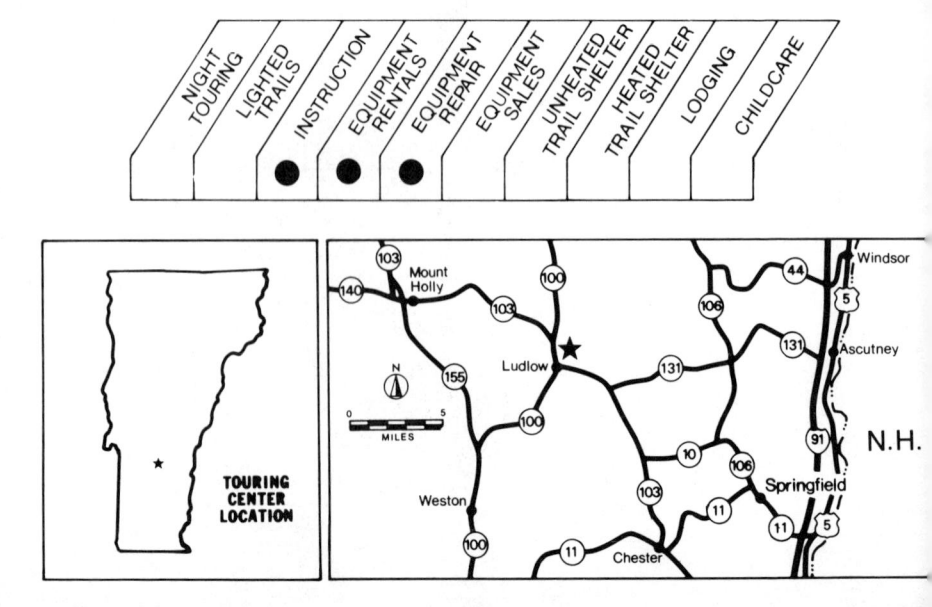

Central Vermont

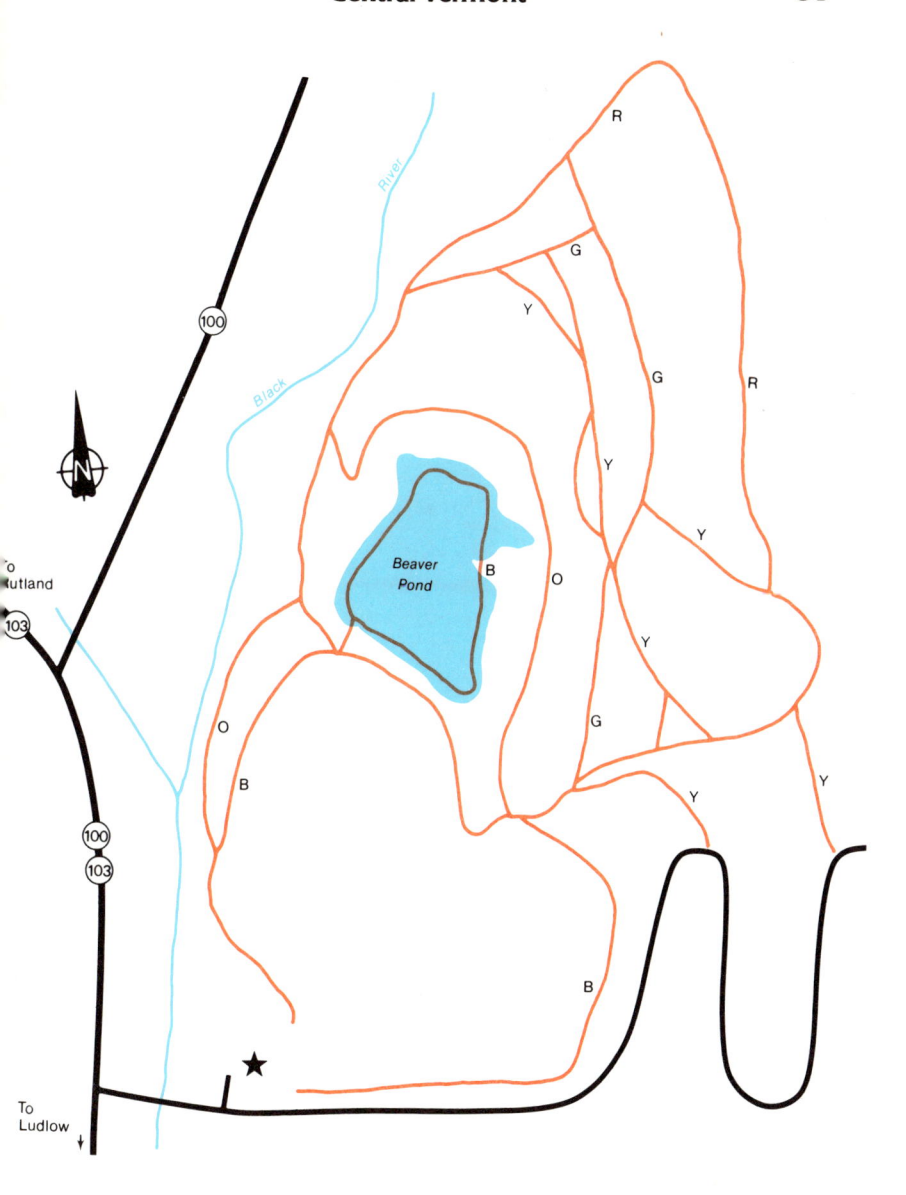

81

"B" Blue - 1.5 km
"O" Orange - 4.0 km
"G" Green - 6.5 km
"R" Red - 9.0 km
"Y" Yellow - 10.0 km

Schematic Representation
Map Is Not Drawn To Scale

SOUTHERN VERMONT

Wild Wings
Ski Touring Center

Box 132
Peru, Vt. 05152
Tel. 802-824-6793

Trail Network: 20 km.
Machine Groomed Trail: 15 km.
Hours of Operation: daily, 9:00 a.m. - 4:00 p.m.
Base Elevation: 1,700 ft.
High Trail: 2,100 ft.
Low Trail: 1,700 ft.

Wild Wings is a small, down home, ski touring center, located in the highlands of the Green Mountain National Forest. The center is in a converted horse barn, with a warming room and rental shop. Heavy snows at the center's 2,000 feet elevation provide long months of skiing

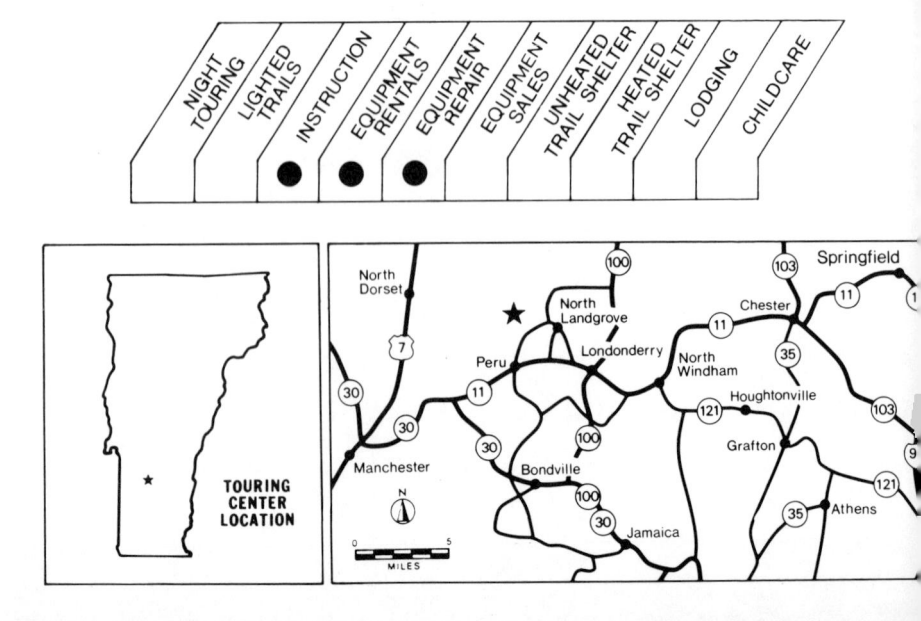

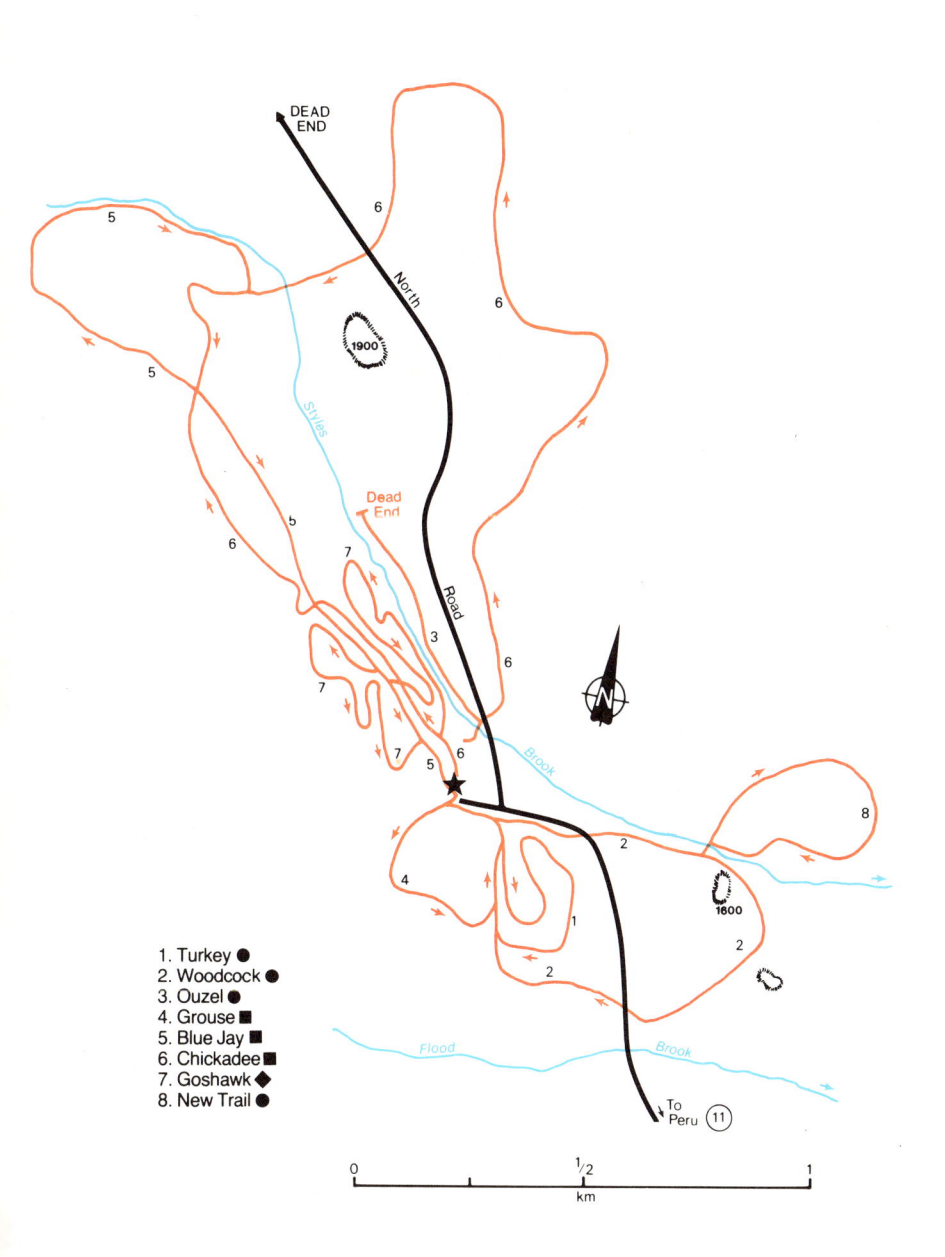

Southern Vermont

85

1. Turkey ●
2. Woodcock ●
3. Ouzel ●
4. Grouse ■
5. Blue Jay ■
6. Chickadee ■
7. Goshawk ◆
8. New Trail ●

Nordic Inn
Ski Touring Center

Box 96, Route 11
Landgrove, Vt. 05148
Tel. 802-824-6444

Trail Network: 20 km.
Machine Groomed Trail: 20 km.
Hours of Operation: daily, 8:30 a.m. - 4:30 p.m.
Base Elevation: 1,350 ft.
High Trail: 1,400 ft.
Low Trail: 1,200 ft.

The Nordic Inn Ski Touring Center's trails take the skier through Red Pine stands in the Green Mountain National Forest, across beaver ponds and by an old colonial cemetary on a hilltop. In addition to 20 km of fine trail skiing, telemark and downhill cross-country skiing classes can be arranged at the nearby Bromley Alpine Ski Area. Dining and drinking beside the Inn's fieldstone fireplace, or in the solarium, are special after-ski treats that should not be missed.

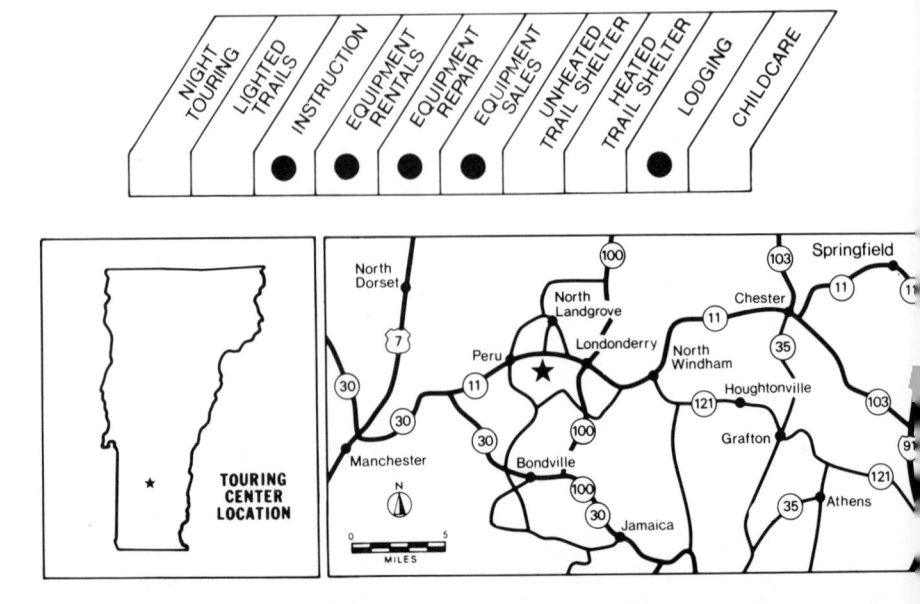

Southern Vermont

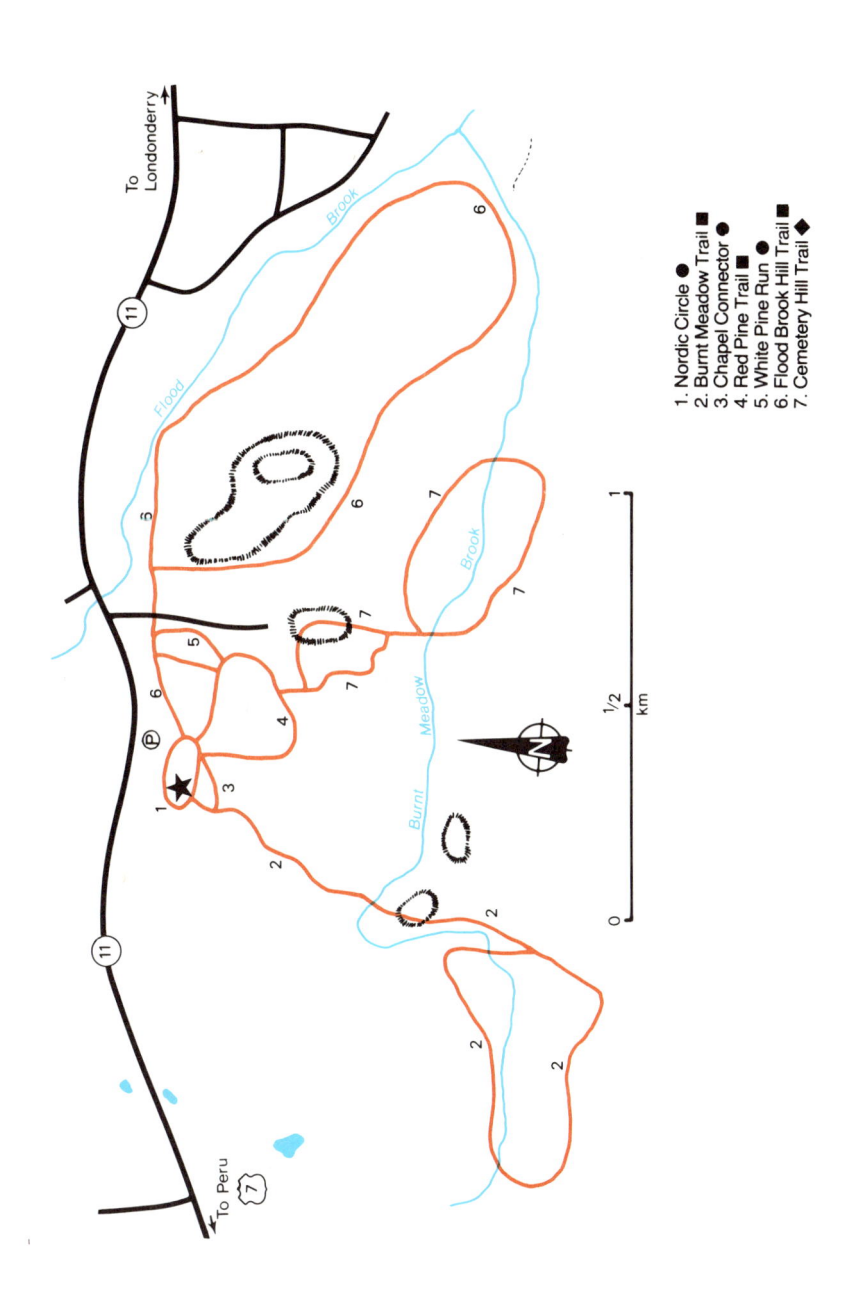

87

1. Nordic Circle ●
2. Burnt Meadow Trail ■
3. Chapel Connector ●
4. Red Pine Trail ■
5. White Pine Run ●
6. Flood Brook Hill Trail ■
7. Cemetery Hill Trail ◆

Viking
Ski Touring Center

Little Pond Road
Londonderry, Vt. 05148
Tel. 802-824-3933

Trail Network: 45 km.
Machine Groomed Trail: 35 km.
Hours of Operation: daily, 8.30 a.m. - 4:00 p.m.
Base Elevation: 1,400 ft.
High Trail: 1,700 ft.
Low Trail: 1,200 ft.

Viking is one of the nation's oldest cross-country ski areas, offering many magnificent views from several locations. The Cobble Hill trail, a 10 km touring loop, has long been a favorite with skiers. The Weston Village trail (10 km one way) connects Viking with the Inn at Weston and the village of Weston. There are two other country inns along the Viking trail system. Inn to inn tours are run throughout the winter.

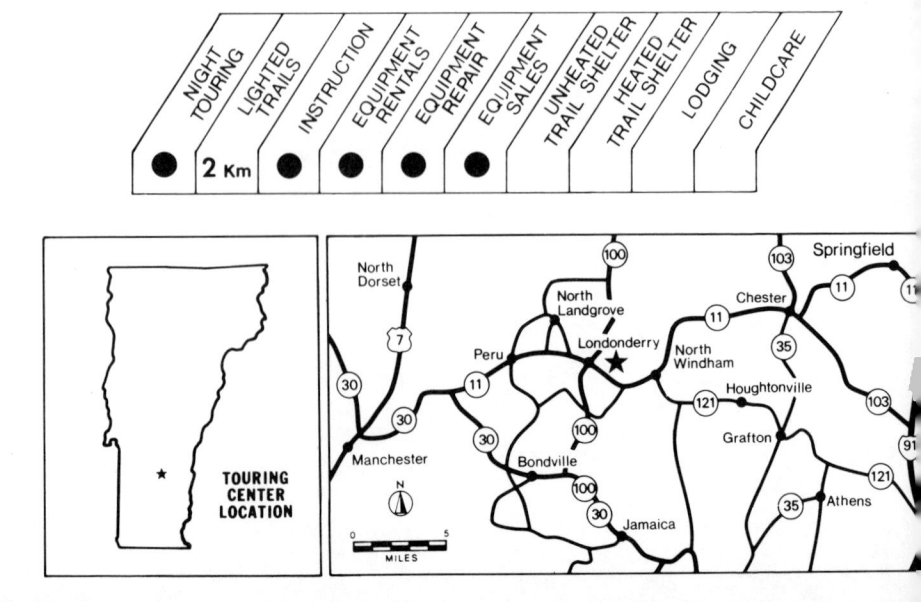

Southern Vermont

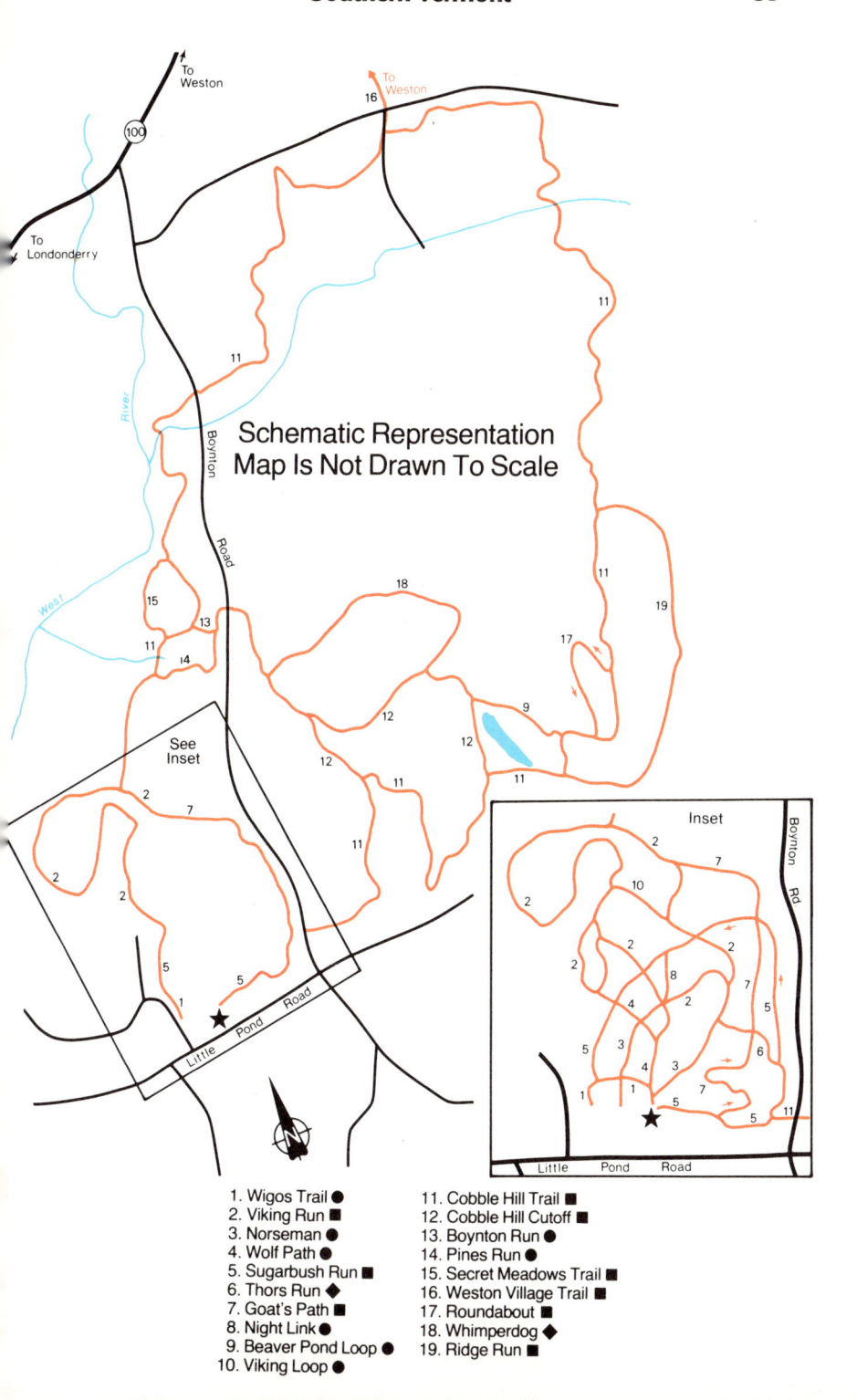

Schematic Representation Map Is Not Drawn To Scale

Inset

1. Wigos Trail ●
2. Viking Run ■
3. Norseman ●
4. Wolf Path ●
5. Sugarbush Run ■
6. Thors Run ♦
7. Goat's Path ■
8. Night Link ●
9. Beaver Pond Loop ●
10. Viking Loop ●
11. Cobble Hill Trail ■
12. Cobble Hill Cutoff ■
13. Boynton Run ●
14. Pines Run ●
15. Secret Meadows Trail ■
16. Weston Village Trail ■
17. Roundabout ■
18. Whimperdog ♦
19. Ridge Run ■

Tater Hill
Cross-Country Ski Center

RFD #1
Chester, Vt. 05143
Tel. 802-875-2517

Trail Network: 40 km.
Machine Groomed Trail: 20 km.
Hours of Operation: daily. 9:00 a.m. - 4:30 p.m.
Base Elevation: 1,780 ft.
High Trail: 1,950 ft.
Low Trail: 1,780 ft.

The Tater Hill Cross-Country Skiing Center is located inside of a 200-year-old farm that houses a restaurant, lounge, and a very comfortable solarium with fine views of snow covered hills, rolling away in the distance. The center's trails journey through open meadow, hardwood and evergreen forests. Special events are planned each month for the entertainment of patrons.

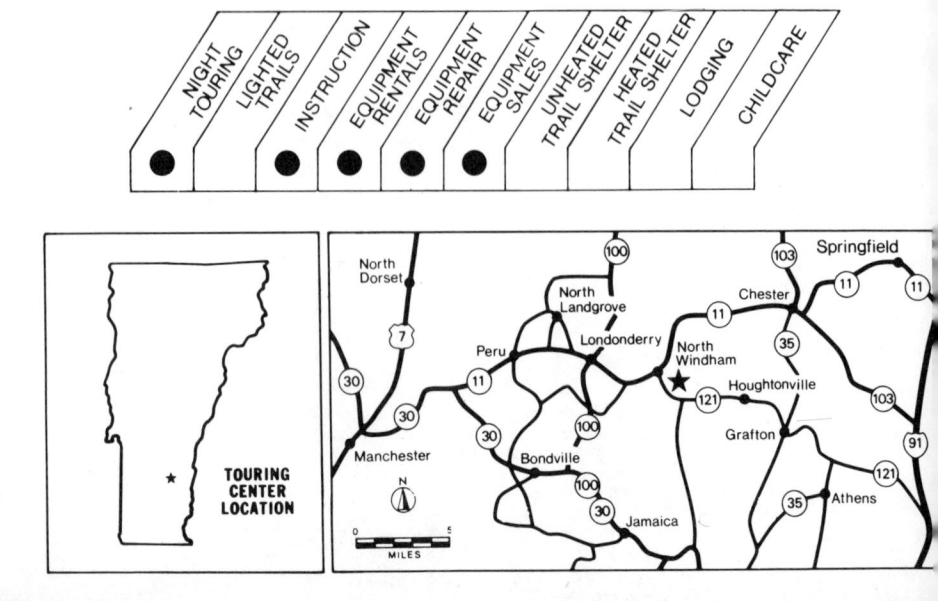

Southern Vermont

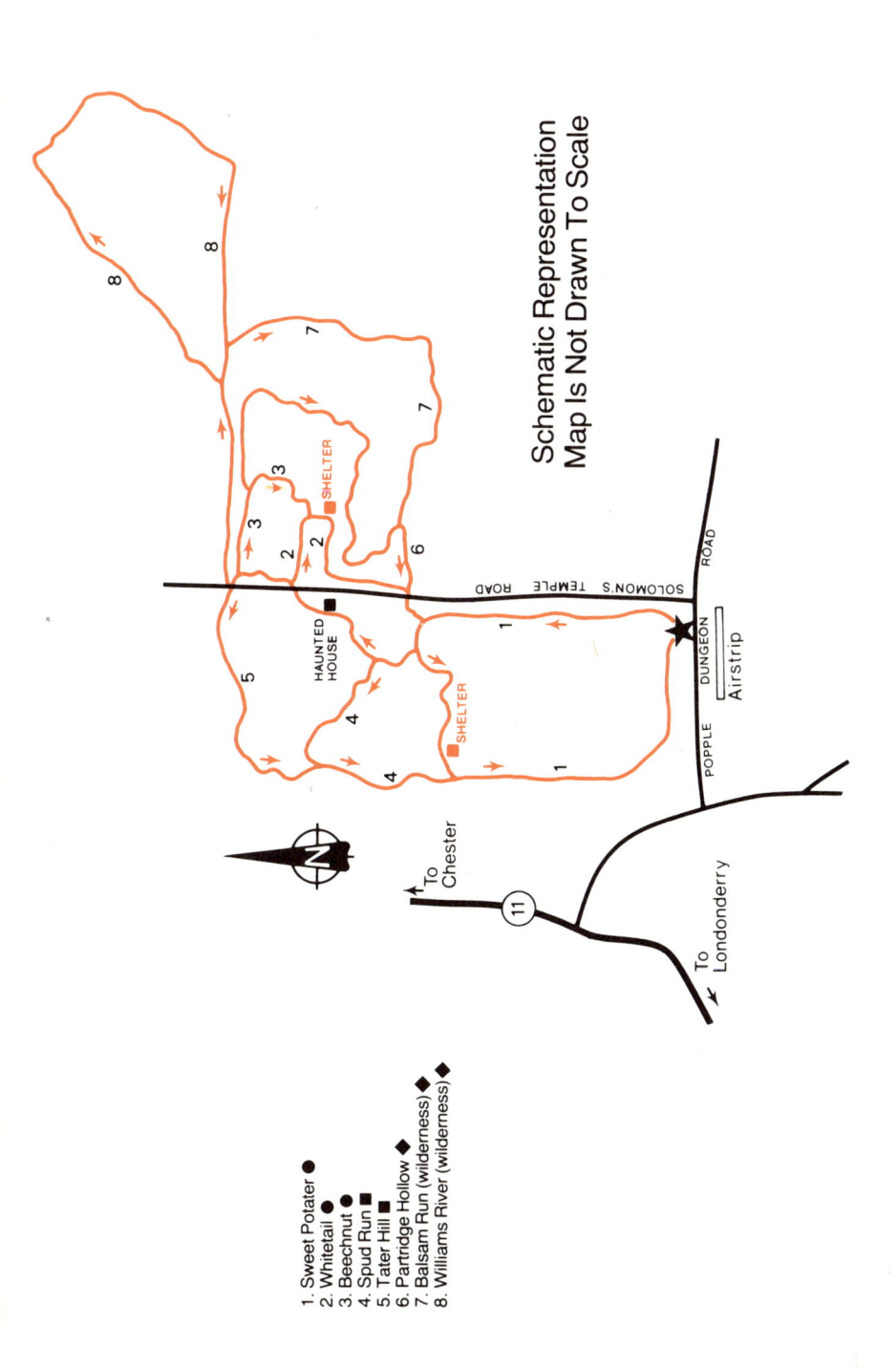

**Schematic Representation
Map Is Not Drawn To Scale**

1. Sweet Potater ●
2. Whitetail ●
3. Beechnut ●
4. Spud Run ■
5. Tater Hill ■
6. Partridge Hollow ◆
7. Balsam Run (wilderness) ◆
8. Williams River (wilderness) ◆

Grafton Cross-Country Ski Shop and Trail System

Townshend Road
Grafton, Vt. 05146
Tel. 802-843-2234

Trail Network: 40 km.
Machine Groomed Trail: km.
Hours of Operation: daily. 9:00 a.m. - 5:00 p.m.
Base Elevation: 900 ft.
High Trail: 1,724 ft
Low Trail: ft.

In the historic village of Grafton, a half mile south of the Old Tavern, located in a rustic log cabin at the foot of Bear Hill, is the Grafton Cross-Country Ski Trail System and Shop. The shop is well stocked with all necessary equipment and clothing for pleasurable outings. The trails wind around and to the top of Bear Hill.

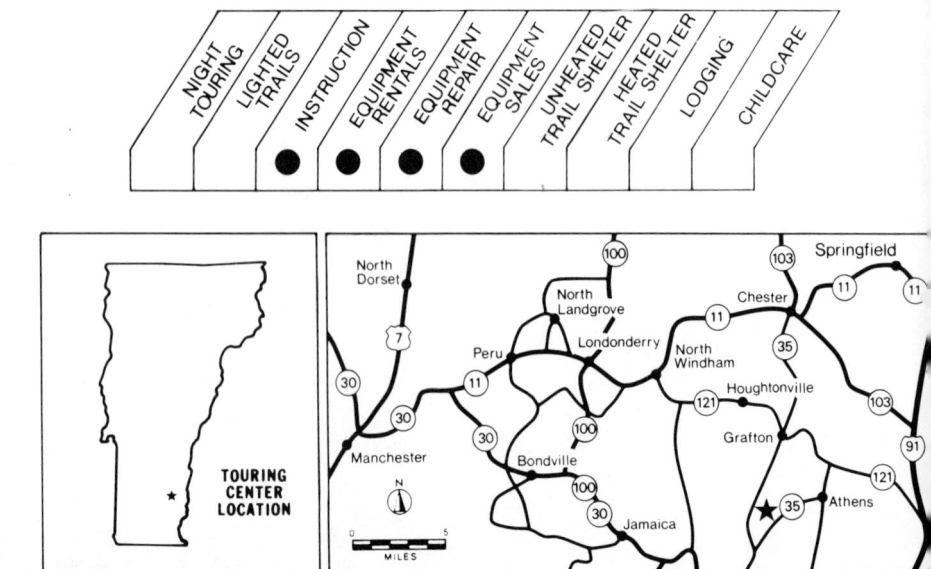

Southern Vermont

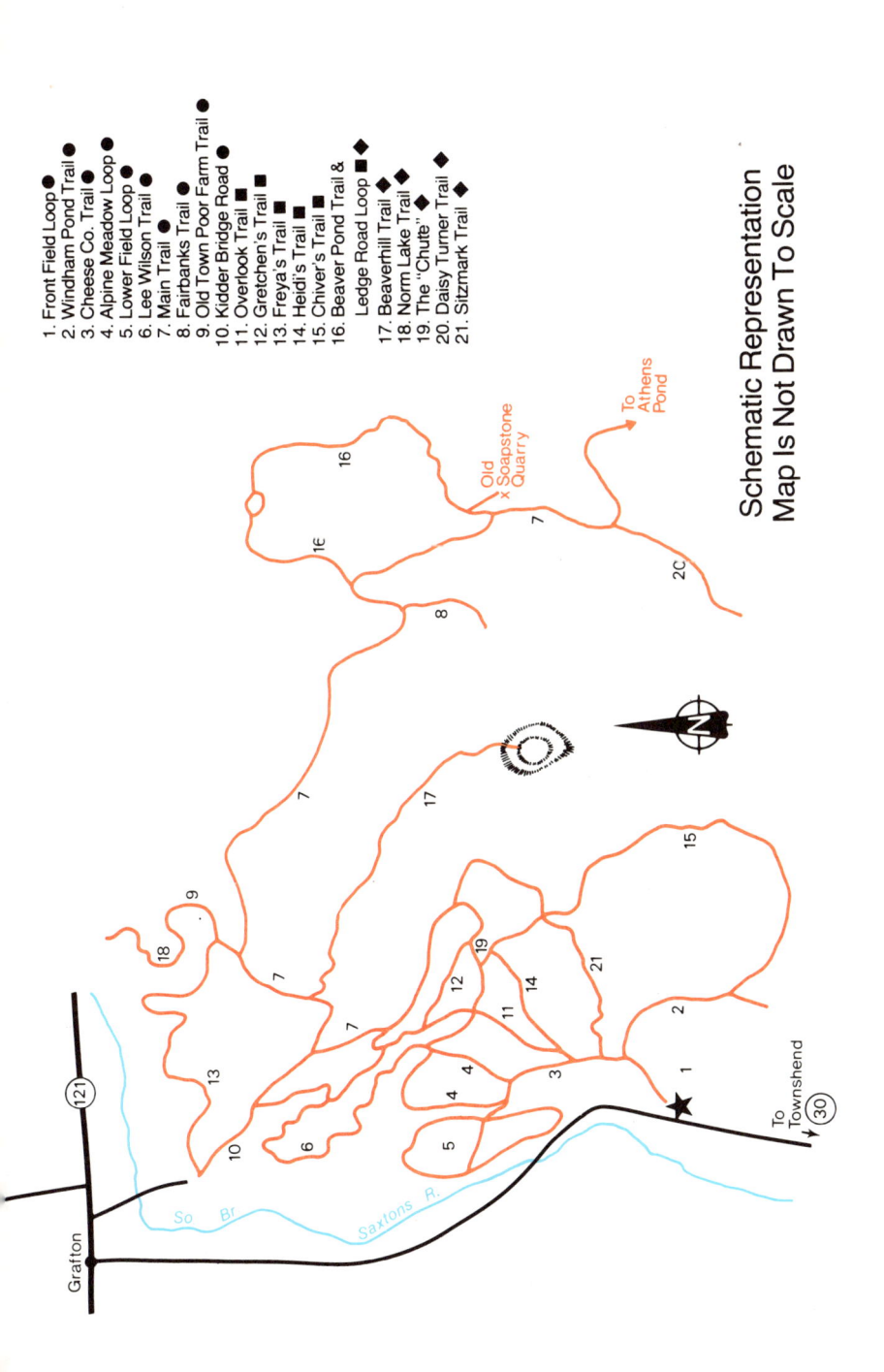

**Schematic Representation
Map Is Not Drawn To Scale**

1. Front Field Loop
2. Windham Pond Trail
3. Cheese Co. Trail
4. Alpine Meadow Loop
5. Lower Field Loop
6. Lee Wilson Trail
7. Main Trail
8. Fairbanks Trail
9. Old Town Poor Farm Trail
10. Kidder Bridge Road
11. Overlook Trail
12. Gretchen's Trail
13. Freya's Trail
14. Heidi's Trail
15. Chiver's Trail
16. Beaver Pond Trail & Ledge Road Loop
17. Beaverhill Trail
18. Norm Lake Trail
19. The "Chute"
20. Daisy Turner Trail
21. Sitzmark Trail

Hildene
Ski Touring Center

Box 377
Manchester, Vt. 05254
Tel. 802-362-1788

Trail Network: 32 km.
Machine Groomed Trail: 26 km.
Hours of Operation: daily, 9:00 a.m. - 5:00 p.m.
Base Elevation: 950 ft.
High Trail: 950 ft
Low Trail: 650 ft.

Skiing at Hildene is more than good, it's an experience in American history. Ski on the touring trails surrounding the 24 room Georgian Revival Manor, the estate of Robert Todd Lincoln, the president's son. A coal parlor stove warms the Ski Center in the Lincoln Carriage Barn. The main house (mansion) is open on holidays, including Abraham Lincoln's birthday. Don't miss the Manchester Winter Carnival.

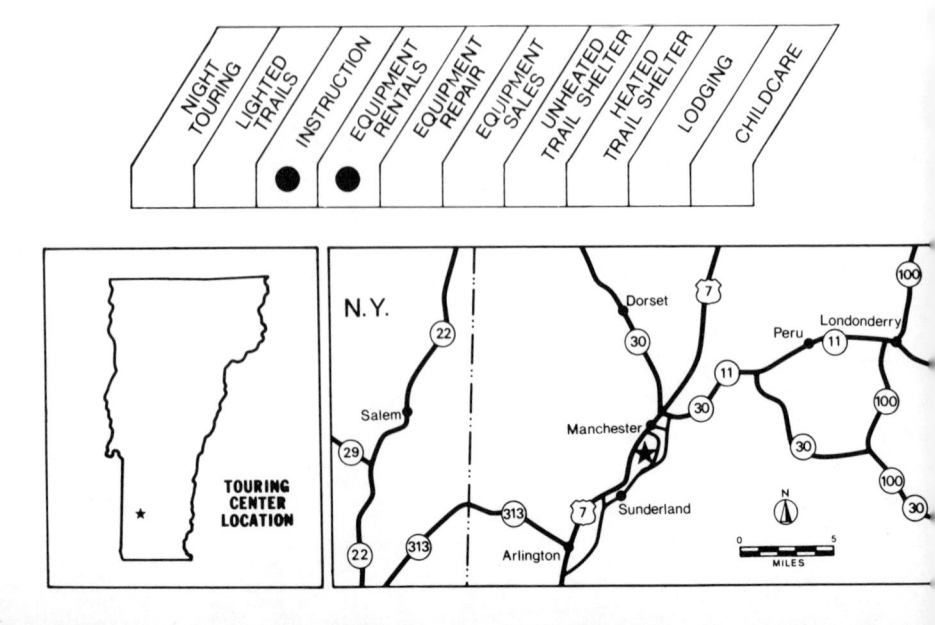

Southern Vermont

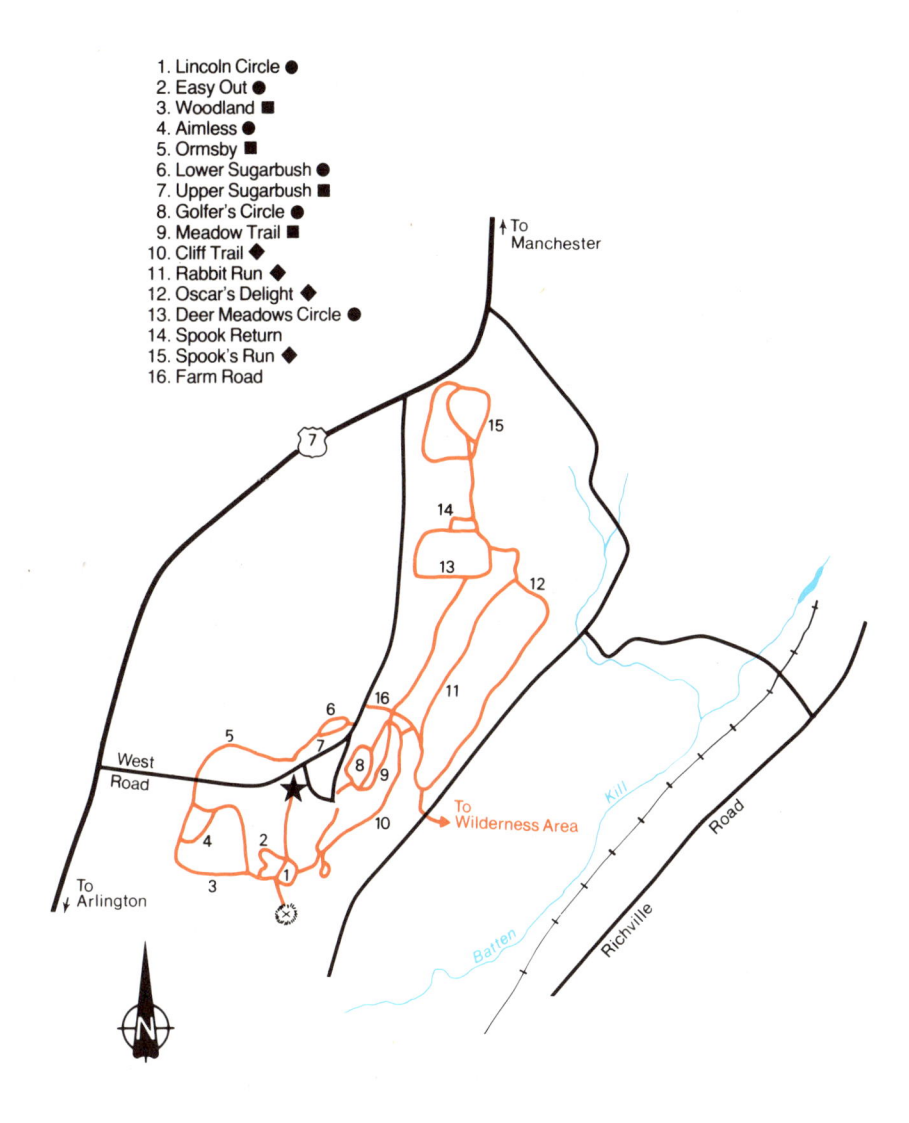

95

1. Lincoln Circle ●
2. Easy Out ●
3. Woodland ■
4. Aimless ●
5. Ormsby ■
6. Lower Sugarbush ●
7. Upper Sugarbush ■
8. Golfer's Circle ●
9. Meadow Trail ■
10. Cliff Trail ◆
11. Rabbit Run ◆
12. Oscar's Delight ◆
13. Deer Meadows Circle ●
14. Spook Return
15. Spook's Run ◆
16. Farm Road

**Schematic Representation
Map Is Not Drawn To Scale**

Stratton Touring Center

Stratton Mountain, Vt. 05155
Tel. 802-297-2200

Trail Network: 20 km.
Machine Groomed Trail: km.
Hours of Operation: daily, 8:30 a.m. - 4:00 p.m.
Base Elevation: ft.
High Trail: ft.
Low Trail: ft.

Stratton Ski Touring Center has recently expanded its trails beyond its golf course network. The more adventurous skier may try the primitive trail up to Stratton Pond. Stratton is a complete winter resort with fine Alpine opportunities close by at Stratton Mountain and Bromley.

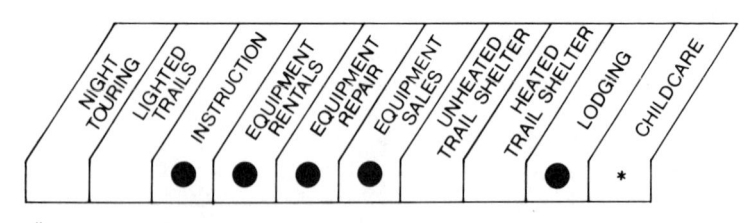

NIGHT TOURING	LIGHTED TRAILS	INSTRUCTION	EQUIPMENT RENTALS	EQUIPMENT REPAIR	EQUIPMENT SALES	UNHEATED TRAIL SHELTER	HEATED TRAIL SHELTER	LODGING	CHILDCARE
		●	●	●	●		●	*	

*Located a mile away

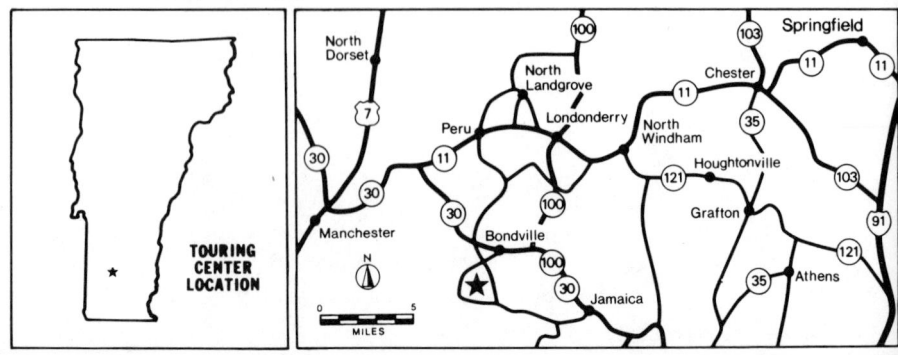

Southern Vermont

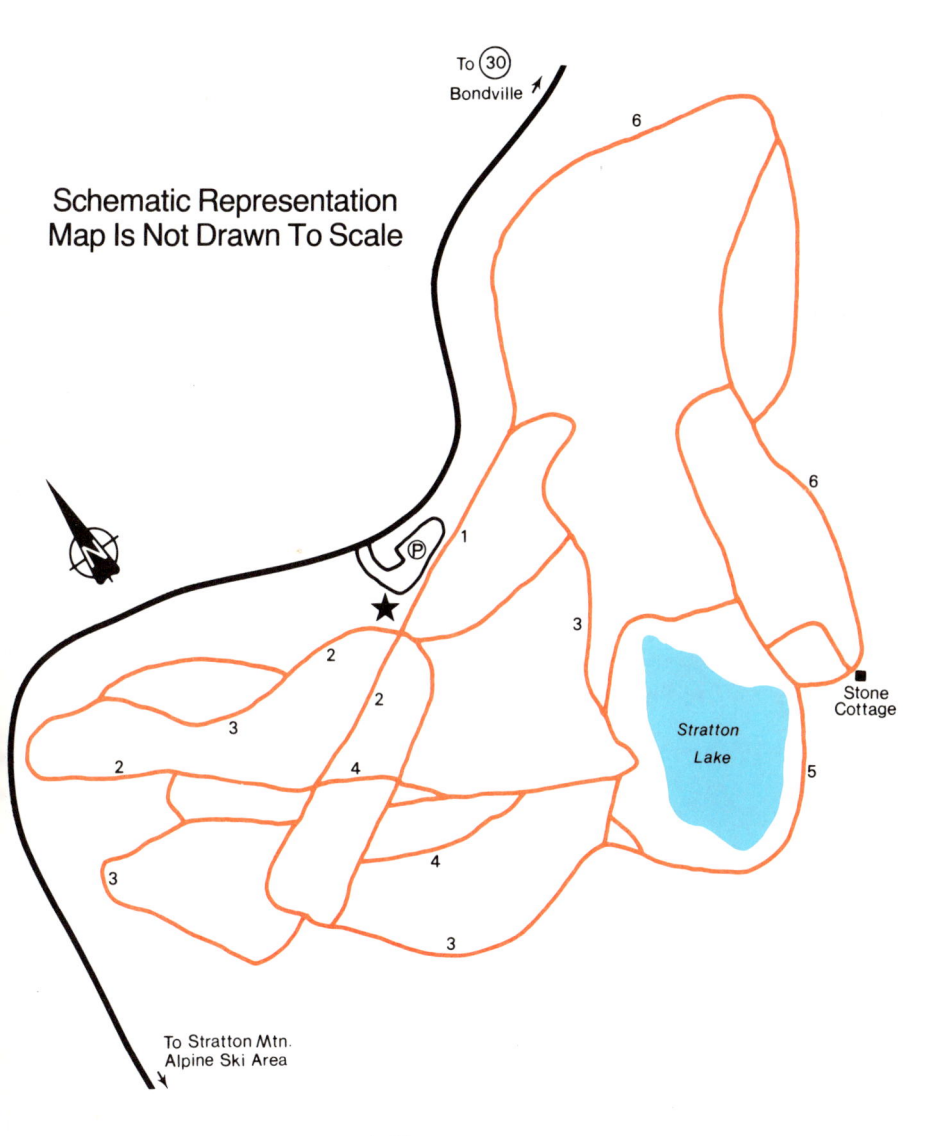

97

**Schematic Representation
Map Is Not Drawn To Scale**

To (30) Bondville

Stratton Lake

Stone Cottage

To Stratton Mtn. Alpine Ski Area

1. .8 km
2. 1.7 km
3. 3.6 km
4. 1.5 km
5. 1.0 km
6. Meadow Trail 5 km

Sitzmark
Ski Touring Center

East Dover Road
Wilmington, Vt. 05363
Tel. 802-464-3384

Trail Network: 32 km.
Machine Groomed Trail: km.
Hours of Operation: daily, 8:00 a.m. - 5:00 p.m.
Base Elevation: 1,400 ft.
High Trail: ft.
Low Trail: ft.

The Haystack-Mount Snow ridge stands in bold profile above and to the west of the Sitzmark Ski Touring Center. The Sitzmark offers a variety of fine trails and touring packages that should be inquired about. One of them is a special 8 km round trip tour from the Sitzmark to the West Dover Inn (built in 1846) for lunch and hot drinks.

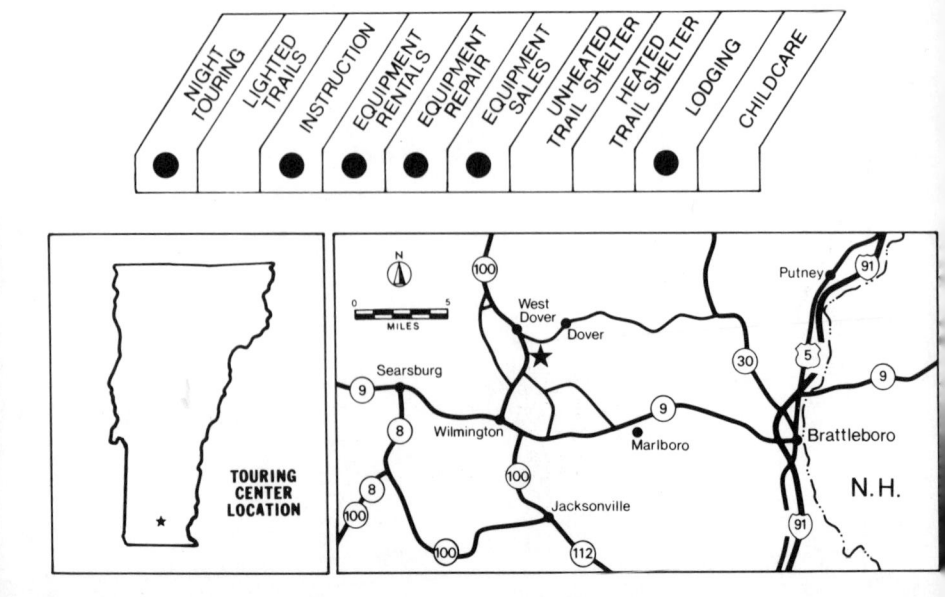

Southern Vermont

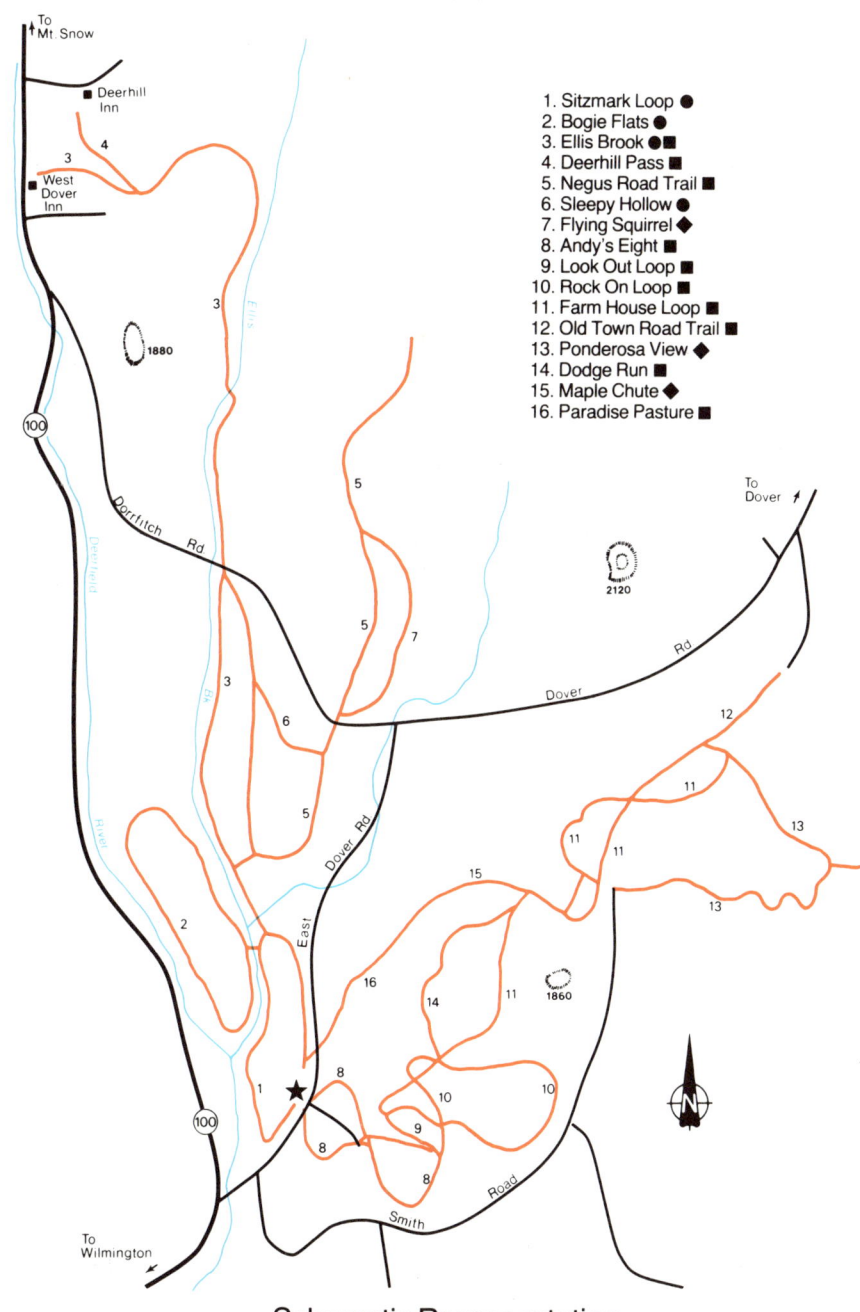

1. Sitzmark Loop ●
2. Bogie Flats ●
3. Ellis Brook ●■
4. Deerhill Pass ■
5. Negus Road Trail ■
6. Sleepy Hollow ●
7. Flying Squirrel ◆
8. Andy's Eight ■
9. Look Out Loop ■
10. Rock On Loop ■
11. Farm House Loop ■
12. Old Town Road Trail ■
13. Ponderosa View ◆
14. Dodge Run ■
15. Maple Chute ◆
16. Paradise Pasture ■

**Schematic Representation
Map Is Not Drawn To Scale**

Hermitage Cross-Country Touring Center

Coldbrook Road
Wilmington, Vt. 05363
Tel. 802-464-3511

Trail Network: 40 km.
Machine Groomed Trail: 30 km.
Hours of Operation: daily. 9:00 a.m. - 4:00 p.m.
Base Elevation: 1,900 ft.
High Trail: 3,550 ft.
Low Trail: 1,800 ft.

The Hermitage Touring Center sits high on the flanks of Haystack Mt. and Mt. Snow. Between these two peaks runs a 3000-foot-plus high ridge over which an exciting cross-country ski route exists designed for advanced skiers. Not only can the Hermitage ski staff help you (guide) up and across this exciting sky line trail, but you can recount your adventures with friends in the charming cocktail lounge after descending from the heights with a favorite hot drink, or a bottle of wine from the Inn's renowned wine cellar.

The Inn's trails lead through pleasing forest and field, even through a working sugarbush, which stocks the shelves of the Inn's gift shop with maple goodies.

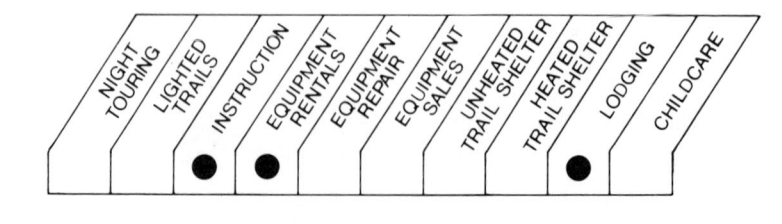

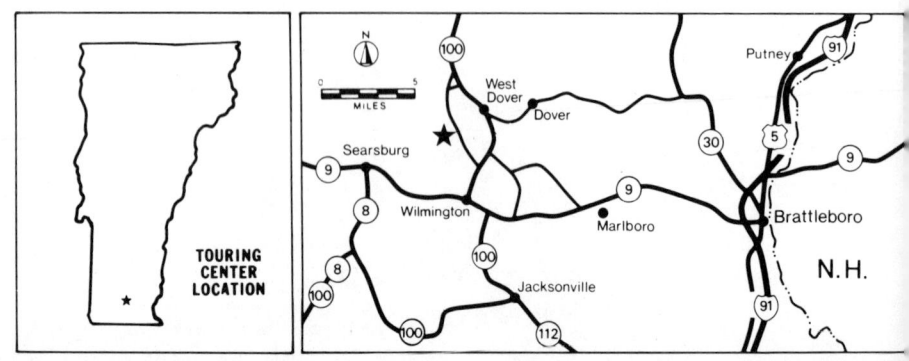

# Southern Vermont

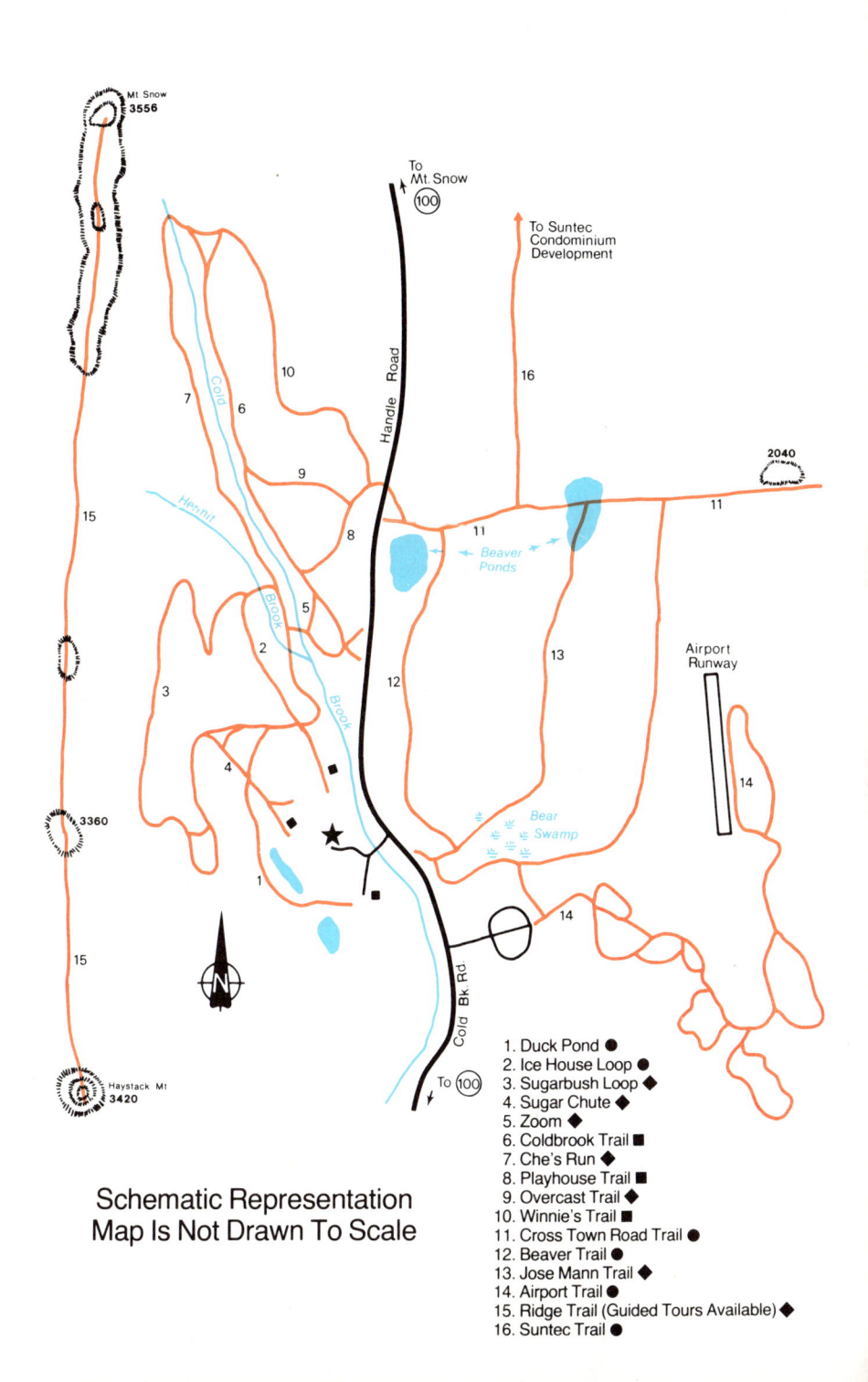

101

Schematic Representation
Map Is Not Drawn To Scale

1. Duck Pond ●
2. Ice House Loop ●
3. Sugarbush Loop ◆
4. Sugar Chute ◆
5. Zoom ◆
6. Coldbrook Trail ■
7. Che's Run ◆
8. Playhouse Trail ■
9. Overcast Trail ◆
10. Winnie's Trail ■
11. Cross Town Road Trail ●
12. Beaver Trail ●
13. Jose Mann Trail ◆
14. Airport Trail ●
15. Ridge Trail (Guided Tours Available) ◆
16. Suntec Trail ●

The White House
Ski Touring Center

Box 757
Wilmington, Vt. 05363
Tel. 802-464-2136

Trail Network: 23 km.
Machine Groomed Trail: 23 km.
Hours of Operation: daily, 9:00 a.m. - 4:30 p.m.
Base Elevation: 1,620 ft.
High Trail: 1,700 ft.
Low Trail: 1,580 ft.

What does romance have to do with skiing? Find out at the White House, which has been selected as one of the ten most romantic places in the world by a seasoned traveler writing for the Boston Herald American. Except for the company of ancient sugar maples surrounding the house, the White House stands alone, emperor of a hilltop overlooking the Mt. Snow Valley. The Ski Center is located in the annex attached to the north side of the house, from whence trails run in all directions. Lose yourself in a winter fantasy on Tolkien's or Merlin's Trail, or end the day on Fool's Run.

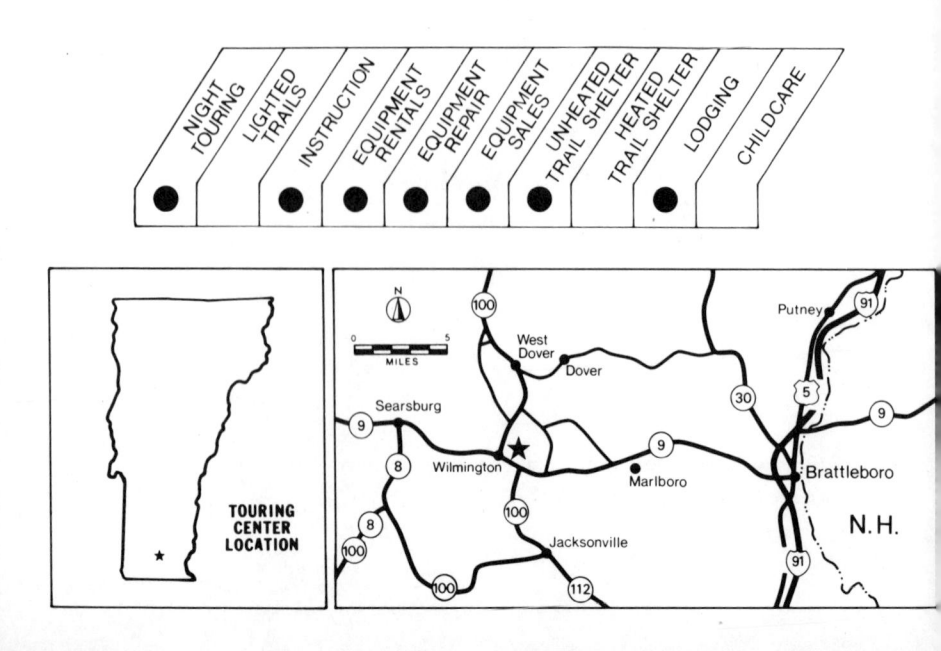

Southern Vermont

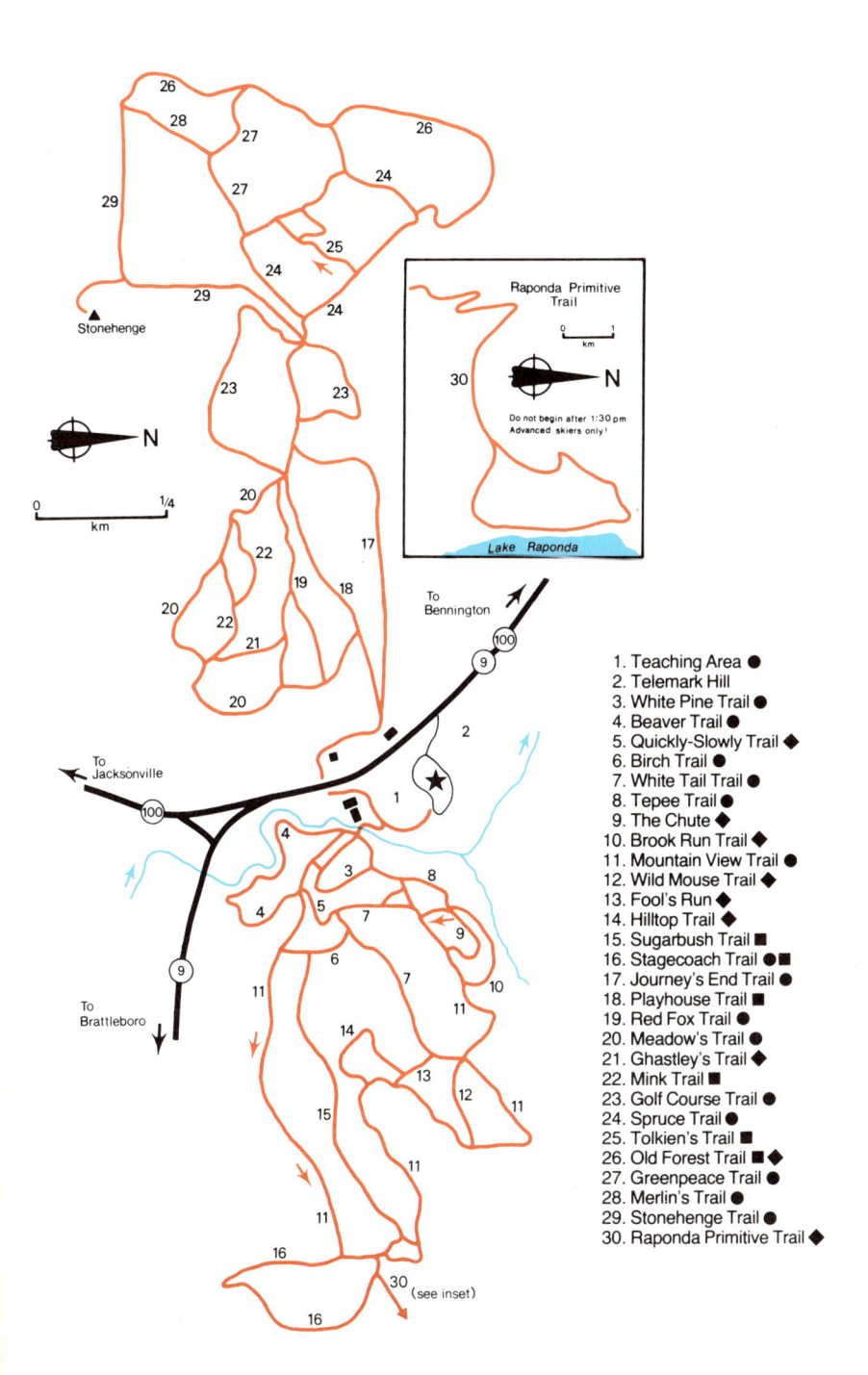

103

Raponda Primitive Trail

Do not begin after 1:30 pm
Advanced skiers only!

1. Teaching Area ●
2. Telemark Hill
3. White Pine Trail ●
4. Beaver Trail ●
5. Quickly-Slowly Trail ◆
6. Birch Trail ●
7. White Tail Trail ●
8. Tepee Trail ●
9. The Chute ◆
10. Brook Run Trail ◆
11. Mountain View Trail ●
12. Wild Mouse Trail ◆
13. Fool's Run ◆
14. Hilltop Trail ◆
15. Sugarbush Trail ■
16. Stagecoach Trail ● ■
17. Journey's End Trail ●
18. Playhouse Trail ■
19. Red Fox Trail ●
20. Meadow's Trail ●
21. Ghastley's Trail ◆
22. Mink Trail ■
23. Golf Course Trail ●
24. Spruce Trail ●
25. Tolkien's Trail ■
26. Old Forest Trail ■ ◆
27. Greenpeace Trail ●
28. Merlin's Trail ●
29. Stonehenge Trail ●
30. Raponda Primitive Trail ◆

Prospect Ski Mountain

34 West Road
Bennington, Vt. 05201
Tel. 802-442-2575

Trail Network: 20 km.
Machine Groomed Trail: 10 km.
Hours of Operation: daily, 10:00 a.m. - 5:00 p.m.
Base Elevation: 2,150 ft.
High Trail: 2,750 ft.
Low Trail: 2,150 ft.

Prospect Mt. is an innovative ski center that offers some well integrated alpine, telemark, and cross-country ski experiences. The cross-country trails have been designed to give the Nordic skier easy access to the mountain's lift lines. The skier has the option of riding the lift to the mountain top and gracing the slopes with telemark turns or departing from the terminus of the lift line and wandering via wilderness trails into some wild highland back country. Snow making equipment will allow the telemarkers time to practice their turns early in the season.

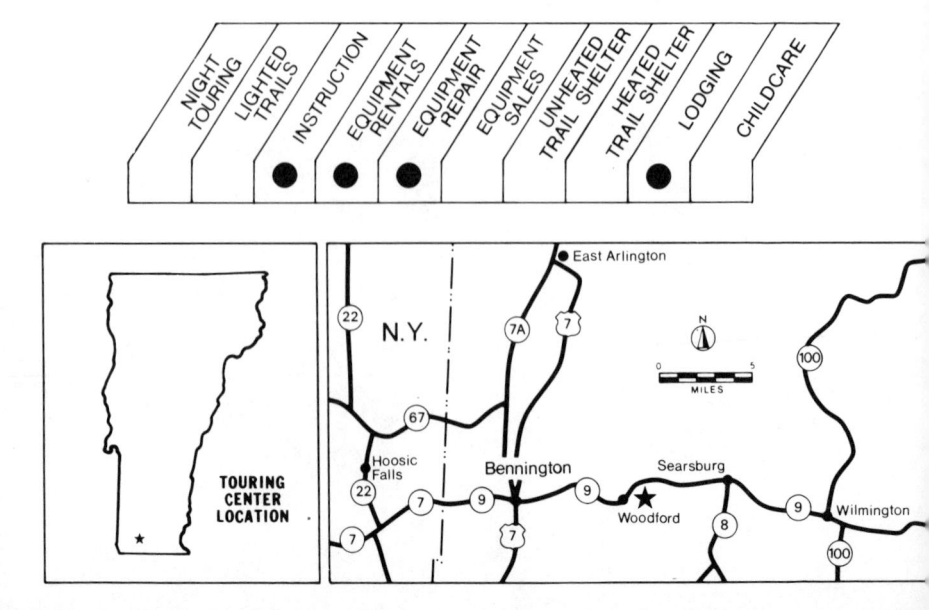

Southern Vermont

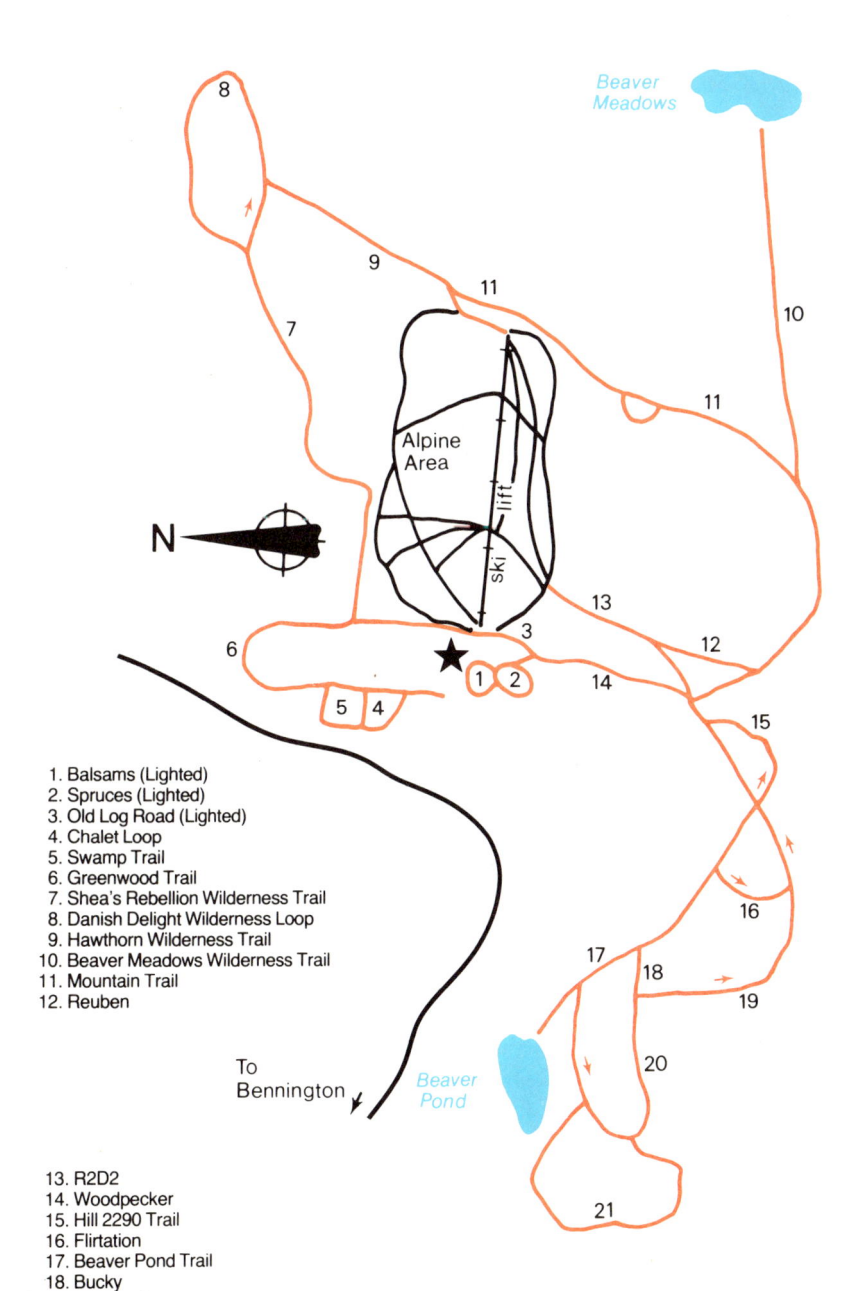

105

Alpine Area

ski lift

Beaver Meadows

Beaver Pond

To Bennington

N

1. Balsams (Lighted)
2. Spruces (Lighted)
3. Old Log Road (Lighted)
4. Chalet Loop
5. Swamp Trail
6. Greenwood Trail
7. Shea's Rebellion Wilderness Trail
8. Danish Delight Wilderness Loop
9. Hawthorn Wilderness Trail
10. Beaver Meadows Wilderness Trail
11. Mountain Trail
12. Reuben
13. R2D2
14. Woodpecker
15. Hill 2290 Trail
16. Flirtation
17. Beaver Pond Trail
18. Bucky
19. Whistlepig
20. Duke's Loop
21. Chickadee Wilderness Trail

**Schematic Representation
Map Is Not Drawn To Scale**

Additional Skiing Information

The state of Vermont annually publishes a free brochure on cross-country skiing which is available by writing or calling:

Vermont Travel Division
134 State Street
Montpelier, Vermont 05602
Tel: 802 828-3236

New England Vacation Center
630 Fifth Avenue
Concourse Level, Shop #2
New York, New York 10020
Tel: 212 307-5780

Vermont Information Center
2051 Peel Street
Montreal, Quebec,
 Canada H3A 1T6
Tel: 514 845-9840

Vermont Welcome Center
 Interstate 89
Highgate Springs, Vermont
Tel: 802 868-7861

Vermont Welcome Center
 Interstate 93
Waterford, Vermont
Tel: 802 748-9822

Vermont Welcome Center
 Interstate 91
Guilford, Vermont
Tel: 802 254-4593

Vermont Welcome Center
 Route 4A
Fair Haven, Vermont
Tel: 802 265-4763

Additional Skiing Information

Every Thursday during the winter season the Vermont Travel Division compiles and releases a statewide report on the ski touring conditions expected for the coming weekend. The report is issued to all Vermont information offices listed above and to major wire services and ski information centers.

Because local weather and snow conditions can vary greatly from day to day, we recommend contacting individual ski tour operators for the latest information.

Guided inn to inn tours can be arranged by contacting:
Nordic Adventures, Box 115, RD 1, Rochester, VT 05767. Tel. (802) 767-3996.
Ski Tours of Vermont, RFD 1-V, Chester, VT 05143. Tel. (802) 875-3631 or 875-3103.
Vermont Voyageur Expeditions, Montgomery Center, VT 05471. Tel. (802) 326-4789.

Also, self-guided tours along well-marked routes may be arranged by contacting:
Inn to Inn Tours, Churchill House Inn, RD 3, Brandon, VT 05733. Tel. (802) 247-3300.

The Vermont Ski Touring Operators Association (VSTOA) provides daily updates on cross-country skiing conditions at many Vermont ski touring centers. Call (802) 775-9754, 24 hours a day, 7 days a week, mid-November through April. VSTOA may also be contacted by writing:
RD 1
Box 146
Waitsfield, Vt. 05673

Epilogue

From Quebec's charming villages to California's Sierra Nevada mountains, cross-country skiing from hut to hut or inn to inn has become increasingly popular. In response to this form of recreation, long distance trails connecting inns and ski touring centers have been built to service the needs of the skiing public. In Vermont the cross-country ski industry is in a dynamic, youthful phase. The time may be right for Vermont to develop and present skiers with the most exciting inn to inn cross-country skiing in North America.

Examples of successful long distance trails exist. Northern Minnesota's Gunflint Trail is 58 miles long and connects eight lodges together. Overnight accommodations are available on an established mountain route between Aspen and Vail, Colorado, about 50 miles. In Canada in the early 1930's the legendary skier "Jack Rabbitt" Johansen created the famous 85 miles long "Maple Leaf Trail" through the Laurentian Mountains.

In Vermont progressive ski touring centers have already extended their trails into regional but not statewide ski networks. This author suggests that the construction of strategically placed new cross-country ski trails might serve to link together regional ski touring networks into a state-length trail, offering lodging nightly enroute from Massachusetts to Canada. The concept of creating and designing an "end to end" cross-country ski trail has been best illustrated by Lance Tapley's historic trans-length cross-country ski of Vermont in 1969. (See *Skiing*, February 1970). While this as yet unnamed trail has been in the past only the stuff of aprés-ski fireside discussions, the ski trail development in the state is now so widespread that there is potential to create a "long trail for skiers" by connecting together pre-existing ski trails. One route (thought, at this point, to be most viable) extends approximately 260 miles from Massachusetts to Canada. This trail would parallel but avoid using the Long Trail by running at lower elevations. It could incorporate or pass near the trail networks of almost two dozen cross-country ski centers. Such a trail could be routed over many highlands above 1500 feet offering skiers spectacular views and, because of the altitude, a long ski season. Careful routing could space inns, overnight lodges and huts so the average skier might travel the length of the state in a month staying at any number of accommodations.

Recent trends in the extension of regional trail networks and the burgeoning interest in cross-country skiing suggest that such a trail will become increasingly feasible. With some bold trail design and construction initiatives, Vermont could become the new frontier in the North American cross-country ski world.

Bibliography

Allaben, Stanton. *Vermont Ski Trail Guide.* Londonderry, Vermont: Stanton Allaben Productions, 1982.

Ford, Sally and Daniel. *25 Ski Tours in the Green Mountains.* Somersworth, New Hampshire: New Hampshire Publishing Company, 1978.

Lousteau, Rod. *Guide to the Ski Touring Centers of New England.* Chester, Connecticut: The Globe Pequot Press, 1980. The Globe Pequot Press, 1981.

Ski Magazine. *Guide to Cross-Country Skiing.* New York: Times Mirror Magazines, Inc. (published annually).

Tapley, Lance. *Ski Touring in New England and New York.* Lexington, Massachusetts: Stone Wall Press, 1976.

Vermont Travel Division. *Cross-Country Skiing, Vermont A Special World.* Montpelier, Vermont: Agency of Development and Community Affairs. (Pamphlet, published annually).

Zieglen, Katey, ed. *Ski Touring Guide to New England.* Peterborough, New Hampshire: Eastern Mountain Sports, 1979.

Index

Blueberry Hill, Goshen, 62
Bolton Valley Cross-Country Center, Bolton Valley, 34
Breadloaf Campus, see Carroll and Jane Rikert Ski Touring Center, Breadloaf, 60
Burke Mountain Touring Center, East Burke, 26
Camel's Hump Nordic Ski Center, Huntington, 32
Carroll and Jane Rikert Ski Touring Center, Breadloaf, 60
Catamount Family Center, Williston, 28
Churchill House, Brandon, 64
Craftsbury Nordic Center, Craftsbury Common, 20
Darion Ski Touring Center, East Burke, 24
Edson Hill Ski Touring Center, Stowe, 42
Fox Run Ski Touring Center, Ludlow, 80
Grafton Cross-Country Ski Shop and Trail System, Grafton, 92
Green Mountain Touring Center, Randolph, 66
Green Trails Touring Center, Brookfield, 58
Hazen's Notch Ski Touring Center, Montgomery Center, 16
Hermitage Cross-Country Touring Center, Wilmington, 100
Highland Lodge, Greensboro, 22
Hildene Ski Touring Center, Manchester, 94
Mad River Glen, see Tucker Hill/Mad River Glen Nordic Ski Centers, Waitsfield, 52
Mountain Meadows Ski Touring Center, Killington, 72
Mountain Top Ski Touring Center, Chittenden, 70
Mount Mansfield Ski Touring Center, Stowe, 44
Nordic Inn Ski Touring Center, Landgrove, 86
Ole's Cross Country Center, Waitsfield, 56
Prospect Ski Mountain, Bennington, 104
Rabbit Hill Inn, Lower Waterford, 48
Sherman Hollow, Richmond, 30
Sitzmark Ski Touring Center, Wilmington, 98
Stark Farm Ski Touring Center, Westford, 18
Stratton Touring Center, Stratton Mountain, 96
Sugarbush Inn Ski Touring Center, Warren, 54
Sugar House Nordic Center, Smuggler's Notch, 46
Tater Hill Cross-Country Ski Center, Chester, 90
Topnotch Touring Center, Stowe, 40
Trail Head Ski Touring Center, Stockbridge, 68
Trapp Family Lodge, Stowe, 37
Tucker Hill/Mad River Glen Nordic Ski Centers, Waitsfield, 52
Viking Ski Touring Center, Londonderry, 88
The White House Ski Touring Center, Wilmington, 102
Wilderness Trails Nordic Ski School and Touring Center, Quechee, 74
Wild Wings Ski Touring Center, Peru, 84
Woodstock Ski Touring Center, Woodstock, 76

About the Editor

Born in Burlington in 1958, Steven Bushey is an avid cross-country skier. Since graduating from the University of Vermont in 1981 he has traveled around North America extensively, crossing the continent once by bicycle. He is presently pursuing graduate studies at Carleton University in Ottawa with research speculating on the development of a Vermont long distance cross-country ski trail. During the 1984 ski season Steve will lead a small group of skiers on a 260 mile trek from the Massachusetts border to Canada. This will be the first documented translength ski tour of Vermont in more than a decade.

The following books are available from Northern Cartographic. Please add $1.50 for postage and handling. Vermont residents add 4% sales tax. Mail orders to:

>Northern Cartographic
>P.O. Box 133
>Burlington, Vt. 05402

Vermont Cross-Country Ski Atlas, 112 pages, $6.95

The Atlas of Vermont Trout Ponds, 100 pages, $5.95

Vermont Lakes In Depth, 84 pages, $4.95

The Atlas of New Hampshire Trout Ponds Volume I: The White Mountains and the North Country, 105 pages, $4.95

The Atlas of New Hampshire Trout Ponds Volume II: The Big Lakes and the Lakes of the South, 112 pages, $4.95

The Wild Side of
MARYLAND
AN OUTDOOR GUIDE

The Wild Side of Maryland: An Outdoor Guide

Molly Dunham, *Editor*
Jerold Council, *Graphics Editor*
Jerry Jackson, *Photo Editor*
Victor Panichkul, *Design Editor*
Andrew Murphy, *Layout Editor*
Emily Holmes, *Graphics Artist*
John Makely, *Photographer*
Marsha Chodnicki, *Illustrator*
Robert Schrott, *Research Editor*
Michael Reeb, *Copy Editor*
Ray Frager, *Copy Editor*

Photos on front and back covers by Jed Kirschbaum.

© 1997 by The Baltimore Sun
All rights reserved under international copyright conventions. No part of the contents of this book may be reproduced or utilized in any form or by any means, electronic or mechanical, including photocopying, recording, or by any information storage or retrieval system without the written consent of the publisher.

Published by

The Baltimore Sun
A Times Mirror Co.
501 N. Calvert Street
Baltimore, MD 21278

ISBN: 0-9649819-4-7   Library of Congress [97-070224]

The wild side of Maryland: an outdoor guide: a publication of The Baltimore Sun - 1997 - Baltimore, MD: Baltimore Sun Co,. 1997

Printed in U.S.A.

The Wild Side of Maryland: An Outdoor Guide

TABLE OF CONTENTS

Introduction v

Parks 1

Geology 18

Flora 34

Wildlife 50

Boating 66

Fishing 104

Hunting 146

Camping 168

Hiking 178

Biking 194

Skiing 206

Appendix 218

Index 230

Map 236

Special thanks to the following for supplying materials for the chapter break photographs: Boat-U.S. Marine Center, Eastern Mountain Sports, Grier Fossil Collection, Maxalea Nurseries, On The Fly Inc., Performance Bicycle Shop, Radebaugh's Florist & Greenhouse, Set's Sport Shop, The Fisherman's Edge, Tochterman's

The world outside our doors

INTRODUCTION

We're calling this an outdoors guide, but it's more like an outside guide. A newspaper's outdoors coverage usually focuses on hunting, fishing and boating, typically the province of men – and some women – who tramp about in duck boots, hip waders or Docksiders without socks. This book stretches that definition to include activities that need no fancy footwear or necessary accessories, just a desire to go outside and explore what's there.

Maryland is an ideal place to do that. This book celebrates the diversity of this compact yet complex state, from the mountains of Garrett County to the dunes of Assateague Island. Hike the Appalachian Trail at South Mountain one weekend and ride bikes beside the marshes of Blackwater National Wildlife Refuge near Cambridge the next. Come winter, one can ski the cross country trails at New Germany State Park near Frostburg, fish for trout on the Big Gunpowder Falls north of Baltimore or hunt fossils at Calvert Cliffs State Park along the western shore of the Chesapeake.

This book is written for residents and visitors alike. Sightseeing on many vacations in the state means a blurry scene from the car window – white pines and signs for Silver Queen corn along U.S. 50 en route to Ocean City or white oaks and gleaming dairy silos beside Interstate 70 on the way to Deep Creek Lake. There's much to be seen in between – just slow down and look around. Many of us have lived here all our lives, yet have never heard the Youghiogheny River as it roars through gorges at Swallow Falls State Park, smelled the cypress swamps at Pocomoke State Park or tasted a fresh perch caught at Sandy Point State Park.

One of the best ways to discover such sensual pleasure is to have a child as a guide. The late Rachel Carson, whose first published writing appeared in The Sun when she was pursuing her masters degree in biology at Johns Hopkins, spent much of her life in Maryland. Best known for "Silent Spring" and "The Sea Around Us," Carson wrote about children and nature in "The Sense of Wonder," a book published after her death in 1964.

"A child's world is fresh and new and beautiful," she wrote, "full of wonder and excitement. It is our misfortune that for most of us, that clear-eyed vision, that true instinct for what is beautiful and awe inspiring, is dimmed

V

INTRODUCTION

and even lost before we reach adulthood.

"If a child is to keep alive his inborn sense of wonder ... he needs the companionship of at least one adult who can share it, rediscovering with him the joy, excitement and mystery of the world we live in."

We wanted to keep children – and the adults who share the outdoors with them – in mind as we put together this book. There are suggestions on how to introduce children to freshwater fishing, saltwater fishing and crabbing. The camping chapter emphasizes family outings. Biking, hiking, fossil hunting, bird watching, skiing ... all are activities families can share.

The natural place to start exploring nature is at a park, and the book opens with a chapter on the seven national parks and 49 state parks, forests and wildlife management areas in Maryland. Next comes a chapter on how it all began: Geologists say the oldest rocks exposed in Maryland are just over 1 billion years old. Here you can find the best sites for hunting fossils of dinosaurs that roamed the state just 70 million years ago.

An amazing array of native plants is the subject of Chapter 3, along with 14 of the best places to find wildflowers and a list of nurseries that sell native species. Chapter 4 covers fauna and focuses on bird-watching, the fastest-growing outdoor recreation activity in America, according to a recent federal survey.

Once readers have the lay of the land, they can launch into chapters on the more traditional outdoor pursuits. More than 200,000 recreational boats are registered in the state, and Chapter 5 goes into detail about opportunities to take to the water, by sailboat, motorboat or canoe. For sailors, there's a suggested seven-day cruise of Chesapeake Bay. The chapter includes safety guidelines for motorboats and 10 trips that sample the canoeing and kayaking possibilities in Maryland.

Chapter 6 covers fishing, from brook trout in the streams of Garrett County to blue marlin off the coast of Ocean City. Hunting is the subject of Chapter 7, with emphasis on deer and waterfowl. Because dates of specific fishing and hunting seasons, as well as catch limits, are frequently subject to change, we have included phone numbers and Internet addresses for the Maryland Department of Natural Resources so that readers can access the most up-to-date regulations.

Suggestions on how to make family camping as trouble-free as possible are covered in Chapter 8. In Chapter 9, hiking is divided into two sections: the more traditional treks on trails and the organized walks of volksmarchers. Chapter 10, on biking, also caters to two distinct participants: the "roadies" and the "off roaders."

INTRODUCTION

Chapter 11 covers outdoor pursuits that require snow: downhill skiing, cross country skiing and snowboarding.

We designed the book to be a one-stop-shopping resource, broad enough to cover a variety of interests and compact enough to slip into a backpack or purse. "The Wild Side of Maryland" includes plenty of destinations that aren't so wild, and that's by design as well. For many families, visiting the wild side of Maryland can be as easy as stepping outside to watch finches at the backyard feeder. Take a child as a guide, as Rachel Carson suggested, and learn from him.

"Is the exploration of the natural world just a pleasant way to pass the golden hours of childhood, or is there something deeper?" Carson wrote in "The Sense of Wonder." "I am sure there is something much deeper, something lasting and significant. Those who dwell, as scientists or laymen, among the beauties and mysteries of the Earth are never alone or weary of life."

Molly Dunham,
Editor

PARKS

State of abundance

BY MICHAEL REEB

From the mountains of Garrett County to the tidal waters of Chesapeake Bay to the seacoast of Assateague Island, Maryland's park system offers panoramic recreational opportunities. Both federal and state parklands are rich in diversity and offer an abundance of flora and fauna — from the mountain laurel of Western Maryland to the wild rice of Eastern Shore wetlands, from the resurging black bear population of the state's western counties to the migratory and shore birds of the Eastern Shore.

Along the way, the park system's hiking trails are the common path. Most of the federal and state parks and wildlife management areas listed below offer hiking trails, which provide our first peeks at the great outdoors. But the federal and state lands listed here also offer much more.

For further looks at what these lands provide, both the federal National Park Service (http://www.nps.gov) and the state Department of Natural Resources (http://www.gacc.com/dnr/) have web sites on the Internet. For information on the federal parks, call the numbers listed below. For information on the state lands, call the numbers below or write: State Forest and Park Service, Tawes State Office Building, 580 Taylor Avenue E-3, Annapolis, Md. 21401, or call: (410) 974-3771.

PERRY THORSVIK
Anglers can get an early start at start parks.

Federal

- Appalachian Trail (Washington and Frederick counties; write: Appalachian Trail Conference, P.O. Box 807, Harpers Ferry, W.Va. 25425-0807, or call (304) 535-6331): Part of a public footpath across 2,155 miles of Appalachian Mountain ridgelines from Maine to Georgia, the 40-mile stretch in Maryland is comprised principally of 38 miles along the ridge crest of South Mountain. It offers a good opportunity for a three- or four-day trip that is never

PARKS

too far from towns or highways. The Appalachian Trail joins the C&O Canal towpath at the Potomac River.

- Assateague Island National Seashore (Worcester County; write: 7307 Stephen Decatur Highway, Berlin, Md. 21811, or call: (410) 641-2120): Contiguous to the Chincoteague National Wildlife Refuge, the site offers numerous adventures: from surf fishing, clamming, hunting (check seasonal state and federal guides), crabbing, canoeing and boating to hiking, backcountry camping, bird-watching and biking.

- Blackwater National Wildlife Refuge (Dorchester County; call: (410) 228-2677): Adjacent to Fishing Bay Wildlife Management Area and just east of Taylor's Island Wildlife Management Area, the refuge is a haven for migratory and shore birds in a marshland setting. The site also affords a good opportunity to observe an eagle. There is a good trail system.

- Catoctin Mountain Park (Frederick County, 10,000 acres; write: Thurmont, Md. 21788, or call: (301) 663-9343): The site offers a variety of trails rated easy, moderate and strenuous through woodlands of chestnut oak, hickory, black birch, hemlock and ash.

- Chesapeake & Ohio Canal: Located beside the Potomac River, the canal runs from Cumberland to Georgetown and provides a byway for hikers and bicyclists. Its watered sections also provide quiet waters

PERRY THORSVIK

A look at Assateague Island from the bay side.

for canoeists, boaters and fishermen.

- Eastern Neck Island National Wildlife Refuge (Kent County; call: (410) 639-7056): Accessible by bridge from Route 445, this area at the mouth of the Chester River is a prime location for migratory birds, especially Canada geese and tundra swans. There is a good trail system.
- Greenbelt Park (Prince George's County, 1,100 acres; write: 6565 Greenbelt Road, Greenbelt, Md. 20770-3207, or call: (301) 344-3948): An oasis of wildlife 12 miles from Washington and 23 miles from Baltimore, the woodland has facilities for hiking, biking and picnicking.

State

Western

- Big Run State Park (Garrett County, 600 acres; write: 349 Headquarters Lane, Grantsville, Md., or call: (301) 895-5453): Located at the mouth of the Savage River, the area has a boat launch, 30 unimproved campsites and a youth group camping area. It also offers fishing, hiking and hunting and is the starting point for a six-mile hiking trail known as Monroe Run.
- Casselman River Bridge State Park (Garrett County, four acres; write: 349 Headquarters Lane, Grantsville, Md., or call: (301) 895-5453): The center of the area is an 80-foot stone arch bridge that was part of the old National Road and, when constructed in 1813, was the largest of its kind in the world.
- Cunningham Falls State Park (Frederick County, 4,946 acres; write: 14039 Catoctin Hollow Road, or call: (301) 271-7574): This park consists of two areas: the Manor Area, located on U.S. Route 15, and the William Houck Area, three miles west of Thurmont on Catoctin Hollow Road. Located in the Catoctin Mountains, the park offers a four-camper cabin, three camper-ready sites and 180 campsites.
- Dans Mountain State Park (Allegany County, 481 acres; write: Water Station Run, Lonaconing, Md. 21539, or call: (301) 777-2139): A day-use park, Dan's Rock offers a view from 2,898 feet and two disabled-accessible features: an overlook at Cresap Monument and a swimming pool.
- Deep Creek Lake State Park (Garrett County, 1,818 acres; write: 898 State Park Road, Swanton, Md. 21561, or call: (301) 387-5563): Fronting a six-square-mile, man-made lake, the area offers camping, swimming, picnicking, a boat launch, interpretative programs and hiking. Water sports of all sorts are possibilities, and in the winter, there are six miles of snowmobile trails.
- Fort Frederick State Park (Washington County, 561 acres; write: 11100 Fort Frederick Road, Big Pool, Md. 21711, or call: (301) 842-2155): Erected in 1756 during

PARKS | western

JOHN MAKELY
Swallow Falls State Park has the state's largest waterfall.

the French and Indian Wars, Fort Frederick is considered the country's best-preserved, pre-Revolutionary stone fort. The C&O Canal passes through the area, which is popular with hikers and bicyclists.

- Gambrill State Park (Frederick County, 1,137 acres; write: 8602 Gambrill Park Road, Frederick, Md.; or call: (301) 271-7574): Scenic overlooks offer views of Frederick on one side of the ridge and the Middletown Valley on the other. Camping is available, and a rustic building may be rented for large group activities.

- Garrett State Park (Garrett County, 6,781 acres; write: 1431 Potomac Camp Road, Oakland, Md. 21550, or call: (301) 334-2038): Given to the state in 1906, the forest was the beginning of the public lands system. It contains a diversity of trees, wildlife and scenery.

- Gathland State Park (Frederick and Washington counties, 140 acres; write: 21843 National Pike, Boonsboro, Md. 21713-9535, or call: (301) 791-4767): The mountain home of Civil War journalist George Alfred Townsend, the site features buildings that he designed and constructed. A day-use park, it contains a stone monument dedicated to war correspondents.

- Green Ridge State Forest (Allegany County, 50,000 acres; write: 28700 Headquarters Dr., NE, Flintstone, Md. 21530-9525, or call: (301) 478-3124): A favorite with deer and wild turkey hunters, the expanse is spread over Town Hill, Polish Mountain and Green Ridge Mountain. There is a wheelchair-accessible overlook at the forest headquarters, as well as a trail.

- Greenbrier (Washington County, 1,288 acres; write: 21843 National Pike, Boonsboro, Md. 21713-9535, or call: (301) 791-4767): A multi-use park, the site has a 42-acre man-made lake, a bathhouse and modern campsites.

- Herrington Manor State Park (Garrett County, 365 acres; write: 222 Herrington Lane, Oakland, Md. 21550, or call: (301) 334-9180): There are 20 log cabins available for rental at the site, which contains a 53-acre lake. In the winter, the park offers cross country ski trails and ski rental.

- Indian Springs Wildlife Management Area (Washington County, 6,400 acres; call (301) 842-2702): Once the home of Native Americans, the site served as a Civil War military signal post at Fairview Mountain. A wildlife haven, the area is a hiker's paradise.

- Mt. Nebo Wildlife Management Area (Garrett County, 2,000 acres; call: (301) 334-4255): Located in the mountains, this tract contains one of the most unique wetlands in the state: a red spruce bog. Bogs are found more typically in northern climates, but the elevation makes ideal conditions for the wetland, a favorite with nature lovers.

- New Germany State Park (Garrett County, 455 acres; write: 349 Headquarters Lane, Grantsville, Md. 21536, or call: (301) 895-5453): Built on the site of a one-time milling center in Savage River State Forest, the park features a 13-acre lake and 11 rental cabins. There are trails for hiking in the summer and cross country skiing in the winter.

- Potomac State Forest (Garrett County, 10,416 acres; write: 1431 Potomac Camp Road, Oakland, Md. 21550): Trout fishermen will find the going good here at the headwaters of the Potomac River. This is rugged mountain forest with an abundance of wildlife.

- Rocky Gap State Forest (Allegany County, 3,240 acres; write: 12500 Pleasant Valley Road, Flintstone, Md. 21530, or call: (301) 777-2139): Located in a saddle created by Evitts Mountain and Martin Mountain, the forest is situated around a 243-acre lake, once home of the state's record-setting largemouth bass. There are also hiking trails, three swimming beaches, a modern bathhouse and a large campground.

- Savage River State Forest (Garrett County, 53,500

acres; write: 349 Headquarters Lane, Grantsville, Md. 21536, or call: (301) 895-5759): The forest, which is classified as a northern hardwood forest, surrounds the Savage River Reservoir. Almost 3,000 acres of the site have been designated as the Big Savage Wildland.

- Sideling Hill Wildlife Management Area (Allegany County, 3,000 acres; write: 11100 Fort Frederick Road, Big Pool, Md. 21711, or call: (301) 842-2702): The forest here is comprised mainly of oak and hickory, and opportunities for observing mountain scenery are excellent, especially in the spring when wildflowers and mountain laurel are in bloom.

- South Mountain State Park (Washington and Frederick counties, 8,039 acres; write: 21843 National Pike, Boonsboro, Md. 21713-9535, or call: (301) 791-4767): The park follows the ridge of South Mountain and includes 40 miles of the Appalachian Trail. The area offers hiking, primitive camping for trail hikers and excellent overlooks.

- Swallow Falls State Park (Garrett County, 257 acres; write: 222 Herrington Lane, Oakland, Md. 21550, or call: (301) 334-9180): Canadian hemlocks can be found in the woods at this site. The Youghiogheny River flows along the park borders, where shaded rocky gorges and rapids are part of the stretch, as well as Muddy Creek Falls, a 63-foot waterfall.

- Warrior Mountain Wildlife Management Area (Allegany County, 4,000 acres; call: (301) 478-2525): A forest covers the ridge and stream valley here, but a power line clearing offers a wonderful view of Western Maryland topography.

- Washington Monument State Park (Washington County, 147 acres; write: 21843 National Pike, Boonsboro, Md. 21713-9535, or call: (301) 791-4767): This day-use park features the first monument dedicated to George Washington, a stone tower erected on a mountainside by the citizens of Boonsboro in 1827.

Central

- Dierssen Wildlife Management Area (Montgomery County, 40 acres; call (301) 258-0817): This marshy tract between the C&O Canal and the Potomac River is a waterfowl sanctuary and a haven for bird-watchers.

- Elk Neck State Forest (Cecil County, 3,465 acres; write: 4395 Turkey Point Road, North East, Md. 21901, or call (410) 287-5333): A variety of game animals can be found in this area, a peninsula between the Elk and North East rivers.

- Fair Hill Natural Resources Management Area (Cecil County, 5,613 acres; write: 376 Fair Hill Drive, Elkton, Md. 21921, or call: (410) 398-1246): The area is used for special events, and is the site of Memorial Day and fall horse-jumping races.

PARKS | central

JERRY JACKSON
The Northern Central Trail is popular with cyclists.

- Gunpowder Falls State Park (Harford and Baltimore counties, 13,020 acres; write: 10815 Harford Road, P.O. Box 5032, Glen Arm, Md. 21057, or call: (410) 592-2897): The area offers opportunities for hiking and trout fishing, in particular. There are four park areas: the Hereford Area (along York Road in Parkton), the Northern Central Trail (from Ashland to Maryland Line), the Sweet Air Area (Route 152) and the Hammerman Area (in Chase near Eastern Avenue). The Hammerman Area offers swimming in the Chesapeake Bay, boat rentals, slip rentals and boat launching.

- Gwynnbrook Wildlife Management Area (Baltimore County, 74 acres; call (410) 356-9272): Originally a game farm for rabbits and quail, the site is the oldest tract of land set aside for wildlife in the state. The mostly forested area, located just off Reisterstown Road in Owings Mills, is a nearby wildlife delight for city residents.

- Hart-Miller Island State Park (Baltimore County, 244 acres; write: 10815 Harford Road, P.O. Box 5032, Glen Arm, Md. 21057, or call: (410) 592-2897): Accessible only by boat, the island is located in the Chesapeake Bay, near the mouth of Middle

River. The western shore offers safe mooring, wading and a 3,000-foot sandy beach.

- Morgan Run Wildlife Management Area (Carroll County, 1,500 acres; write: 8020 Baltimore National Pike, Ellicott City, Md. 21043, or call: (410) 461-5005): This site offers hiking and equestrian trails. Morgan Run is a designated catch-and-release trout stream.

- North Point State Park (Baltimore County, 1,310 acres; write: P.O. Box 176, Fort Howard, Md. 21052, or call: (410) 477-0757): The Defenders' Trail, used during the War of 1812, runs through this Chesapeake Bay waterfront, day-use park. The site is also the location of the old Bay Shore Amusement Park.

- Patapsco Valley State Park (Baltimore, Howard, Carroll and Anne Arundel counties, 12,699 acres; write: 8020 Baltimore National Pike, Ellicott City, Md. 21043, or call: (410) 461-5005): The park, which follows the Patapsco River, consists of five recreation areas: the Glen Artney Area (near Route 1 in Relay), the Hilton Area (south of Frederick Road in Catonsville), the Hollofield Area (adjacent to Route 40 in Ellicott City), the Pickall Area (North Rolling Road to Fairbrooke Road to Johnnycake Road) and the McKeldin Area (off Marriottsville Road).

- Patuxent River State Park (Howard and Montgomery counties, 6,529 acres; write: 11950 Clopper Road, Gaithersburg, Md. 20878, or call: (301) 924-2127): Located along the Patuxent River Valley, the area offers a self-guided nature trail for hikers and wildlife enthusiasts.

- Rocks State Park (Harford County, 855 acres; write: 3318 Rocks Chrome Road, Jarrettsville, Md. 21084, or call: (410) 557-7994): Deer Creek, which meanders through the park, is known for its fishing and tubing. The King and Queen Seat, a rock outcropping, is visible several hundred feet above the creek.

- Seneca Creek State Park (Montgomery County, 6,109 acres; write: 11950 Clopper Road, Gaithersburg, Md. 20878, or call: (301) 924-2127): This site, a day-use park with a 90-acre lake, houses old mills, stone quarries and an old schoolhouse.

- Soldier's Delight Natural Environment Area (Baltimore County, 2,000 acres; write: 8020 Baltimore National Park, Ellicott City, Md. 21043, or call: (410) 461-5005): This area is home to at least 39 rare, threatened and endangered plant species, as well as rare insects, rocks and minerals. There are marked hiking trails, but horses and cycling are prohibited because of the sensitive nature of the area.

- Susquehanna State Park (Harford County, 2,639 acres; write: 3318 Rocks Chrome Road, Jarrettsville,

MICHAEL LUTZKY

Gulls fly over water in Susquehanna State Park.

Md. 21084, or call: (410) 557-7994): Hikers can discover a diverse topography through the Susquehanna River Valley, exploring heavy forest and massive rock outcroppings. A 19th-century farm houses the Steppingstone Museum, which is operated by a private foundation.

Southern

- Calvert Cliffs State Park (Calvert County, 1,313 acres; write: P.O. Box 48, Scotland, Md. 20687, or call: (301) 872-5688): This day-use park has a hiking trail that leads to the beach, a fossil-hunter's paradise, and mighty cliffs overlooking Chesapeake Bay. The cliffs contain fossils from the Miocene period, 15 million years ago.

- Cedarville State Forest (Prince George's and Charles counties, 3,697 acres; write: 11704 Fenno Road, Upper Marlboro, Md. 20772, or call: (301) 888-1410): There are opportunities for freshwater fishing and hiking in a woodland setting, and a visitors' center is open during the summer at the state's only warm-water fish hatchery.

- Greenwell State Park (St. Mary's County, 596 acres; write: P.O. Box 48, Scotland, Md. 20687, or call: (301) 872-5688): A day-use park, the site offers opportunities for hiking, fishing, hunting, canoeing and kayaking. There are areas that are handicapped-accessible.

- Merkle Wildlife Sanctuary (Prince George's County,

PARKS | southern

1,600 acres; write: 11704 Fenno Road, Upper Marlboro, Md. 20772, or call: (301) 888-1410): A prime area to observe Canada geese on the Western Shore, the area is comprised of marshland, woodlands, farm ponds and fields.

- Point Lookout State Park (St. Mary's County, 528 acres; write: P.O. Box 48, Scotland, Md. 20687, or call: (301) 872-5688): The attractions here include beaches, a boat launch area, a 710-foot fishing pier and camping. Point Lookout served as a Civil War prison for Confederate soldiers.

- Rosaryville State Park (Prince George's County, 982 acres; write: 11704 Fenno Road, Upper Marlboro, Md. 20772, or call: (301) 888-1410): A day-use park, the site is home to the Mt. Airy Mansion Plantation, which can be toured by appointment.

- Sandy Point State Park (Anne Arundel County, 786 acres; write: 1100 East College Parkway, Annapolis, Md. 21401, or call: (410) 974-2149): Perhaps the most visible of the state's parks, it stretches along the western edge of the Bay Bridge spans. Sandy Point offers swimming, surf fishing, boating and windsurfing and is also a great place for bird-watching.

- Smallwood State Park (Charles County, 629 acres; write: Route 1, Box 64, Marbury, Md. 20658, or call (301) 888-1410): Located on Mattawoman Creek, the site was the home of Revolutionary War General William Smallwood. His house has been restored and is open to visitors. There are also 50 boat slips and access to Potomac River fishing.

- St. Clement's Island State Park (St. Mary's County, 40 acres; write: P.O. Box 48, Scotland, Md. 20687, or call: (301) 872-5688): Accessible only by boat, the Potomac River island was the site of the first landing of English settlers in Maryland in 1634. There is a cross dedicated to their memory here.

- St. Mary's River State Park (St. Mary's County, 2,176 acres; write: P.O. Box 48, Scotland, Md. 20687, or call: (301) 872-5688): A flood-control dam for a 5,600-acre watershed has created a 250-acre lake here, the site of great bass fishing.

Eastern

- Assateague State Park (Worcester County, 756 acres; 7307 Stephen Decatur Highway, Berlin, Md. 21811, or call: (410) 641-2120): This is the state's only ocean park and contains two miles of frontage on the Atlantic Ocean, in addition to marshes on Sinepuxent Bay. A variety of activities, including beachcombing, sunbathing, fishing, surfing and bayside canoeing, are possible. The park was selected by National Geographic Traveler in 1994 as one of the 10 best state parks in the country.

- Cedar Island Wildlife Management Area (Somerset County, 3,000 acres; call: (410) 543-8223): A bird lover's paradise, the area is a haven for black ducks with its tidal marsh, ponds and creeks.

- Choptank River Fishing Pier (Talbot and Dorchester counties, 25 acres; write: 29761 Bolingbroke Point Drive, Trappe, Md. 21673, or call: (410) 476-3795): When the Frederick C. Malkus Bridge was completed, this older span was converted into a pier, which is lighted and offers night fishing. White perch, striped bass, hard head and sea trout are among the varieties taken from the span.

- Deal Island Wildlife Management Area (Somerset County, 13,000 acres; call (410) 543-8223): This is a prime spot to watch, photograph and hunt ducks and geese (check federal guidelines). There is an abundance of pondweed and widgeongrass, on which waterfowl feed.

- Fishing Bay Wildlife Management Area (Dorchester County, 21,000 acres; call: (410) 376-3236): Tidal marshes interspersed with islands of loblolly pine make this a prime area to observe waterfowl. Adjacent to Blackwater National Wildlife Refuge, the area is the site of early Native American settlements.

LLOYD FOX
Herons are one variety of bird found in parks on the bay.

- Isle of Wight Wildlife Management Area (Worcester County, 200 acres; call: (410) 543-8223): Located across the Isle of Wight Bay from Ocean City, the Isle of Wight is sheltered from the Atlantic Ocean by the same coastal island that supports Ocean City. Visitors to the

PARKS | eastern

seaside resort might want to check out the waterfowl and marsh birds here.

- Janes Island State Park (Somerset County, 3,147 acres; write: Route 2, 40 Alfred Lawson Drive, Crisfield, Md. 21817, or call: (410) 968-1565): The area offers rental cabins, camping and miles of shoreline and marsh areas, prime territory for waterfowl.

- Martinak State Park (Caroline County, 107 acres; write: 137 Deep Shore Road, Denton, Md. 21657, or call: (410) 479-1619): A one-time home of Native Americans, the area consists of hardwood and pine forests on the Choptank River and Watts Creek. Modern campsites and boating access are available.

- Millington Wildlife Management Area (Kent County, 3,800 acres; call: (410) 928-3650): This area serves several roles: hunting, wildlife management and protection of endangered species of plants. Once the home of the Lenni Lenape Indians, artifacts from the period are on display.

- Pocomoke River State Park (Worcester County, 914 acres; write: 3461 Worcester Highway, Snow Hill, Md. 21863, or call: (410) 632-2566): The park consists of two sites: Milburn Landing, which is surrounded by creeks and marshlands, and Shad Landing Area, a river park with a swimming pool.

- Pocomoke State Forest (Worcester County, 13,276 acres; write: 3461 Worcester Highway, Snow Hill, Md. 21863, or call: (410) 632-2566): The forest is known for its

ROBERT K. HAMILTON
Fall foliage can enhance a picnic in the park.

stand of loblolly pines and the cypress swamps that border the Pocomoke River, along which good fishing is found.

- Taylor's Island Wildlife Management Area (Dorchester County, 1,100 acres; call (410) 376-3236): Just west of Blackwater National Wildlife Refuge (see above), the area is representative of bay tidal marsh with its islands of loblolly pine and cedar.
- Tuckahoe State Park (Caroline and Queen Anne counties, 3,498 acres; write: 13070 Crouse Mill Road, Queen Anne, Md. 21657, or call: (410) 820-1668): Tuckahoe Creek runs through the park, and a 20-acre lake offers boating and fishing. The Adkins Arboretum, a 500-acre site in the park, propagates and displays trees, plants and shrubs indigenous to Maryland.
- Wye Oak State Park (Talbot County, 29 acres; write: 13070 Crouse Mill Road, Queen Anne, Md. 21657, or call: (410) 820-1668): The park surrounds its 400-year-old white oak, which is the largest in the United States. Periodically, the Forestry Division of the DNR sells seedlings from the tree.

Trash-free policy

Maryland's state parks and forests are "trash-free." That means that trash cans have been removed to improve the appearance of the areas and provide a more enjoyable experience for all.

The Maryland State Forest & Park Service asks that you take all trash with you when you leave and that you recycle. Trash bags are distributed at all developed areas of state parks. Those renting shelters or using pavilion areas for large groups are asked to bring their own large trash bags.

The Forest & Park Service advocates a policy of reduce-reuse-recycle. You can reduce waste by buying reusable products and avoiding individually wrapped items. You can reuse resources by using washable tablecloths, napkins and towels; placing food waste in a separate bag for composting; and using reusable dishes rather than disposable ones. You can recycle glass bottles and jars, metals cans and paper and plastic products.

The result: The park will be just as clean for tomorrow's visitors as it was for today's. And no one will have to contend with a smelly, overflowing, bee-infested garbage can.

PARKS | amenities

	Boat launch	Boat rental	Canoeing	Cabins	Camper cabins	Campsites	Hookups	Dumping stations	Camp store	Fishing	Hunting	Picnicking	Swimming	Bicycle trail	Hiking trail	Horseback trail	Cross country skiing
Federal																	
A. C&O Canal	◆	◆				◆						◆		◆	◆	◆	
B. Appalachian Trail						◆									◆		
C. Catoctin Mountain						◆						◆			◆		
D. Greenbelt Park						◆						◆			◆	◆	
E. East. Neck Refuge															◆		
F. Blackwater Refuge															◆		
G. Assateague Island	◆		◆			◆		◆	◆	◆	◆	◆	◆	◆	◆		
State – Western																	
1. Herrington Manor	◆	◆	◆	◆						◆	◆	◆	◆		◆		◆
2. Swallow Falls						◆		◆		◆		◆			◆		◆
3. Garrett Forest						◆				◆	◆				◆	◆	◆
4. Deep Creek Lake	◆	◆	◆			◆		◆	◆	◆	◆	◆	◆		◆		
5. Potomac Forest						◆				◆	◆	◆	◆		◆	◆	◆
6. Savage River	◆		◆			◆				◆	◆	◆		◆	◆	◆	◆
7. New Germany	◆	◆	◆	◆		◆		◆	◆	◆		◆	◆		◆		◆
8. Casselman River										◆		◆					
9. Big Run	◆		◆			◆				◆		◆			◆		
10. Dans Mountain										◆		◆	◆		◆		
11. Rocky Gap	◆	◆	◆			◆	◆	◆	◆	◆	◆	◆	◆		◆		
12. Green Ridge	◆		◆			◆				◆	◆	◆		◆	◆	◆	
13. Sideling Hill												◆					
14. Fort Frederick	◆	◆	◆			◆			◆	◆		◆			◆		◆
15. Gathland												◆			◆		◆
16. South Mountain						◆					◆	◆			◆		◆
17. Greenbrier	◆	◆	◆			◆	◆	◆	◆	◆	◆	◆	◆		◆		◆
18. Wash. Monument												◆			◆		◆
19. Gambrill						◆		◆		◆		◆			◆		◆
20. Cunningham Falls	◆	◆	◆		◆	◆		◆	◆	◆	◆	◆	◆		◆		◆
State – Central																	
21. Seneca Creek		◆	◆							◆	◆	◆		◆	◆	◆	◆
22. Patuxent River			◆							◆	◆				◆	◆	◆
23. Patapsco Valley			◆			◆	◆	◆		◆	◆	◆		◆	◆	◆	◆
24. Morgan Run										◆	◆				◆	◆	
25. Soldier's Delight												◆			◆		
26. Gunpowder Falls	◆	◆	◆							◆	◆	◆	◆	◆	◆	◆	◆
27. Rocks			◆							◆	◆	◆			◆		
28. Susquehanna	◆		◆			◆				◆		◆			◆	◆	◆
29. Fair Hill NRMA										◆	◆	◆		◆	◆	◆	
30. Elk Neck	◆	◆	◆	◆		◆	◆	◆	◆	◆	◆	◆	◆			◆	◆
31. North Point			◆							◆		◆		◆	◆		◆
32. Hart-Miller Island						◆				◆		◆	◆		◆		
State – Southern																	
33. Sandy Point	◆	◆								◆		◆	◆		◆	◆	◆

PARKS | amenities

	Boat launch	Boat rental	Canoeing	Cabins	Camper cabins	Campsites	Hookups	Dumping stations	Camp store	Fishing	Hunting	Picnicking	Swimming	Bicycle trail	Hiking trail	Horseback trail	Cross country skiing
State – Southern																	
34. Rosaryville												◆					
35. Merkle Wildlife															◆	◆	
36. Cedarville										◆	◆	◆			◆	◆	
37. Smallwood	◆	◆	◆			◆	◆			◆		◆			◆		
38. St. Clement's Isl.										◆		◆			◆		
39. St. Mary's River	◆		◆							◆	◆	◆			◆		
40. Point Lookout	◆	◆	◆			◆	◆	◆	◆	◆		◆	◆	◆	◆		
41. Calvert Cliffs										◆	◆	◆			◆		
State – Eastern																	
42. Tuckahoe	◆	◆	◆				◆			◆	◆	◆				◆	
43. Wye Oak												◆					
44. Martinak	◆	◆	◆	◆		◆		◆		◆		◆			◆		
45. Choptank River										◆							
46. Janes Island	◆	◆	◆	◆		◆	◆	◆		◆		◆	◆				
47. Pocomoke			◆							◆	◆			◆	◆	◆	◆
48. Pocomoke River	◆	◆	◆			◆	◆	◆	◆	◆		◆	◆	◆	◆		
49. Assateague	◆	◆				◆			◆	◆	◆		◆	◆	◆		

Cabin and campsite breakdowns

IA: impaired accessible; **P:** primitive campsite; **U:** unimproved campsite; **I:** improved campsite; **R:** reservations; **CR:** camper ready; **E:** electrical hookup; **S:** sewer hookup; **W:** water hookup.

Herrington Manor   IA 20 cabins
Swallow Falls   IA 6, IR 64, CR 5 campsites
Garrett State Forest P 17 campsites
Deep Creek Lake IA 4, IR 112 campsites
Potomac   P 22 campsites
Savage River   P 42 campsites
New Germany   IA 11 cabins, IA 5, 139 campsites
Big Run   U 30 campsites
Rocky Gap   IA 11, IR 278 campsites, E
Green Ridge   P 97, U 99 campsites
Fort Frederick   U 30 campsites
South Mountain P 7 campsites
Greenbrier   IR 165 campsites, E
Gambrill   IR 35 campsites
Cunningham Falls   IR 180, CR 5, IA 150 campsites
Patapsco Valley IR 84, IA 4 campsites, E
Hart-Miller   P 22 campsites
Susquehanna   IR 75 campsites
Elk Neck   9 cabins, IR 302, IA 8 campsites, ESW
Smallwood   IR 16 campsites, E
Point Lookout   IR 143, IA 5 campsites, ESW
Martinak   1 cabin, 163 campsites
Janes Island   IA 4 cabins, IR 104, IA 3 campsites
Pocomoke River IR 250 campsites
Assateague   IR 311, IA 4 campsites

15

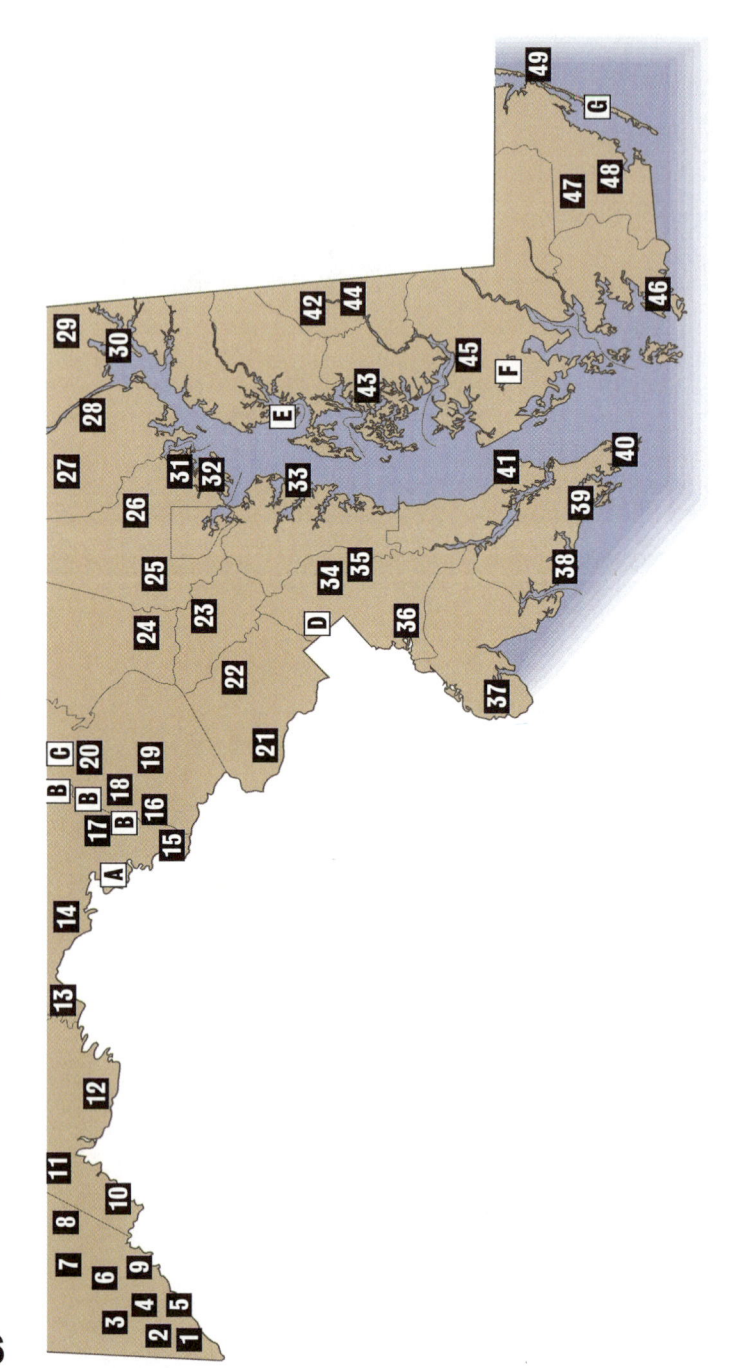

Federal and state parks in Maryland

16

Federal and state parks in Maryland

FEDERAL

A. Chesapeake & Ohio Canal
B. Appalachian Trail
C. Catoctin Mountain Park
D. Greenbelt Park
E. Eastern Neck Island Nat'l Wildlife Refuge
F. Blackwater Wildlife Refuge
G. Assateague Island Nat'l Seashore

STATE

Western

1. Herrington Manor State Park
2. Swallow Falls State Park
3. Garrett State Forest
4. Deep Creek Lake State Park
5. Potomac State Forest
6. Savage River State Forest
7. New Germany State Park
8. Casselman River Bridge State Park
9. Big Run State Park
10. Dans Mountain State Park
11. Rocky Gap State Park
12. Green Ridge State Forest
13. Sideling Hill Wildlife Mgmt. Area
14. Fort Frederick State Park
15. Gathland State Park
16. South Mountain State Park
17. Greenbrier State Park
18. Washington Monument State Park
19. Gambrill State Park
20. Cunningham Falls State Park

Central

21. Seneca Creek State Park
22. Patuxent River State Park
23. Patapsco Valley State Park
24. Morgan Run Natural Envir. Area
25. Soldier's Delight Natural Envir. Area
26. Gunpowder Falls State Park
27. Rocks State Park
28. Susquehanna State Park
29. Fair Hill Natural Resources Mgmt. Area
30. Elk Neck State Park
31. North Point State Park
32. Hart-Miller Island State Park

Southern

33. Sandy Point State Park
34. Rosaryville State Park
35. Merkle Wildlife Sanctuary
36. Cedarville State Forest
37. Smallwood State Park
38. St. Clement's Island State Park
39. St. Mary's River State Park
40. Point Lookout State Park
41. Calvert Cliffs State Park

Eastern

42. Tuckahoe State Park
43. Wye Oak State Park
44. Martinak State Park
45. Choptank River Fishing Piers
46. Janes Island State Park
47. Pocomoke State Forest
48. Pocomoke River State Park
49. Assateague State Park

GEOLOGY

Dig that rock

BY FRANK D. ROYLANCE

Maryland's roots are showing. And that's good news for anyone seeking a glimpse of the tremendous geological forces and vast time scales that have formed the land as we see it today. But we have inherited a complex geological puzzle.

Colliding continents have pushed up mountains, and eons of erosion have repeatedly worn them down. The skeletons of microscopic marine animals have accumulated over millions of years to form deep beds of limestone. Ancient forests have fallen and turned to seams of coal. Ages of erosion and deposition have formed sandstones, mudstones, siltstones and slates. And the fossil shells and bones of species now vanished from the planet remain in Maryland's rocks and gravel cliffs to speak of life that came before us.

Geologists say the oldest rocks exposed in Maryland are just over 1 billion years old. They are the metamorphic rocks. You can find them in outcrops, highway and railroad cuts in parts of Baltimore City, Baltimore County and central Howard County. They comprise all of Sugarloaf Mountain in southeastern Frederick County, and are found in other parts of the Piedmont, from Montgomery to western Harford County.

These ancient rocks were formed at the bottom of warm, shallow seas in Precambrian times. The Earth then was already 3.5 billion years old, but the first complex life forms had not yet begun to appear, so these

Chesapecter nefrens Miocene pelecypod can be found at Calvert Cliffs.

rocks hold no fossils. The sedimentary deposits were later buried, heated and squeezed by geological forces that transformed them into hard, crystalline minerals. These have since been lifted up, and erosion of the younger, softer deposits above them has exposed them again to view.

About 570 million years ago, at the start of the Cambrian period, what would one

GEOLOGY

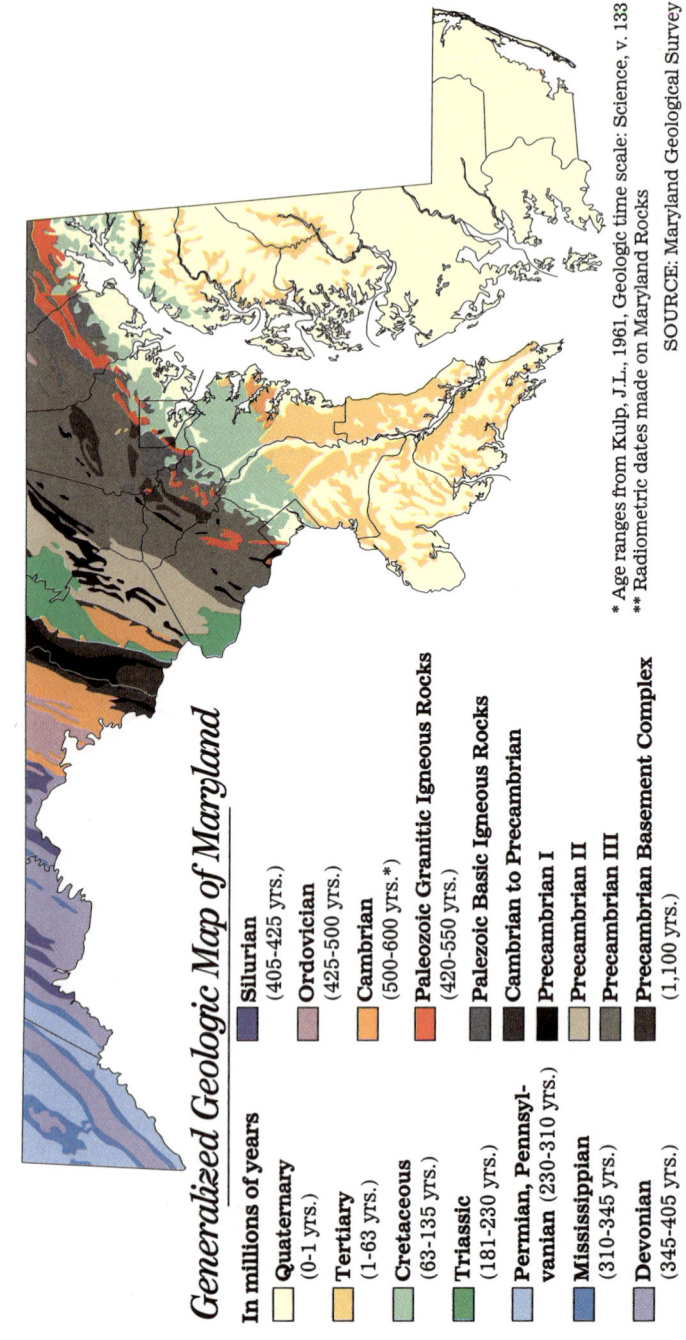

Generalized Geologic Map of Maryland

In millions of years

- **Quaternary** (0-1 yrs.)
- **Tertiary** (1-63 yrs.)
- **Cretaceous** (63-135 yrs.)
- **Triassic** (181-230 yrs.)
- **Permian, Pennsylvanian** (230-310 yrs.)
- **Mississippian** (310-345 yrs.)
- **Devonian** (345-405 yrs.)
- **Silurian** (405-425 yrs.)
- **Ordovician** (425-500 yrs.)
- **Cambrian** (500-600 yrs.*)
- **Paleozoic Granitic Igneous Rocks** (420-550 yrs.)
- **Paleozoic Basic Igneous Rocks**
- **Cambrian to Precambrian**
- **Precambrian I**
- **Precambrian II**
- **Precambrian III**
- **Precambrian Basement Complex** (1,100 yrs.)

* Age ranges from Kulp, J.L., 1961, Geologic time scale: Science, v. 133
** Radiometric dates made on Maryland Rocks

SOURCE: Maryland Geological Survey

This example of Miocene coral is astrhelia palmata.

day become Maryland was at tropical latitudes, covered by a shallow sea. At the bottom of that sea, the accumulating remains of marine organisms were forming the limestone deposits that can now be found in Washington and central Frederick counties. The most dramatic example in Maryland is found at Crystal Grottoes near Boonsboro.

Crystal Grottoes is a classic and beautiful limestone cavern. Groundwater seeping through cracks in the bedrock over hundreds of millions of years has dissolved enough of the limestone to open extensive caverns. The dripping, flowing water also has left behind mineral deposits in a variety of exotic formations. Stalactites, stalagmites, columns and flowstones are just a few. The caverns are open for guided tours daily from 9 a.m. to 6 p.m., April through October, and on weekends during the rest of the year. Phone (301) 432-6336.

By 400 million to 500 million years ago, in the Ordovician and Silurian periods, the continental plates that carry North America and Europe began to move toward each other. It was a time of volcanic eruptions and mountain-building in eastern North America. The layered sedimentary deposits were wrinkled like a loose carpet, and thrust skyward to form mountains.

As the new mountains later began to erode away, mud and silt deposits washed into shallow waters. They accumulated there and became the shales, slates, siltstones and conglomerates visible today in Allegany and central Washington counties.

Trilobites such as this Odontocephalus, are found in Western Maryland.

By the late Devonian period, 360 million years ago, the European and North American plates were headed for each other again, and

GEOLOGY

GEOLOGY

JOHN MAKELY

Sideling Hill road cut near Hancock offers exhibit center.

mountains were again being pushed up along the eastern edge of North America. Mud and sand were again washing into the coastal seas. They formed the fossil-rich shales, siltstones and sandstones found today in parts of Washington, Allegany and Garrett counties. These rocks are rich with fossil bivalves, gastropods, brachiopods, crinoids (sea lilies) and corals.

During the next 100 million years, thick forests and swamps covered the region. From time to time, sea level changes would bury the forests in marine sediments and begin turning them into coal. These rocks from the Pennsylvanian and Mississippian periods can be found at the Savage River Dam, and other parts of Garrett and western Allegany counties. Fossils in those rocks include ferns and shellfish, corals and trilobites.

Mountain-building resumed 230 to 240 million years ago, as the North American plate again ran up against the European and North African plates. The collision formed the ancestors of today's Appalachian Mountains, which geologists believe rose to Himalayan proportions.

The power of this collision is dramatically evident at Sideling Hill, six miles west of Hancock. There, in 1984, highway workers blasting a $20 million shortcut through the mountain for Interstate 68 exposed almost 810 feet of layered and sharply folded sedimentary rock. The U-shaped bend in the rocks forms what geologists call a "syncline."

The disappearance of the rocks that once extended upward from the ends of the "U" bear striking witness to the eons of erosion that have worn down the towering Appalachians, leaving the relatively gentle hills and valleys we see today in Western Maryland.

The state has constructed a rest stop and exhibit center at the Sideling Hill road cut. It offers visitors interpretive displays and a film explaining the area's geology and natural history. For information, call (301) 842-2155.

As those high Appalachians were eroding, dinosaurs came to dominate the Earth, and some found their way into what is now Maryland. Sediments were washing out of the mountains and filling basins to the east, forming the red shales and red sandstones typical of the Triassic period, 181 million to 230 million years ago. These deposits can be found in parts of Frederick and western Carroll counties. Dinosaur footprints were found in 1895 at a quarry near Emmitsburg.

But the dinosaurs' heyday in Maryland was 70 to 90 million years ago, during the Cretaceous period. Sediments and fossils from that time can be found along a 7-mile-wide band that runs from Cecil County to Washington, D.C. The stretch from Baltimore to Washington came to be known as "Dinosaur Alley" because of the fossil discoveries.

The fossilized remains of cycad trees were found in the last century in fields near Hanover, in Anne Arundel County. Since 1859, iron ore pits near Bladensburg, and Muirkirk in Prince George's County, have yielded fossilized dinosaur bones and teeth. Among them are the remains of Astrodon, the first sauropod named and described in North America. The story of the discovery of these and other Maryland dinosaur fossils is well told in "Dinosaurs of the East

GEOLOGY

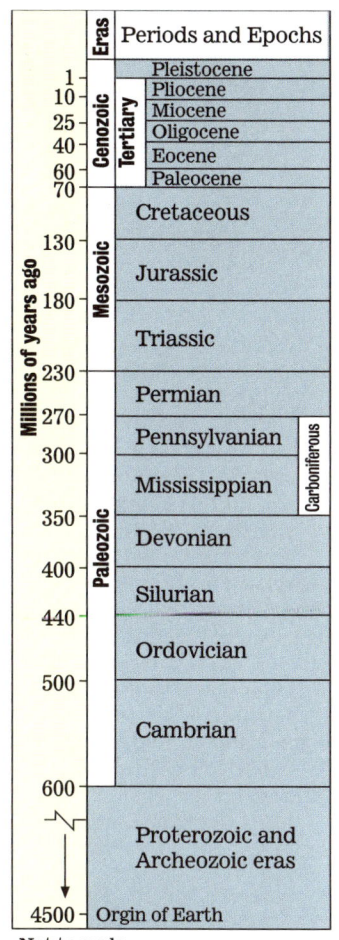

Millions of years ago	Eras	Periods and Epochs
1	Cenozoic	Pleistocene
10	Tertiary	Pliocene
25		Miocene
40		Oligocene
60		Eocene
70		Paleocene
130	Mesozoic	Cretaceous
180		Jurassic
230		Triassic
270	Paleozoic	Permian
300		Pennsylvanian (Carboniferous)
350		Mississippian (Carboniferous)
400		Devonian
440		Silurian
500		Ordovician
600		Cambrian
4500		Proterozoic and Archeozoic eras / Orgin of Earth

-Not to scale
Reprinted with permission. Maryland Geological Survey. Department of Natural Resources.

23

GEOLOGY

Crocodile teeth from Miocene period are found in Southern Maryland.

Coast," by David B. Weishampel and Luther Young (Johns Hopkins University Press, 1996).

The counties of Southern Maryland and the Eastern Shore lie atop sediments less than 20 million years old. Washed from the eroding Appalachian Mountains into coastal seas, these clays, sands and gravels still have not consolidated to form rock.

Most deposits on the Eastern Shore are less than one million years old. As much as 8,000 feet thick at the ocean beaches, they were built up by sediments flowing from ancestors of today's Delaware and Susquehanna rivers. Most are rich in marine invertebrate fossils, like snails and clams.

The sediments that form the Calvert Cliffs, on the Chesapeake in Calvert County, are 6 to 20 million years old. They constitute a world-famous source of Miocene fossils, including abundant remains of shellfish, coral, crocodiles, rays, whales and porpoises. But the most sought-after are the fossil shark teeth.

Notor hynchus cow shark teeth are from the Miocene period.

Scientists believe the region was a favored calving area for marine mammals, and that they attracted sharks. Most were small, but the 4-inch teeth sometimes found at Calvert Cliffs attest to beasts whose jaws could have accommodated several full-grown humans.

The Calvert Marine Museum in Solomons has reconstructed one of these 37-foot sharks. It also houses one of the best collections of Mio-

Stingray plates are in sediments at Calvert Cliffs.

These pieces of petrified wood are from Cretaceous period.

cene fossils anywhere. For information, call (410) 326-2042.

Marine deposits from the same period in nearby Delaware also have yielded the remains of terrestrial mammals that washed into this coastal sea 17 million years ago. They included extinct beaver, rhinoceroses and small, prehistoric horses. The bones of other extinct mammals of more recent pre-history — perhaps the last million years — turned up in the now-closed "Bone Cave" near Cumberland, where early explorers found the remains of camels, giant bears and sabre-tooth cats.

Unfossilized cypress stumps and wood, leaves and other organic matter are occasionally found in sand and gravel quarries in Southern Maryland. They are evidence of the warmer, forested environment that prevailed here within the last 5 million years.

The Chesapeake Bay itself is the most dramatic evidence of the state's more recent geological change. It is actually the drowned valley of the Susquehanna River, whose present channel south of Havre de Grace has been gradually inundated by rising sea levels since the end of the last Ice Age, 12,000 years ago. Evidence of the rising water and shore erosion is most dramatic at Turkey Point, in Elk Neck State Park in Cecil County.

Eventually, geologists say, the bay will fill with sediment, and the Susquehanna will again meander across its broad plain. When sea levels fall again, the river's pace will quicken, the waters in its channel will bite into the sediments and carve a deeper, broader gorge. Still later, sea levels will rise again to flood the gorge and create a new Chesapeake Bay.

Field guide to fossils

The best way to find fossils is to hunt with an experienced collector. Rock and

GEOLOGY | fossil sites

fossil clubs (two are listed at the end of this chapter) provide a good way to start. Or, with a few inexpensive maps and guides, and some simple equipment, you can strike off on your own. Start with some of the sites listed in this guide. They were recommended by collectors or geologists as productive and safe, and they should reward you with some fossils to take home.

In Maryland, the fossil-collector's best bets are in Garrett, Allegany and Washington counties in Western Maryland, and in Southern Maryland at the western edge of the Coastal Plain, where fossil-bearing sediments are exposed at the surface.

In the west, marine deposits laid down 450 million to 300 million years ago, between the Silurian and Mississippian periods, have been preserved as shales, mudstones and limestones. They contain the fossilized remains of extinct corals, shellfish, sea lilies, trilobites and snails, as well as terrestrial plants, such as ferns and trees.

In the east, dinosaur fossils less than 100 million years old have been found in a narrow band of Cretaceous sediments in Prince George's County.

But the most abundant and rewarding fossil beds are found in Southern Maryland, where the sand, gravel and clays laid down in coastal seas, primarily during the Miocene period less

Ecphora gardnerae is Maryland's official state fossil.

than 20 million years ago, have preserved the fossil remains of shellfish, shark teeth, stingrays, crocodiles and marine mammals such as manatees, dolphins and whales.

Best sites

Look for fossils anywhere your maps or guides indicate exposures of fossil-bearing sedimentary deposits or rock. Likely spots include highway and road cuts, the bases of cliffs and quarries, and eroded stream banks. Do not dig large holes in cliffs or stream banks. You may undermine them and trigger a dangerous landslide.

Along Chesapeake and Potomac beaches, search along the high-water mark, or in the swash. Use your sifter to search the fine sands. Winter, after a storm has stirred up the beach, can be a good time to go.

Here are some of the best and most easily accessed fossil-hunting spots recommended by Maryland geologists and collectors (see map at end of chapter):

Matoaka Cottages

What: A private Chesapeake Beach shore site. Rental cottages available May through October. Beach access available year-round for a small fee. Miocene fossils, about 14 million years old. A good spot to find Ecphora shells, the Maryland State Fossil. Also shark teeth, extinct sand dollars, oyster shells, crocodile teeth, whale and porpoise bones.

Where: South on Maryland Rt. 4 to Calvert County. Watch for signs for St. Leonard. Turn left on Calvert Beach Road. Drive about 0.9 miles beyond (east of) St. Leonard. Turn left onto dirt road and follow signs for Matoaka rental cottages. (410) 586-0269. Drive to the end of the road. Pay at the cottage office. Collecting is permitted on the beach and from fallen blocks of sediment from the cliff. Digging in the cliff is dangerous and illegal.

Brownie's Beach

What: A private Chesapeake beach site with open access. Miocene marine fossils, including teeth from 20 species of extinct sharks, stingray dental plates, teeth from extinct horses, camels, peccaries, porpoises and whales.

Where: South on Rt. 4 to Maryland Rt. 260. Turn left (east) toward Chesapeake Beach. In Chesapeake Beach, turn right (south) on Rt. 261. Continue south for just under a mile, to the bottom of a big hill, and past a swamp on your left. Turn left onto a dirt road and follow it to a parking area on your right. Hike east to the beach, then south toward the cliffs. Do not dig into the cliffs. Do not go past the metal fence.

Calvert Cliffs State Park

What: A public park, open year-round. Abundant Miocene fossil shells, shark teeth, corals, crocodile and ray teeth, 11.5 million to 14 million years old. The cliff area has been closed because of rock falls, but fossils may be collected on the beach. For more information, call Point Lookout State Park, (301) 872-5688.

This sand dollar, Abertella aperti, is from Miocene period.

GEOLOGY | fossil sites

GEOLOGY | fossil sites

MARK BUGNASKI

Connie Dadago, left, and Pat Dize examine fossils at Calvert Cliffs.

Where: Drive south on Rt. 4, 14 miles south of Prince Frederick. Park entrance and parking lot are on your left. Trail through the woods to the beach is 1.8 miles long. Be sure to leave time for the hike back before sunset. There is a chemical toilet at the beach. Bring something to eat and drink.

Purce State Park

What: An undeveloped state park on a Potomac River beach. Scan or sift the river swash zone for small Paleocene shark teeth, 60 million to 70 million years old. You also may find stingray dental plates and fossil mollusks.

Where: Drive south on Maryland Rt. 224, 1.9 miles south of Liverpool Point Road. Look for a small parking lot on the left. The beach trail begins on the right, opposite the lot.

Big Spring Quarry

What: An abandoned Washington County quarry. It contains Devonian siltstone and shale 350-400 million years old. Splitting the slabs reveals fossils of sea lilies (crinoids) and shellfish (brachiopods). Trilobites also may turn up.

Where: Above the road, on the north side of Maryland Route 56, 2.1 miles west of Big Spring, near McCoys Ferry Road.

Piscataway Creek

What: A creek ravine in Prince George's County 8 miles south of Washington, D.C. containing fossil remains of sharks, rays and whales from the Miocene.

Where: Drive south from Washington on Maryland Rt. 210. About 0.6 of a mile south of Old Fort Road, the highway cuts through the bank of the ravine. A short distance to the south, the road crosses a bridge over Piscataway Creek. The fossils are in the dense, clayey, olive-green to brown sand in the ravine wall to the west. The best spot has been the section just north of the bridge.

Henson Creek

What: Low stream banks in Prince George's County containing fossil bivalves and gastropods from the Paleocene, 60-70 million years old. Among them is Cucullaea, a large extinct clam, up to 6 inches wide.

Where: Take Oxon Hill Road east from the Rt. 210 exit from the Capital Beltway, to Brinkley Road. Park in a pulloff opposite Brinkley Road's intersection with Fisher Road. About 150 feet west of the intersection, a stream passes under Brinkley Road. The fossils are in the stream banks beginning 100 feet south of the bridge.

Wheeler Road

What: A road cut just outside Washington containing fossils from the Upper Cretaceous period, just before the extinction of the dinosaurs. The gray-black sandy marl contains fossil shells, fish, and bones and teeth from crocodiles, turtles and other marine reptiles.

Where: Take Wheeler Road less than a mile east from the District into Prince George's County. Look for a road cut on the north side.

Etiquette

First, make sure you have permission to collect. Most of the sites listed here are public areas, or private land open to collectors. Some are on private property and require permission and/or payment of a small fee. Please respect private property. To avoid disappointment, the best approach is to join an established fossil club or travel with an experienced collector or guide.

Porpoise teeth like these can be found in Southern Maryland.

GEOLOGY | resources

Equipment

Wear appropriate clothing. You may have to hike a fair distance on difficult terrain, or wade in shallow water. Bring a rock hammer, chisel (and safety glasses if you plan to split rocks), a magnifying glass and something you can pack your specimens in so they won't break. Wading boots, a shovel and a sand sifter with a quarter-inch screen may help in the soft sands, clays or gravels of the coastal plain. A fossil guide book (several are listed at the end of this chapter) will help you identify what you've found.

Resources

Publications available from the Maryland Geological Survey, 2300 St. Paul Street, Baltimore, Md. 21218-5210, (410) 554-5500:

"Studies in Maryland Geology (Special Publication No. 3)," edited by David K. Brezinski and James P. Reger, Maryland Geological Survey.

"Collecting Fossils in Maryland," by John D. Glaser, Maryland Geological Survey (1979, revised 1995).

"Dinosaurs in Maryland (Educational Series No. 6)," by Peter M. Kranz, Maryland Geological Survey.

"General Geological Map of Maryland," Maryland Geological Survey (1967).

Books and guides available in bookstores:

"Fossil Collecting in the Mid-Atlantic States," by Jasper Burns. The Johns Hopkins University Press, (1991).

"Dinosaurs of the East Coast," by David B. Weishampel and Luther Young. Johns Hopkins University Press (1996).

"Fossils," by Cyril Walker

Dinosaurs in Maryland?

Yes, once there were dinosaurs in Maryland. Their fossil remains still turn up, but many of the best sites are private property. The best way to hunt for them is with an experienced collector.

Dr. Peter Kranz is a geologist and former public school science teacher who received his Ph.D from the University of Chicago. He has become an expert on Maryland's dinosaurs. He often takes volunteers with him to help excavate dinosaur remains. He also runs paid field trips, school presentations and assemblies, and even dinosaur birthday parties for children.

Dr. Kranz can be reached at 818 G Street SE, Washington, D.C. 20003. Telephone :
(202) 547-3326.
Email him at dinosaur fund@juno.com

GEOLOGY | resources

MARK BUGNASKI

Sorting through rocks for fossils at Calvert Cliffs beach.

and David Ward. Dorling Kindersley Inc. (1992).

"Fossils: A Guide to Prehistoric Life (A Golden Guide)," by Frank H.T. Rhodes, Herbert S. Zim, Paul R. Shaffer. Golden Press (1962).

Organizations

Calvert Cliffs Fossil Club, c/o Mike Ellwood, president; 1918 Pagebrook Road, Silver Spring, Md. 20903.

Maryland Geological Society, 8052 Kavanagh Road, Baltimore, Md. 21222. (410) 554-5500.

Calvert Marine Museum, Solomons, Md. (410) 326-2042.

31

GEOLOGY | fossil map

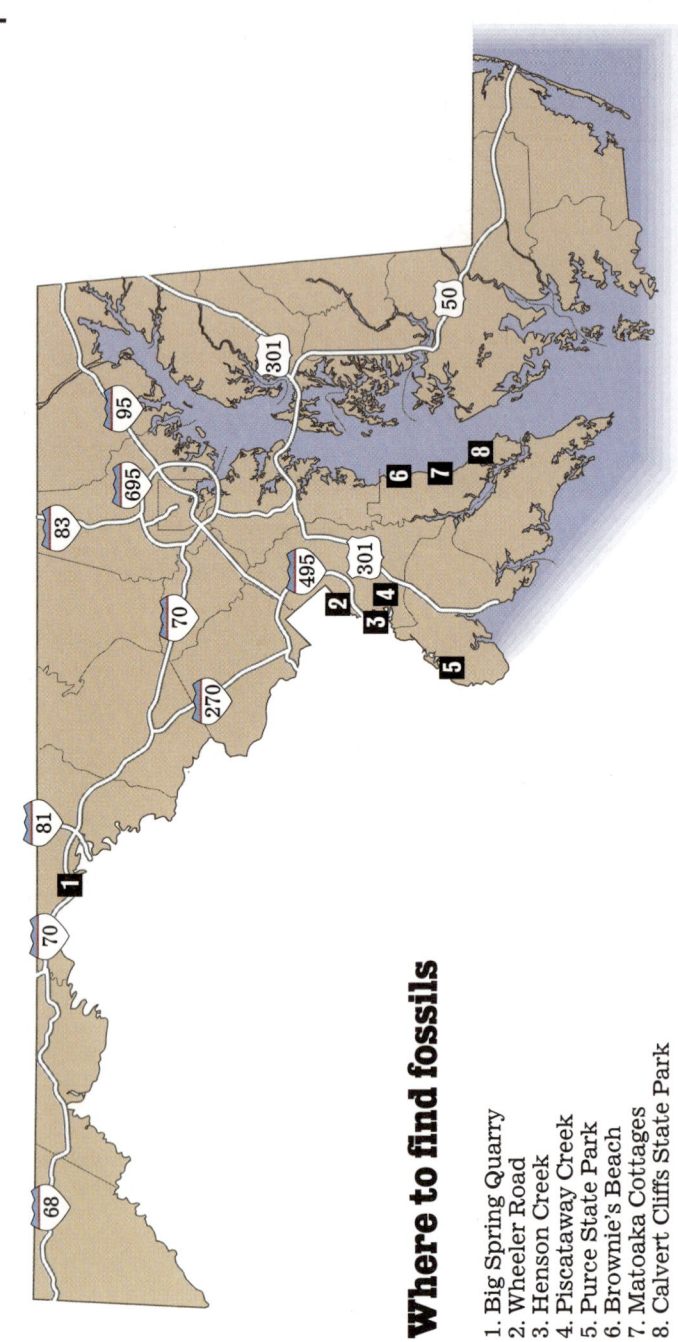

Where to find fossils

1. Big Spring Quarry
2. Wheeler Road
3. Henson Creek
4. Piscataway Creek
5. Purse State Park
6. Brownie's Beach
7. Matoaka Cottages
8. Calvert Cliffs State Park

32

Minerals to find in Maryland

Selenite

Talc

Marcasite

Calcite

Limonite

GEOLOGY

FLORA

Hidden beauty blooms

BY MIKE KLINGAMAN

Think of Maryland's native flora, and what comes to mind? Black-eyed Susans and the Wye Oak.

Two down, and 2,400 to go. That's how many plant species are indigenous to the Free State, from the delicate woodland orchids of Western Maryland to the rugged bald cypress on the Eastern Shore; from the sea of spring ephemerals beside the rushing Susquehanna to a lonely prickly pear cactus on the beach near Calvert Cliffs.

All are as much a part of the state's horticultural heritage as its heralded white oak and daisies.

Though a number of Maryland's own can be seen from the highway — a copse of silvery beeches, a glinty field of goldenrod, a towering stand of wild rice — many of the trees, shrubs and flowers that rooted here long ago grow in shy obscurity, in woods and meadows and marshes off the beaten path. How else would they survive?

Native plants — those that occur naturally in an ecosystem, without human interference — have flourished for hundreds, often thousands of years across the state. Most were anchored in Maryland soil long before European settlers arrived. The majestic rose

MARK BUGNASKI
Sure, Maryland has Black-eyed Susans, but also much more.

FLORA

mallows rising from the shallows of the Nanticoke River, along Route 50 in Dorchester County, greet beach-goers as they did the tribes who once roamed there. Campers in New Germany State Park, in Garrett County, sleep amid beds of painted trillium, a tiny wildflower, just as their pioneer ancestors did.

How diverse is Maryland's flora? Thirty-seven species of wild asters live here, 33 types of goldenrod and 30 violets. Some vegetation finds a cozy niche and explodes. Botanists count 15 kinds of wild orchids in Frederick County's Catoctin Mountain Park alone.

Though most native plants grow in soil or sand, a few struggle up out of rock or water. Moss phlox, a thin, wispish wildflower, rises stoically from the fissures of ancient boulders along aptly named Billy Goat Trail, beside the Potomac River in Montgomery County. At the Jug Bay Wetlands Sanctuary (Anne Arundel), butterflies flit around the purple-flowering pickerelweed, whose heart-shaped leaves climb inexorably from the murky depths of the Patuxent.

It's no surprise that some of Maryland's most cherished plants hug the banks of its largest rivers. For eons, scraps of vegetation have washed down distant creeks and streams that feed the Potomac and Susquehanna. Eventually, the bits of floral flotsam come aground and germinate, their odyssey complete.

Dozens of plants, some rare and unusual, are sequestered along the shores of the Potomac, near Great Falls in Montgomery County: wildflowers with exotic names like the white trout lily, which migrated up from the Mississippi Valley, and the star false Solomon's seal, which floated down from northern climes.

Other wayfaring plants took the high road, arriving by way of the Eastern Continental Divide, a daunting ridge of high ground that runs through the Appalachians and separates the major watersheds. To the west, rivers run toward the Gulf of Mexico; to the east, the Atlantic Ocean.

For centuries, different seeds and berries have found

MARK BUGNASKI
Maiden pink stands out in a field in Finksburg.

FLORA

GENE SWEENEY, JR.

The State Highway Administration has sown wildflowers along roads such as I–83.

their way to the crest of that ridge, which crosses Maryland in Garrett County.

"All a seed need do is wash down the Maryland side of that ridge, and — presto — something is growing here that would normally be further west," says Joe Metzger, a horticulturist in Western Maryland.

Witness dwarf larkspur, with its brilliant blue spikes, and pink-flowering shooting star, its petals swept back to mimic its namesake. Midwesterners both, these plants made it as far east as

FLORA

PERRY THORSVIK
Beach heather decorates dunes on Assateague Island.

Sharpsburg, huddling on the pH-friendly limestone bluffs above the historic Washington County town.

The state's diverse terrain — mountains, wetlands, plains — accommodates a wide range of plants, all within a few hours' drive. Theoretically, you could see swamp azaleas at dawn, in Pocomoke State Park, and mountain pimpernels at dusk, in Green Ridge State Forest (Allegany County). Except you'd probably want to squeeze in a visit to Soldier's Delight Natural Environmental Area, a rocky barren near Randallstown, for a glimpse of the globally rare fringed gentian, a federally endangered, cobalt-blue wildflower that retreated there.

Maryland's moderate climate offers refuge for warm- and cool-loving vegetation. "We're at the southern edge of the range for northern species and the northern edge for southern plants," says Cris Fleming, co-author of the book "Finding Wildflowers in the Washington-Baltimore Area." "Plants from Canada and New England just touch the northern edge of Maryland, while Southern species creep up as far as St. Mary's County and the Eastern Shore."

Here, one finds ancient plants with old-fashioned names like dutchman's breeches and possumhaw holly; ominous sobriquets like bloodroot and rattlesnake plantain; and colorful ones like green dragon and pink lady's slipper.

Some of them multiply freely throughout the state. Others survive in isolated pockets, or microclimates, whose quirky conditions fit their needs.

On a steep, wooded hillside in Patapsco State Park, in Howard County, an unpretentious wildflower struggles on. The plant has placed itself wisely — a north slope with little sunlight for one that likes the cold. Nodding trillium, a species more common in Canada, has lasted here for who can say?

"How did it get here? Birds. The river. Who knows?" says Fleming. "Maybe it came thousands of years ago, when the climate was cooler, and has just hung on since.

"But it's one of Maryland's own. You've got to admire plants like that."

Field guide

Whether you're seeking a glimpse of the rare fringed gentian at Soldiers Delight Natural Environmental Area in Baltimore County or pining for a peek at a prickly pear in bloom at Calvert Cliffs State Park, you have plenty of plants to choose from in Maryland.

The following are 16 native plants that wildflower hunters can stalk in the state.

Bloodroot

Toothwort

Rattlesnake Plantain

Nodding Trillium

FLORA | field guide

FLORA | field guide

Black-eyed Susan

Lady's Slipper

Larkspur

Dutchman's Breeches

Wild Rice

Wild Azalea

Fringed Gentian *Skullcap*

FLORA | field guide

Prickly Pear *Wild Geranium*

Hepatica *Cardinal Flower*

41

FLORA | sites

Best sites
(See map at the end of chapter)

1. Cranesville Swamp — Cranberries, purple-fringed orchids and speckled alders highlight this cool, damp, 400-acre bog in Garrett County, accessible by boardwalk and owned by the Nature Conservancy. Many northern plant species found here. Swamp entrance on Lake Ford Road, near Thayerville and Swallow Falls State Park. Phone (301) 656-8673.

2. New Germany State Park — Campgrounds and stream banks covered with flashy painted trillium and white clintonia, a lily that ought to be a presidential favorite. New Germany Road, 5 miles south of Grantsville (Garrett County). Phone (301) 895-5453.

3. Green Ridge State Forest — Scramble up steep, slippery shale barrens in search of native plants. Rewards include a glimpse of the rare yellow-flowering mountain pimpernel and Kate's mountain clover. On Star Route in Flintstone (Allegany County). Phone (301) 478-3124.

4. Snyders Landing — Walk the old C&O Canal towpath through "limestone alley," a unique habitat filled with sinkholes, springs and limestone caves. Wild ginger, whose flower resembles a little brown jug, grows from rocks dripping overhead. Hepatica and twinleaf thrive here, near the rarer dwarf larkspur and shooting star. On Snyders Landing Road, in Sharpsburg (Washington County). Phone (301) 432-5124.

MARK BUGNASKI
Colorful flowers deserve colorful names. This is flea bane.

5. Catoctin Mountain Park — This national park is home to Camp David, the presidential retreat, and a good source of various oaks, beeches, mountain laurel and 15 species of orchids. Also a half-dozen types of violets, some with large, pansy-sized flowers. On Maryland Route 77, west of Thurmont (Frederick County). Phone (301) 663-9388.

6. C&O Canal National Historical Park — a nearly 200-mile tract that runs from Washington, D.C., to Cumberland. Botanists rave about a lush section in western Montgomery County, filled with unusual plants. One naturalist has counted 100 species of wildflowers in three hours there, near the Great Falls Tavern Visitors Center (11710 MacArthur

Blvd., Potomac). Phone (301) 299-3613.

7. Soldier's Delight Natural Environmental Area — The only known source of fringed gentian, a fall-blooming wildflower, is found on this largest (2,000-acre) serpentine barren in Maryland. Admire the few native plants that can tolerate a thin soil so rich in metals, it's toxic to much vegetation. 5100 Deer Park Road, between Randallstown and Owings Mills (Baltimore County). Phone (410) 922-3044.

8. Irvine Natural Science Center — Several miles of self-guided nature trails on the grounds of St. Timothy's School. Bloodroot, trillium, wild geranium displayed. 8400 Greenspring Ave., Stevenson (Baltimore County). Phone (410) 484-2413.

9. Cylburn Arboretum — A 176-acre nature preserve includes a wildflower trail, with plants labeled for beginners. Some species are native to Maryland, others are not. 4915 Greenspring Ave. (Baltimore City). Phone (410) 396-0180.

10. Susquehanna State Park — Many spring-flowering plants bloom along the three-mile, blue-blazed river trail below Conowingo Dam, including erect trillium, Dutchman's breeches and Virginia bluebells. 801 Stafford Road, Havre de Grace (Harford County). Phone (410) 836-6735.

11. Jug Bay Wetlands Sanctuary — Anne Arundel County's largest (500-acre) park offers woods, wetlands and meadows. Magnificent marshes, accessible by boardwalk trail, boast some of the largest stands of wild rice on the East Coast, plus pickerelweed, fragrant sweet flag and climbing hempweed, a pink-flowering vine that climbs up water plants without smothering them. Near Upper Marlboro. Phone (410) 741-9330.

12. Battle Creek Cypress Swamp Sanctuary — This Nature Conservancy park features what is thought to be the most northerly stand of bald cypress trees in the United States. Also summer-blooming lizard's-tail and cardinal flower. On Gray's Road, near Prince Frederick (Calvert County). Phone (410) 535-5327.

13. Flag Ponds Nature Park — Woodlands and wetlands, freshwater ponds and saltwater beaches offer botanical diversity at this 330-acre park near Calvert Cliffs. Of special interest are the prickly pear (the only native Eastern cactus), rare sand plum tree and climbing milkweed. About 10 miles south of Prince Frederick, on Maryland routes 2 and 4 (Calvert County). Phone (410) 535-5327.

14. Pocomoke River State Forest and Park — Paddle canoes out to an island filled with flowering viburnums, swamp azaleas, winterberry hollies and the delicate white fringe tree. Nice stand of bald cypress trees. 3461 Worcester Highway, Snow Hill (Worcester County). Phone (410) 632-2566.

FLORA | resources

MARK BUGNASKI

In Finksburg, coral honeysuckle blooms.

Equipment

Binoculars, for viewing hard-to-reach plants
Camera with close-up lens
Compass (though most parks have marked trails)
Field guide to native plants or wildflowers
10-power hand lens
Waterproof bag (for wetlands areas)

Etiquette

Stay on nature trails.
Don't pick flowers.
Respect private property.
Pick up litter.
Don't lay cameras or other equipment on plants.

Potpourri

Spring is the best time to hunt native plants — woodland species bloom in March and April. Summer is good for wetlands. Fall offers flowering meadows of wild asters and goldenrod.

Beginners should take field trips in small groups, accompanied by a knowledgeable guide.

Consult on-site naturalists in public parks for best plant locations.

Railroad tracks and old road cuts offer good wildflower viewing.

You needn't walk miles to see native plants. They may be thriving beside the sunny parking lot in any state park.

Resources

Books

"Audubon Society Field Guide to North American Wildflowers — Eastern Region," by William A. Niering and Nancy C. Olmstead; Alfred A. Knopf.

"Chesapeake Bay, Nature of the Estuary, A Field Guide," by Christopher P. White; Tidewater Publishers.

"Finding Wildflowers in the Washington-Baltimore Area," by Cristol Fleming, Marion Blois Lobstein and Barbara Tufty; Johns Hopkins University Press.

"Newcomb's Wildflower Guide," by Lawrence Newcomb; Little, Brown.

A purple coneflower attracts a butterfly.

GENE SWEENEY, JR.

"Peterson Field Guides: Wildflowers," edited by Roger Tory Peterson and Margaret McKenny; Houghton Mifflin.

Organizations

Maryland Native Plant Society, P.O. Box 4877, Silver Spring, Md. 20914-4877.

National Audubon Society, Mid-Atlantic Region, 1104 Fernwood Ave., Suite 300, Camp Hill, Pa. 17011. Phone (717) 763-4985.

Sources of native plants

Clear Ridge Nursery, 217 Clear Ridge Road, Union Bridge, Md. 21791. Phone (410) 848-4789.

Conebrook Nursery, P.O. Box 177, 2737 Grier Nursery Road, Forest Hill, Md. 21050. Phone (410) 838-4747.

Environmental Concern, Inc., P.O. Box P, 210 W. Chew Avenue, St. Michael's, Md. 21663. Phone (410) 745-9620.

Richard Falcone, Waldorf, Md. Phone (301) 870-8038 (by appointment only).

Kollar Environmental Service, 5200 West Heaps Road, Pylesville, Md. 21132. Phone (410) 836-0500.

Lower Marlboro Nursery, P.O. Box 1013, Dunkirk, Md. 20754. Phone (301) 855-7654.

Wildlife Landscapes, Baltimore, Md. Phone (410) 256-1777 (by appointment only).

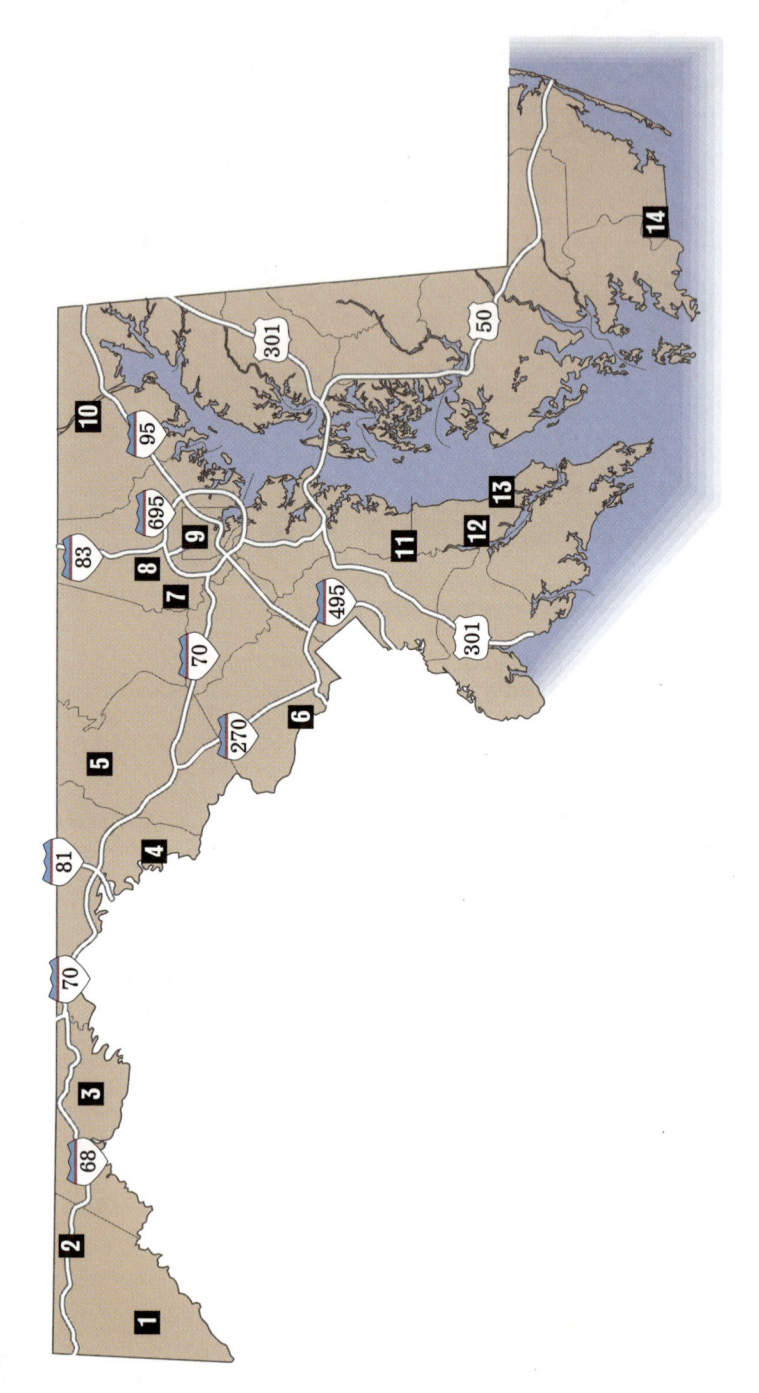

Where to find wildflowers

46

Where to find wildflowers

1. Cranesville Swamp
2. New Germany State Park
3. Green Ridge State Forest
4. Snyders Landing
5. Catoctin Mountain Park
6. C&O Canal National Historical Park
7. Soldier's Delight Natural Environmental Area
8. Irvine Natural Science Center
9. Cylburn Arboretum
10. Susquehanna State Park
11. Jug Bay Wetlands Sanctuary
12. Battle Creek Cypress Swamp Sanctuary
13. Flag Ponds Nature Park
14. Pocomoke River State Forest

FLORA | fall foliage

JED KIRSCHBAUM

Maple leaves are awash in color come autumn.

Fall foliage on display

You don't have to trek to New England and battle the legions of leaf-peepers to enjoy the kaleidoscope of autumn colors: Every fall, Maryland decks itself out in waves of crimson and gold.

The transformation begins in Garrett County, usually in the last couple weeks of September, and rolls east toward the Chesapeake. By mid-November, most of the deciduous trees on the Eastern Shore have shed their leaves.

Leaves change color as autumn progresses, sap-flow slows and chlorophyll, the chemical that gives leaves their green color, disappears. Warm sunny days and cool nights help trap some of the sugar in leaves, which results in brilliant colors.

The Maryland Office of Tourism Development, in conjunction with the Depart-

FLORA | fall foliage

AMY DAVIS

Loy's Station covered bridge, one of three covered bridges in Frederick County, is a scenic destination for folks traveling near Thurmont to see the fall foliage.

ment of Natural Resources, offers a fall foliage hot line with weekly updates of where to see leaves at their peak. The toll-free hot line — (800) LEAVES-1, or (800) 532-8371 — is in operation from the middle of September to the end of November.

In addition, the service includes information on weekend fall festivals and other events that leaf-peepers might want to visit. One of the first festivals on the calendar is Oakland's Autumn Glory Festival. Held each year in early October, it attracts about 50,000 people.

The U.S. Forest Service also operates a toll-free recorded service that gives foliage forecasts throughout the country: (800) 354-4595.

ROBERT K. HAMILTON

Trees like these, in Howard County's Centennial Park, brighten the state's hillsides with color each autumn.

WILDLIFE

Bird-watching is looking up

BY MIKE KLINGAMAN

Maryland is home to so many different birds, the only trick is knowing where to find them. In the Free State, it's as simple as looking up.

"Open your eyes anywhere here, and bird life is all around you," says Bob Rineer, president of the Maryland Ornithological Society.

There are oceanic birds, the shearwaters and petrels that buddy up to fishing boats off the coast; marsh birds (rails, bitterns) that feed on the rich, squiggly life along the Chesapeake; and forest birds — warblers and thrushes — that thrive in the deep woods of Western Maryland.

The coastal plains, rolling hills and rugged mountains provide a diversity of habitats for the more than 400 species of birds native to the state. A number of them live here year-round, from the blue jays at backyard feeders to the bald eagles wintering in trees near Conowingo Dam. Some, like the Baltimore oriole, are fair-weather friends, migrating to and from the region as the seasons change. Others, like the stilt sandpiper, are simply tourists passing through on the Atlantic flyway, an aerial highway that cuts a busy swath through Maryland's skies en route from Canada to South America.

Millions of birds take that path, delighting the state's 1.5 million bird-watchers. Each spring, Bob Rineer roosts at Fort Smallwood, in Riviera Beach, and counts hawks flying north from Florida. But he's also content watching birds from his urban workplace. Rineer, who works at Johns Hopkins Hospital in downtown Baltimore, has seen 68 species there.

PERRY THORSVIK
Bald eagle soars at Eastern Neck Island Refuge.

Maryland birds run the gamut, from black crows to white swans; from four-inch hummingbirds to eagles with wing spans of seven feet or more. Here, one finds cardinals that seldom leave their neighborhoods, and chimney swifts that winter in South America ... orioles that nest in treetops and kingfishers that burrow into stream banks ... ring-billed gulls

WILDLIFE | birds

KIM HAIRSTON

A night heron surveys the water while atop a branch.

that circle burger joints for handouts and ospreys hovering over schools of fish in the bay... vultures that dine on road kill and cedar waxwings that feed on fruit.

"For its size, Maryland ranks very, very high in its variety of birds," says Chandler Robbins, a federal wildlife biologist and author of a popular field guide for bird-watchers. "You don't have to go anywhere in particular. In any one year, I can see 100 species within 100 feet of my house in Laurel."

Weekends, wildlife enthusiasts flock to state parks, reservoirs and marshes that harbor colorful or unusual birds — golden-crowned kinglets and saw-whet owls that nest in the cool bogs of Cranesville Swamp, in Garrett County... gulls and snow buntings that winter on the empty beaches at Sandy Point State Park, in Anne Arundel County... wild turkeys and grouse rustling in the brush at Indian Springs Wildlife Management Area, in Washington County... leggy herons and longspurs that revel in the solitude of the wetlands and dunes of Assateague Island.

Scenic Assateague is a bird-watcher's paradise during fall migrations, says Mark Hoffman, a wildlife official for Maryland's Department of Natural Resources: "It's the last pit stop before the ocean for a lot of species heading south" — and a good place to see exotic water birds blown off course by storms at sea.

For the less adventurous, try bird-watching in a local park. Any green space in an urban setting is a natural

WILDLIFE | birds

oasis for migrating species passing overhead.

Bird-watching is the fastest-growing outdoor recreation activity in America, increasing by more than 150 percent since the 1980s, according to a 1995 federal survey. Maryland is on the cusp of that boom: Each year, Blackwater National Wildlife Refuge near Cambridge draws more than 100,000 binocular-carrying bird-watchers seeking everything from bald eagles to the brown-headed nuthatch.

A bird-watchers' hot line, (301) 652-1088, provides weekly updates on where to find unusual species. The state also plays host to one of the nation's first bird-watching festivals. Each April, the Eastern Shore counties of Somerset, Worcester and Wicomico stage the Delmarva Birding Weekend, a two-day fete that features guided canoe trips down the Pocomoke River and Nassawango Creek to see water birds and a boat ride to Deal Island for a glimpse at its peregrine falcons.

"Birds in Maryland are never boring," says Robbins. "They're coming and going, constantly changing, always the unexpected. Every month, another species comes through — and watching them can be tremendously relaxing, when it's done at your own speed."

LLOYD FOX

Canada geese gather to feed in a Kent County field.

WILDLIFE | birds

Field guide

Great blue heron: A large, leggy water bird found near ponds, lakes and marshes throughout the state, year-round. Herons nest in colonies in treetops in early spring. When flying, they curve their heads back against their necks in a distinct "S" shape.

Wood duck: Less conspicuous than other ducks, it frequents wooded streams and ponds, and rarely travels in large numbers. Occasionally winters here, in warmer climes. Unusually long tail makes it easy to spot in flight.

Bald eagle: On the comeback in Maryland, this regal, hardy bird is seen more on the Eastern Shore, but can be spotted fishing anywhere along the Chesapeake or its tributaries. Favorite site: the Blackwater National Wildlife Refuge.

Osprey: Migratory black-and-white bird that summers here, building large nests of wood atop buoy markers or on platforms specifically erected for it over water. Wings have distinctive crook, or bend. Spectacular to watch when fishing.

WILDLIFE | birds

American kestrel: Attractive, somewhat solitary in nature, usually found in rural areas teeming with mice. Sits on utility wires while hunting food. Nests in old woodpecker holes in dead trees or abandoned barns, mostly west of the Chesapeake. Lives here year-round.

Wild turkey: Omnivorous bird making a comeback, its range has expanded from Western Maryland to include the whole state. Found mostly in wooded areas or in fields adjacent to forests. Broods often come to grassy areas at edge of woods to find insects.

Eastern screech owl: One of smaller owls, common but rarely seen in the region. Roosts in tree cavity by day, and hunts rodents, insects and other birds at night. Imitate its call after dark, and the owl may fly close enough to be seen by flashlight.

Common nighthawk: More often heard than seen, this cryptically colored bird nests on flat rooftops in urban settings. Its call, a nasal *peent*, sounds after dusk. Though nocturnal by nature, it is one of the few land birds to migrate by day, flying south in late summer.

55

WILDLIFE | birds

Chimney swift: Noted birding author Roger Tory Peterson called it "a cigar with wings" because of its distinct shape. It nests in chimneys and is frequently seen in cities. Plain plumage, bowed wings. Makes a chippering call. This insect-eater winters in South America.

Ruby-throated hummingbird: A popular summertime favorite of Maryland homeowners, who go to great lengths to entice it to their gardens. Hummingbirds feed on the nectar of many of the same flowers that attract butterflies.

Belted kingfisher: Common near freshwater and saltwater ponds and marshes, especially in winter, when more northerly habitats are frozen. Perches on bridges and utility lines over water. Nests by burrowing into banks of streams or in cliffs along the bay.

Downy woodpecker: Tiny, black-and-white, sparrow-sized bird that favors woodlands, but can be drawn to backyard feeders filled with suet. This species will drum on trees, but not as frequently as the more common red-bellied woodpecker.

WILDLIFE | birds

Blue jay: Noisy, colorful, large-crested favorite at suburban feeders, where it prefers sunflower seeds and nuts. Feed them in winter, and jays respond by eating thousands of garden insects in summer. Some northern birds migrate to Maryland in colder months.

Tufted titmouse: A small, bluish-gray bird found statewide. Extremely vocal in summer, it makes a loud peter-peter-peter whistle. Easily drawn to feeders filled with sunflower seeds and to nest boxes placed in the woods for them.

White-breasted nuthatch: An interesting species that moves down trees, head-first, on short legs, poking under loose bark in search of bugs. Distinct yank-yank-yank call. Eats nuts and seeds, notably sunflowers in winter.

Eastern bluebird: Rebounding in Maryland, thanks to growing number of nesting boxes placed outside for them. Eats fruit, not seeds, in winter. Travels in pairs in summer and in flocks in colder months. Prefers open farmland; sometimes found near stables.

WILDLIFE | birds

Cedar waxwing: Odd-looking little bird with black mask, tawny crest, yellow belly and reddish-white wings. Rarely seen at feeders, it will visit yards filled with fruit-bearing shrubs and trees. Lives here year-round.

Scarlet tanager: Brilliant red-and-black species whose song sounds like a robin with a sore throat. Migratory bird that likes large, unbroken tracts of forest land. Usually makes bird-watchers come to it.

Northern cardinal: A regular patron of winter feeders, this showy, familiar species is not at all bashful despite its bright colors. Loves suburbia for its sunflower seeds and fruit, and is one of the last birds to leave feeding trays at dusk.

Baltimore oriole: Migratory orange-and-black bird that heads south shortly after baseball season. More common on Western Shore, it tends toward wooded areas near streams, staying high in treetops. Song is a series of loud, flute-like whistles.

Best sites

This is a quick reference list to favorite bird observation spots in all parts of the state (see map, next page).

1. Cranesville Swamp. Along state line between Cranesville, W.Va., and Browning Mill, Md., 4 miles NW of Swallow Falls. Nesting warblers, golden-crowned kinglet, saw-whet owl.

2. Herrington Manor. 5 miles NW of Oakland on Swallow Falls Rd. Nesting sapsuckers, thrushes, warblers.

3. Swallow Falls State Forest and Recreation Area. 8 miles N of Oakland and 6 miles W of Thayersville. Follow signs. Northern warblers.

4. Dans Mountain State Park. Turn E from Rt. 36, 1/2 mi. N of Lonaconing. Warblers. For hawk migration, ravens, Bewick's wren, return to Rt. 36, go N through Midland, E to Dans Rock.

5. Oldtown. C & O Canal 14 miles SE of Cumberland on Rt. 51. Warblers, vireos, flycatchers.

6. Indian Springs Wildlife Management Area. Leave I-70 at Indian Springs, go W on U.S. 40 and Old U.S. 40 to Pectonville Rd. (1/2 mile W of Licking Creek). Work N toward Pa. line (5 miles); also try side roads. Turkey, grouse, Bewick's wren, maybe Bachman's sparrow.

7. Monument Knob. At Frederick-Washington Co. line on Alt. U.S. 40, turn N and drive 1 mile to Washington Monument State Park. Watch migrating hawks from tower.

8. Seneca. C & O Canal towpath from mouth of Seneca Creek, E to Violets Lock off Rt. 190 (River Rd.) and W along towpath or along River Rd. and Old River Rd. to Sycamore Landing, and "Hughes Hollow" (at Hughes Rd. and Old River Rd.). Warblers, ducks, bitterns, rails, gallinules.

9. C & O Canal National Monument. Access through roads running S from Rt. 100 such as Great Falls or Swain's Lock, or reached by MacArthur Blvd. bus by getting off at Brookmont or Walhonding Roads and walking to Potomac River. Warblers, vireos, flycatchers.

10. Patapsco State Park. U.S. 1 to River Rd. in Elkridge or Md. 103 to Ilchester Rd. Warblers, migrants.

11. Susquehanna State Park. Churchville to Level on Rt. 155, then E 3 miles on Rock Run Rd. Cerulean, prothonotary and other warblers, hawks, ducks.

12. Elk Neck State Park. Rt. 272, 10 miles S of North East. Wintering waterfowl, nesting and migrating warblers.

13. Remington Farms. W from Chestertown on Rt. 20; 1.2 miles S of Rt. 21 go left on unnumbered road for 0.6 mi. to sign. Canada, blue and snow geese, ducks.

14. Eastern Neck Island National Wildlife Refuge. From Chestertown, Rt. 20, then Rt. 445 to southern tip of Kent County. Wintering waterfowl, migratory songbirds.

WILDLIFE | birds

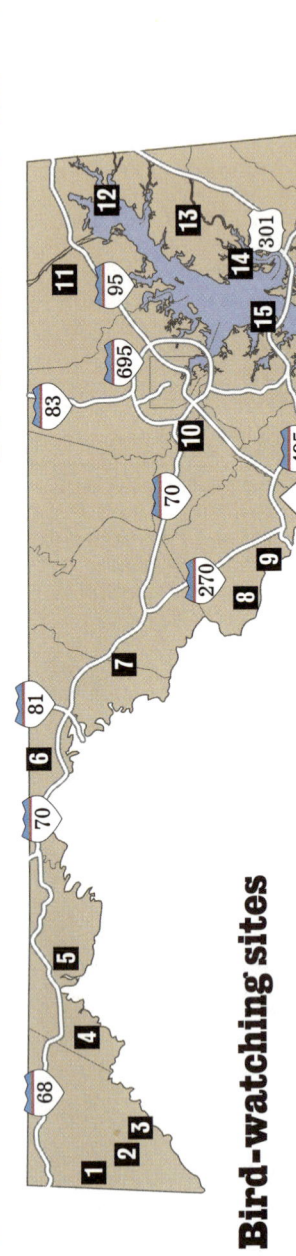

Bird-watching sites

1. Cranesville Swamp
2. Herrington Manor State Park
3. Swallow Falls State Forest
4. Dans Mountain State Park
5. Oldtown
6. Indian Springs Wildlife Management Area
7. Monument Knob
8. Seneca
9. C&O Canal National Monument
10. Patapsco State Park
11. Susquehanna State Park
12. Elk Neck State Park
13. Remington Farms
14. Eastern Neck Island National Wildlife Refuge
15. Sandy Point State Park
16. Patuxent Marshes
17. Battle Creek Cypress Swamp
18. Blackwater National Wildlife Refuge
19. Deal Island Wildlife Management Area
20. Pocomoke State Forest
21. Assateague Island National Seashore
22. Ocean City

WILDLIFE | birds

BO RADER

There are an estimated 1.5 million bird-watchers in Maryland.

15. Sandy Point State Park. U.S. 50 & 301, W end of Bay Bridge. Waterfowl, marsh birds, gulls, shorebirds, migrant hawks, snowbunting.

16. Patuxent marshes. U.S. 301 to Md. 382 to Croom Airport Rd. Also Md. 4 at Hill Bridge. Rails, blackbirds, marsh wren, waterfowl.

17. Battle Creek Cypress Swamp. On Rt. 506, 2 miles E of Bowens. Nesting southern warblers.

18. Blackwater National Wildlife Refuge. From Cambridge, Rts. 16 and 335 or 16 and Egypt Rd. Waterfowl, eagles, brown-headed nuthatch.

19. Deal Island Wildlife Management Area. Rt. 363 from Princess Anne. Waterfowl, herons, shorebirds.

20. Pocomoke State Forest. Best areas are Shad Landing State Park, 3 mi. S of Snow Hill on Rt. 113, and Milburn Landing, 7 mi. SW of Snow Hill on Rt. 364. Land birds.

21. Assateague Island National Seashore. Rt. 611 from West Ocean City. Sea and shorebirds, herons, sparrows, longspurs.

22. Ocean City. Check especially the Inlet, tidal flats at W end of 3rd St., and fresh pond 1/2 mi. N of Elliott's service station on mainland.

Bird-watching equipment

Binoculars (7- to 10-power)
Birding field guide
Camera
Hat
Insect spray
Notebook
Spotting scope (20-to 60-power)
Sunglasses
Sunscreen lotion
Tape recorder

WILDLIFE — snakes

Etiquette

- No trespassing on private land.
- Never disturb nesting areas.
- Avoid "flushing" birds — making them fly saps their energy for migration.
- Leave habitat as you found it.
- Leave pets at home.
- Educate children before bringing them along.

Resources

Organizations

Maryland Ornithological Society, Cylburn Mansion, 4915 Greenspring Ave., Balto., Md. 21209. Phone (800) 823-0050.

Audubon Naturalist Society of Central Atlantic States, 8940 Jones Mill Rd., Chevy Chase, Md. 20815. Phone (301) 652-9188.

Books

"Finding Birds in the National Capital Area," by Claudia Wilds, Smithsonian Institution Press.

"Field Guide to the Birds of North America," National Geographic Society.

"A Field Guide to the Birds of Eastern and Central North America," Roger Tory Peterson, Houghton Mifflin.

"A Guide to Field Identification: Birds of North America," Chandler Robbins, et al, Golden Press.

"Field List of the Birds of Maryland," Marshall Iliff, Robert Ringler and James Stasz, Maryland Ornithological Society.

Watch out for snakes

Bird-watching in the woods? Careful where you walk. There are 20 types of snakes in Maryland, two of them poisonous — the copperhead, common throughout the state, and the timber rattler, found only in the mountainous areas of Maryland.

The copperhead, which frequents stream bottoms and rock outcroppings, has copper- to cream-colored skin and a dark brown hourglass pattern running down its back. Copperheads are docile, unless agitated or stepped upon. Ditto the timber rattler, which uses the brownish-black rattles at the base of its tail as a warning before it strikes. The snake is yellow-brown or black-brown in color, with a diamond pattern on its back.

Most snakes in Maryland are non-venomous, including the common black rat snake, which, if cornered, vibrates its tail against dry leaves to mimic a rattler. Others include the black racer, slightly smaller (three feet), thinner and faster than the black rat snake; common garter snake (greenish-brown with tan stripes); and ring-neck snake, a small, dark species with a cream-colored neckband.

More aggressive is the northern water snake, which, though not poisonous, will bite. Often mistaken for the deadly water moccasin, or cottonmouth, which is not

Northern water snake

Black rat snake

Black racer

Common garter snake

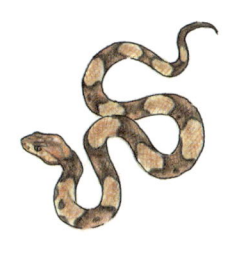

Copperhead

Eastern hognose snake

Timber rattlesnake

Ring-neck snake

WILDLIFE | snakes

63

WILDLIFE

JOHN MAKELY
Garter snake, common in the state, is harmless.

found in Maryland, the northern water snake is dark brown and usually found in ponds, tidal creeks and brackish, slow-moving waters near the bay.

On the Eastern Shore, look for the Eastern hognose snake, a dark brown species with a nose resembling a pig snout. Approach it and the hognose snake either rolls over and plays dead or vomits its last meal. Defensive tactics, both.

Other wildlife

In pursuit of birds, expect to cross paths with some of the other fauna native to Maryland, including 60 mammals, 50 reptiles, 40 amphibians, thousands of insects and hundreds of thousands of other invertebrates, like spiders, snails and worms.

A look at the larger critters:

Deer. There are two species in Maryland, white-tailed and sika, the latter a small, elusive deer introduced from Asia 60 years ago and found only on the lower Eastern Shore.

Squirrels. Besides the common grey, there's the red squirrel (in mountainous areas) and the fox squirrel, the largest in Maryland with its big, bushy tail. Also two types of Delmarva fox squirrels, both endangered, on the Eastern Shore.

Foxes. Red foxes, more common, like open farmland. Grey foxes are more secretive and stick to the woods.

Bears. Rarely seen, they live mainly in Western

LLOYD FOX
White-tailed deer are a common site in outer suburbs.

Maryland, but have been spotted as far east as Baltimore County.

Raccoons. They scavenge at night all over the state.

Groundhogs. Also called woodchucks, they like open grasslands and are found everywhere but on the Eastern Shore, where the soil is too wet for them to live underground.

Opossums. These nocturnal grey mammals with long pointed snouts and naked tails are the most common road-kill animal in Maryland.

Muskrats. Live near water, most often seen at dawn or dusk.

Turtles. Wooded areas have box turtles; ponds and creeks are home to painted and snapping turtles.

Salamanders. The largest salamander in North America, the two-foot hellbender, frequents the Youghiogheny River in Garrett County.

List of endangered species

The following animals, known to be from Maryland, are listed as federally threatened or endangered:

Indiana bat
Delmarva fox squirrel
Eastern cougar
Bald eagle
Peregrine falcon
Piping plover
Roseate tern
Red-cockaded woodpecker
Green sea turtle
Hawksbill sea turtle
Kemp's ridley sea turtle
Leatherback sea turtle
Loggerhead sea turtle
Maryland darter
Shortnose sturgeon
Dwarf wedge mussel
Northeastern beach tiger beetle
Puritan tiger beetle
American burying beetle

JED KIRSCHBAUM
This shortnose sturgeon, an endangered species, was returned to the Chesapeake Bay in Cecil County.

BOATING

On the water, take it to the limit

BY PETER BAKER

A boat, it has been said, is a hole in the water into which one pours money — and in Maryland many thousands of people do so happily, buying, using and maintaining everything from inexpensive aluminum canoes to mega-yachts that run into the millions.

From whitewater kayakers in Garrett County to blue-water anglers off the state's Atlantic Coast, people have registered more than 200,000 boats in the state for use on bays, rivers, creeks, ponds, lakes and reservoirs.

According to a recent study of recreational boating in Maryland, there were 100,087 registered trailerable powerboats, 60,021 registered powerboats kept in the water and 30,328 registered sailboats — and boat ownership continues to be on the upswing.

How much money do people pour into these holes in the water?

How about $1.01 billion a year? That's the figure spent on recreational boating here in 1993, according to the study, funded by the Department of Natural Resources and the Marine Trades Association of Maryland. The average boater spends $5,311 per year.

But anyone who shoots the rapids, paddles still water, competes in club races, cruises or fishes from a boat knows that boating is not mainly about money. It is about the pleasure of being on the water and of prudently discovering one's limits in the process.

Throughout the tidewater, there are racing, cruising and fishing clubs, many of which have junior programs to introduce newcomers to the various types of boating.

AMY DAVIS
Young sailors can practice skills at Annapolis Yacht Club.

BOATING | sailing

The DNR, with the assistance of volunteer instructors, teaches a boating safety education course at many locations each year, and everyone born on or after July 1, 1972, is required to pass the course before being allowed to operate a registered or documented vessel in Maryland. For more information, call (410) 974-2040.

The DNR has also put its boating safety course on a CD-ROM that boaters can use to replace classroom courses. The course explains right-of-way rules and navigational charts and how safely to anchor a boat. The course can be taken free at the Maryland Natural Resources Police headquarters at the Tawes State Office Building in Annapolis. The headquarters also is the place to pick up the course on CD-ROM; a $20 refundable deposit is required.

To reserve study time on a computer or to borrow a copy of the course on CD-ROM, call the Natural Resources Police headquarters at (410) 974-2248 during regular business hours.

U.S. Power Squadrons, the Coast Guard Auxiliary and other groups also teach courses that meet state standards. For Power Squadron courses, call (410) 686-5926 or (410) 282-6464. For Coast Guard courses, call (800) 336-BOAT.

The Alexandria Drafting Company's "Waterproof Chartbook of the Chesapeake" contains indispensable charts and is available from marinas and tackle shops. It also has a list of marinas and launching areas. The ADC also produces a street map book for each county.

The Department of Game and Inland Fisheries, 4010 W. Broad Street, Richmond, Va. 23230-1104, phone (804) 367-1000, will provide — free of charge — "Chesapeake Bay & Susquehanna River and its tidal tributaries, Public Access Guide" in both booklet and foldout map forms. It's an excellent resource that includes all boat ramps in Maryland.

Federal and state laws require certain safety equipment to be on all boats, whether sitting at the dock or under way. Be certain you know the requirements and meet all of them. They are listed below in the subsection on motorboats.

Rhythm of speed

At 7 or 8 knots, believe it or not, speed under sail can be a very heady thing — the bay breaks away in one wave stem to stern, the hull vibrates softly, the rigging hums and beyond the wheel or tiller, the rudder settles into tight rhythm. Until it is time to change course and retrim and the rhythm of speed is found again.

Throughout Maryland's Chesapeake Bay and tidal rivers, whether in 8-foot dinghies or 60-foot

Basic sailboat

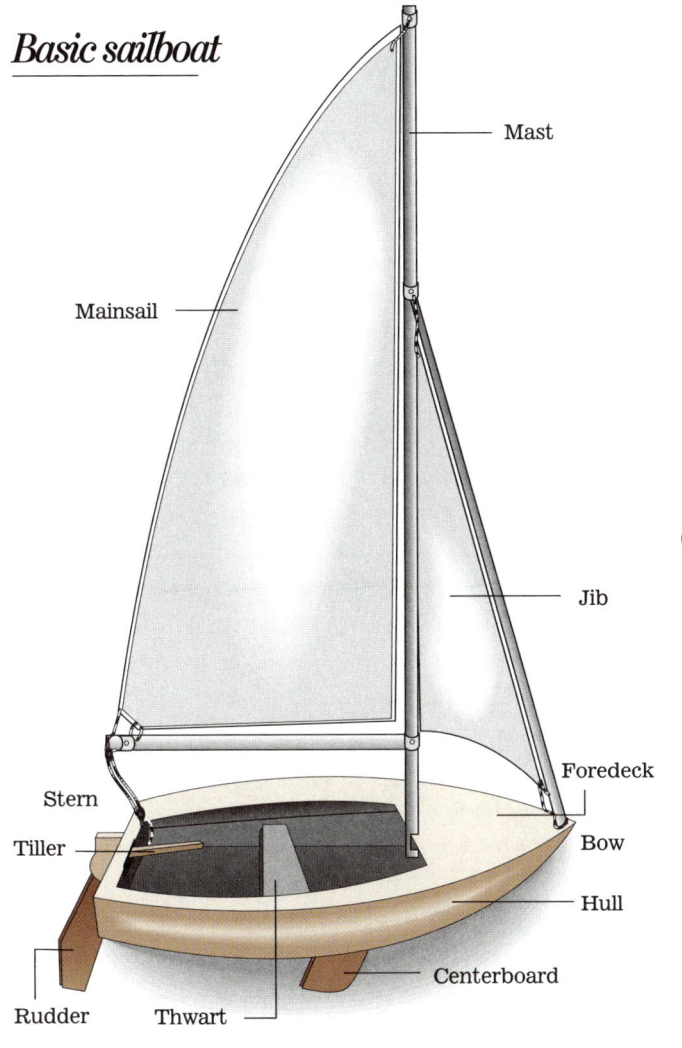

- Mast
- Mainsail
- Jib
- Foredeck
- Stern
- Bow
- Tiller
- Hull
- Rudder
- Thwart
- Centerboard

BOATING | sailing

DNR courses introduce beginners to sailing terms.

schooners, the rhythm of sailing vibrates among racers, day sailors and cruisers.

The tidewater encompasses hundreds of snug anchorages and bustling harbors, secluded and populated river reaches, tricky straits and narrows and open water that can be roiled by sudden squalls or severe storms.

69

BOATING | sailing

Sloop
Single mainmast

Cutter
Two headsails in front of mast.

Ketch
Mainmast is taller with mizzenmast in front of steering position.

Schooner
Second mast higher

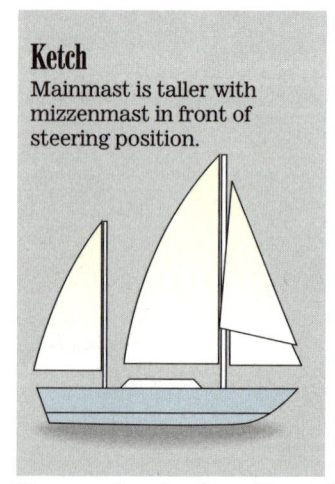

Here are four basic sailboat designs.

Or the tidewater can be flat as a mirror as far as one can see — until an ocean-going freighter rises on the horizon and rumbles along the shipping channel at 15 knots, spreading its rolling bow wave from shore to shore.

But on most days, winds can be expected to be under 15 knots and seas two feet or less, conditions that make the bay and its backwaters ideal for sailing.

Most of the more than 30,000 registered sailboats are home-ported in Baltimore and Anne Arundel counties. And on any given weekend there is a regatta or cruise organized by yacht clubs, sailing clubs or cruising clubs — from traditional log canoe races on Eastern Shore rivers to national racing championships off Annapolis, from multihull cruises to Alberg 30 raft-ups.

Baltimore and Annapolis are the major racing centers on the bay, with weeknight and weekend racing. Both ports and many others through the tidewater have yacht clubs, sailing clubs and sailing schools with training programs for sailors of all ages, starting with pre-teens in dinghies and extending through big boat sailing.

The sailing season never really ends in Maryland; there are frostbite regattas held in many areas over the winter months. But in general, the season runs from late April or early May through mid-November in warmer years.

While Anne Arundel and Baltimore counties are home ports to the greatest number of sailboats in the state, the best cruising grounds are away from the hubbub of heavy weekend boating traffic and regattas.

North of the Bay Bridge, a dozen rivers branch off into quiet anchorages where sea nettles are little or no problem at all during most of the cruising season. In this part of the tidewater, the shorelines are steep, for the most part, and the channels well defined.

The Chester, Magothy, Sassafras, Susquehanna, North East, Elk and Bohemia rivers are the best for cruising sailors.

From the Bay Bridge to the Little Choptank River on the Eastern Shore, and the Patuxent River on the western shore, nine more rivers carry sailing depths well up their lengths.

From Solomons south to the Virginia border, cruising grounds include six smaller rivers and the Potomac, which is navigable from its confluence with the bay at Point Lookout to Washington, 90 miles upstream.

Add in Pocomoke and Tangier sounds along the Eastern Shore, and rivers and bays in Virginia's portion of the Chesapeake, there are some 6,000 miles of shoreline, some three dozen rivers, a multitude of tributaries and hundreds of good anchorages to explore.

At its narrowest, the bay measures about 3.5 miles and at its widest about 25 miles.

Yet in many areas, especially below the Choptank River, where the Eastern Shore is girdled by extensive marshes, the water is crossed by shoals. Up-to-date charts and good navigation skills are necessary to avoid groundings.

The main stem of the bay also is a shipping lane to Baltimore, which is frequented by ocean going ships day and night, so vigilance is advisable.

Cruising on the bay can be very good.

The wildlife is abundant: bald eagles and osprey, herons, cormorants, ducks, geese and, in the more southern areas, skimmers and brown pelicans.

BOATING | sailing

LINDA COAN

Governors Cup is one of the area's most popular races, attracting more than 150 boats a year.

The fishing can be excellent, and a sailor with a tidal sportfishing license can with a little patience and minimal gear catch a dinner of perch, spot, croaker, sea trout, rockfish, blues or flounder.

Hard crabs, too, are easily caught with collapsible traps or hand lines, and soft crabs can be found in the marshy shallows.

Once away from the hubbub of busy harbors, there is an intriguing mix of man and nature, a serenity that is hard to find elsewhere.

Safety

In warm weather, afternoon thunderstorms can rise quickly over the western shore and scoot across the bay with little warning — and some are powerful enough to endanger small craft. So a weather radio is a necessary item to have aboard — and it should be listened to on a regular schedule.

Tides and currents are minimal, with most Maryland waters having tidal differences of one to two feet, unless there are exacerbating conditions. A northwester lasting several days, for example, will hold the tide out of many rivers and harbors on the western shore and pile up the tides on the Eastern Shore.

Major navigational hazards are generally limited to shoals and a handful of areas used for weapons testing by the military and closed to navigation during active testing. Aberdeen Proving Ground in the upper bay, the Navy testing range below Dahlgren on the Potomac, Bloodsworth Island and the target ships near the Middle Grounds off Point Lookout are restricted to navigation at certain times.

Minor hazards include fish traps, crab pots and trotlines used by commercial fishermen. Although many entrance channels are said to be clear of crab pots, each of which is marked by a float, it is not uncommon for pots to drift and for a handful to work their way into supposedly open waters. A sharp lookout and good helmsmanship will keep you clear of trouble.

Bay cruisers also will encounter jellyfish, flies and mosquitoes at times, but good cabin and hatch screens will take care of the flying pests. Swimmers should check for jellyfish before jumping in.

First aid kits should include bug repellent, topical treatments for bites or stings and extra sunscreen. Stow an aerosol can of bug killer aboard just in case.

Planning ahead

The best Chesapeake Bay cruises start well before you leave the dock. Buy the most current and complete chartbook you can find, sit down at a table and plot where you would like to go and then determine what is realistic.

BOATING | bay cruises

Calculate your average boat speed over a series of day sails in a variety of conditions, and then decide how many hours in a day you are willing to sail. Multiply the number of hours by your boat's average speed, and the resulting figure will provide what should be a workable range for each day of cruising — 5 knots times six hours, for example, gives a daily range of 30 nautical miles.

Next, go to the chartbook and plot a circle of 30 nautical miles, using your home port as the center point. The rivers and harbors within that circle should be reachable.

Repeat the process from each ensuing anchorage, keeping in mind that the last leg of the cruise must result in a workable sail home.

Resources

Books

"Guide to Cruising Chesapeake Bay," published by Chesapeake Bay Magazine. Write 1819 Bay Ridge Ave., Annapolis, Md. 21403, or call (410) 263-2662.

"Guide for Cruising Maryland Waters," a chartbook that covers the upper part of the Chesapeake. Write Dept. of Natural Resources, Consumer Services, P.O. Box 1869, Tawes State Office Building, 580 Taylor Ave., B-1, Annapolis, Md. 21401, or call (410)974-3211.

"Cruising the Chesapeake: A Gunkholer's Guide," by William H. Shellenberger, International Marine Publishing/McGraw Hill (800-822-8158).

"The Chesapeake Bay Book: A Complete Guide," by Allison Blake, Berkshire House Publishers (800 321-8526). Includes lists of recommended marinas, charter boats, cruise and excursion boats and sailing schools.

"Chapman's Piloting, Seamanship and Small Boat Handling," published by Hearst Marine Books.

"Reed's Nautical Alamanac," published by Thomas Reed publications.

"Learning to Sail," by Di Goodman and Ian Brodie, published by International Marine/McGraw-Hill.

Numbers to call:
Coast Guard boating safety answers, 800-368-5647

Baltimore County Sailing Center — sailing programs, 410-321-6909

Bay cruises

A seven-day cruise on Chesapeake Bay

From Baltimore harbor, many cruising areas of the upper bay are well-suited to overnight trips, but getting out into the tidewater treasures that lie south of

A day's sail on the bay

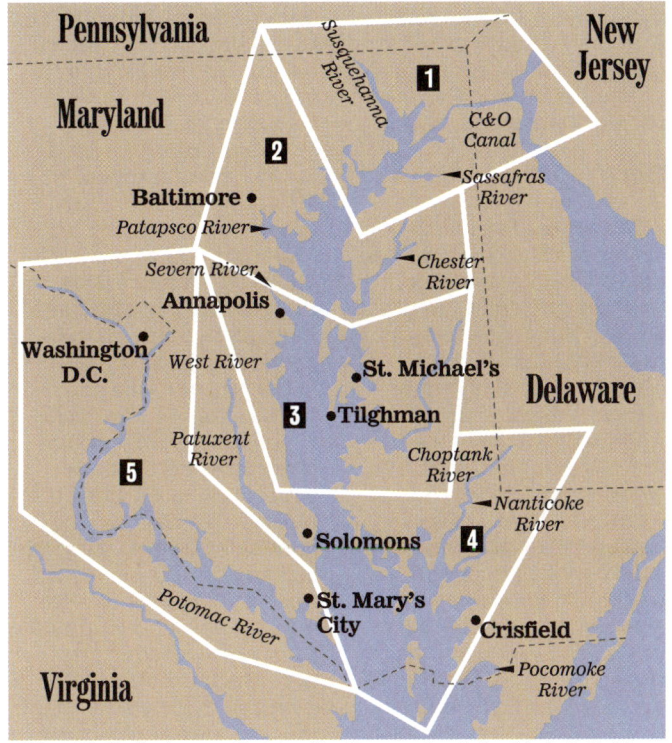

William H. Shellenberger. Cruising the Chesapeake: A Gunkholer's Guide © 1990. Reprinted with permission. International Marine Publishing, a division of the McGraw Hill Companies.

Within each of the five regions shown, you can sail point-to-point in a day trip

the Bay Bridge can take a little more planning.

The following cruising destinations plumb some of the usual and unusual haunts for cruising sailors willing to spend their days sailing and only the early morning and summer evenings traipsing about tidewater tourist traps and towns.

The following are suggested for experienced sailors, and the longer daily runs might be beyond the range of sailboats with an average speed of less than 5 knots.

Cruisers who cannot make 5 knots or more might want to check the options listed and shorten their daily runs to avoid periods of nighttime sailing. The options also are intended to allow cruisers to vary their destinations when persistent head winds, stormy

BOATING | bay cruises

weather or calms could impede their progress.

No one should undertake a cruise without up-to-date nautical charts, proper safety equipment and thorough preparation and vigilance.

Day 1

Baltimore Harbor to Annapolis Harbor, approximately 29 nautical miles.

- Things to do: The State House, Naval Academy and the city's historic district all are served by tour companies, although all are within walking distance of the docks. Shopping is plentiful, whether for trinkets or a wardrobe. Boat shows are held in the spring and fall, each July 4 there is a fireworks display and on any given weekend or Wednesday night there is top-notch racing to watch. Details are available from an information booth at the city docks.

- Dockage/anchorage: Dockage can be had along the city docks, on municipal moorings or at transient slips in many marinas, but the port often is busy and it pays to check with the harbor master or marina offices early. The harbor master's office is located in the center of the plaza at the foot of the public docks where the tour boats tie up. Anchoring is restricted in certain areas marked by buoys, but the outer harbor, off the Naval Academy sea wall and Spa Creek above the bridge hold many good possibilities. Back Creek also has a number of good anchorages. The head of the city docks offers free dinghy docking, as does the landing at Truxtun Park, toward the head of Spa Creek. Water taxi service runs through the season.

- Groceries/food services: Several restaurants are along the city docks, and many more are within easy walking distance along Main and West streets as well as State Circle and Maryland Avenue. Groceries can be bought at the Marketplace in the center of the plaza at the head of the city docks.

- Marine supplies/services: Fawcett's marine supply is located along the bulkhead at the city docks, and Viking marine supply is in Eastport just across the Spa Creek Bridge. Several other supply and equipment firms are located in Eastport. Back Creek and Spa Creek each have several fine marinas with travel lifts and facilities for repairs on boats of all sizes. Diesel fuel and gasoline are readily available.

- Options: From Baltimore, Annapolis should be readily reached in a day's sail or motor. But should you find yourself losing the wind or the light or both, the Magothy River offers several good anchorages a short distance within its mouth, which is located on the Western Shore just north of the Bay Bridge, and Whitehall Bay, along the western shore below the bridge, provides sheltered anchorages.

Day 2

Annapolis Harbor to St. Michael's Harbor, approximately 24 nautical miles.

- Things to do: Both the Chesapeake Bay Maritime Museum and the St. Mary's Square Museum are worth seeing, and the maritime museum gives an excellent view of traditional lifestyles of the Chesapeake Bay area. Shopping. Antiques. Bric-a-brac.
- Dockage/anchorage: Three marinas in town offer transient slips, and the maritime museum has dockage for members only. The town has a public dinghy dock for those anchored out. Close-in anchoring can be a problem during busy summer weekends, so check the charts for nearby anchorages such as Leeds Creek, Hunting Creek and Shaw Bay.
- Groceries/food services: There are more than a half-dozen restaurants and almost as many sandwich shops and carryouts in this small colonial town. Groceries, a pharmacy and a laundromat are within walking distance of the waterfront.
- Marine supplies/services: Supplies and repairs to rigging, shipboard systems and engines are available. Diesel fuel and gasoline available.
- Options: If the wind is blowing out of Eastern Bay, the 6.5-mile beat to Tilghman Point can be discouraging, but once around it, there is an easy, six-mile reach up the Miles River. Crab Alley Bay and the mouth of Cox Creek can provide adequate overnight anchorage, but services will not be readily available. If you must, run out Eastern Bay and turn west-northwest to the West River and sail into Galesville, where there is a good anchorage, water taxi service and groceries, restaurants and boat services and supplies are readily available. The trip to Solomons on Day 3 will still be possible.

TIFFANY H. HOUSE
Practicing a spinnaker peel prior to the start of a race.

Day 3

St. Michael's Harbor to Solomons Harbor, approximately 45 nautical miles.

- Things to do: The Calvert Marine Museum is a highlight for history or maritime buffs. A short walk from the harbor and anchorages are antique shops, fish houses, the J.C. Lore Oyster Processing House and the Chesapeake Biological Laboratory, part of the University of Maryland system. Harbor tours are available during the boating season, and the area still supports strong charter fishing and commercial watermen.

- Dockage/anchorage: There are several nice marinas and waterfront hotels that offer overnight dockage for transients. Mill Creek and Back Creek offer good anchorages, and water taxi service is available.

- Groceries/food services: Grocery stores, carryouts and several very good restaurants are within easy walking distance.

- Marine supplies/services: Yacht repair facilities are more than adequate, and parts or supplies are readily available. Diesel fuel and gasoline are readily available.

- Options: In the case of head winds or light winds, head into the Choptank River to Cambridge or Oxford or a half-dozen creeks on the northern shore that offer good anchorage. The Little Choptank River also is a decent anchorage. Solomons will be reachable on Day 4, but Crisfield, well to the southeast, probably will have to be dropped from the itinerary.

Day 4

Solomons Harbor to Crisfield Harbor, approximately 40 nautical miles, using Kedges Strait.

- Things to do: Two historical sites are the Governor J. Millard Tawes Historical Museum and the Albert LaVallette House. But Crisfield is still a waterman's town, with the lifestyles tied to commercial crabbing. Through the boating season, there is a parade of festivals in town in July and August, including July 4 celebrations, the J. Millard Tawes Crab

MICHAEL LUTZKY
Members of St. Mary's College sailing team go through drills.

and Clam Bake, the Watermen's Folklife Festival Arts and Crafts Show and the National Hard Crab Derby and Fair on Labor Day weekend.

- Dockage/anchorage: The state-operated Somers Cove Marina is virtually the only game in town, with more than 500 total slips and 100 of those targeted for transients. Limited open anchorage and a fee required for dinghy tie-ups.
- Groceries/food services: A half-dozen restaurants and carryouts are within easy walking distance, as are two supermarkets.
- Marine supplies/services: Marine supplies and hardware, diesel fuel and gasoline available.
- Options: With the exception of a hard beat through Kedges Strait, the trip to Crisfield should be do-able. But should contrary conditions arise, one might opt to turn and run to St. Mary's City on Day 4 rather than on Day 5.

Day 5

Crisfield Harbor to St. Mary's City, approximately 37 nautical miles.

- Things to do: St. Mary's City, the first capital of Maryland, is something of a miniature Williamsburg — without the high prices, big crowds or elaborate displays. Especially worth seeing are a replica of the first statehouse and the 57-foot Dove, a re-creation of the sailing ship that brought the first settlers to Maryland. Also nearby are a visitor's center, museum, an archaeological-historical exhibit and a reconstructed 17th century inn.
- Dockage/anchorage: Anchorages are numerous but are best off St. Mary's College, host to the annual Governor's Cup Race. The college has a courtesy dinghy dock.
- Groceries/food services: Limited.
- Marine supplies/services: Available at Dennis Point Marina on Carthagena Creek or Point Lookout Marina on Smith Creek at the entrance to the St. Mary's River.
- Options: Once committed to St. Mary's City, the options are few. St. Jerome's Creek above Point Lookout off Chesapeake Bay is accessible to shoal draft boats; Cornfield Harbor at Point Lookout State Park inside Point Lookout can offer emergency anchorage in certain conditions; the Yeocomico and Coan rivers on the Virginia shore of the Potomac inside Smith Point also are possible options.

Day 6

St. Mary's City to Tilghman, approximately 57 nautical miles.

- Things to do: Tilghman is a watermen's town with its focal point being Knapps Narrows, a dredged channel that connects Chesapeake Bay and the Choptank River. While there are periodic

BOATING | bay cruises

PERRY THORSVIK

Schooners are frequent sights in Inner Harbor.

watermen's fairs and an annual Tilghman Days celebration, there is little to be done here but shop in small stores, restock provisions and rest for the final leg home to Baltimore.

- Transient slips are available at a couple of marinas in the Narrows and at a country inn on nearby Dogwood Harbor, which recently was dredged. Anchoring out is best done up Harris Creek at Dun Cove or Waterhole Cove.

- Groceries/food services: Tilghman has several good restaurants along the Narrows or a short walk south, where there also is a market.

- Marine supplies/services: All services and supplies are available at the Narrows, along with diesel fuel and gasoline.

- Options: On this longest leg of the cruise, the Little Choptank River on the Eastern Shore and Solomons on the western shore offer good alternatives should head winds or calm slow the going — but on most summer days southerlies should push you along nicely.

Day 7

Tilghman to Baltimore Harbor, approximately 34 nautical miles.

- Things to do: The Inner Harbor area is chock full of side trips, top-notch restaurants and shopping: the Maryland Science Center, the National Aquarium, Harborplace, World Trade Center, Baltimore Maritime Museum, Pier 6 Concert Pavilion and festivals and shows at the newly expanded Convention Center complex, to name a few.

- Dockage/anchorage: Whether in the Inner Harbor or the Middle Branch of the Patapsco River, there are good anchorages available. Several marinas offer slips for transients, and in the Inner Harbor there is excellent water taxi service.
- Groceries/food services: Markets are within walking distance, along with very good restaurants, bars and night clubs. Fells Point and Little Italy are excellent areas to investigate.
- Marine supplies/services: Repairs of all types and supplies and hardware are readily available, along with diesel fuel and gasoline.
- Options: Annapolis, of course, is the perfect short stop, but closer to home is the Magothy River, just above the Bay Bridge.

Upper Bay Overnighters

1. Baltimore to Rock Hall, eight nautical miles
- Things to do: There are 10 restaurants along or near the waterfront of this busy, commercial harbor, and even more marinas. Shopping is limited but interesting. The Rock Hall Museum offers a glimpse of Eastern Shore life in a town grown from a watermen's economy.
- Dockage/anchorage: Overnight anchorage is best in nearby Swann Creek.

2. Baltimore to Worton Creek, 23 nautical miles
- Things to do: This quiet anchorage, with good depths for sailboats, offers nettle-free swimming and a handful of restaurants.
- Dockage/anchorage: Three marinas on the creek have transient slips, although weekends can be busy. Many good anchoring areas, from the outer creek into Green Point Wharf.

3. Baltimore to Dobbins Island on the Magothy River, 21 nautical miles
- Things to do: Dobbins Island is a popular bay anchorage, offering deep water in close to the northern shore of the island, which is a good picnic area. If you go, take your trash out with you.
- Dockage/anchorage: Best anchorage is in Sillery Bay, south of the cable area.

4. Baltimore to Gunpowder River, approximately 18 nautical miles
- Things to do: Shoreside activities are limited, but if you take along a dinghy, there is wonderful fishing along the marshy shorelines of Saltpeter and Dundee Creeks and at Carroll Point. A good place to drop the hook for lunch. Shoreside activities on Aberdeen Proving Ground are restricted.
- Dockage/anchorage: Depths of 6 feet plus run upriver beyond Maxwell Point, but best holding ground is below Maxwell Point.

Whitbread Round the World Race

In April 1998, the Whitbread Round the World Race will sail up Chesapeake Bay to Fort McHenry, finishing a 900-mile sprint from Fort Lauderdale, Fla. The Whitbread is the premier distance sailing race in the world, a nine-leg, 32,000 nautical mile circumnavigation in state-of-the-art offshore racing boats. It is a spectacle enjoyed by some of the largest shoreside and television audiences in the world. Yet it is relatively unknown in the United States.

Race organizers and Chessie Racing, Maryland's team in the Whitbread, hope to change all that. Chessie Racing will have a new boat built for the race. Its Whitbread 60 is designed by Bruce Farr and Associates of Annapolis.

"This is a great event with the best sailors and boats in the world," said Mark Fischer, CEO of the Blakeslee Group in Baltimore and a man deeply involved with Chessie racing. "We don't just want to compete. We want to do it right and we want to win."

Syndicates registered for the race include 41 teams from 17 countries, including six from the United States.

The value of the Whitbread layover in 1998 – a period of 10 days to two weeks that will be split between Baltimore and Annapolis – has yet to be determined by city and state officials, but they speculate that the race has the potential to pay off big.

Lee Tawney, director of international economic development for Baltimore, said the Whitbread gets tremendous exposure through computer networks as well as television coverage around the world–in addition to hundreds of thousands of people who travel to layover ports.

In Auckland, New Zealand, during the last Whitbread, for example, more than 815,000 people passed through the Whitbread Village. The Whitbread Village in Baltimore will be set up at Rash Field, along the Inner Harbor.

Philippa Beresford, who coordinates onshore activities at Whitbread layovers around the world, calls the race a "festival of sailing," a place where sailors and non-sailors alike can learn about racing a 70-foot sailboat around the world and the technology that makes 400-mile days possible.

Satellite technology, oceanography, geography, mathematics, weather forecasting and many other sciences all are involved in completing the race — along with expert seamanship.

Satellite uplinks now create video feeds that enable television stations to track the racing around the world, from the struggle to find wind in the Doldrums to either side of the Equator, to the battle to harness it in the 50-foot seas of the southern

BOATING | whitbread race

ALGERINA PERNA

George Collins, CEO of T. Rowe Price, will sail the area's first-ever Whitbread entry.

reaches of the Indian, Pacific and Atlantic oceans.

The Whitbread is a knuckle-busting, high-endurance athletic event that now lasts nine months and 32,000 nautical miles. And perhaps that is why people come from around the world to see the boats and sailors and learn what makes them and the race tick.

Whitbread schedule

The Whitbread Round the World Race begins in Southampton, England, on Sept. 21, 1997, and arrives in the Baltimore-Annapolis area on April 22-23, 1998.

In all, there are nine legs in the 32,000-nautical mile sailing race:

Leg 1 to Cape Town, South Africa.

Leg 2 to Fremantle, Australia, starting Nov. 8, 1997.

Leg 3 to Sydney, Australia, starting Dec. 13, 1997.

Leg 4 to Auckland, New Zealand, starting Jan. 4, 1998.

Leg 5 to Sao Sabastiao, Brazil, starting Jan. 31, 1998.

Leg 6 to Fort Lauderdale, Fla., starting March 14, 1998.

Leg 7 to Baltimore-Annapolis, starting April 19, 1998.

Leg 8 to La Rochelle, France, starting May 3, 1998.

Leg 9 to Southampton, starting May 22, 1998.

83

BOATING | lighthouses

Lighthouses of the bay

Amoung the many sights that attract sailors to the Chesapeake Bay are the lighthouses that stand guard along the shorelines. The standing lighthouses are located on the following map.

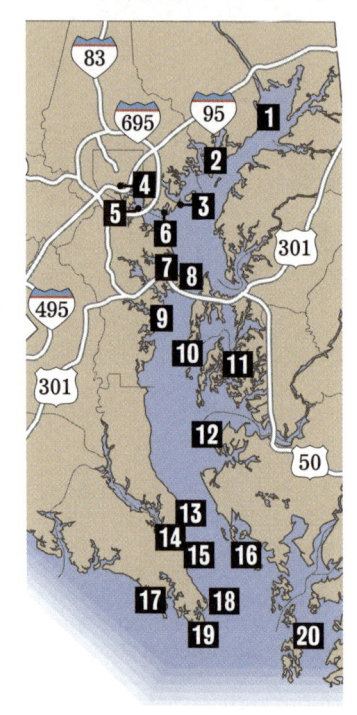

PERRY THORSVIK
Coast guardsmen paint the Sandy Point Lighthouse, a landmark on bay cruises.

AMY DAVIS
Pooles Island Lighthouse, built in 1825; is oldest still standing in state.

1. Turkey Point
2. Pooles Island
3. Craighill Lower Range (front and rear)
4. Lazaretto
5. Fort Carroll
6. Craighill Upper Range (front and rear)
7. Baltimore
8. Sandy Point
9. Thomas Point
10. Bloody Point
11. St. Michael's
12. Sharps Island
13. Cove Point
14. Drum Point
15. Cedar Point
16. Hooper Island
17. Piney Point
18. Point No Point
19. Point Lookout
20. Solomons Lump

Local Whitbread events

The tentative schedule for events in the Baltimore-Annapolis area is as follows, according to Whitbread Chesapeake, the group organizing events for the Maryland layover of the Whitbread fleet:

1997

May 1: Whitbread boats gather at the Inner Harbor in preparation for East Coast Tour from Baltimore to Annapolis to New York City.

May 4: Assembled fleet sails to Annapolis for two days of final preparations.

May 6: Leg to New York scheduled to start off Whitehall Bay at the mouth of the Severn River near Annapolis. Fleet will sail out the mouth of Chesapeake Bay before turning north to New York.

1998

April 14: Baltimore-Annapolis media center opens.

April 16: Baltimore Race Village opens at West Wall of Inner Harbor, kicking off the Whitbread Festival.

April: Annapolis Race Village opens (site TBA).

April 19: Racing fleet leaves Fort Lauderdale, Fla.

April 22-23: Fleet finishes off Fort McHenry at entrance to Inner Harbor. Also, welcoming ceremonies.

April 29: Embassy Day luncheon and awards ceremony at Baltimore Convention Center.

May 1: Race fleet leaves for Annapolis.

May 1: Chesapeake Bay Foundation benefit.

May 1: Annapolis party.

May 3: Race fleet starts leg to La Rochelle, France, from the Bay Bridge in conjunction with annual Bay Bridge Walk.

Powerboats differ widely

Ken Penrod positioned his bass boat before a chute of water rushing between a pair of boulders on the upper Potomac River near Lander in Frederick County, smiled and said, "Watch this."

He eased the boat ahead, goosed the throttle and slid up over the rocky ledge to the pool above.

"Got to have the equipment to get to the fish up here," he said, chuckling. "Try that with a regular outboard, and you'd lose the prop in no time."

Instead, Penrod, who owns the Life Outdoors Unlimited fishing and hunting guide service, uses an outboard with a jet drive unit to fish the rocky upper Potomac.

"But down below, on the tidal Potomac, I use a conventional outboard," Penrod said on a fishing trip, when the smallmouth bass were hitting hard and often. "If you are going to spend time on the water, not only do you have to have the right equipment, you have to know how to use it, too."

BOATING | powerboats

AMY DAVIS
A boater motors in the shadow of bridges over the Susquehanna.

The powerboats in use in this state differ widely – from reservoir rigs with multiple batteries and multiple electric motors, to bay cruisers to high-performance muscle boats and competition ski boats.

Trailered powerboats are by far the most numerous registered recreational craft in Maryland, with a recent study funded by the DNR and the Marine Trades Association of Maryland showing 100,087 of them in the state in 1993. The study also showed 60,021 registered powerboats that are kept in the water.

Bass boats. Jon boats. Jet boats. Baybuilts. Skiffs. Runabouts. Tin boats, fiberglass boats, wood boats.

Boats for rocky rivers and placid lakes and pools above the fall line. Boats for slalom courses and race courses, fishing and cruising.

But while each type of boat serves a separate purpose, the elements of safe operation are largely the same: know the rules of the road, the characteristics of the water in which you operate, the limitations of your skills and your boat – and make certain you have all required safety gear on board at all times.

Safety

1. Equipment for recreational boats

■ Personal flotation devices (PFDs): All boats must be equipped with wearable PFDs for each person aboard. Boats over 16 feet also must have a throwable PFD (ring, seat cushion, horseshoe, etc.). PFDs must be Coast Guard-approved.

■ Visual distress signals: All vessels used on coastal waters and those waters connected directly to them up to a point where they are less than two miles wide must be equipped with visual distress signals. Recreational boats less than 16 feet, boats participating in organized events such as parades, regattas or races, open sailboats less than 26 feet without propulsion machinery and manually propelled boats are exempt when in use during daylight. These, too, must carry signals when used at night. Check with Coast Guard regulations, approved devices and regulations for storage and use.

■ Fire extinguishers: Boats must carry approved types of fire extinguishers if any of the following conditions exist: inboard engine, closed compartments under thwarts and seats where portable fuel tanks can be stored; double bottoms not sealed to the hull or which are not completely filled with flotation materials; closed living spaces; closed storage compartments where combustible or flammable materials are stored; permanently installed fuel tanks. Minimum number of hand-held extinguishers required are: one B-I type for boats less than 26 feet or approved fixed system; two B-I or one B-II for boats 26 feet to less than 40 feet or one B-I with approved fixed system; three B-I or one B-II and one B-I for boats 40 feet to 65 feet or two B-I or one B-II with approved fixed system.

■ Backfire flame arresters: All boats with gasoline engines installed after April 25, 1940, must have a Coast Guard-approved system to control backfire flame from the carburetor.

2. Required non-approved equipment

■ Natural ventilation of engine and fuel tank compartments: All vessels with enclosed gasoline engines and or fuel tank compartments built after April 25, 1940, and before Aug. 1, 1980, are required to have natural ventilation for those compartments. Vessels built after July 31, 1978, but before Aug. 1, 1980, are not required to have natural ventilation of the fuel tank compartment if

ALGERINA PERNA
Properly fitted personal flotation devices are a must.

BOATING | powerboats

there is no electrical connection in the compartment and the compartment vents to the outside of the vessel.

- Powered ventilation of engine and fuel tank compartments: Vessels built after July 31, 1980, that have gasoline engines with a starting motor, for electrical generation, mechanical power or propulsion in a closed compartment are required to have a Coast Guard-approved powered ventilation system.

3. Sound signals

Though Coast Guard regulations do not require vessels under 12 meters in length to carry a whistle, horn or bell, the rules of navigation require sound signals under certain situations – such as meeting, crossing and overtaking another vessel. Recreational vessels also are required to have sound signals in times of reduced visibility such as fog. Mouth-operated whistles or horns, a hand-struck bell or an air-powered horn are acceptable equipment.

4. Good gear and good advice

- Getting home: Boats under 16 feet should carry an alternate source of power on board – paddles, a set of oars or a separate engine that can operate on a separate fuel system and starting circuit.
- Anchoring: All boats should carry an anchor of suitable weight and design for the size of boat and types of bottom normally encountered. Length of anchor line should be at least five to

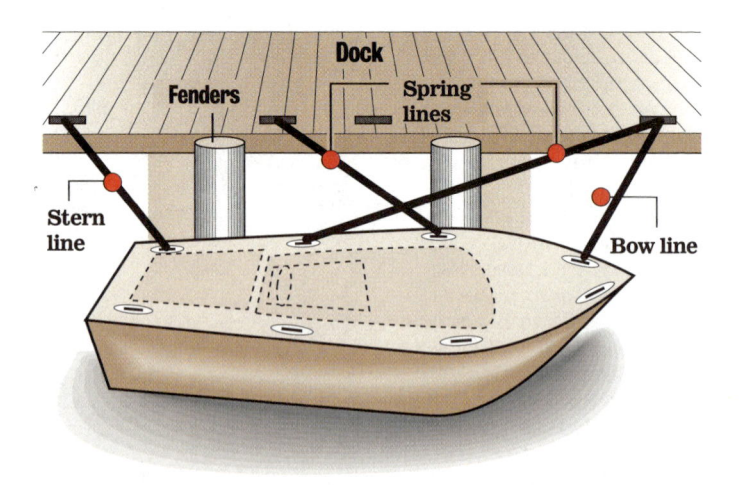

How to properly dock a boat.

seven times the depth of the water anchored in. Anchoring should be done from the front of the boat with the bow into the wind by lowering the hook rather than throwing it, which could cause the anchor line to wrap around the anchor and make it ineffective. Do not anchor by the stern, because the transom, loaded with engine weight, is heavier and closer to the water than the bow. Anchoring by the stern can cause the boat to capsize or cause the stern to be pulled under by current.

- Bailers: In addition to whatever electrical or installed manual systems are on board, every boat also should be equipped with a portable manual pump, bucket or scoop for emergency use.

- First aid: Take a first-aid kit along on every trip and know how to use it.

- Loading up and vessel trim: In general, keep the load low and level, especially in small boats. Check the Coast Guard maximum capacities for people, engines and gear, usually located on a plate attached to the hull, and do not exceed them. If there is no capacity plate, the following formula can be used to determine the maximum number of persons (average of 150 pounds) that can be carried in calm weather: length (from transom to point of the bow) times width divided by 15.

- Fueling: Portable tanks should be filled off the boat. Before refueling boats with on-board tanks, close all hatches and ports. Extinguish smoking materials. Shut off all electrical equipment, radios, stoves and other appliances. Stop all engines and motors. After filling, wipe up all spills immediately. Open all hatches and ports to ventilate the boat. Run the electric blower for five minutes and then check the bilges for fuel vapors before starting the engine. Never start an engine while vapors are present; there will be a danger of explosion.

- Fuel management: Use one-third of your fuel going out, one-third coming back and keep one-third in reserve.

- Float plans and weather: Before setting out, tell a friend or relative where you are going, when you expect to get there and when you expect to return. Include a description of your vessel and pertinent telephone numbers or radio call signs. Check weather reports before leaving shore and keep an eye out for changing weather patterns. If you have a VHF radio aboard, tune to the weather band periodically for updates. Portable weather-band radios are available for under $30.

- Survival and hypothermia: To minimize body heat loss in cold water or extended periods in warmer waters, do not remove your clothing. Instead, tighten collars, cuffs, shoes and hoods. Keep your head covered to reduce heat loss, up to 50 percent of

BOATING | water sports

which can escape from your head. Put on a life jacket immediately if one is available. Make every effort to get out of the water by boarding a swamped or capsized boat (vessel built after 1978 or designed to support you even if swamped or capsized), raft or floating debris. Swim only to reach a nearby floating object or person. If you can't get out of the water, huddle with other people or hold your knees to your chest, wrap your hands around your legs and keep them clasped. Remain as still as possible, moving only enough to keep afloat.

- For Coast Guard boating safety answers, call (800) 368-5647.

Making sport of the water

Water skiing

When done correctly, this is a three-person team sport– boat driver, observer and skier.

In Maryland, in fact, there must be at least two people in the boat when towing a water skier, and both must be at least 12 years old.

It is the responsibility of the driver to know the rules of safe boat operation and to follow them. The responsibility of the second person in the boat, the observer, is to watch the skier being towed and to inform the driver of the skier's progress and of boats that could be approaching from blind spots.

Skiers must wear Coast Guard-approved personal flotation devices.

To get a skier up, ease the boat forward until the slack is out of the tow line, and wait for the skier to signal that he or she is ready. Then, check around to make sure the way ahead is clear of traffic and apply enough power to slip the skier onto plane.

Once the skier is up, ease off on the power to a speed the skier is comfortable with. Skiers should signal the observer with hand signals - thumbs down for slower, thumbs up for faster, thumb and forefinger circled and the other three fingers upright for OK.

When skiers are down in the water, they also should signal the boat about their condition - hands clasped high over the head for OK, hand on top of the head for back to the dock. Skiers in the water should, if possible, hold their skies upright in the water to make themselves more readily visible to boats around them.

While towing a skier, turns should be wide and smooth and a safe distance should be maintained from all docks, obstructions and hazards. Tow ropes are suggested to be 75 feet in tidal waters and 50 feet inland. Distances from docks and obstructions should be twice those lengths.

To pick up a skier, circle slowly to bring the rope to

the skier. When bringing skiers aboard, shut down the engine and bring them in over the stern.

Board sailing

This is a fast, exciting sport that is inexpensive to get into and relatively easy to learn - but as with all water sports, safety should be a primary concern.

When board sailing, the law requires that a Coast Guard-approved personal flotation device be worn, and in waters below 65 degrees, use of a wet suit is advisable to reduce the chances of hypothermia.

Once you have learned the rules of right of way on the water, which apply to sailboards as well as other craft, start out slowly. Practice in shallow, protected water when the weather conditions are warm and the winds are manageable and step up as your skill level increases.

Because board sailing can be physically challenging, limit the time spent on the water to an hour or so before resting. It is better to be fresh when knocked down than tired and struggling to retrieve board and sail.

Many state and county parks are accessible to board sailors. Sandy Point State Park (1100 East College Parkway, Annapolis, Md. 21401, 410-974-2149) is popular; check with DNR (800-830-3974) for other state facilities. Windsurfing Unlimited in Annapolis (410-573-9436) offers rentals and public board sailing.

Personal watercraft

Personal watercraft, often known by the brand name Jet Skis, can be a lot of fun or incredibly dangerous depending on how and when they are used.

PERRY THORSVIK
Personal watercraft are subject to same rules as larger craft.

BOATING | canoes and kayaks

And while they are fast and highly maneuverable, Jet Skis are powerboats and subject to the same rules of the road as larger craft.

Jet Skis also must carry the same required equipment as conventional inboard-powered boats.

Good practices to follow are:

- Always wear a Coast Guard-approved personal flotation device.
- Wear eye protection to reduce the effects of spray.
- Wear gloves and shoes.
- Wear a wet suit when the water is 65 degrees or colder to reduce the chances of hypothermia. Wet suits also will provide protection for the sun.
- In Maryland, those over the age of 14 who have earned a boating safety certificate can operate personal watercraft - although in the last couple of years there have been bills in the legislature aimed at further restricting use. Check with the Natural Resources Police (410-974-2248) for up-to-date information.

Various boats, on a trip afloat

By Michael Reeb

The decision to take up canoeing, whitewater kayaking or sea kayaking will depend on a number of factors: The type of person you are, what you are expecting from your trip afloat and the type of water in your area.

From the mountain-fed creeks and rivers of Western Maryland to the estuaries of the Chesapeake Bay, canoes and kayaks offer their operators a view that often is unavailable from larger craft. While large sections of the Chesapeake are navigable by bigger boats, the only choices when it comes to the smaller waterways of Western Maryland are canoe, kayak and small boats.

For those intent on exploring the whitewater of the Youghiogheny, Casselman or Gunpowder rivers, a canoe or whitewater kayak is the way to go. And for solo paddlers looking to make time on open water, a sea kayak may be the vessel of choice.

In any event, a trip by canoe or kayak will reveal much about the world at large – but in small doses. Canoe or kayak is the perfect access to a tidal marsh, a freshwater creek, a secluded cove otherwise unaccessible. Although the view at times may be microscopic, the overall picture it reveals will be panoramic.

The rewards can be enormous, particularly in the case of the Chesapeake Bay. The Chesapeake is the nation's largest body of water where salt and fresh water mix. Because of this, the resulting brackish water is rich in nutrients and supports an incredibly diverse ecological system that changes from river to river.

BOATING | canoes and kayaks

KENNETH K. LAM

A kayaker shoots the falls on the C&O Canal.

A trip down the bay's main channel may allow a glimpse at the forest, but forsake examination of the trees. An ideal way to see the trees is by smaller craft.

For both canoeists and kayakers, Maryland offers abundant opportunities. Says the Chesapeake Bay Foundation's John Page Williams Jr. about the road sometimes not taken: "Those people who think the Choptank River ends at Cambridge, there's an old steam boat landing 15 miles up from Cambridge. It's deep, it's plenty deep."

Says Lee Jones of Water Dogs Kayaking: "The kayaking in this area ranges from some fantastic stuff on the beginner's level to some very expert-level stuff. You don't have to drive far to get to an incredible level of experience of whitewater kayaking."

93

BOATING | canoes and kayaks

Whitewater kayak

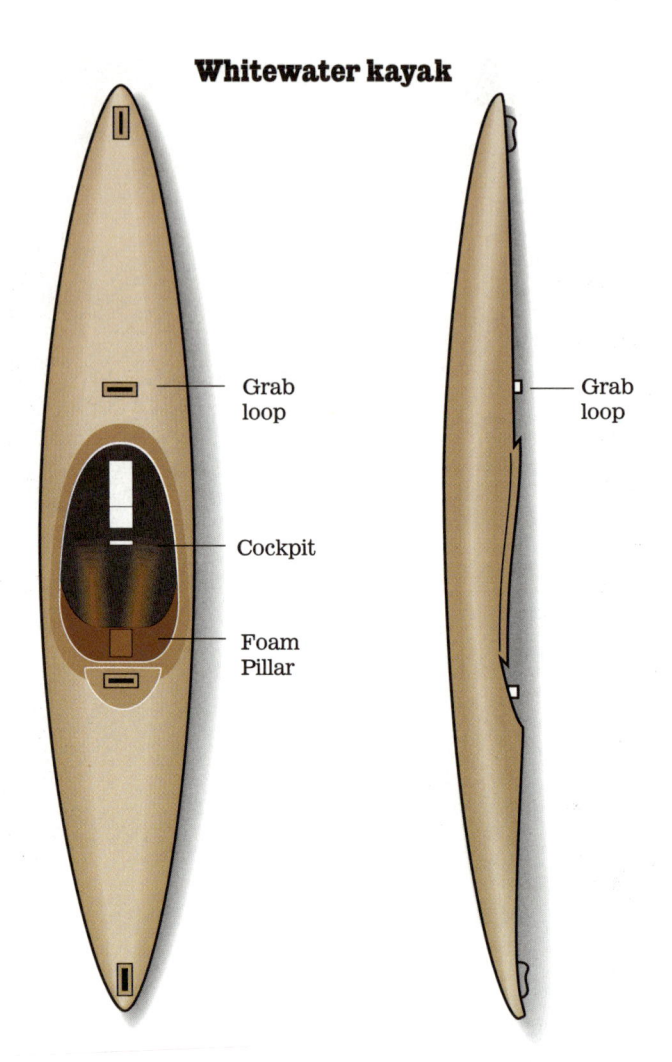

- Grab loop
- Cockpit
- Foam Pillar
- Grab loop

That level of experience also will apply to waters best accessible by canoe and kayak. "I got raised in outboard skiffs," says Williams. "I've been running stuff between 15 and 18 feet for 30 years. When I went to work for the Chesapeake Bay Foundation, I ended up running canoes. Even though I had fished the tidal areas, I didn't know them very well. I gradually began to learn some of the freshwater marsh plants, which are a little more difficult than the saltwater ones. I began to see this world which not many people were familiar with."

It did not take him long to get hooked. "Up the river,

Sea kayak

- Bow
- Deck
- Hatch
- Hatch
- Stern
- Rudder

BOATING | canoes and kayaks

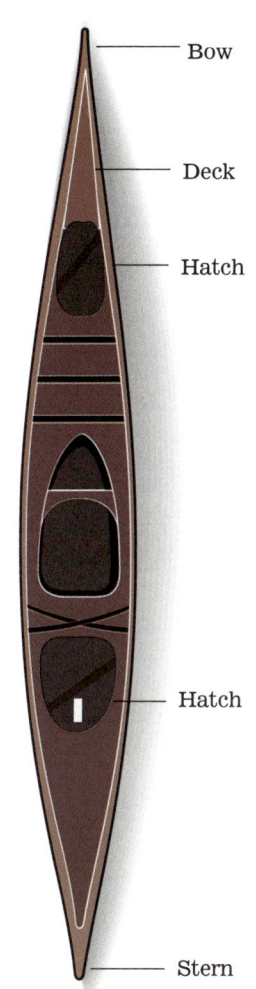

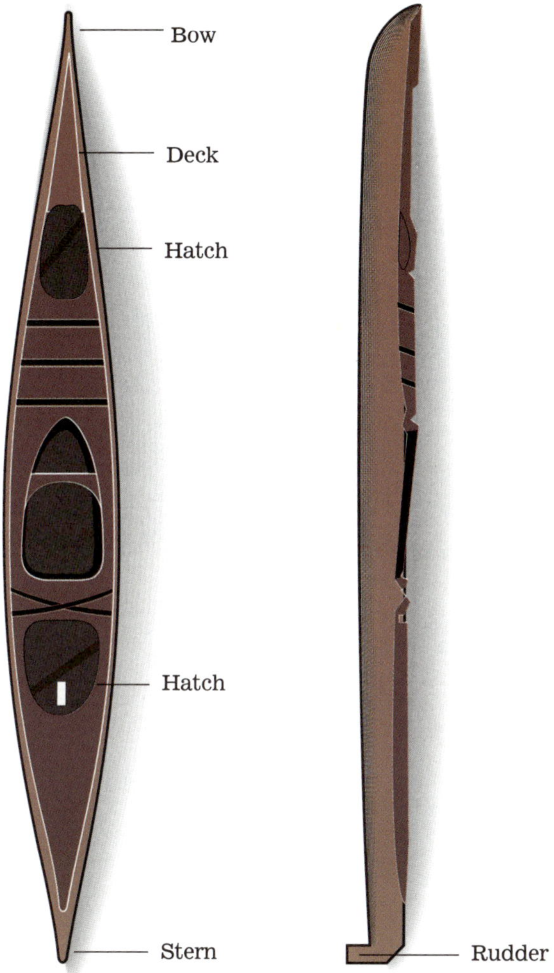

you can catch a dozen types of fish and shellfish, some of which have spent some time on the continental shelf and some of which came from a few hundred yards downriver," he says. "These rivers are a heart-stopper. I drove over all these rivers trying to get to true religion. My point of view got stretched a whole lot having to run those canoes."

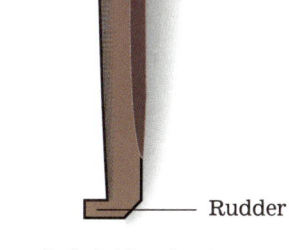

Safety

Lessons for both canoeing and kayaking are crucial. Contact the local chapter of Red Cross, (410) 764-4609, for instructional classes that

95

BOATING | canoes and kayaks

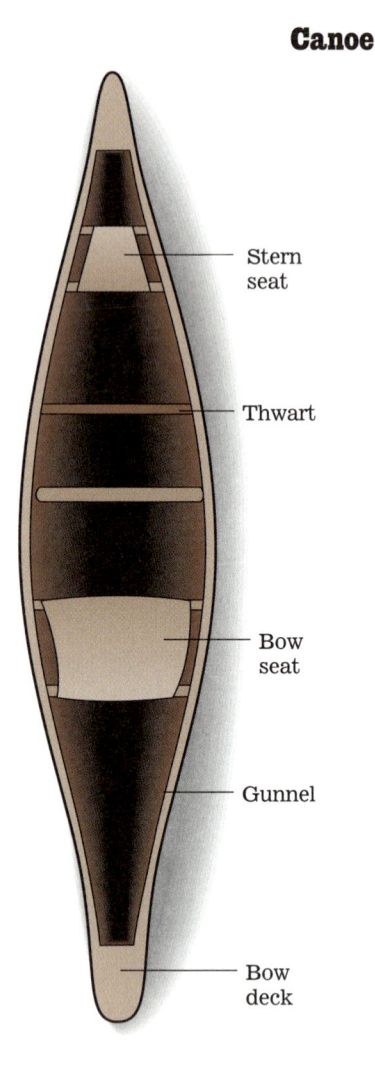

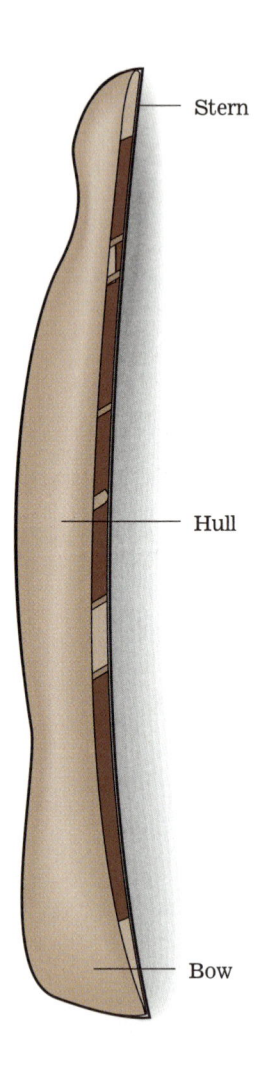

Canoe

- Stern seat
- Thwart
- Bow seat
- Gunnel
- Bow deck

- Stern
- Hull
- Bow

will teach you safety, basic maneuvers and strokes and how to read the water. Water Dogs Kayaking is a Baltimore area-based, American Canoe Association-certified group that teaches whitewater kayaking on local rivers, including the Patapsco and Gunpowder. Water Dogs also has a summer whitewater program for youths aged 12 to 15.

Although canoeing appears deceptively simple, the need for some instruction is just as critical as it is with kayaking. In fact, novice kayakers might be better prepared than novice canoeists because a novice whitewater kayaker probably wouldn't think of going out without some instruction, whereas a novice canoeist might. The following organizations can provide information on instruction:

- Whitewater kayaking: Water Dogs Kayaking, P.O. Box 918, Sparks, Md. 21152, (410) 329-3688.
- Sea kayaking: Chesapeake Paddlers Association, P.O. Box 3873, Fairfax, Va. 22038.

Equipment

- Renting vs. buying: Purchasing a canoe or kayak is a big decision and can be costly. Your decision also will be based on how you plan to use your craft. If you wish to kayak on flat or tranquil waters, then a sea – or touring - kayak will fill your needs. If you wish to kayak on whitewater, then a whitewater kayak will fill your order.

It may be wiser to rent one or several different craft one or more times out before making the decision to buy a boat.

- Before making a purchase, verse yourself in the craft's basic terminology: All canoes have a hull, which is made of one of several materials, but probably wood, aluminum, fiberglass or plastic laminate. Gunnels are attached to the top of the hull. Both gunnels and thwarts, which run across the inside of the boat, are used to stiffen the boat.

Rocker is the amount of curve in a canoe's hull from bow to stern. A canoe with a straight keel has no rocker, is easy to move in a straight line but is more difficult to turn. A canoe with a more rounded keel has a rocker, is more difficult to move in a straight line but is easier to turn. Boats also have become more specialized and cater to a variety of needs – touring, whitewater and racing.

- Whitewater kayaks: Usually from 10 to 12 feet in length, they are broader than sea kayaks and have a harsher entry into the water. A whitewater kayak has a foam pillar inside that runs the length of the boat. Flotation bags that are filled with air sit on either side of the foam pillar.
- Sea kayaks: Usually from 15 to 18 feet in length, they are more narrow than whitewater kayaks and have a softer entry into the water. A sea kayak has a beam – or width – that often is two feet or less. There are only a few inches of deck above water, and this permits less resistance for quicker travel on open water. Sea kayaks come equipped with hatches to store equipment. They also usually come equipped with a spray skirt - a covering from the paddler's chest to the cockpit that keeps out water.

Springriver Corp. both rents and sells and has three locations: Annapolis (410) 263-2303, Catonsville (410) 788-3377 and Rockville (301) 881-5694. All three locations

BOATING | canoes and kayaks

rent touring and whitewater canoes; recreational, whitewater and sea kayaks; and sit-on-tops, another class of kayaks.

■ As for purchasing a craft, Springriver's Richard Bruce says: "A lot of times with the canoes, usually if you can give us what type of water, it's easy to narrow it down to one or two boats. When you get into kayaks, it's much more of a personal issue, and you might want to rent one for a few times out. I could narrow it down to one or two for me, but you might hate them. An inch in a kayak is a lot. The general rule of thumb for kayaks is, for each foot of length of you have, you can subtract an inch on width."

Etiquette

Observing these few, common-sense practices will make your water adventure a safer and happier place for all concerned - fishermen, waders, landowners and other boaters:

1. When putting in, taking out, camping or resting on public land, secure permission from the landowner before entering or crossing his property.

2. Act responsibly by hauling out all trash you bring in with you.

3. Respect fishermen's space by paddling well out of their range when possible.

4. Communicate with other paddlers, particularly on whitewater. Respect their space and yield the right of way when they have entered the flow.

5. Don't cut into a commercial trip. Your day - and theirs - will be better if you allow them to go their way.

Resources

The following two books, in addition to being valuable references, provide vital field-guide details for a number of paddling trips:

"Maryland and Delaware Canoe Trails, A Paddlers Guide to Rivers of the Old Line and First States," by Edward Gertler. Silver Spring, The Seneca Press, 1996.

"Exploring the Chesapeake in Small Boats," by John Page Williams, Jr. Centreville, Tidewater Publishers, 1992.

Field guide

The following 10 trips are samples of the canoeing and kayaking possibilities in Maryland. Within a week of a heavy spring rain, trips 1, 2 and 5 offer varying degrees of whitewater. The outings have been picked in an attempt to represent the varied topography of the state and to give a representative look at western, central, southern and Eastern Shore canoeing and kayaking locations:

1. Youghiogheny River
County: Garrett
Put in: Herrington

BOATING | canoes and kayaks

Manor Road
Take out: Swallow Falls Road
Distance: 7.2 miles
Width: 30 feet
Difficulty: Easy to very difficult

Description: This section of the "Upper Yough" runs through a scenic wooded gorge. The river is mostly smooth with a few riffles through the first 3-mile section before Miller's Run, where the river becomes more difficult. The next 3 miles are relatively calm, but high ledges and boulders follow the next mile before Swallow Falls State Park. All but the most experienced paddlers should get out here because Swallow Falls is a hundred yards downstream from that point, and 2 miles of rapids follow that. Expert paddlers might want to put in at Swallow Falls, take out around the falls and continue on through exceedingly difficult waters.

2. Casselman River
County: Garrett
Put in: Maple Grove Road
Take out: River Road
Distance: 5 miles
Width: 20 feet
Difficulty: Easy to medium difficult

Description: The Casselman, the largest tributary of the Youghiogheny, cuts through scenic countryside and offers a good run for intermediate paddlers. The put-in at Maple Grove Road is just below the confluence of the North and South branches of the Casselman. It flows through a gorge and below U.S. 68 and the stone-arch Casselman Bridge, built in 1813 to carry the National Highway across the river.

3. Potomac River
County: Washington
Put in: Fort Frederick State Park
Take out: Williamsport
Carry: Dam No. 5
Distance: 16 miles
Width: 200 yards
Difficulty: Easy

Description: The first 2 miles, with a backdrop of wooded hills, are flat but

BOATING | canoes and kayaks

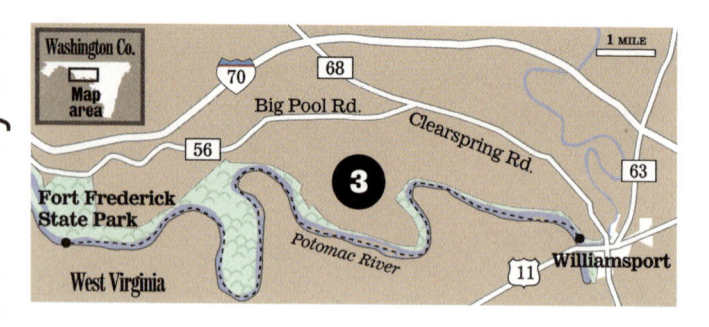

with a strong current. At that point, at McCoys Ferry Road, the river begins to back up by Dam No. 5, which calls for a carry on the left side of the river. The take-out is just below the convergence of Conococheague Creek.

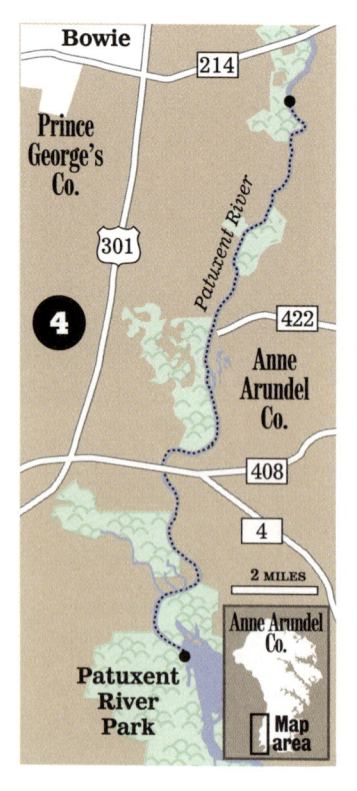

4. Patuxent River
County: Prince George's
Put in: Queen Anne Bridge
Take out: Jackson's Landing, Patuxent River Park, Upper Marlboro
Distance: 10 miles
Width: 40 feet
Difficulty: Flat water
Note: Patuxent River Park can arrange for a shuttle to a put-in at Queen Anne Bridge, 10 miles upstream from Jackson's Landing.

Description: The Chesapeake Bay Foundation's John Page Williams Jr. says: "If I'm going to take one person out for one day, I would handpick a creek. It could be the Mataponi or King's Creek on the Choptank. I would take them out there in late August when everything's in bloom and all the those fish - maybe a chain pickerel or two, a largemouth bass - are moving about, when the marsh is in bloom, the hibiscus is in bloom. That's one of the peaks in the season."

5. Gunpowder Falls
County: Baltimore
Put in: Maryland Route 45 (York Road), 2 miles south of Parkton

100

BOATING | canoes and kayaks

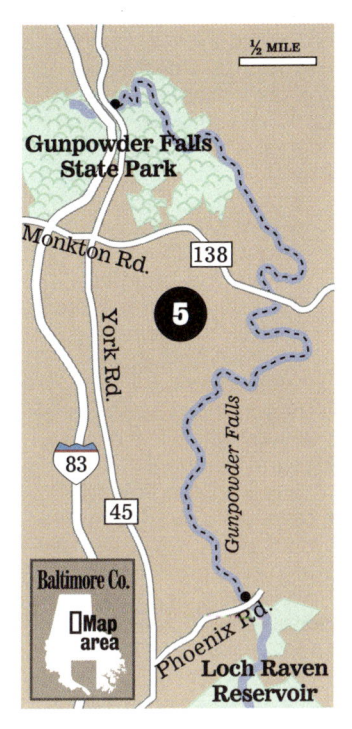

Take out: Phoenix Road
Distance: 12 miles
Width: 40 feet
Difficulty: Easy
Description: This is picturesque territory, a mixture of wooded gorge and rolling farmland. The water is runnable within a week of a heavy rain in winter or spring. There are a few riffles along the stretch, but it is generally a good run for novices. Those seeking more whitewater should try Little Falls, which is runnable within a week of a hard rain in winter or spring. Access can be gained from Route 45, just south of Parkton. It converges with the main stem of the Gunpowder Falls just south of Blue Mount Road.

6. Sassafras River
Counties: Kent, Cecil
Put in: Gregg Neck Public Landing
Take out: Foxhole Public Landing
Distance: 5 miles
Width: 100 yards
Difficulty: Flat water
Description: This is one of two trips - the other being the Bohemia - representative of upper Eastern Shore topography. Freshwater marsh and farms envelope the river. Above the Route 213 bridge that spans the river between Georgetown on the Kent County side and Fredericktown on the Cecil County side, there is little boat traffic. Largemouth bass fishing is good here.

7. Eastern Neck Island National Wildlife Refuge
County: Kent
Put in: Shipyard Creek
Take out: Bogles Wharf
Distance: 9 miles
Width: Opens to main stem of Chester River
Difficulty: Flat water, although winds may result in waves on otherwise tranquil waters.
Description: Eastern Neck Island is a refuge for

101

BOATING | canoes and kayaks

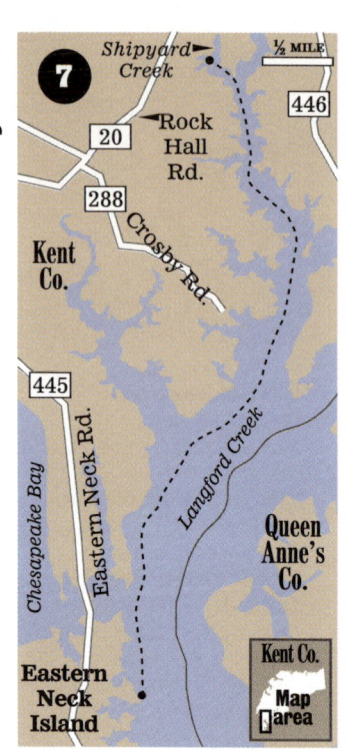

migratory birds in the fall, particularly tundra swans, but in the summer, zebra and monarch butterflies are in abundance. A serene paddle on the northern end of the island may turn up a great blue heron, an osprey, a red-tailed hawk, sandpipers and king and Virginia rails.

8. Wye River
County: Talbot
Put in: Wye Landing
Take out: Skipton Landing
Distance: 11 miles
Width: 600 yards
Difficulty: Flat water, although winds may necessitate caution on the leg to Skipton Landing.

Description: This trip allows a paddler to explore the straight of Wye Narrow, which separates Wye Island from the Talbot County mainland and connects the Wye and Wye East rivers. Follow the same path back and take out at Skipton Landing at the head of Skipton Creek.

9. Nassawango Creek, Pocomoke River
County: Worcester
Put in: Red House Road

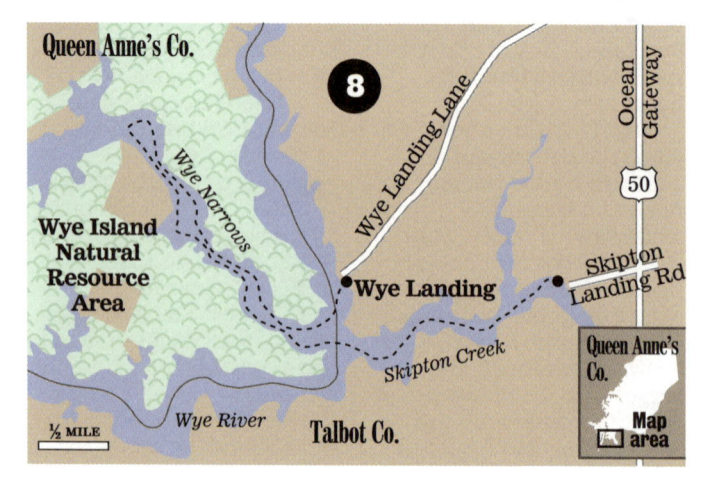

102

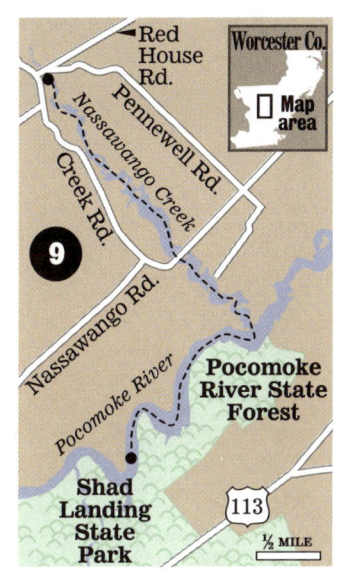

BOATING | canoes and kayaks

Take out: Shad Landing State Park
Distance: 5 miles
Width: 60 feet
Difficulty: Flat water
Description: This section of the river is lined with cypress trees, one of two deciduous conifers native to North America, and this secluded trip will give the paddler an opportunity to observe the tree in its northernmost outpost.

10. Assateague Island National Seashore
County: Worcester
Put in: Ferry Landing Road
Take out: Ferry Landing Road
Distance: 8 miles
Width: 2,500 feet
Difficulty: Flat water, although winds may kick up the waters of Chincoteague Bay. 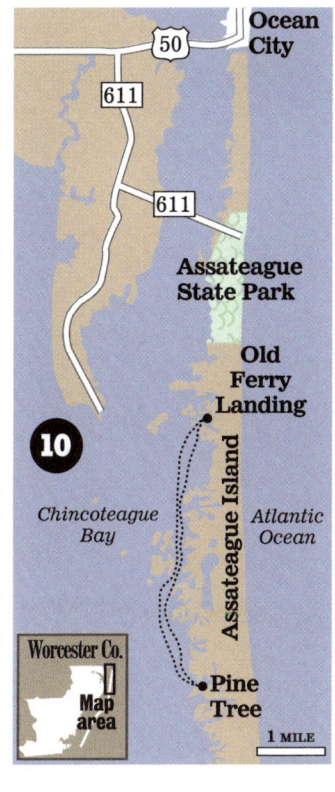
Description: There are four canoe-in campsites, which sit among pine trees and are accessible from the Ferry Landing Road launch. Backcountry-use permits are required and must be obtained by mid-afternoon. Each site has a chemical toilet and a picnic table but no drinking water. This trip is a good occasion to explore the Chincoteague Bay side of Assateague Island and its marshes, where the great blue heron, the snowy egret and black-crowned night heron may be seen.

103

FISHING

From ocean to bay to stream - a large cast

BY PETER BAKER

Maryland is a small state, but within its borders it is possible to fish a variety of species, from marlin and tuna off the Atlantic Coast to native brook trout in the cold mountain streams of the state's western counties.

In between the geographic extremes, the Chesapeake Bay and the state's rivers, reservoirs, lakes, ponds and streams can provide excellent angling for bank fishermen, waders and float-tubers, stream stalkers and boaters.

Many tidal rivers feeding the Chesapeake Bay hold black bass, yellow perch, catfish and chain pickerel in their upper reaches and striped bass, white perch, bluefish, spot and croaker in the lower stretches, where the rivers widen and are more heavily influenced by saltwater tides.

Above the fall line, depending on the areas fished, anglers can encounter smallmouth, largemouth and rock bass, walleye, tiger muskies, rainbow, brown and brook trout, crappie, bluegill, pumpkinseed, northern pike, muskellunge, catfish and land-locked striped bass.

Along the Atlantic Coast, the tidal back bays are popular for rockfish, flounder, blues, sea trout, croaker and spot, and surf and inshore anglers can add sea bass, tautog and whiting to the list of possibilities. Offshore, fishermen can battle shark, dolphin, bluefin and yellowfin tuna and white and blue marlin.

KARL MERTON FERRON
Fishing is a natural sport for families to share.

Public access to walk-in fishing areas is good in most counties, state-maintained or commercial launch ramps are numerous, and fishing guides and charter boats are readily available for virtually all types of freshwater and saltwater fishing.

Maryland is a small state, but the possibilities are many — whether fly-fishing, casting, trolling, chumming

FISHING | trout

or bottom fishing best suits you. For up-to-date information on Department of Natural Resources regulations, call (410) 974-3365 or check DNR's website on the Internet: http://www.gacc.com/dnr/.

We've included sections geared to getting kids involved in freshwater and saltwater fishing, as well as crabbing. Children as young as 3 can start putting a line in the water, as long as there's an adult to bait the hook or tie the chicken neck to the crab line. DNR also has a program worth checking out — Hooked on Fishing, Not on Drugs — with clinics at various sites during the summer for ages 7-13. For more information, call (410) 974-8474.

Trout fishing on the rise

By Dan Rodricks

That winter afternoon, with snow on the banks of the Big Gunpowder Falls below Prettyboy Reservoir Dam in Baltimore County, sunlight sliced through the clouds and brightened the dark water of Central Maryland's blue-ribbon trout stream.

Within a few minutes, brown trout started dimpling the surface, sipping at tiny black insects known as midges, barely visible to the human eye. A half-dozen stream-bred browns

AMY DEPUTY
David Gerhardt fly fishes on the Gunpowder River.

snapped at tiny dry flies, tied from feathers to resemble the naturals and knotted at the end of fine leaders. It was a Friday in February, a superb day for fishing. All the trout, which were between 12 and 16 inches long, were returned alive to the river.

A lot of people find it hard to believe, but trout fishing in Maryland is not just a springtime activity anymore. Such a January-to-December pleasure would not exist without the vital fishing restrictions on the Gunpowder and other rivers that have become home to stream-bred trout. If not for the no-bait, catch-and-release designation — and the willingness of the fishing public to understand the rules and abide by them — there would be few trout rising to midges in midwinter. And there would be

FISHING | trout

KIM HAIRSTON

Art Nierenberg teaches his son, Matthew, how to fly fish on the platform for disabled anglers on Morgan Run.

fewer rivers where men and women could enjoy trout fishing any time the weather and the spirit moved them.

For sure, there are plenty of places in Maryland to catch trout for the dinner table. The state Department of Natural Resources stocks thousands of hatchery rainbows in dozens of streams, creeks, reservoirs and ponds across the state. Men and boys, women and girls can hit those streams when the put-and-take season opens and, if they're lucky, take their daily limit home. A lot of the streams designated put-and-take are considered marginal for trout. (Trout can only live in water that remains clean and cold all year; most of the streams that get stocked with trout become too warm through the summer.)

Put-and-take streams still dominate the list of places where you can fish for trout. But the fact that there's more catch-and-release water is a testament to progressive stream management and the efforts of the state and conservation groups to restore our rivers to their historic best.

Now, from the Big Gunpowder north of Baltimore to the Savage River deep in Western Maryland, trout are thriving and reproducing in impressive numbers. There's a simple reason for the catch-and-release restrictions — without them, there would soon be no year-round fishery for the growing number of anglers who like to prospect for wild trout from January to December.

In most of these places — the Gunpowder, the Savage,

107

FISHING | trout

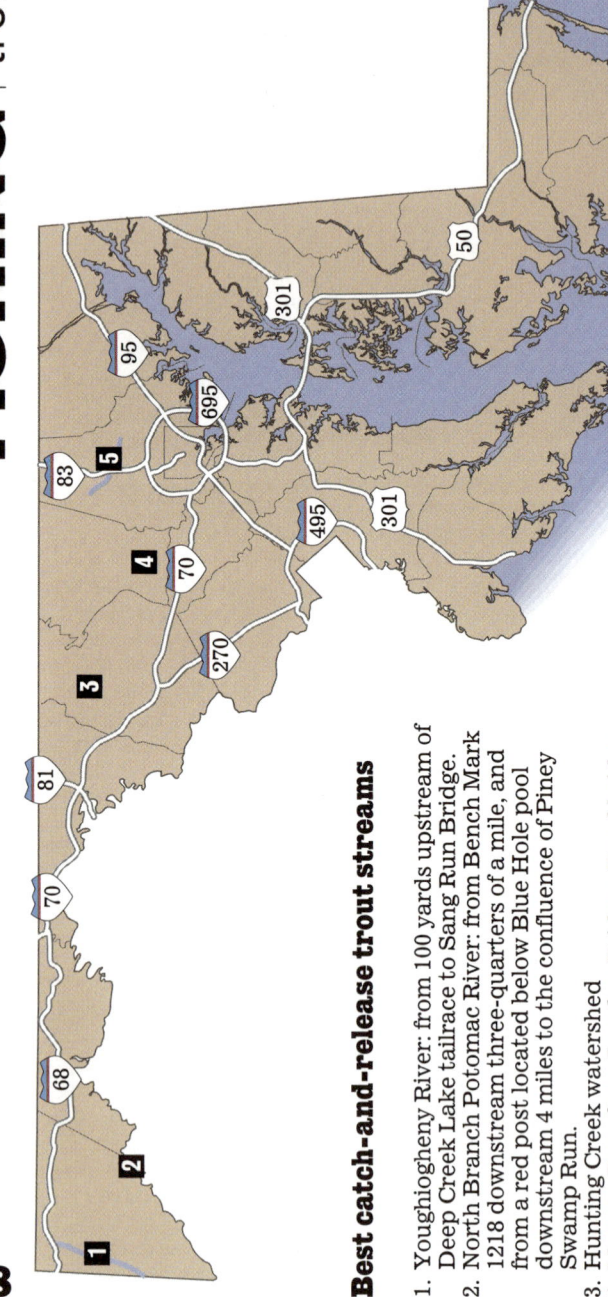

Best catch-and-release trout streams

1. Youghiogheny River: from 100 yards upstream of Deep Creek Lake tailrace to Sang Run Bridge.
2. North Branch Potomac River: from Bench Mark 1218 downstream three-quarters of a mile, and from a red post located below Blue Hole pool downstream 4 miles to the confluence of Piney Swamp Run.
3. Hunting Creek watershed
4. Morgan Run: from London Bridges Road bridge upstream to Route 97 bridge.
5. Gunpowder Falls: main stem from Prettyboy Reservoir Dam downstream to Corbett Road.

the Youghiogheny, Morgan Run and the North Branch of the Potomac — you can witness one of the exciting wonders of the natural world: trout rising to feed on flies that emerge from under rocks in the streambed, hatch and ride on the surface of the rushing water.

But don't get the idea that wild trout in catch-and-release rivers are for fly anglers and their $400 graphite rods exclusively. Anglers who prefer casting small metal spinners into whitewater riffles and deep, mysterious pools can do just as well — some say better. But you cannot and should not fish those streams with with artificial lures or flies (barbless hooks advised). That way, your chances of mortally wounding a trout are greatly reduced.

Look for good year-round trout fishing in the Gunpowder, Morgan Run in Carroll County, Big Hunting Creek near Thurmont and in Western Maryland streams with special designations. The Youghiogheny has four miles of catch-and-release water now, and, with careful state management, a stretch of it is emerging as a prime trout stream. The same is true for the North Branch of the Potomac, a big, western-looking river in renaissance after decades of abuse.

GENE SWEENEY, JR.

The Gunpowder River's success as a trout stream is testament to catch-and-release program.

bait, such as worms or corn. Save that for put-and-take fishing. When you fish a catch-and-release stream, you're in a special place. The state says you must fish

There's also great fishing, albeit under a different set of circumstances and rules, in the Casselman River. It has a delayed harvest restriction, another innovation that

FISHING | trout

makes for good fishing beyond the relatively short put-and-take season.

The delayed harvest rule means you can take the fish, but only after a certain date. In the Casselman, the harvest date does not commence until June 15. So, for the first six months of the year, sporting anglers can try to catch some of the big brown trout stocked by the state, as long as they're released.

While wading the Gunpowder, Big Hunting Creek or any of the Western Maryland streams, make sure you stop to enjoy the scenery. It's a vital part of the trout fishing experience. If the river is clean and cold and the trout are wild, you're probably standing in a beautiful place. In fact, you're probably dressed in hip boots or chest-high waders (felt soles to avoid slipping), immersed in the water, knee-deep in the trout's world. Catching is a challenge, catching is fun. But being there is the thing.

One summer day on the Gunpowder, about an hour into fishing, I looked up and saw an osprey winging its way down the river, right above me. There was a foot-long brown trout in its talons (some Gunpowder regulars are exempt from the catch-and-release rule). That was the only fish I saw that particular day, but it made my day.

Equipment

A pair of waterproof and warm waders, with felt soles, are highly recommended for anyone desiring to fish for

Mickey Finn

Clouser minnow

Black wooly bugger

Bead head wooly bugger

Muddler minnow

Crayfish

Some streamers worth checking out.

FISHING | trout

A sampling of dry flies to try.

Flies shown: Adams, Royal Wulff, Royal Coachman, Light Cahill, Blue-winged Olive, March Brown, Hendrickson, Quill Gordan, Ant, Griffith's gnat, Elk-hair caddis, Tan Comparadun, Sulphur Emerger, Mayfly, Spinner.

trout in Maryland streams. Young or old, whether you're fishing with fly or worm, you need to be sure-footed; the felt soles prevent slipping while you're in the water.

If you're new at wading, you might want to tether a walking staff to your belt and use it when moving in the stream.

A snug hat and a pair of Polaroid sunglasses (for spotting trout) also are suggested.

A cotton fishing vest with lots of pockets helps keep your fishing stuff — split-shot sinkers, additional lures, a snack — handy. If you're spin-fishing and want to try a variety of lures by a variety of manufacturers, keep them in a small compartmentalized box that will fit in one of the vest pockets. You should tuck a hiker-size roll of bathroom tissue in a vest pocket, too.

111

FISHING | trout

Gold-ribbed hare's ear *Prince* *Stone fly*

Black bead head *Green bead head* *Brassy* *Green Weenie*

San Juan worm

Some nymphs to try for bottom-feeding trout.

A fly-fisher's starter kit: Some popular flies (with sizes).

STREAMERS (wet flies that imitate minnows)
  Wooly bugger (6-10)
  Black-nose dace (10-12)
  Clouser minnow (8-10)
  Mickey Finn (8-10)
  Grey Ghost (8-10)

DRY FLIES (for surface-feeding trout)
  Royal Coachman (12-14)
  Royal Wulff (12-14)
  Adams (12-16)
  Light Cahill (14-16)
  Tan caddis (14-18)
  Griffith's gnat (18-22)
  Blue-Winged Olive (18-20)

NYMPHS (for bottom-feeding trout)
  Stone fly (14-18)
  Bead head (16-18)
  Gold-ribbed hare's ear (12-18)
  Pheasant tail (14-18)
  Prince (14-18)

Etiquette

Don't leave monofilament line or lead split shot on the stream banks or in the water. There's a reason for all those pockets in fishing vests — trash. Take yours with you.

Don't crowd other fishermen. On rivers, if you're fishing downstream and come upon an angler who is casting upstream, get out of the river, hike a bit and return to the water below the other angler.

AMY DAVIS
Cutthroat trout like this one are stocked by DNR.

Resources

Maryland Fly Anglers
(410) 435-1646
Freestate Fly Fishers
(410) 544-4861
Federation of Fly Fishers
(301) 663-3966
Trout Unlimited-national
office, (703) 522-0200

Some Tackle shops to check out:

On the Fly
(410) 329-6821
Fisherman's Edge
(410) 719-7999
Tochterman's
(410) 327-6942
Wolf's Fly Fishing and
Fine Guns (410) 465-1112.

Matching fly hatches

Match the hatch. It's a principle of fly-fishing. Trout eat a lot of different aquatic insects. These insects hatch in streambeds and emerge on the water's surface as adult flies. The trick is to match the naturals with artificial flies, made from bird feathers and animal hair. The charts on the following pages tell anglers what flies they should expect to see on Maryland streams with significant hatches.

Gunpowder River

Fly	J	F	M	A	M	J	J	A	S	O	N	D
Tan Caddis					■				■	■		
Olive Caddis					■				■	■		
Hendrickson				■								
March Brown					■							
Sulphur Dun					■	■						
Lt. Cahill						■						
Beetles						■	■	■	■			
Ants							■	■	■			
Blue-winged Olive		■							■	■		
Midges	■	■	■	■	■	■	■	■	■	■	■	■
Brown Stone		■	■									
Black Stone	■	■										

Reprinted with permission. On the Fly, Monkton, Md.

FISHING | fly hatches

Big Hunting Creek

Fly	J	F	M	A	M	J	J	A	S	O	N	D
Black Stone	■	■			■					■	■	
Brown Stone		■	■									
Blue Quill, Dun				■	■							
Quill Gordon				■								
Hendrickson					■							
Red Quill					■							
March Brown					■							
Grey Fox					■							
Yellow Sally					■							
Pale Evening Dun					■							
Lt. Cahill					■							
Salmon					■							
Green Drake					■							
Yellow Drake					■	■						
Wht-Gloved Howdy					■	■						
Cream Drake					■	■						
Sm. Cream Drake						■	■	■	■	■		
Big Brown Drake							■					
White Miller							■					
Tricos						■	■	■	■	■		

Reprinted with permission.

Casselman River

FISHING | fly hatches

Fly	J	F	M	A	M	J	J	A	S	O	N	D
Bitch Creek		▬										
Sculpin		▬										
Crayfish												
Midges												
Black Stone		▬										
Brown Stone			▬									
Quill Gordon				▬								
Hendrickson				▬								
Red Quill				▬								
Tan Caddis				▬▬								
B.W. Olive				▬								
March Brown					▬							
Grey Fox					▬							
Green Drake												
Olive Caddis						▬▬						
Lt. Cahill						▬						
Cream Variant						▬						
Sulphur												
Interpunctatum												
Dun Variant							▬					
Hoppers							▬▬					
Stimulator							▬					
Crickets								▬				
Flying Ants									▬			
Crane Fly												

Source: Department of Natural Resources

FISHING | fly hatches

Youghiogheny River

Fly	J	F	M	A	M	J	J	A	S	O	N	D
Bitch Creek	■	■									■	■
Sculpin	■	■									■	■
Crayfish	■										■	■
Midges	■											
Black Stone		■	■									
Brown Stone			■									
Quill Gordon				■								
Hendrickson				■								
Red Quill				■					■			
Tan Caddis				■	■				■	■		
B.W. Olive				■				■	■			
March Brown					■							
Grey Fox					■							
Green Drake					■							
Olive Caddis						■						
Lt. Cahill						■						
Cream Variant						■						
Sulphur						■						
Interpunctatum							■	■				
Dun Variant							■					
Hoppers							■	■				
Stimulator												
Crickets								■				
Flying Ants								■	■			
Crane Fly									■	■		

Source: Department of Natural Resources

Savage River

FISHING | fly hatches

Fly — Month

Fly	J	F	M	A	M	J	J	A	S	O	N	D
Bitch Creek	■	■									■	■
Sculpin	■	■									■	■
Crayfish	■										■	
Midges	■											
Black Stone			■									
Brown Stone				■								
Quill Gordon				■								
Hendrickson				■								
Red Quill				■					■			
Tan Caddis					■				■			
B.W. Olive					■			■	■			
March Brown						■						
Grey Fox						■						
Green Drake						■						
Olive Caddis						■						
Lt. Cahill						■						
Cream Variant						■						
Sulphur						■						
Interpunctatum							■	■				
Dun Variant							■					
Hoppers							■	■				
Stimulator							■	■	■			
Crickets								■				
Flying Ants								■	■			
Crane Fly									■			

Source: Department of Natural Resources

FISHING | fly hatches

Upper North Branch Potomac River

Fly	J	F	M	A	M	J	J	A	S	O	N	D
Bitch Creek	■	■									■	■
Sculpin	■	■									■	■
Crayfish	■										■	■
Midges												
Black Stone		■	■									
Brown Stone			■									
Quill Gordon				■								
Hendrickson												
Red Quill												
Tan Caddis				■	■					■		
B.W. Olive												
March Brown												
Grey Fox												
Green Drake												
Olive Caddis						■	■					
Lt. Cahill						■						
Cream Variant						■						
Sulphur												
Interpunctatum												
Dun Variant							■					
Hoppers							■	■				
Stimulator							■	■				
Crickets								■				
Flying Ants								■	■			
Crane Fly								■	■			

Source: Department of Natural Resources

Lower North Branch Potomac River

Fly	J	F	M	A	M	J	J	A	S	O	N	D
Bitch Creek	■										■	■
Sculpin	■	■									■	■
Crayfish	■										■	
Midges	■											
Black Stone		■										
Brown Stone			■									
Quill Gordon				■								
Hendrickson				■								
Red Quill				■					■			
Tan Caddis				■	■				■			
B.W. Olive				■				■	■			
March Brown					■							
Grey Fox					■							
Olive Caddis						■						
Lt. Cahill						■						
Cream Variant						■						
Sulphur						■						
Interpunctatum							■	■				
Dun Variant								■				
Hoppers								■	■			
Stimulator								■	■			
Crickets									■			
Flying Ants								■	■			
Crane Fly									■	■		

Source: Department of Natural Resources

FISHING | bass

ROBERT K. HAMILTON
The Susquehanna lures bass fishermen to its rocky shallows.

Bassin' is boomin'

BY PETER BAKER

Thirty years ago, an Alabama businessman dared to introduce competition to bass fishing, and, in the decades since, a billion-dollar, nationwide industry has grown from that far-fetched idea.

"I had no idea at the time, of course, that this thing would take off the way it did," said Ray Scott, the 63-year-old founder of the Bass Anglers Sportsman Society, which has some 500,000 members around the world. "But, my, did it ever — and it is still growing in popularity."

Within a 50-mile radius of Baltimore, Scott said, there are 20,392 households that include current or recent members of B.A.S.S. Within a 70-mile radius, he said, there are 30,615.

PETER BAKER
Duke Nohe, president of the Maryland Aquatic Resources Coalition, holds up a nice bass taken from Prettyboy Reservoir.

Yellow Black Fury   *Aglia long*   *Aglia #1*   *Lightnin'*   *Red Black Fury*

A sampling of spinners from Mepps.

"There are more B.A.S.S. fishing households in the Baltimore area than within the same distances around Dallas," Scott said, "and Texas, as everybody knows, is a bassin' hotbed."

But in Maryland, too, the fever runs high.

From the tidal rivers of the eastern and western shores of Chesapeake Bay, up the Potomac River and across the state's reservoirs, lakes and ponds, bassers and bass competitions are numerous.

Not that all bass fishermen are competitors or members of B.A.S.S. Many more are simply out for the sport of hooking a big largemouth in Mattawoman Creek in Charles County or a feisty smallmouth from the upper Potomac River near Brunswick.

And in Maryland, the opportunities to do so

Mepps Syclops

Blue Fox Super Vibrax

#4 Panther Martin

Other spinners to try.

FISHING | bass

are plentiful, whether by conventional tackle or fly-fishing gear.

More than 100 public reservoirs, lakes and ponds hold bass. Twenty-six major tidal rivers or creeks hold bass in their main stems and a myriad of feeder streams. The upper Potomac River, above Great Falls near Washington, offers good bass fishing along much of its run upriver into Western Maryland and in many of its feeder streams and major tributaries.

"You could spend a lifetime fishing for bass in this state and never get bored with it," said Ken Penrod, Life Outdoors Unlimited outfitter and author. "I've fished most of it and written books about how to fish it, but I've never gotten tired of it."

Tidal bassin' in the state can be separated into three major areas — the rivers of the Eastern Shore, the rivers of the western shore of the Chesapeake Bay and the tidal Potomac River, especially from the Route 301 bridge to Washington.

The best of the Eastern Shore rivers are the Bohemia, Sassafras, Chester, Choptank, Nanticoke, Wicomico and Pocomoke, although the Blackwater, Transquaking and Manokin are worth exploring in small boats.

On the western shore, the Susquehanna-Gunpowder complex has excellent bass fishing, including the Back, Middle, Bush, Northeast and Elk rivers, Dundee Creek and the Susquehanna Flats.

A few years ago, the B.A.S.S. Masters Classic, the Super Bowl of tournament bass fishing, came to Baltimore and ran its fishing operations out of the state marina on Dundee Creek — and the best bassers in the country canvassed the rivers, creeks and tributaries on both shores above the Bay Bridge.

"You know, I grew up here and started fishing here a lot of years ago," Roland Martin, a top touring pro for many years, said during practice for the 1991 Classic. "But you come back here and fish, and the difference between then and now is amazing. It seems to me that there are a lot more and bigger fish nowadays."

And indeed, many of the tidal rivers have benefited from DNR stocking programs designed to augment natural reproduction in tidal waters.

But it is the tidal Potomac that supports the most prolific largemouth fishery in the state and carries the heaviest tournament traffic.

In September 1996, Dan Morehead, a young pro angler from Paducah, Ky., got his first taste of tournament bass fishing on the river in the Bassmaster Maryland Invitational.

Fishing exclusively on Broad Creek, a shallow bay near Fort Washington, for all three days of competition, Morehead won the tournament with 54 pounds, 11 ounces — an average of more

ROBERT K. HAMILTON
Canoe provides access to the Susquehanna near Rock Run.

than 3.5 pounds per fish.

"This place was absolutely unbelievable," said Morehead, who was fishing an area most anglers pass by. "There was a huge milfoil bed, and when the tide was going out, it cleared the water and I could see where the fish were and where they were going.

"The first time I saw that, it scared me to death."

Which prompted someone in the interview area to quip, "Hey, welcome to bass fishing, Maryland style."

Fly-fishing for bass

Increasing numbers of fishermen are turning to fly fishing for largemouth and smallmouth bass and panfish, with many anglers building their own rods and tying the flies they use.

Beginners, however, are better advised to start out at a good tackle store, where a salesman experienced in fly-fishing can help assemble a functional outfit suited to your skill level and budget.

Before buying, try out a comparable rig to ensure you are comfortable with it and able to cast 50 or more feet with accuracy.

If you have never used a fly rod, there are clubs throughout the state that welcome new members and readily share information and techniques. There also are a number of videos and books on the market, the best of which probably are Lefty Kreh's book, "Longer Fly Casting," and

FISHING | freshwater

KIM HAIRSTON

Kids learn casting at "Hooked on fishing, not drugs" clinic.

his video, "All New Casting Techniques."

For largemouth and smallmouth bass, 6, 7, or 8 weight rods from eight to nine feet in length work well. The best starter line is one that is weight-forward and floating.

Leaders are not as specialized as for trout fishing, so store-bought leaders seven to nine feet in length, tapering to 6-pound test are fine.

A single action reel with a good drag system will be perfectly functional.

Popular flies for panfish are: surface poppers, sponge spiders, hellgrammite patterns, Clouser crayfish, wooly buggers and weighted hare's ear.

For bass, good flies are deer hair bugs and mouse, deceiver patterns, and muddler minnows, wooly buggers and leeches, Clouser crayfish and Clouser minnows.

Once the basics are mastered, one can add extra spools loaded with sink-tip lines, shooting heads and other special lines that will help get your fly to the fish in varying conditions.

Freshwater fishing for kids

Largemouth and smallmouth bass often draw the attention of experienced anglers in Maryland's fresh waters, but a child's initiation to angling might begin with panfish — pumpkinseed, green and yellow-bellied sunfish, bluegills, crappie, white and yellow perch, rock bass or warmouth.

For young children, these fish are best hunted

with live baits fished under a bobber. The bait attracts the fish, and the bobber gives the young angler a marker to watch for a strike.

A light spinning outfit and 6-pound test line should get the job done. Clip a bobber far enough above the hook (Nos. 1, 2, 3, or 4) to keep your bait from falling to the bottom and crimp a couple of split-shot weights midway between bobber and hook. The weights will keep the bait down, but the length of line beyond will allow it to move freely.

Nightcrawlers, small minnows, grubs, mealworms and hellgrammites are good baits, depending on which species is targeted. Crappie, for example, will readily take small minnows, but sunfish rarely do.

When you buy your bait, ask the salesperson what's hitting most frequently in the specific area you plan to fish.

Most panfish are cover-oriented and hang close to beaver huts, undercut banks, blow-downs, brush piles, bridge pilings and boat docks — and that often makes them accessible from shore.

Determine the depth you'll be fishing, set the bobber, crimp the weights, bait the hook, gently cast close to cover and watch the bobber.

When the bobber is pulled below the water, the fun begins.

JOHN MAKELY
Freshwater fishing is year-round sport on Deep Creek Lake.

FISHING | freshwater

Freshwater fish

Largemouth bass

Muskellunge

Black crappie

Smallmouth bass

Chain pickerel

White crappie

Brook trout

Rainbow trout

FISHING | freshwater

Northern pike

Yellow perch

Walleye

Bluegill

Brown trout

Channel catfish

Blue catfish

Carp

127

FISHING | chesapeake bay

PETER BAKER

Wayne Dyott holds 28-inch rockfish and the spoon that caught it off the mouth of the Choptank River.

128

Rockfish now thriving in bay

By Peter Baker

It is an hour before dusk in early September, and the air is sultry as thunderheads build over the western shore. Chesapeake Bay rolls away from the boat transom toward Love Point, its satin surface mirroring the sunset.

A single fish breaks the surface, the sound a lone echo in the silence of the late-summer calm — and suddenly there is chaos, as a half-acre of water is churned by hundreds of rockfish feeding heavily.

Gulls wheel and shriek and dive, snapping up scraps. Baitfish jump from the water, with hungry stripers in hot pursuit, and a pair of fishermen lob small spoons into the fray, catching and releasing rockfish on almost every cast, until suddenly there is silence again.

Most of us who fish Maryland's part of the Chesapeake Bay have been there, done that on some stretch of water between the mouth of the Susquehanna River and the Maryland-Virginia border.

It is heady stuff these days — intense, rewarding.

But such was not always the case. In the 1980s, rockfish were threatened by overfishing, and recreational and commercial fisheries for the species were closed for five years.

In this decade, however, rockfish (striped bass) have come close to completing a carefully orchestrated recovery, and in spring, early summer and fall, recreational anglers again can catch their fair share of the rock.

"I have no doubt that the moratorium is the reason that there are as many rockfish as there are here now," said Capt. Buddy Harrison, who has fished the bay for more than 40 years and runs recreational and commercial enterprises in Tilghman on the Eastern Shore.

"There are more and bigger rockfish in this bay than any time I can remember."

Few will quarrel with Harrison's assessment of the Chesapeake Bay's stocks of rockfish, and the stripers' life cycle almost guarantees varied seasons of sportfishing on the bay.

But though rockfish have become the backbone of the bay fishery, many other species are available — bluefish, flounder, sea trout and speckled trout, channel catfish, Spanish mackerel, croaker, spot, white perch, black drum, channel bass and occasionally cobia in the southern reaches of Maryland waters.

Generally, more species are available from the Choptank River south, where the salinity is greater through most of the season. But in dry years, even a few channel bass will make their way as far north as the Bay Bridge.

In the early spring, large, sexually mature rockfish,

FISHING | chesapeake bay

which have spent the rest of the year migrating north and south along the Atlantic seaboard, swim up the bay's rivers to spawn.

And by the first of May each year, a special season is held to target a small portion of them as they leave the bay to resume their migration.

According to William P. Jensen, whose Tidewater Fisheries Division of the DNR was instrumental in the coastal recovery of stripers, the month-long spring season does not harm the burgeoning population.

But it does afford fishermen the chance to catch the striper of a lifetime, fish that can run more than 50 inches in length and more than 50 pounds.

Rockfish season has also been open during June and the first four days of July in recent years. But the season then closes until September, when the fall season opens and runs into November.

In the spring, trolling is the best method for intercepting the big stripers as they move out of the bay, and big spoons, bucktails and parachutes are the best lures.

Upper bay

The waters of the Chesapeake Bay above the Bay Bridge offer a type of fishing for just about anyone who wants to wet a line — spinning, casting, bottom fishing, trolling or fly-rodding.

The creeks and rivers hold perch, bass, pickerel, carp and catfish, and, at different times of the year, the bay is host to rockfish, blues, white perch and even sea trout at the southern limit of the area.

The best of the bay action below Poole's Island, however, is for white perch and rockfish.

Capt. Ed Darwin, who frequently runs the charter boat Becky D in the prime fishing areas from Thomas Point, a short distance below the Bay Bridge, to the mouth of the Patapsco River, has made an art of fishing for both species.

Darwin, a former shop teacher in Baltimore, said on one fishing trip that he isn't fond of trolling, a favorite method of many bay fishermen.

"The skill is in finding the fish," Darwin said, as we sat

PETER BAKER
Fishing for rockfish (striped bass) draws thousands of anglers to the Chesapeake.

atop mixed schools of fat white perch and rockfish, keeping only the largest perch and releasing the stripers. "And if you are good enough to know where they are, then you don't have to troll around looking for them."

Through the years, Darwin has kept a log of prime fishing spots. He guards it carefully and volunteers little information.

But the basic tactics are few and uncomplicated: Find an area of hard or shell bottom exposed to tidal movements and current, and you probably will find fish.

The one season that even Darwin concedes requires trolling is the spring trophy season for rockfish. But by mid-May, once the majority of the big stripers have moved through, Darwin usually can be found working a chum line to attract lingering big stripers near Hackett's, Tolley Point, Thomas Point or the deeper edges above the bridge.

From June 1 through July 4, the minimum size limit for rockfish drops from 32 inches to 26, but the creel limit remains at one per day. So once the waters have warmed, many upper-bay anglers begin bottom fishing for white perch, croaker and spot, along with occasional catches of flounder.

Best baits for perch, spot and croaker are bloodworms, peeler crab and grass shrimp. Flounder are best caught on minnows drifted across the drop-offs, along which flounder naturally ambush their prey.

Through the heat of late July and August, jigging bucktails will work well for catch-and-release rockfish, blues and sea trout.

Come September and the start of the fall rockfish season, trolling, chumming and bottom fishing will work for stripers over the 18-inch minimum — but the best of it is finding schools of rockfish breaking on the surface.

Middle bay

In the middle bay area, Harrison, too, trolls for the big spring stripers, preferring to work the edges of the main shipping channel, where the bottom drops away to 50 or more feet.

"This spring season," Harrison said, "will make you understand why they call it fishing instead of catching. But it doesn't take a lot of these big fish in a day to make a trip worthwhile, either."

Even though the best fishing is where the water is deep, most of the fish are taken from the top of the water column.

Harrison likes to run long, lightly weighted lines and big spoons in the spring.

But by late May, the boats out of Harrison's Chesapeake House will go to chumming for stripers, while keeping an eye out for the arrival of black drum, which begin to show up at the Stone Rock and

FISHING | chesapeake bay

Saltwater fishing hot spots

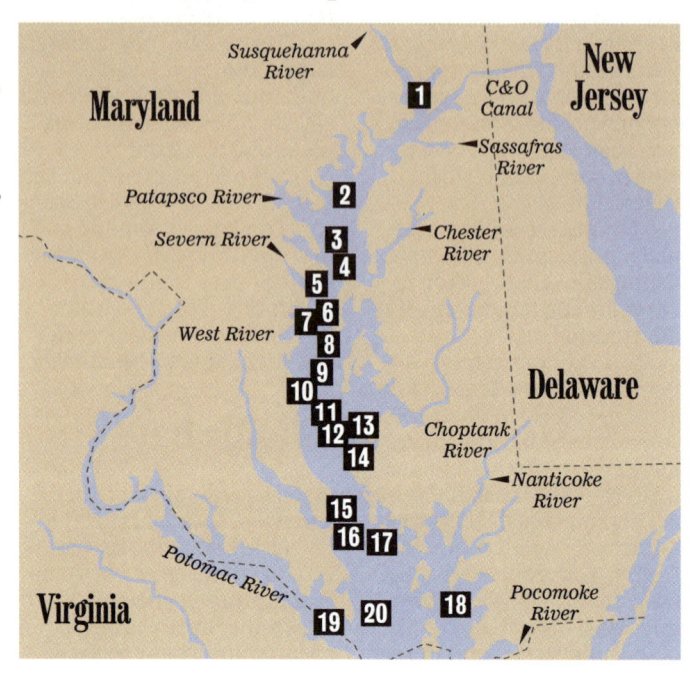

1. Susquehanna Flats: largemouth bass, rockfish, white perch, catfish, chain pickerel
2. Hart-Miller Island: catfish, white perch, rockfish
3. Belvidere Shoal: rockfish, white perch, bluefish, spot
4. Love Point: rockfish, bluefish, white perch
5. Hacketts Bar: rockfish, bluefish, white perch, spot
6. Brickhouse Bar: rockfish, white perch, bluefish, spot
7. Thomas Point Light: rockfish, bluefish, white perch, spot, croaker
8. Bloody Point: rockfish, bluefish, white perch, spot, croaker
9. Poplar Island: rockfish, bluefish, white perch, spot, croaker
10. Chesapeake Beach: rockfish, bluefish, Spanish mackerel, white perch, spot, croaker, sea trout
11. Stone Rock: rockfish, bluefish, sea trout, spot, croaker, flounder, black drum
12. Sharps Island: rockfish, bluefish, sea trout, spot, croaker, flounder
13. The Diamonds: spot, croaker, bluefish, sea trout, rockfish, flounder, Spanish mackerel
14. James Island: rockfish, flounder, sea trout
15. Cove Point: rockfish, bluefish, spot, croaker, sea trout, flounder, Spanish mackerel
16. Cedar Point: rockfish, bluefish, sea trout, spot, croaker, white perch, Spanish mackerel
17. Hooper Island: rockfish, bluefish, sea trout, spot, croaker, flounder, Spanish mackerel, black drum
18. Tangier Sound: sea trout, flounder, croaker, spot, bluefish, rockfish
19. Cornfield Harbor: rockfish, bluefish, flounder, sea trout, spot, croaker
20. Point Lookout: rockfish, bluefish, Spanish mackerel, sea trout, flounder, croaker

Poplar Island around Memorial Day.

The drum run usually is short and unpredictable, but for the two or three weeks they are around, the action can be hot and heavy for 40- to 70-pound fish.

By July, croaker have begun to show up in good numbers at the mouth of the Choptank, and the action switches to bottom fishing with peeler crab or bloodworms. In most years, sea trout and spot will mix with the croaker, and the edges at the Diamonds, Stone Rock and Sharps Island Light can turn up enough fish to fill a cooler in a hurry — and the sea trout action can carry on into early October, well after the croaker and spot have moved south.

Flounder, too, can be taken from the edges, although the last couple of years have been hit or miss for flounder from the Choptank north.

By late summer, when the heat of August makes it more comfortable to fish the early or late hours of the day, schools of snapper bluefish will have moved as far north as Love Point, above the Bay Bridge, and will be breaking on the surface, providing fast, furious action for anglers casting small spoons or bucktails.

When the rockfish season reopens in September, the early action is controlled by chumming for 18- to 20-inch fish, but as the season wears into October and November, boats from Chesapeake Beach, Solomons and Tilghman turn again toward trolling, working the western shore edges for stripers that often exceed 30 inches — and occasionally running into a fall run of bluefish in the 5-pound range.

Lower bay

Capt. Bruce Scheible has been fishing the lower Chesapeake Bay and the mouth of the Potomac River for decades, and he is not shy about evaluating the area.

"Without a doubt, this is the best area in Maryland to fish for the most species," Scheible said on a trip out of Scheible's Fishing Center in Ridge. "Bluefish, rockfish, sea trout, croaker, Norfolk spot, flounder, you got it all here, and you got it longer than anyone else on the bay."

In the spring, big rockfish and blues congregate south of the Middle Grounds near the Virginia-Maryland border, but rather than troll, Scheible prefers to chum, drawing the fish from deep water along a trail of ground menhaden ladled over the side.

Anglers with lightly weighted lines drift cut bait into the chum lines, where stripers and blues often hit with a bang and fight well against light spinning tackle.

As the spring trophy season for rockfish ends, the fishing in the Point Lookout-Smith Island area heats up — small bluefish and rockfish begin to break regularly on

133

the surface and croaker and spot move onto the Middle Grounds, soon to be followed by sea trout and flounder.

In July and August especially, when rockfish season is closed, the lower bay offers a variety of fishing that is hard to match in other Maryland waters at that time of the year.

Sea trout usually are plentiful, along with croaker and spot, and all can be caught by bottom fishing with bloodworms, peeler crabs, squid or shrimp.

Bluefish and Spanish mackerel travel close to the surface, where small spoons trolled at five or six knots will readily catch them. And flounder are available along the drop-offs with minnows and squid baits.

But it is in the fall — especially late September and October — that rockfish begin to congregate on the Middle Grounds and along the channel edges and bigger sea trout begin to feed heavily in deep water.

Free tidal fishing areas

North East — North East Community Park, mouth of the North East Creek.

Chestertown — Maryland Route 213 Bridge over Chester River.

Cambridge — Long Wharf south end of city-owned bulkhead near Municipal Yacht Basin.

Charlestown — Stone wharf at Conestoga and Water streets.

Denton — Crouse Memorial Park Pier north of Maryland Route 404 bridge.

Sharptown — Pier and town dock off Ferry Street on Nanticoke River.

Salisbury — City-owned bulkhead between Mill Street and Division Street.

Snow Hill — Byrd Park, Sturgis Park and city bulkhead next to municipal parking lot; Potter's Crossing Road bridge west of U.S. Route 113.

Pocomoke City — City docks from Laurel Street boat ramp to U.S. 113 overpass and Winter Quarter dock on Pocomoke River. County-owned dock at Cedar Hall Landing near western terminus of Route 371 on the Pocomoke River.

Princess Anne — Manokin River Park approximately 350 feet off the south bank of Manokin River west of bridge at Somerset Avenue and west side of that bridge.

Havre de Grace — Designated area of Tydings Memorial Park and pier at the end of Congress Street.

Baltimore County — Cox's Point on Back River and Deep Creek.

Baltimore City — Canton Recreational Pier at Boston Street, Hull Street Recreational Pier, and Middle Branch Park from fishing pier south of Hanover-Potee Street bridges to Hanover Street Bridge over Middle Branch.

Annapolis — North end of old Route 450 bridge over the Severn River.

Worton — Bridge No. K-004 over Still Pond Creek on Still Pond Creek Road near Chestertown.

Tyaskin — Tyaskin Park on Wetipquin Creek west of Route 349.

Friendship Landing — County-owned pier and property off Friendship Road southeast of Ironside Riverside Road (Route 425) on Nanjemoy Creek.

Saltwater fish

Rockfish (striped bass)

White perch

Weakfish

Spot

Black drum

Copia

Red drum

FISHING | saltwater

135

FISHING | saltwater

Atlantic croaker

White marlin

Bluefish

*Southern whiting
(Southern kingfish)*

Spotted sea trout

Cod fish

Northern porgy

Black sea bass

Dolphin

Bluefin tuna

FISHING | saltwater

Wahoo

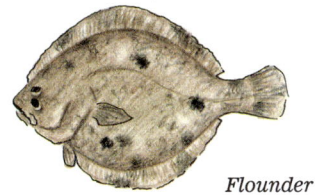

Tautog

Flounder

Albacore

137

FISHING | saltwater

PERRY THORSVIK

Holly Burnham baits a hook for Kenny Laws.

Saltwater fishing for kids

One of the best ways to get kids interested in fishing is to keep the tackle simple and the fish plentiful, and in Chesapeake Bay waters that often means white perch, spot or croaker.

White perch, spot and croaker generally are smallish fish, but a 12-inch perch or spot or a 14-inch croaker will feel like a sizable rockfish to a child handling a light rod for the first time.

If you haven't a suitable rig, for about $30 you can purchase a composite graphite rod and a basic reel that will be resistant to the common abuses of childhood. When buying, be certain the salesman knows who will be using the rig and what type of fishing you will be doing.

Add a double bottom rig, with No. 2 or No. 1 bait hooks, enough weight to hold bottom (half an ounce to an ounce, unless the current is running strong), and a bag of bloodworms and you are good to go.

Each hook on the rig should be baited with a one- or two-inch length of bloodworm, and sent to the bottom. Reel up slack line until the weight can be felt in contact with the bottom — and hold on. All three species hit with a distinctive tug. When they do, set the hook with an upward tug and reel in.

If bloodworms are not available, grass shrimp, clam or crab baits will work well for all three.

These species frequent oyster bars, other shell bottoms and barnacle-encrusted bridge pilings and move in schools — so once you catch one, there usually are many more nearby.

White perch are more common north of the Bay Bridge, especially along the western shore, and spot and croaker more often are found on bars and humps south of the bridge. Perch, spot and croaker often will share the same hard-bottom areas from Thomas Point to the bridge.

If you have access to a boat, so much the better. If not, there are head boats and charter boats throughout the bay area that can put you on the fish.

However you get the fish, keep only what you will eat and quickly release the rest.

Conservation is a lesson best learned early.

Crabbing for kids

Few things are as enjoyable as spending a couple of hours with children along the water crabbing from a dock, public pier or shoreline — and in Maryland there are many public areas where the crabbing can be easy.

All that is needed for dock or shoreline crabbing is several lengths of light line, a package of chicken necks, bull lips or salted eel, some light weights, a net and a container to store the catch in.

ALGERINA PERNA

Youngsters with string, bait and a net can learn quickly to catch crabs.

Cut the bait into one- or two-inch lengths, tie the bait and sinker to one end of the line and attach the other to the dock or shore. Lower the bait into the water, with just enough line out to let it touch bottom.

When a crab takes the bait, it will start to move off with it, and the line will stretch out, signaling that a crab has taken the bait.

Slowly retrieve the line until the crab can be seen on the bait, scoop the net under both bait and crab and bring it quickly up out of the water.

There are several kinds of nets available, but for ease of getting the crab out of the net, wire baskets are best.

For crabbing from a boat or high pier, the equipment list is a little more extensive, but simple in both cases.

For crabbing from high piers, such as the old bridge that has been made into a public fishing pier over the Choptank River near Cambridge, it is better to use collapsible traps rather than lines and nets, because of the distance from water level to the pier. Traps are available at bait and tackle shops and many hardware stores.

Using the same variety of baits but in larger sizes, tie them to the base of the trap on the inside. Tie a long line to the trap, following the directions on the package so the sides of the trap will close easily and quickly when the long line is pulled.

Lower the trap to the bottom and wait a while before retrieving the trap, which hopefully will accumulate a few crabs on each haul.

Crab sizes, catch limits, number of traps allowed, lengths of trot lines and seasons are subject to change. So it's best to check with the DNR (410-974-8480) for the most up-to-date information.

Atlantic offers big game

By Peter Baker

Early each August, dozens of offshore sportfishing yachts crawl through the last of Monday morning darkness from marinas and private docks into the inshore basin at the Ocean City inlet — diesel engines rumbling and captains, crew and anglers mumbling while anticipating the dawn.

At first light, a radio call goes out and the White Marlin Open begins with the yachts speeding out the inlet, the roar of engines echoing off stone jetties, 50-foot hulls coming up onto plane and slamming across waves and wakes.

For many anglers in the field, it is a well-rehearsed race toward glory and, perhaps, big bucks. For others, it will be an initiation into the mysteries of searching the offshore canyons for white and blue marlin, sailfish, tuna, dolphin, wahoo and sharks.

FISHING | atlantic ocean

ART BALTROTSKY
Gearing up in pre-dawn darkness at Ocean City Fishing Center.

And at the end of the five-day tournament, the one angler who catches the largest white marlin of the week can lay claim to the lion's share of a prize pool in excess of a half-million dollars.

Bob Bell was entered in a recent White Marlin Open after many years spent hunting billfish away from the Maryland coast.

"The fishing here got so bad [in the 1980s]," said Bell, who has fished around the world, "that I took the boat to Florida, and, for several years, we just never came back."

But in this decade, fishing for marlin and tuna has improved, and anglers like Bell have returned to fish the canyons 60 and more miles offshore from Ocean City, which bills itself as the White Marlin Capital of the World.

Baltimore, Washington, Wilmington, Norfolk and Poor Man's canyons can hold good numbers of game fish when the weather and

141

FISHING | atlantic ocean

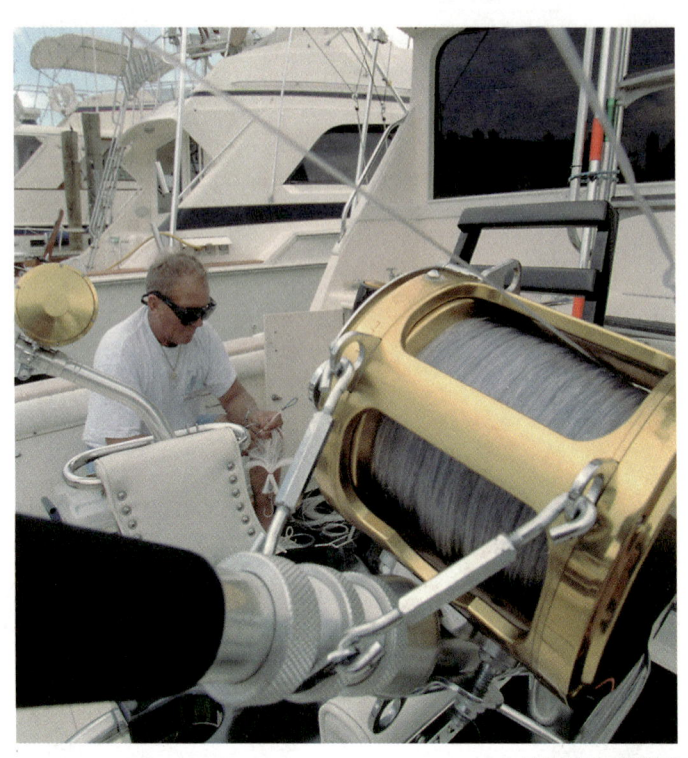

ART BALTROTSKY

Big-game fishing reels carry spools of 80-pound line.

currents are right. Knowing when the right conditions will be where, takes years of experience — or a little bit of luck.

"To find the fish, to decide where they are or where they might be — the temperatures, the reefs, the change of currents — that is what makes fishing so interesting," said Carlos Bentos, a Washington and Annapolis restaurateur who was the top angler at the 1996 White Marlin Open.

But tournament fishing — even with a boatload of experience, money and technology — boils down to luck.

"Let me tell you something about this," Bell said after catching an 80-plus-pound white marlin. "You know, we just happened to run over the fish today. We were fishing big baits for blue marlin. So sometimes, it is just a matter of luck."

For Bell and most anglers, offshore angling is a team effort in which captain, mate and fishermen must mesh boat-handling and angling skills in the fight against big fish.

But for Bentos, the business of fishing offshore is a solitary pursuit.

FISHING | atlantic ocean

"It is a matter of independence and quietness," said Bentos, who almost always fishes alone. "I am with people all the time in my restaurants.... I like the introspection of it, the opportunity of being by yourself.

"But not only do you go for fish, you go for the sunrises. To see the porpoises running with the boat, the bait breaking on the surface, the birds trying to make their own day, the magnificence of the nature."

By late May each year, shark fishing begins to pick up off Ocean City and is peaking in mid-June, when the annual Shark Tournament is held at the Ocean City Fishing Center.

By mid-July, the tuna runs should be strong, just in time for the O.C. Tuna Tournament. A few weeks later, the White Marlin Open kicks off the best of the billfish season, which will carry over until the water temperatures drop in September. Tuna fishing can extend into October in years when the weather stays warm.

Hunting billfish and tuna offshore is the high-profile, high-dollar side of fishing along Maryland's Atlantic Coast, but inshore, there are angling activities to suit any budget or mind-set — from pier, surf and jetty fishing for rockfish, sea trout, tautog and bluefish, to drifting for flounder, croaker or spot.

In most years, the action begins to heat up in late February or early March, when the head boats from the Ocean City Fishing Center and Bunting's Dorchester Street Docks try to hook up with the schools of mackerel migrating northward along the coast.

But with the resurgence of rockfish over the past decade, early spring anglers also will have a shot at big stripers as they move along shore or inshore to spawn. Along the Atlantic Coast, the minimum size limit for rockfish is 28 inches, and, in the open season, anglers can catch up to two per day.

Usually by the first week of May, summer flounder have started to move into the inlet and back bays from the spawning grounds offshore. As the weather warms, flounder will disperse through the back bays and be available along underwater ledges until fall, when they again will move offshore to spawn.

Bluefish will blitz the inlet and back bays from time to time from late spring to fall, and once the water warms in late May or early June, sea trout will move in, although the best action for trout usually is in the fall.

Croaker and spot move in once the water warms and stay until early fall, and are great targets for kids.

Whatever your skill level or attention span, there can be decent fishing down the ocean year-round, and one needn't remortgage the house to pay for it.

143

FISHING | resources

Head boats run half- or full-day trips out to the wrecks to fish for sea bass, croaker, tautog, blues, stripers and small sharks.

Surf anglers can fish from ocean beaches during certain hours and from Assateague at all hours.

Pier fishermen can choose from piers oceanside or bayside, although a small fee is required.

Jetty fishermen can work either side of the inlet at all hours for the cost of bait and gear.

Even the Route 50 bridge leading into Ocean City can be a fishing hot spot and often is lined with anglers.

Small boats can be rented from a number of establishments, along with rods and reels if necessary, and a boat opens up the back bays and its wildlife. Fill a cooler with sodas and sandwiches, strap on a life jacket and set out to see something of the watery side of Ocean City's world.

Equipment

You've got the fishing gear together — rods, reel, line, lures, etc. Now add the following to your boat, car or backpack:

- Properly fitted personal flotation device
- Foul weather gear — hat, jacket, pants.
- Waders and non-skid shoes or boots for wading.
- Clean, soft-cotton gloves for handling fish to be released.
- Warm-weather sun gear, including long-billed cap, lightweight wind breaker pants and jacket.
- Sun screen and polarized, UV blocking sunglasses
- Knife — folding pocket model or short-bladed sheath knife.
- Pliers — Combination set with wire cutter and small nose.
- Landing net.
- Small first aid kit for treatment of minor burns, cuts, abrasions, etc.

Resources

DNR, tidewater
 (410) 974-3558
DNR, freshwater
 (410) 974-3061
 (410) 974-3683 TDD
Clyde's Sports Shop
 (410) 247-3474 – recording
Potomac River Stage Reports
 (703) 260-0305
Maryland Saltwater Sportfishermen's Association
 (410) 768-8666
Anglers Sports Center
 (410) 757-3442
Tochterman's tackle shop
 (410) 327-6942

Books

"Longer Fly Casting," by Lefty Kreh, published by Lyons and Burford

"Saltwater Fly Patterns," by Lefty Kreh, published by Lyons and Burford

"Chesapeake Stripers," by Keith Walters, published by Aerie House

FISHING | resources

"Catching Striped Bass," by Keith Walters, published by Aerie House

"Fishermen's Knots, Rigs and How to Use Them," by Bob McNally, published by McNally Outdoor Publications

"Tidewater Bass Fishing," by Ken Penrod, published by PPC Publishing

"Fishing the Rivers of the Mid-Atlantic," by Bill Anderson, published by Tidewater Publishers

"The Art of Trolling," by Ken Schultz, published by Ragged Mountain/McGraw-Hill

"Reading the Water," by Dave Hughes, published by Stackpole Books

"Bug Making," by C. Boyd Pfeiffer, published by Lyons and Burford

"Lou Tabory's Guide to Saltwater Baits and Their Imitations," published by Lyons and Burford

"Northeast Guide to Saltwater Fishing and Boating," published by McGraw-Hill

"Life in the Chesapeake Bay," by Alice Jane Lippson and Robert L. Lippson, published by Johns Hopkins Press

"Chesapeake Bay: Nature of the Estuary, A Field Guide," by Christopher P. White, published by Tidewater Publishers.

HUNTING

Duck, duck, goose and beyond

BY PETER BAKER

For hunters, Maryland is a state full of opportunities, from the waterfowl of the Atlantic Coast and Chesapeake Bay tidewater to white-tailed deer and wily wild turkeys among the high ridges and mountains of the western counties.

Although the fall migrations of tremendous flocks once made the state famous for Canada goose hunting, in the last few years the state's hallmark has become its excellent hunting for whitetails and the secretive sika deer.

The Atlantic Flyway population of migratory Canada geese has been greatly diminished by over-hunting and a decade of poor breeding success in northern Quebec Province in Canada. As a result, the U.S. Fish and Wildlife Service has declared a moratorium on hunting these birds throughout the flyway until the breeding population reaches acceptable levels.

While the Canadas have struggled, deer and turkey have flourished in the state, with all counties open in the spring for bearded turkeys and all counties open in the fall for deer.

The fall season for wild turkey is open only in the western portion of the state.

Bow season for deer opens in September and runs through the end of January, and in between there are two muzzleloader seasons and a two-week firearms season.

Even without the Canada goose season, waterfowl hunting is good in the state for ducks, brant, snow geese and sea ducks.

Possibilities for upland game include rabbit, quail and pheasant.

Other forest game seasons include squirrel and ruffed grouse. In future years, there is a possibility of a limited black bear season.

Webless migratory birds hunted in the state are doves, king and clapper rails, Virginia and sora rails, woodcock and snipe.

There are more than 250,000 acres of public land open to hunting in the state, including barrier islands along the Atlantic Coast, swamps and marshes along the tidewater areas of the lower Eastern Shore, fields and wood lots in the agricultural belts of central Maryland and the forested ridges and mountains of the western counties.

Whether the draw is the bugling of a sika deer in a fog-shrouded swamp or a big white-tailed buck strutting through the rut, hunters can hit the mark in Maryland.

HUNTING — deer

More than 360,000 people in Maryland are active hunters, according to the Department of Natural Resources. We have included general guidelines on the various seasons, regulations and licensing procedures, but anyone who hunts is advised to contact DNR for updated information at (410) 836-4550 or on the Internet at http://www.gacc.com/dnr/.

From whitetails to sikas

By late November in most years, when the firearms season for deer opens statewide, the wind blows cold along the high ridges and through the hollows of Garrett County and snow cover is widespread along the western and northern faces of some of the oldest mountains on earth.

It is at once a stark and awesome landscape, a wild and modestly forbidding part of Maryland.

But cross over a ridge on a sunny day and the world begins to change. Open fields, clear cuts and forest edges drip or run with snowmelt, small bare patches appear and the vegetation of the edges breaks loose from the cold grip of winter in late autumn.

Work east across the state and the changing landscape continues, from the mountains and high plateaus down across the Piedmont to the coastal plain — from bleak mountain forests in the western counties to Eastern Shore field edges that can produce shoots and hardy berries well into December in warmer years.

Across the 238 miles Maryland runs from its border with West Virginia to the Atlantic Ocean, deer hunting changes with the landscape, too.

Through most of the state, the hunting is for white-tailed deer, but in the marshy lands of Dorchester County and on Assateague Island in Worcester County, a tiny elk named the sika deer is hunted.

Sika deer were introduced from Asia in the early 1900s, and the exotic species draws hunters from around the country.

The estimated deer population in Maryland exceeds 225,000 and may be approaching 300,000, according to the DNR. In some areas the number of deer is being controlled by hunting seasons, while in others the herd continues to expand.

"In Western Maryland, there is tremendous hunting pressure and the population dynamics are somewhat different than the rest of the state," said Doug Hotton, deer project manager for the DNR. "In those western counties, with the use of antlerless permits, we are able to manage the population more precisely than in other parts of the state."

By fluctuating the number of antlerless permits and

HUNTING | deer

Sika deer, right, are smaller than whitetails.

the days on which they can be used, Hotton said, the breeding population can be kept in check. When the breeding population is too large, use of antlerless permits is wider than in other years.

"We are back in a growth phase after a couple of down years there," Hotton said. "Antlerless deer are the whole key to getting the population where you want it to go."

Through the rest of the state, where the choice of antlered or antlerless deer is left largely to the hunter, Hotton said, "Overall, we are in a growth phase and we have reached a level where it needs to be flattened out or decreased."

With the exception of the western counties, Hotton said, the take in the rest of the state is roughly 50 percent antlerless deer.

In suburban counties such as Anne Arundel, Montgomery, Prince George's, Howard and Baltimore, the take of deer during the firearms season has increased dramatically since 1991, the last year in which Maryland had a one-week gun season.

But the increase might be due as much to increasing numbers of deer as to the change to a two-week season, which started in the fall of 1992.

"The two-week season has not caught on as well as we thought it might," said Hotton. "After the first week of the season, the pressure falls off, and the numbers fall off with it."

HUNTING | deer

Overall, deer hunting is big business in Maryland, with the DNR estimating that bow, muzzleloader and firearms seasons create more than 3,200 jobs and in excess of $209 million in economic activity each year.

Bow season opens in early September and runs through the end of January. Bow hunting is increasingly popular in the state, especially in suburban counties where rifles or shotguns are impractical.

The muzzleloader season is split, with an early, three-day season opening on the third Thursday in October and a second split opening around Christmas and running into early January.

On opening day of the firearms season — the Saturday after Thanksgiving every year — nearly 100,000 hunters can be expected to be in the field from the wetlands and hard edges in Worcester County to the high ridges in Garrett County.

The success rate of hunters has increased from 20 percent in 1985 to 40 percent in recent years.

Although there are large numbers of deer available, 73 percent of successful hunters in 1995 took only one deer; 20 percent bagged two; five percent killed three; two percent killed four or more.

Hotton said that the DNR has begun work on a new statewide deer management plan to address areas of the state where the deer population continues to expand rapidly.

"One possibility — and it is only a possibility at this time — is to increase the number of areas where hunters would be required to take antlerless deer," Hotton said. "But those details will be worked out after meetings with hunters, other user groups, landowners and others."

PERRY THORSVIK

Hunting can cut across the generations as with the Fletchers of Cumberland.

Waterfowl opportunities

A half-dozen heads peered upward through the narrow opening in the blind, looking into the wind and listening to the sounds of geese — Canadas — coming to Ray Marshall's spread of decoys.

Marshall, a top outfitter on the Eastern Shore, stood outside the blind on the downwind edge calling to the Canadas, talking the flight of a dozen or so within range of the hunters.

When it was time, the top of the blind was slid back, the hunters took their shots and four Canadas fell, while the others wheeled and struggled for altitude and quickly were out of range.

"It really doesn't get any better than that, does it?" said Marshall, who runs parties for ducks and geese. "They came in beautifully."

For many years, large numbers of Canadas migrated south to Maryland's Eastern Shore counties from the Choptank River north. The goose hunting was superb.

But over the past decade, the migratory population of Canadas has been diminished by late winters and poor breeding conditions on the Ungava Peninsula in northern Quebec.

Also, hunters from New England to Virginia, waterfowl biologists said, were killing so many juvenile birds that too few were left

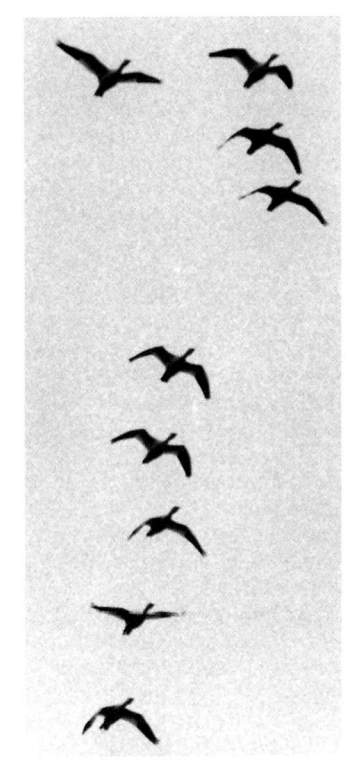

KIM HAIRSTON
The Canada goose population has been diminished

to offset years in which natural conditions limited breeding success.

As a result, the U.S. Fish and Wildlife Service declared a moratorium on hunting Canadas throughout the Atlantic Flyway. The moratorium will stand until the breeding population reaches acceptable levels.

Maryland Waterfowl Project Manager William Harvey has flown the breeding ground survey with USFWS and the Canadian Wildlife Service several times, but in 1996 he got his first look at a

HUNTING | waterfowl

migratory population that in large part passed the winter in Maryland with deaths only from natural causes.

What he saw on the vast emptiness of the Ungava Peninsula, Harvey said, was both encouraging and discouraging.

"It is good news and bad news, really," said Harvey. "The bad news was the [habitat] conditions. But through the area we saw a substantial increase in pairs."

The state of the habitat is out of anyone's control, of course. But the number of geese paired off waiting to breed, nest and raise young is good news.

"If you were to add up all the birds, the total probably is down . . . but more were pairs," Harvey said. "I interpret that to mean the closure increased the survival of birds, allowed more breeding pairs to return to the breeding grounds and allowed more younger birds to reach breeding age."

Although there are more migratory Canadas, hunting for them will remain closed.

Waterfowl hunters in the state have other opportunities, however.

DNR, with the approval of the USFWS, has opened a September hunting season for resident Canada geese in 21 counties and is experimenting with a January-February season in six western counties. Resident geese do not join the annual migrations of the Canadas that summer in Quebec and winter largely on the Eastern Shore.

While numbers of Canada geese have declined, snow geese numbers have grown substantially on the Eastern Shore and the DNR is aggressively trying to reduce those numbers with season splits that run from late October into early March.

As yet, a cottage industry centered on snow geese has not fully developed. It is simply too hard to predict what snow geese will do, said Marshall.

"I have put out hundreds of decoys for them and spent a lot of time trying to figure them out," said Marshall. "But try as I might, I just can't. It just seems a matter of luck when they show up."

In the last few years, duck populations have also increased in Maryland. Mallards, teal, pintails, wood ducks, black ducks and canvasbacks are possibilities, with the fast-moving canvasback making a comeback in Maryland in recent years.

Dates for duck seasons are set by the USFWS and Maryland generally has 40 or 50 days separated into October, November and December-January splits, with restrictions on when black ducks and canvasbacks can be hunted.

For hunters who like their shooting faster and even more challenging, there are sea duck zones, where scoters, eiders and old squaw are plentiful in most years.

HUNTING | waterfowl

LLOYD FOX

The duck hunter waits in a blind with his retriever

153

HUNTING | upland and forest game

Wild turkey success

While deer and waterfowl traditionally have drawn the most attention from Maryland hunters, other game in the state — most notably wild turkey — provides additional recreational opportunities.

Over the greater part of the past two decades, wild turkeys have been re-introduced throughout the state, and in 1995 the spring season for bearded birds was opened in all counties.

And while some species have faltered through the years, wild turkeys have been a tremendous success through the work of DNR.

Calvert County ranks fourth in the state for turkey hunting success, and before 1979 wild turkeys had not existed in that county for decades.

Wildlife biologists re-introduced the birds to Calvert County, as they have since throughout the state, by trapping turkeys in Western Maryland and transplanting them. Natural reproduction has filled out many areas of suitable habitat.

Maryland has two turkey hunting seasons each year, the statewide hunt for bearded birds only, from mid-April to mid-May, and the fall hunt early in November. The fall hunt is limited to Garrett and Allegany counties and Washington County west of Interstate 81.

The spring season is the more popular, drawing approximately 13,500 hunters in 1995. The fall season draws about 7,000 hunters, according to DNR.

Other forest game seasons include squirrel and ruffed grouse.

According to DNR statistics, the number of squirrel hunters has been declining since the early 1980s, with a 1993 mail survey indicating there were 33,049 squirrel hunters, down from nearly 62,000 a decade earlier.

As the number of hunters has decreased, so has the

PETER BAKER
The re-introduction of wild turkeys has been success story for DNR.

harvest. But the success rate of the remaining hunters has remained the same.

The ruffed grouse season is closed in Charles County, where efforts continue to re-introduce the species. But, according to DNR, grouse transplanted in the county have not established a significant number of birds in the area.

Overall, interest in ruffed grouse hunting has lessened in the last few years, according to DNR, and the number of grouse hunters has decreased as well. The take of grouse over the past 10 years has been stable, but is beginning to show a slight decline.

Upland hunting opportunities include seasons for cottontail rabbit, quail, pheasant, woodchuck and crow — but pheasant and quail numbers have been in sharp decline for many years.

DNR's winter survey that studies trends in pheasant populations in Washington, Frederick, Baltimore and Carroll counties noted only four males in 1996, the lowest number on record.

Over the past 17 years, the USFWS's annual Breeding Bird Survey suggests a decline of 82 percent in the quail population.

According to DNR, bobwhite quail are now scarce in Western Maryland, although in Southern Maryland and on the lower Eastern Shore there are still fair numbers of birds.

In both cases, habitat lost because of land development and changing farming techniques is believed to be the cause of population decline.

A rite of early September is the opening of mourning dove season, the first of a handful of hunts for species of webless migratory birds.

Dove populations have been stable in the state for 10 years, and many wildlife management areas offer excellent public hunting opportunities.

The peak of the dove season usually comes in October, when resident birds mix with migrants making their way south for the winter.

Woodcock hunting is still good at times in areas with good bottomland hardwoods, but overall woodcock populations have been declining for many years, largely because of habitat destruction.

Rails and snipes can be found in wetland areas in the tidewater and elsewhere in the state, and there are hunting seasons for four species of rails — sora, Virginia, king and clapper — and the common snipe.

Rules to hunt by

- Sunday hunting — There is no hunting on Sundays, except for woodchucks, which can be hunted any day year-round.
- Licenses — To buy a hunting license in Maryland, you must be able to prove you were a licensed hunter

HUNTING | regulations

before July 1, 1977, have proof of completion of a firearms and hunter safety education course (required for junior hunters, under the age of 16), prove that you hunted on private land before July 1, 1977, and were exempt from purchasing a license, or provide certification that you are purchasing a non-resident license and will hunt only waterfowl.

Maryland has two types of licenses for residents, a basic license that allows all legal game to be hunted except deer and waterfowl, and a consolidated license that allows all legal game to be hunted in season, including deer with bow, modern firearms or muzzleloader. Deer (bow, muzzleloader and firearms) and waterfowl stamps can be purchased along with the basic license. HIP permits are required to hunt migratory game birds and state and federal migratory waterfowl stamps must be purchased to hunt waterfowl.

License fees (as of 1996-97):

Resident basic junior hunting license: $6.50

Resident consolidated junior hunting license: $15.50

Resident basic hunting license (ages 16 through 64): $15.50

Resident consolidated hunting license (ages 16 through 64): $24.50

Resident senior consolidated lifetime license (65 or older): $12.50

Resident senior consolidated annual license (65 or older): $1.25

Nonresident three-day small game and waterfowl license: $35

Nonresident basic hunting license: $120.50

For state stamps fees, check with the DNR. Federal migratory waterfowl stamp is $15.

■ Handicapped hunters — Hunters with mobility impairments certified by a doctor can obtain permits to hunt from vehicles under certain parameters. For more information, contact the DNR Wildlife and Heritage Division, (410) 974-3195.

■ Hunter orange — A color not found in nature, daylight fluorescent orange, is required of all people who hunt wildlife or accompany, aid or assist another person in the field or on the water. Minimum requirements are a cap of solid hunter orange, a vest or jacket with front and back panels of at least 250 square inches of hunter orange or an outer garment of at least 50 percent hunter orange camouflage worn above the waist.

Hunters using their own property are exempt, as are deer hunters in bow season, hunters who use raptors and those who hunt or assist in the hunting of brants, coots, ducks, gallinules, geese, mergansers, rails, snipes, crows, doves or wild turkeys.

■ Hunting private property — It is unlawful to hunt on private land without written permission of the landowner or the landowner's agent or lessee.

Chris McAvinue uses a compound bow. — KIM HAIRSTON

Seasons and bag limits

The DNR recently began approving hunting dates and bag limits for two seasons in succession, rather than the traditional method of approving one season at a time.

Opening dates for various seasons change somewhat year to year, and the following are general guidelines. Check with DNR for up-to-date information.

Deer

■ Bow — For white-tailed deer and sika deer, the season usually opens on the second Saturday in September and runs through the end of January in all counties. While bow hunters can continue to hunt during the firearms and muzzleloader seasons, they must wear hunter orange and abide by the regulations for those seasons on those days. The bag limit is one deer, antlered or antlerless, and one more is possible with a bonus stamp. In Dorchester County, however, the regular bag limit is two deer and no bonus stamp is necessary. Other counties also might have two-deer limits in years when the deer population is excessive. Only one deer per day may be taken in Allegany, Carroll, Frederick, Garrett and Washington counties.

■ Muzzleloader — An early, three-day season opens statewide the third Thursday of each October, with a bag limit of one sika or white-tailed deer. Bonus stamps do not apply during the early season. Antlered or antlerless in all counties except Allegany, Carroll, Frederick, Garrett and Washington, which are antlered only. The late

HUNTING | regulations

season usually runs from shortly before Christmas into the first week of January, with a bag limit of one deer or two with a bonus stamp. Deer can be antlered or antlerless in all counties except Allegany, Frederick (Zone 1), Garrett and Washington (Zone 2), where deer must be antlered or can be antlerless with a permit. Bonus deer in those counties must be antlered.

Note: Check DNR Guide to Hunting and Trapping in Maryland for explanation of bonus deer stamps and allowable take of antlerless or antlered deer.

- Firearms — The two-week firearms season for white-tailed and sika deer opens statewide the Saturday after Thanksgiving, with a bag limit of one deer. In Dorchester County, two deer can be taken. Elsewhere, a second deer can be taken with a bonus stamp. In all counties except Allegany, Carroll, Frederick (Zone 1), Garrett and Washington, deer can be antlered or antlerless. In Washington (Zone 1) and Carroll counties, deer must be antlered only for the first week of the season, and may be antlered or antlerless during the second week. In Allegany, Frederick (Zone 1), Garrett and Washington (Zone 2) counties, deer must be antlered only except the last two days of the season, when hunters with permits can take antlerless deer.

For annual changes, check the current DNR Guide to Hunting and Trapping in Maryland, which is issued when a hunting license is purchased.

PETER BAKER

Steve Holt calls Canada geese into a blind.

Waterfowl

Shooting hours are 30 minutes before sunrise to sunset.

The USFWS sets parameters under which Maryland may select its waterfowl seasons each year. The following are generalizations based on when seasons have fallen the last few years. For up-to-date season and bag-limit information, contact DNR.

- Canada geese, migratory: closed season.
- Canada geese, resident, early season: From early to mid-September in Anne Arundel, Calvert, Caroline, Cecil, Charles, Dorchester, Harford, St. Mary's, Somerset, Talbot, Wicomico and Worcester counties and those parts of Prince George's, Baltimore and Howard counties east of I-95. Bag limit five. Early September to late September in Allegany, Carroll, Frederick, Garrett, Montgomery and Washington counties and those portions of Prince George's, Baltimore and Howard counties west of I-95. Bag limit five. Season closed in Queen Anne's and Kent counties.
- Canada geese, resident, experimental late season: Mid-January to mid-February in Allegany, Carroll, Frederick, Garrett, Washington and Montgomery counties west of I-270 and I-495 from Virginia line to intersection of I-495 and I-270. Bag limit three.
- Snow geese: Late October to late November, mid-December to mid-January and late January to early March. Bag limit eight.
- Brant: Three-day split in late November and late December to mid-January. Bag limit two.
- Ducks: Generally there are three splits to the season, with limits on when canvasbacks and black ducks can be hunted. First split comes early in October, second split is mid- to late November and third split is mid-December to mid-January. Black ducks usually are open in November and December-January splits, and canvasbacks are open in the December-January split. Bag limits vary year to year, but may include no more than one hen mallard, one pintail, two wood ducks, one redhead, one fulvous tree duck, one mottled duck, one black duck (in season), one canvasback (in season).
- Sea ducks: Early October through mid-January. Limits will vary.

Upland game

- Eastern cottontail: In Allegany and Garrett counties, the season opens early in November and runs through the end of January. In all other counties, the season opens and closes a week later. Bag limit is four, possession limit is eight.
- Bobwhite quail: The season opens early in November and closes in the middle of January in the area of the state west of I-83

south to I-695 to I-95 to the Virginia line, excluding Allegany and Garrett counties. In the area of the state east of that line, the season opens early in November and closes in the middle of February. Bag limit is six, possession limit is 12.

- Pheasant (male only): Mid-November to the end of December in all counties. Bag limit is one. Possession limit is two.
- Crow: Mid-August to mid-March on Wednesday, Thursday, Friday and Saturday only. No bag limit or possession limit.
- Woodchuck: An unprotected species, woodchuck can be hunted year-around, including Sundays. There are no bag limits.

Webless migratory birds

Shooting hours are 30 minutes before sunrise to sunset, except for early split of dove season, when dove hours are noon to sunset.

- Mourning doves: The season usually has three splits, early September to mid- October, mid-to-late November and late December to early January. Daily limit is 12.
- King and clapper rails: Early September to early November. Bag limit is 10, singly or in aggregate.
- Sora and Virginia rails: Early September to early November. Bag limit is 25, singly or in aggregate.
- Woodcock: Usually two splits, late October to late November and mid-to-late December. Daily limit is three.
- Common snipe: Mid-September to late November and mid-December to mid-January. Daily limit is eight.

Forest game

- Squirrels: Gray and Eastern fox squirrels can be hunted from early in October until end of January, with a bag limit of six and a possession limit of 12. Red or piney squirrels can be hunted during same season, with no bag limits.
- Wild turkey (fall): The season runs Monday through Saturday early in November

KIM HAIRSTON
Care must be taken when mounting a tree stand.

only in that part of the state west of I-81 in Washington, Allegany and Garrett counties. In years when there is a good hatch, there are provisions for an extension of the season. Bag limit is one.

- Wild turkey (spring): Mid-April to mid-May in all counties for bearded birds only with a bag limit of one. If no turkey was taken in the previous fall season, then two bearded birds can be taken in the spring. In either case, daily bag limit is one.

- Ruffed grouse : The season runs from early October through Jan. 31 with a bag limit of two and a possession limit of four. Season closed in Charles County.

Guidelines for staying safe

Firearms safety

Treat every gun as if it is loaded.

Always be aware of the direction the muzzle is pointed, and be able to control its direction if you should stumble.

Keep the barrel and action clear of obstructions, and double check to ensure you have the right ammunition for the gun you are carrying.

Identify your target and what lies beyond it before shooting.

When not in use, unload your gun, disengage or open the action, and keep it cased on the way to the shooting area.

Never point a gun at anything you don't intend to kill.

Do not climb a tree or jump over ditches or obstacles with a loaded gun. Put the gun down where it can be retrieved safely, butt end first.

Do not shoot at flat, hard surfaces or water.

Store guns and ammunition separately, out of the reach of children or people untrained in handling firearms.

Avoid alcoholic beverages before and during shooting.

Tree stand safety

Inspect your tree stand and related equipment before the season begins and then daily afterward, to ensure it maintains designed strength and integrity.

Always use a climbing belt when ascending or descending a tree. Most accidents happen on the way up or down.

Wear a safety belt when on the tree stand — clip it on as soon as you are aboard and leave it on until you are ready to go down.

Before climbing to the stand, unload your weapon and rig a hand line, so your gun and gear can be hauled up safely.

Use extra care when weather conditions are wet, snowy or icy, all of which can make tree stand steps slippery and dangerous.

Steel shot and choke recommendations

Bird	range	shot size	choke
Teal	all	6, 5	improved cylinder, modified
Ducks	under 40 yards	6, 5, 4, 3	improved cylinder
Ducks	30 to 50 yards	4, 3, 2	improved cylinder, modified
Ducks	beyond 50 yards	2, 1	modified, imp. mod., full
Brant	under 50 yards	1, BB	improved cylinder, modified
Snow geese	under 50 yards	1, BB	improved cylinder, modified
Canada geese	all	B, BBB, T	modified, improved modified
All geese	beyond 50 yards	B, BB, T	modified, improved modified

Weapons

Shotguns

Shotguns can be used for upland and forest game, migratory game birds and woodchuck, opossum, nutria, fishers and raccoons. Magazine and chamber can hold a total of no more than three shells, except when deer hunting, when the number is restricted to eight.

Deer hunters must use a rifled slug, pumpkin ball or sabot, except in Dorchester County, where No.1 buckshot or larger can be used. Shotguns smaller than 20 gauge are not allowed for deer hunting.

Shotguns larger than 10 gauge cannot be used to hunt waterfowl. Nontoxic shot larger than No. T cannot be used for waterfowl. The use or possession of lead shot while hunting waterfowl is prohibited in Maryland.

For hunting wild turkey in the spring season, shot is restricted to no larger than No. 4 and no smaller than No. 6.

Rifles

It is illegal to hunt with automatic weapons, and rifles used for deer hunting must develop muzzle energy of at least 1,200 foot pounds. Clips are limited to no more than eight cartridges or bullets.

Rifles can be used to hunt upland and forest game except turkey in the spring season.

Soft point bullets and all military, full metal jacketed, incendiary or tracer bullets are prohibited.

Breech-loading rifles cannot be used to hunt deer in Anne Arundel, Baltimore, Calvert, Caroline, Charles, Frederick (south of I-270), Harford, Howard, Kent, Montgomery, Prince George's, Queen Anne's, St. Mary's, Talbot and portions of Worcester counties.

Muzzleloaders

Muzzle-loading rifles and shotguns can be used to hunt upland and forest game and woodchuck, fox, opossum, nutria, fisher and raccoons, but cannot be used for wild turkey in the spring season.

Muzzleloaders used for deer must be .40 caliber and use a minimum of 60 grains of black powder or an equivalent amount of Pyrodex and propel one all-lead, lead alloy or copper soft-nosed or expanding bullet or ball. Sabot loads are legal.

Only iron sights are allowed during the deer season, although hunters with serious vision problems can apply for a permit allowing the use of a telescopic sight.

Muzzleloaders can be used to hunt deer in all counties, except on certain military lands.

Both flintlock and percussion caps are legal in Maryland, but only blackpowder weapons loaded from the muzzle or the front of the cylinder on handguns are legal.

Bows

Archery can be used for hunting all game birds and game mammals.

Bows must be hand held, hand drawn and held in drawn position by hand. Release aids are permitted but poisoned arrows are not.

For deer hunting, arrows must have a sharpened broadhead with a minimum blade width of seven-eighths of an inch.

Bows must have a full draw and pull of not less than 30 pounds.

Hunting with crossbows is illegal unless a physical disability prohibits the use of a traditional bow and the disabled hunter has met certain requirements and received a special permit from DNR.

Other equipment

After the basic hunting gear has been inspected and readied for the day afield, add the following for use should the need arise:

Foul weather gear – hat, jacket, pants in colors or camouflage that meet state

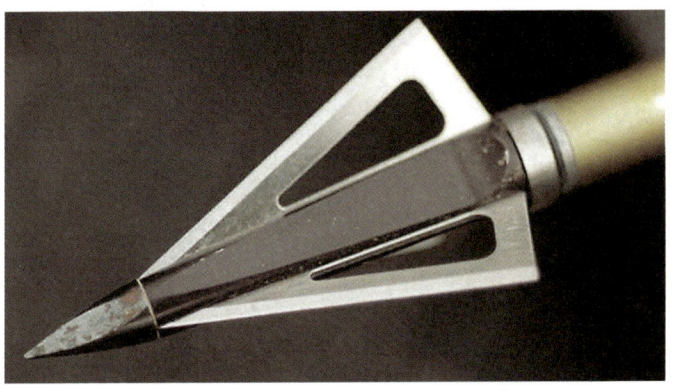

KIM HAIRSTON

Arrows such as this are used to hunt deer

HUNTING | resources

requirements for hunter orange.

Sun screen and polarized, UV blocking sunglasses

Knife – folding pocket model or short-bladed sheath knife.

Pliers – Combination set with wire cutter and small nose.

Rope – a 10- to 15-foot length of quality, five-sixteenths inch line will serve a variety of purposes, from hauling gear to a tree stand to making a bridle for dragging deer up steep inclines to emergency gun slings, pack straps or even splint ties.

Small first aid kit for treatment of minor burns, cuts, abrasions, etc.

Resources

Numbers to call

Natural Resources Police
800-628-9944

Federal violations, U.S. Fish and Wildlife Service, Enforcement Division, Cambridge 410-228-7991

Reporting banded birds
800-327-BAND

State Catch-a-poacher hotline - 800-635-6124
(TTY 410-974-3683)

Hunter safety courses
410-974-2040

Hunter Harvestshare
410-974-3195

DNR Wildlife and Heritage Division - 410-974-3195

Hunting Permits:

- Gwynnbrook 410-356-9272
- Millington 410-928-3650
- Myrtle Grove 301-743-5161

Maryland Bow Hunters Society
800-434-0811

Heart of Maryland Bowhunters 410-795-1542

LLOYD FOX

Former Baltimore Colts great Ordell Braase hunts ducks with Labradors.

HUNTING | resources

LARRY C. PRICE

Hunters who use muzzle-loading rifles might use traditional powder flasks such as this one in antique brass.

Ruffed Grouse Society,
national headquarters
412-262-4044

Books

"Deer and Deer Hunting, The Serious Hunter's Guide," by Robert Wegner, Stackpole Books.

"Real World Whitetail Behavior," by Jim Roy, published by Derrydale Press

"NRA Hunter Skills Series Waterfowl Hunting," published by the National Rifle Association

"NRA Firearms Fact Book," published by the National Rifle Association.

165

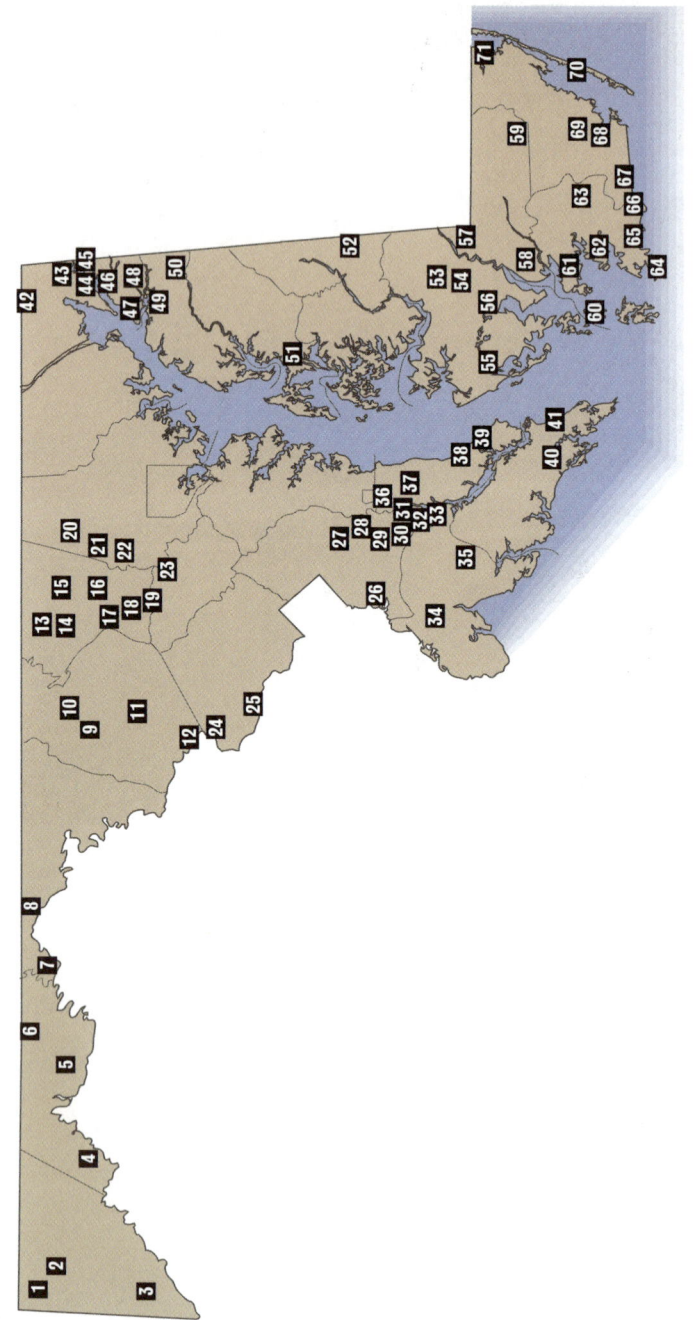

Public hunting lands in Maryland

166

Public hunting lands in Maryland

1. Youghiogheny Reservoir CWMA
2. Youghiogheny Wild River NRMA
3. Mt. Nebo WMA
4. Dans Mountain WMA
5. Warrior Mountain WMA
6. Billmeyer-Bellgrove WMA
7. Sideling Hill WMA
8. Indian Springs WMA
9. Heater's Island WMA
10. Thurmont Watershed CWMA
11. Frederick City Watershed CWMA
12. Monocacy NRMA
13. Sawmill CWMA
14. Speigel CWMA
15. Harper CWMA
16. Maring CWMA
17. Farver CWMA
18. Woodbrook CWMA
19. Morgan Run NRMA
20. Prettyboy Watershed
21. Dover CWMA
22. Liberty Watershed
23. Hugg-Thomas WMA
24. Cherrington CWMA
25. McKee-Beshers WMA
26. NPS Blind Sites
27. Cheltenham WMA
28. Nottingham NRMA
29. Spice Creek NRMA
30. Milltown Landing NRMA
31. Patuxent River Park-Jug Bay
32. Aquasco Farm CWMA
33. Bowen WMA
34. Myrtle Grove WMA
35. Indian Creek NRMA
36. Hall Creek NRMA
37. Huntingtown NRMA
38. Hughes Tree Farm CWMA
39. Hag Ponds Park CWMA
40. Walton CWMA
41. Elms CWMA
42. Fair Hill NRMA
43. C&O Canal Lands-Elk Forest
44. C&O Canal Lands-Welch Point
45. C&O Canal Lands-Bethel
46. C&O Canal Lands-Courthouse Point
47. C&O Canal Lands-Stemmers Run
48. Earleville WMA
49. Sassafras River NRMA
50. Millington WMA
51. Wye Island NRMA
52. Idylwild WMA
53. Linkwood WMA
54. LeCompte WMA
55. Taylor's Island WMA
56. Fishing Bay WMA
57. Nanticoke River WMA
58. Ellis Bay WMA
59. Johnson WMA
60. South Marsh WMA
61. Deal Island WMA
62. Fairmount WMA
63. Wellington WMA
64. Cedar Island WMA
65. Pocomoke Sound WMA
66. MD Marine Properties WMA
67. Hickory Point National Heritage Area
68. E.A. Vaughn WMA
69. Pocomoke River WMA
70. Sinepuxent Islands WMA
71. Isle of Wight WMA

CAMPING

A tent-full of possibilities

By Jon Morgan

As family vacations go, it lacks the sleepy pace of a trip to the beach. The bears aren't nearly as courteous as they are at, say, Disney World. And the restrooms are unlikely to pass muster with Conde Nast. Or with the surgeon general, for that matter.

But if you don't mind working for your food — and for your heat and shelter — then a family camping trip can be a great experience. There's enough work for everyone to stay engaged. The lack of modern distractions, i.e. television, virtually guarantees better communication, even with teen-agers. And there's a certain spirituality to waking up to a sunrise rather than the banter of "Good Morning America."

As luck would have it, Maryland is a great place to camp. The diversity of options is breathtaking. There are the 1930s-era cabins at Herrington Manor State Park in Western Maryland. The cabins have huge, rough-stone fireplaces, and some fabulous waterfalls are a short — and easy — hike away.

At the other extreme, there are the Assateague state and national parks "downyocean." These offer camping virtually on the surf, as well as such kid-friendly activities as shell collecting, wild-horse watching,

CAMPING

JOHN MAKELY
At New Germany Park, you can camp in a log cabin.

CAMPING

clamming and begging Daddy to drive to Ocean City for chili dogs.

In between are the Catoctin Mountains, where you can hike near — but not too near — the president at Camp David, and Patapsco Valley State Park outside Ellicott City, which proves you don't have to drive 100 miles for a good hike.

The key to enjoyment, let alone survival, is preparation. When you immerse yourself in nature, you take the good, the bad and the buggy. But the right equipment and a little common sense can minimize the complaints of little ones as well as the frenzied trips to the ranger's cabin. Setting everything up for an overnight excursion in the back yard is a good way to test both the equipment and your junior rangers.

You don't have to spend a fortune on Spandex-backed, Gortex-lined woollies. On the contrary, a camping vacation can and should be inexpensive. Getting back to nature is as much getting back to basics as it is being outdoors. Just remember that everything is a little more, well, extreme. What may be viewed from the living room window as a gentle spring shower might as well be the sequel to Hurricane Hugo if you forgot to pack some ponchos. Temperatures, too, swing wider than you'd think. So bring clothes that will be comfortable for an 80-degree day and 50-degree night. That means T-shirts and sweat shirts, blue jeans and shorts and ponchos and ponchos (did we mention the ponchos?).

Bring extras of everything, especially shoes, so you always have something dry to wear. Clothes dampened by rain can lead to hypothermia (see: ranger's cabin, and fast).

Renting a cabin is a good way to taste the camping experience. But these fill up and often exceed hotels in cost. And besides, the point is being outside, remember? Sleeping under the stars has a romantic aura to it, but if you can get a family to sleep happily through the night with all of nature's wiggly, nuzzling night-feeders, then you don't need a vacation. Go to work and volunteer for some stressful assignments.

The best place for families to camp is at an organized campground where you pull the car up to the assigned space and set up the tent.

JOHN MAKELY

After a soggy weekend of camping, dry out the tent in the sun.

CAMPING

JOHN MAKELY

Packing for the elements is a key part of camping.

Save the backwoods excursions for later, when even the youngest member of the family can confidently track, capture and gut a wild rabbit.

Tents can be reasonably cheap to buy or rent and, as long as you don't come back from the first trip still arguing about how to start a campfire, should provide years of service. Don't forget about borrowing, too; most of your pine-scented friends would probably be glad to see their equipment being used when they are unable to get outdoors.

With children, the options are to buy several small tents or one large one. The small ones tend to be quicker to put up and offer more privacy. Youngsters, however, may find it hard to fall asleep, alone, in an unfamiliar structure.

Parental visions of bear attacks usually prompt Dad to sleep with one youngster in one tent while Mom does duty in the other. This, of course, doesn't enhance togetherness. A number of good quality family tents are on the market, and they can be put up in something less than the time it takes to canoe the Mississippi end to end. Their idea of privacy is generally just a flimsy curtain that doesn't quite touch the ground. But there's room for dressing, diaper-changing and other necessities. You can even fit a small porta-crib in many of them. The biggest problem with these is once your kids refuse to go camping with you, you are stuck with a tent the size of a garage.

Sleeping bags are important, too. Try to match them

171

CAMPING

Tent types

A-frame

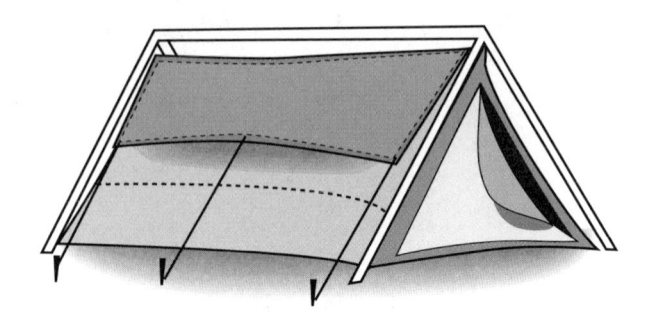

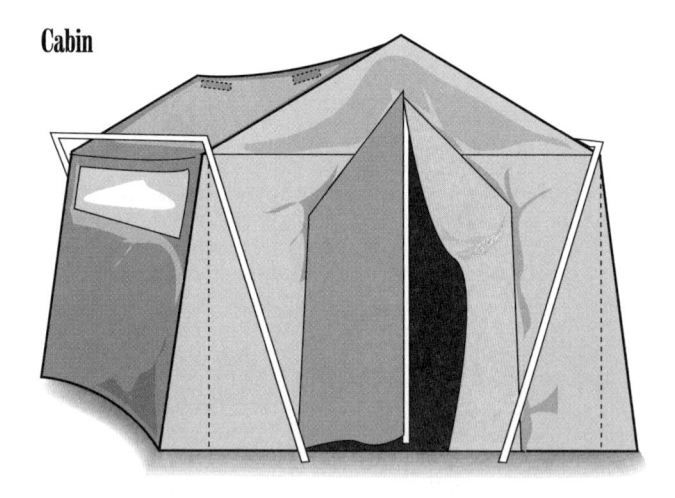

Cabin

to the temperatures you'll be encountering. No sense perspiring through the night in Sir Edmund Hillary's Arctic Explorer if you're just bivouacking at Susquehanna State Park in July. Splurge for an inexpensive foam pad, too. These go underneath the sleeping bag and keep the acorns and tree roots from feeling like a surprise appendectomy. Serious couples, or serious campers, should get a compatible make of sleeping bags so they can be zipped together to form a double. There's nothing so cozy.

From there, the sky is, literally, the limit. But keep it simple. Most campgrounds offer built-in charcoal grills.

One-man

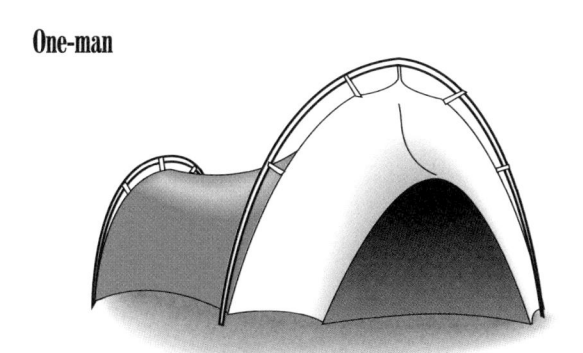

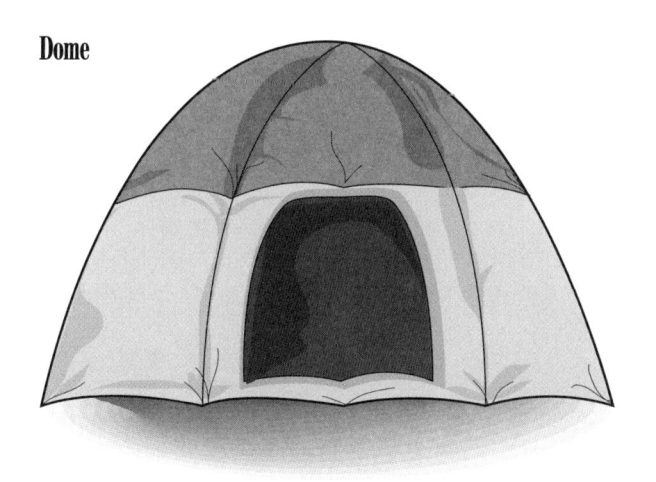

Dome

You can get away with packing some old pots and pans you don't mind permanently blackening. Coffee never tastes better than out of a $4 grill-top percolator.

You can't have enough flashlights and lanterns because, under the laws of nature, half of them cease working at nightfall. Battery-powered lanterns offer a measure of safety with small children around, but propane versions are cheaper and last longer without a change of power. Forget about the liquid-oil lanterns. Your grandparents hated them, and so will you.

With infants, a porta-crib is a good idea, both for

CAMPING

sleeping and as a playpen free of sharp rocks and biting snakes. A good-quality baby backpack — for carrying the baby on your back — extends your range and enjoyment immeasurably. And you'll gain new appreciation for the durability of the species when you see an infant sleep through a 3-mile hike alongside roaring waterfalls.

Sunscreen and bug repellent are a must. Don't forget some rainy-day amusements too. Games, coloring books and reading books may be sanity savers during an unexpected monsoon. And don't be shy about heading to a nearby mall until the clouds pass. (Did we mention ponchos?)

One final thought: Woody Guthrie was right. This land is your land and my land. So don't mess it up. Take this opportunity, through both example and spoken lesson, to stress conservation. Clean up after yourselves. Bring back everything you brought to the campground. Eschew paper plates and napkins. Use cloth napkins and rugged plastic ware for eating, and clean for reuse. All Maryland state parks and forests have done away with garbage cans, to save money and stress conservation. Bring your own garbage bags and heed the warnings about animals getting into them. As they say, take only photos and leave only footprints.

Equipment

Don't try to bring the entire indoors outdoors with you. Just bring what you'll need. Remember, you are roughing it.

Try out your equipment in advance. Set up the tent once in the back yard to be

PERRY THORSVIK
Before setting up on your trip, put up the tent at home.

sure there are no missing poles, stakes or other necessities. Same with lanterns, stoves, etc.

Some things you're likely to forget: a dishpan and biodegradable dish soap, towels, garbage bags, clothesline for wet clothing, can/bottle opener, cutting board, toilet paper.

Safety

Bring clothing that will keep you comfortable in a variety of weather conditions.

A course in first aid is a good investment.

A well-stocked first aid kit, available in most camping supply stores, is essential.

Be aware of your limitations. Don't hike farther, swim deeper or climb higher than you safely can.

Heed any animal or weather warnings posted at the ranger station. There really are bears out there.

Extinguish your campfire and grill before leaving.

Don't store food in your tent. This will attract animals, possibly unfriendly ones.

Etiquette

Remember that sound travels easily through nylon tents, so keep it quiet after other campers have gone to bed.

If you're meeting friends and think you may be staying up late, ask the campground rangers if they have any closed sections of campsites they could open for your party.

Pick up after yourself. That means even cigarette butts.

Resources

A number of pages have been opened on the Internet with useful information. The Maryland Department of Natural Resources (http://www.gacc.com/dnr/) offers links to individual parks and even a weather forecast. The Great Outdoor Recreation Pages, or GORP (http://www.gorp.com), offers links nationwide to suppliers, campgrounds and other camping-related pages (including one specific to Maryland).

The DNR camping information line has a recorded message detailing which parks are open and offering information on seasonal activities: (410) 461-0052.

The U.S. Park Service maintains a toll-free number for information and to make reservations at campgrounds: (800) 365-2267.

The Maryland Association of Campgrounds is a group of private campgrounds (listed on map on next page). For a brochure that lists amenities at each campground, call (301)271-7012.

Campgrounds to check out

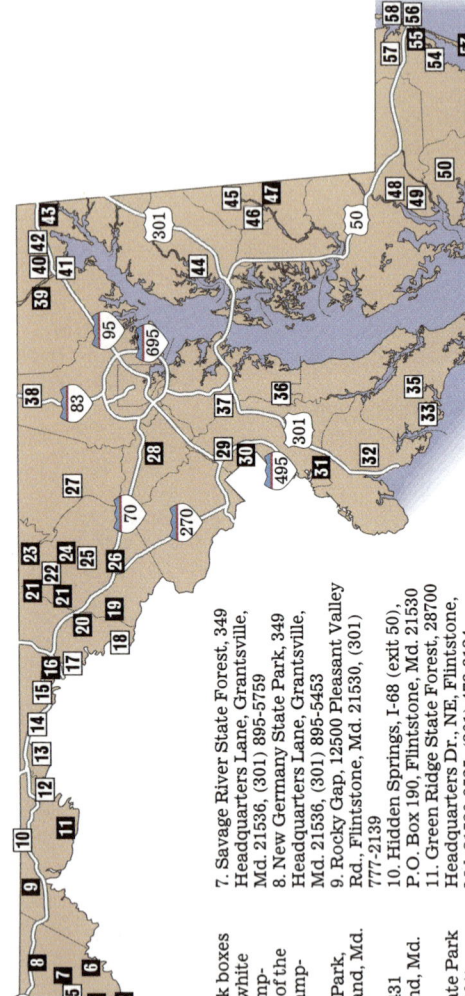

The sites marked with black boxes are public; the numbers in white boxes represent private campgrounds that are members of the Maryland Association of Campgrounds.

1. Herrington Manor State Park, 222 Herrington Lane, Oakland, Md. 21550, (301) 334-9180
2. Potomac State Forest, 1431 Potomac Camp Rd., Oakland, Md. 21550
3. Deep Creek Lake, 898 State Park Rd., Swanton, Md. 21561, (301) 387-5563
4. Garrett State Park, 1431 Potomac Camp Rd., Oakland, Md. 21550, (301) 334-2038
5. Double G Campground, P.O. Box 25, McHenry, Md. 21514, (301) 387-5481
6. Big Run State Park, 349 Headquarters Lane, Grantsville, Md. 21536, (301) 895-5453
7. Savage River State Forest, 349 Headquarters Lane, Grantsville, Md. 21536, (301) 895-5759
8. New Germany State Park, 349 Headquarters Lane, Grantsville, Md. 21536, (301) 895-5453
9. Rocky Gap, 12500 Pleasant Valley Rd., Flintstone, Md. 21530, (301) 777-2139
10. Hidden Springs, I-68 (exit 50), P.O. Box 190, Flintstone, Md. 21530
11. Green Ridge State Forest, 28700 Headquarters Dr., NE, Flintstone, Md. 21530-9525, (301) 478-3124
12. Little Orleans Campground, Rt. 1, Box 148, Little Orleans, Md. 21766, (301) 478-2325
13. Happy Hills Campground, 12617 Seavolt Rd., Hancock, Md. 21750, (301) 678-7760
14. Indian Springs Campground, 10809 Big Pool Rd., Big Pool, Md. 21711, (301) 842-3336

15. Hagerstown KOA, 11759 Snug Harbor Lane, Williamsport, Md. 21795, (301) 223-7571 or (800) 562-7607
16. Fort Frederick, 11100 Fort Frederick Rd., Big Pool, Md. 21711, (301) 842-2155
17. Safari Campgrounds, 16519 Lappans Rd., Williamsport, Md. 21795, (301) 223-7117 or (800) 421-7116
18. Maple Tree, 20716 Townsend Rd., Gapland, Md. 21736, (301) 432-5585
19. South Mountain State Park, 21843 National Pike, Boonsboro, Md. 21713-9535, (301) 791-4767
20. Greenbrier State Park, 21843 National Pike, Boonsboro, Md. 21713-9535, (301) 791-4767
21. Appalachian Trail, P.O. Box 807, Harpers Ferry, W.Va. 25425-0807, (304) 535-6331
22. Ole Mink Farm, 12806 Mink Farm Rd., Thurmont, Md. 21788, (301) 271-7012
23. Cunningham Falls State Park, 14039 Catoctin Hollow Rd., Thurmont, Md. 21788, (301) 271-7574
24. Catoctin Mountain Park, Thurmont, Md. 21788, (301) 663-9343
25. Crows Nest, P.O. Box 145, Thurmont, Md. 21788, (301) 271-7632 or (800) 866-1959
26. Gambrill State Park, c/o Cunningham Falls State Park, 14039 Catoctin Hollow Rd., Thurmont, Md. 21788, (301) 271-7574
27. Ramblin Pines Family Campground, 801 Hoods Mill Rd., Woodbine, Md. 21797, (410) 795-5161
28. Patapsco Valley State Park, 8020 Baltimore National Pike, Ellicott City, Md. 21043, (410) 461-5005
29. Cherry Hill Park, 9800 Cherry Hill Rd., College Park, Md. 20740, (301) 937-7116
30. Greenbelt Park, 6565 Greenbelt Rd., Greenbelt, Md. 20770-3207, (301) 344-3948
31. Smallwood State Park, Route 1, Box 64, Marbury, Md. 20658, (301) 888-1410
32. Aqua Land Campground, P.O. Box 355, Newburg, Md. 20664, (301) 259-2575
33. Goose Bay, 9365 Goose Bay Lane, P.O. Box 58, La Plata, Md. 20693, (301) 932-0885
34. Point Lookout State Park, P.O. Box 48, Scotland, Md. 20687, (301) 872-5688
35. Dennis Point Marina and Campground, Rt. 1, Box 118A, Leonardtown, Md. 20650, (301) 994-2288
36. Duncan's Family KOA, KOA 5381 Sands Rd., Lothian, Md. 20711, (410) 741-9558
37. Capitol KOA, 768 Cecil Ave., Millersville, Md. 21108, (410) 923-2771
38. Morris Meadows Recreation Farm, Inc., 1523 Freeland Rd., Freeland, Md. 21053, (410) 329-9636
39. Susquehanna State Park, 3318 Rocks Chrome Rd., Jarrettsville, Md. 21084, (410) 557-7994
40. Riverside Ponderosa Pines Campground, 1435 Carpenter's Point Rd., Perryville, Md. 21903, (410) 642-3431
41. Woodlands Camping Resort, 265 Starkey Lane, Elkton, Md. 21921, (410) 398-4414
42. Bittonwood Beach, Earleville, Md. 21919-0028, (410) 275-2108
43. Elk Neck State Forest, 4395 Turkey Point Rd., North East, Md. 21901, (410) 287-5333
44. Duck Neck, Rt. 1, Box 262, Chestertown Md. 21620, (410) 778-3070
45. Holiday Park, P.O. Box 277, Greensboro, Md. 21639, (410) 482-6797
46. Lake Bonnie Campsites, P.O. Box 42, Goldsboro, Md. 21636, (410) 482-8479
47. Martinak State Park, 137 Deep Shore Rd., Denton, Md. 21657, (410) 479-1619
48. Sandy Hill Family Camp, 5753 Sandy Hill Rd., Quantico, Md. 21856, (410) 873-2471
49. Roaring Point Waterfront Campground, P.O. Box 104, Nanticoke, Md. 21840, (410) 873-2553
50. Princess Anne Campground, Rt. 13, Box 427M, Princess Anne, Md. 21853, (410) 651-1520
51. Jane's Island State Park, Route 2, 40 Alfred Lawson Dr., Crisfield, Md. 21817, (410) 968-1565
52. Pocomoke River State Park, 3461 Worcester Highway, Snow Hill, Md. 21863, (410) 632-2566
53. Assateague Island National Seashore, 7307 Stephen Decatur Highway, Berlin, Md. 21811, (410) 641-2120
54. Frontier Town, P.O. Box 691, Ocean City, Md. 21842, (410) 641-0880
55. Assateague State Park, 7307 Stephen Decatur Highway, Berlin, Md. 21811, (410) 641-2120
56. Eagle's Nest, Sinepuxent Bay, Rt. 611, Ocean City, Md. 21842, (410) 213-0097
57. Bali-Hi, St. Martins Neck Rd., P.O. Box 618, Ocean City, Md. 21842, (410) 352-5477
58. Ocean City Travel Park, 105 70th St., Ocean City, Md. 21842, (410) 524-7601

HIKING

Hit a trail that fits your stride

BY ERNEST F. IMHOFF

Hikers in Maryland can heed the advice of a legendary West Coast runner, Walt Stack. His secret was to "start slowly and taper off." Or they can start easily with one-mile strolls and build up to hikes of several days. The state has scores of wooded trails that satisfy these extremes and those in between. Day hikes are plentiful for children, normally active adults and super-walkers.

Thurston Griggs, an 80-year-old Arbutus tramper who has hiked the state's trails for decades, suggested that beginners start with hiker-biker trails north and south of Baltimore, then graduate to parks like Gunpowder State Park and Soldier's Delight.

"Good footwear is of prime importance," he says, "but find out whether your feet like light shoes or heavy boots. Feet are different."

Twice president of the Maryland Mountain Club, Griggs said its favorite mountain for years is outside the state, 130 miles from Baltimore — Old Rag Mountain, 3,291 feet high, in the Shenandoah National Park, Virginia.

"We still go twice a year," he said. Its rocky Ridge Trail and open summit draw fans from the entire mid-Atlantic region, but on summer weekends, it got too popular. The National Park Service began

GEORGE W. HOLSEY

Thurston Griggs, left, assists hikers on the Appalachian Trail from April to Thanksgiving.

HIKING | best sites

charging a $3 fee in 1996 to help limit the crowds.

In Maryland, Sugarloaf Mountain and South Mountain are two prime examples of easy and more difficult hikes, not far from Baltimore and suburban Washington.

Best sites

- Sugarloaf Mountain. You can drive partway up Sugarloaf Mountain, off state Route 95 in Frederick County, and stroll with children on gentle trails from a few hundred yards to two miles long. The partly open summit at 1,281 feet offers peaceful views of the Frederick Valley. Deer and foxes might linger on backwoods trails.

The hill stands alone, a 2,350-acre mountain bought piecemeal by Gordon Strong, a Chicago railway magnate. Since his death in 1954, a nonprofit foundation, Stronghold, Inc., has managed the land for public use. From the top, federal troops spotted Robert E. Lee's army crossing the Potomac at White's Ford headed for Gettysburg.

- South Mountain. For a greater challenge, put your boots on for the 36-mile quartzite ridge that runs between Frederick and Washington counties. This path is better known as the Maryland portion of the Appalachian Trail from Pen Mar, near Route 491 in Washington County, on the Pennsylvania border to Weverton Cliffs, near Route 340 at the Potomac River. Call (301) 791-4767.

For years, from April to Thanksgiving, Griggs has driven to the trail and patrolled different sections five days a week, partly to assist hikers.

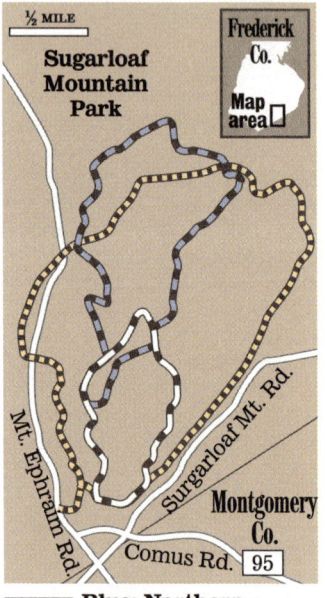

Blue: Northern Peaks Trail
Starts at West View parking. Five miles of nice scenery and hiking.

White: Mountain Loop Trail
A 2.5-mile loop around the summit, or 7 miles with the Northern Peaks trail.

Yellow: Saddleback Horse Trail
A 7-mile loop around the base of the mountain.

Sugarloaf Mountain offers three trails to try.

180

Marathon walkers can do this trail in one long day, ending two miles away in Harpers Ferry, W.Va., or in bite-sized sections one at a time. Parks, shelters and lookouts mark the washboard-type trail of ups and downs crossed by several highways.

Curiosities abound. The Devil's Racecourse is a large boulder field created by freezing and thawing over centuries. Washington Monument State Park is one of the choice spots in Central Maryland for hawk watching. Gathland State Park features a monument to Civil War correspondents.

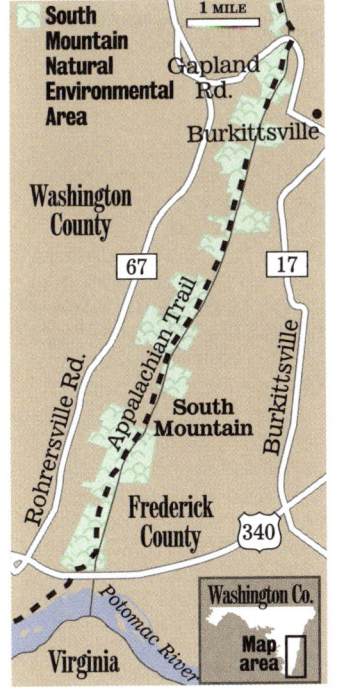

Trail at South Mountain straddles Frederick and Washington counties.

Weverton Cliffs hangs over the broad Potomac.

Here are some other venerable hikes in the Free State:

- Hiking to the highest point in Maryland, Hoye Crest on Backbone Mountain, 3,360 feet high, in Garrett County, is not a tough climb, but has other challenges. It requires a 225-mile drive from Baltimore and a dogleg detour into West Virginia for a starting point 25 miles southwest of Oakland. An informal sign on Route 219 in the Monongahela National Forest starts the walk. Once you begin, pay attention. The hike goes up only 650 feet in altitude, but follows a variety of directions that hint at trails.

Informal markers take you past blow-downs, undergrowth and prickly bushes. Unlike many publicly owned state summits, Hoye Crest, near a ridge-top vacation home development, is actually owned by a Texas company. It is wooded, and you see virtually no landscapes from the summit announced by a sign. But there are nice outlooks along the way. And you have bragging rights as one of the few to have climbed the state's summit.

- Savage River State Forest, Garrett County, is a wild place far from the city. The Big Savage Mountain Hiking Trail is a 17-mile trail along the crest of the mountain with overlooks, rough and flat parts and elevation change of 1,700 feet. With permits, camping is allowed anywhere

HIKING | best sites

181

HIKING | best sites

HILLERY SMITH

Reach the heights of Maryland on top of Backbone Mountain.

in the 53,000-acre state forest. Call (301) 895-5759.

Take Exit 29 off I-68, four miles west of Frostburg. Head south on Beall School Road 1.25 miles to a T intersection. Turn left and drive 1.25 miles to the St. Johns Rock trail head. For overnight camping permits, go to Savage River Complex headquarters, in Grantsville: Take Exit 24 and drive eight miles, following signs for New Germany State Park, Savage River State Forest. Call (301) 895-5759.

- The Chesapeake and Ohio Canal Trail is 184.5 miles from tidewater Georgetown in Washington to Cumberland on the Allegheny Plateau. The trail, except when flooded out, is flat and smooth, originally 12 feet wide for mules pulling canal boats. Rising 605 feet gently northwest, the walkway is between the river on the left and the canal's remains on the right.

Highlights include the Great Falls of the Potomac, spectacular but sometimes fatal whitewater for careless hikers. The Billy Goat Trail is a five-mile circuit there. Other historic sites are Harper's Ferry, the Antietam Battlefield and the 3,118-foot-long Paw Paw Tunnel. Nearby roads provide good access for short hikes. Visitors centers are at Cumberland, Hancock, Williamsport, Great Falls and Georgetown. Call (301) 299-3613.

- Catoctin Mountain Park, a national park, and Cunningham Falls State Park, just west of Thurmont, are adjacent and divided by

Route 77. They offer an intriguing variety of mountain trails and vistas.

Drive three miles west on Route 77 to the Catoctin visitors center parking lot for information and trails. Call (301) 663-9388 for Catoctin and (301) 271-7574 for Cunningham Falls.

Catoctin offers the Blue Ridge Loop of 4.6 miles, the Wolf Rock Loop of four miles or a combination hike of eight miles. The Catoctin Trail is a 20-miler going south through Cunningham Falls to Gambrill State Park northwest of Frederick. Cunningham Falls nature trail, leading to a beautiful waterfalls, is an easy .3-mile walk linked with other paths of different lengths. The Cat Rock Circuit Trail, for instance, takes you nine miles up 1,120 feet to beautiful views at the Bobs Hill Overlook, 1,562 feet altitude.

■ Calvert Cliffs State Park allows you to look for fossils 15 million years old along the Chesapeake Bay beach after leaving your car and walking two miles through a forest of pine, beech and oaks. Several other trails meander through the park. Sharks' teeth, fish bones and shells are among the 600 species of resident fossils. You may keep what you get. Climbing is not allowed on the unstable cliffs. Drive south on Route 3, Route 301 and Route 4 to southern Calvert County. The park entrance is on the east side. Call (301) 872-5688.

■ Blackwater National Wildlife Refuge is a cornucopia of birds, mammals, reptiles and plants in a setting of marshlands, fields and forests. You can find gentle walks of 1/3 mile and 1/2 mile and a wildlife drive of five miles that's easy to walk.

The rewards of strolling in the public portions are memorable. Year-round and seasonal denizens are plentiful. Bald eagles live there all year, and ospreys come in early spring and fly south in August. Many varieties of ducks dominate the area at times. There are also egrets, swans, Canada geese, muskrats, Delmarva fox squirrels, blackbirds, wrens and diamondback terrapins and many more.

The visitors center is open all year except for weekends in July and August, when bird activity is lowest. For information, call (410) 228-2677. A two-hour drive from Baltimore, the refuge is located on Key Wallace Drive, off Route 335 south of Cambridge in Dorchester County.

Safety

Difficulty or remoteness of hikes determines preparation. Get your legs in shape and learn about the route beforehand. Let family or friends know your plans. Stay on trails and don't hike alone unless you are experienced and know how to use a compass. Be careful going down mountains; most accidents happen then. Know when to turn around.

HIKING | walks

Sites for rock climbing

Carderock Recreation Area, Montgomery County, at the Potomac River, off the Clara Barton Parkway, northwest of Washington.

Great Falls National Park, Fairfax County, Va., at the Potomac, off Route 193, also near Washington.

Rocks State Park, off Route 24, Harford County, (410) 557-7994.

Seneca Rocks, W.Va., Spruce Knob-Seneca Rocks National Recreation Area, at the intersection of West Virginia Route 55 and U.S. 33.

Resources

Two "Audubon Society Field Guides to the Natural Places of the Mid-Atlantic States": "Inland" By Susannah Lawrence and Barbara Gross and "Coastal" by Susannah Lawrence, Pantheon Books.

"Country Walks Near Baltimore" by Alan Fisher and "Day Trips in Delmarva," Rambler Books.

The Mountain Club of Maryland. Call (410) 377-MCOM and leave your name and address on the answering machine; the club will mail you a hiking schedule and club description.

Walks on the mild side

BY LOWELL E. SUNDERLAND

So you don't have time or the willpower to get out of the house and climb a mountain, no matter how exciting and adventurous that might seem. "Let me walk," you say, "closer to home." That's OK. You have lots of company, and you're in a great place, Maryland, to do just that.

This is about regular walking — as in walking the dog, walking around the block or going for a walk in a park. You always can walk by yourself, but, to play off the famous song, you also need never walk alone. This is America, and that means even walking has been organized. More in a moment.

Why walk regularly? As one walking group's bumper sticker puns: "Walk for the health of it." Doctors will tell you regular walking can help your health. It's, shhhh, exercise. Combine brisk walks with a reduced-fat, low-salt diet and, over time, you're apt to drop some weight. Try covering a mile every 15 minutes for 30 or 45 minutes, which is brisk but far from Olympian.

In time, your blood pressure may drop, too. And for a while, some stress will melt away as you see in totally new ways your neighborhood, and when you really get serious, parts of the Mid-

HIKING | walks

Columbia's Lake Kittamaqundi entices hikers in all seasons.

ANDRE F. CHUNG

dle Atlantic you'd probably never visit otherwise.

The easiest way to walk is, to quote Michael Jordan's shoemaker, "just do it" — daily or, at a minimum, three to five times a week — in your own community. Don't concern yourself initially with form, or the "right" shoes and clothes or the season or the weather (although bag it if lightning's around). If you get serious, all those "right" things will fall into place soon enough.

Many folks find extended neighborhood walks satisfying enough, but for others, organized walking eventually becomes irresistible. People seek out walking clubs to be with others who like not only to exercise but also explore. What's interesting? What's that town or park or historic spot up the road like?

To find what clubs are doing, call the numbers in this chapter and watch the papers. Check local recreation and parks department, too. Howard County's recreation department, for example, conducts an annual series of walks on the Appalachian Trail and in the Catoctins.

Group walks are conducted somewhere almost every weekend by the Mountain Club of Maryland and various Sierra Club units, with the focus mainly on parks and watersheds in Maryland and neighboring states, with typical trails being five to eight miles long. Events are led by knowledgeable walkers and hikers (really, the distinction's blurry). Participants often meet and car pool to the trail head. Non-member fees are minimal, and additional costs are split. Respectable, not heroic, physical condition is all you'll need to keep pace in most of these walks.

For more information:

Mountain Club of Maryland, (410) 377-MCOM. Leave a message and the club will send you a list of its events.

Sierra Club, area telephone contacts:
Baltimore City, Baltimore and Harford counties
(410) 752-0104
Catoctin (Carroll, Frederick, Washington counties):
(301) 831-7606
Eastern Shore:
(410) 634-2491
Howard County:
(301) 831-3306
Washington metro area:
(202) 547-2326

Volksmarches

If you want to tailor a walk more to your own convenience and pace, try a "volksmarch" — German for "people's walk." Mainly, a volksmarch lets you start whenever you want to, usually between 8 a.m. and 1 p.m. Then, proceed at your own pace — it's not a race. If you want to stop for lunch or to shop or to smell the roses, that's fine. You can walk alone, with family, friends or new acquaintances. Just return, usually by 4 p.m.

Using some historical, geographical or other attraction as a centerpiece, volksmarch clubs clearly define a 10-kilometer (6.2 miles) "trail" with colorful, easy-to-follow ribbon or markers. Most folks, even beginners, can finish typical trails in two hours or less.

Walking these weekend events is free, although if you get into it, optional souvenir patches or medals and sustained record-keeping adhering, believe it or not, to international guidelines are available for a few dollars. Depending on trail rules, you might take the dog, too (as long as you can abide with local leash and pooper-scooper laws).

Volksmarch courses provide an array of experiences and terrain — in all kinds of weather, pretty much 52 weeks a year. Many walks are easy; some are relatively challenging, depending on terrain. To illustrate, Maryland clubs in 1996 conducted more than 80 different walks, among them "trails" in areas as diverse as downtown Baltimore, on the Appalachian Trail, along Columbia's ubiquitous blacktop pathways, in various communities around the Baltimore beltway, by the Chesapeake Bay at Downs Park in Anne Arundel County and along an obscure river on the Eastern Shore in Tuckahoe State Park.

Participation, not form or speed, is what counts in volksmarching, which started in walking-crazy Germany and spread in the '80s into this country. It arrived mostly via military personnel who got into the habit in Europe and wanted to continue here.

But volkswalking, as some call it, is not a military thing. Maryland, and the Middle Atlantic, constitute a hotbed of volksmarching activity —

ANDRE F. CHUNG

Markers identify each 10-kilometer volksmarch route.

indeed, on some weekends you can pick from two or three events from Northern Virginia into southern Pennsylvania, some attracting more than 1,000 walkers.

Baltimore and every Central Maryland county, except for Harford, have at least one volksmarch club.

If you really get into it, you can find volksmarches in more than 20 nations these days, as well as in all 50 states. In fact, the second person to finish a volksmarch in each state is a Marylander, Roger Turczynski, who lives in Severn.

For more information about volksmarching:

American Volkssport Association, (210) 659-2112. Web site: www.teleport.com//walking/avaclub.htm

Maryland Volkssport Association, (410) 296-1707.

A sampling of Maryland volksmarch clubs:

Anne Arundel: Annapolis Amblers, (410) 757-6983

Baltimore city and county: Baltimore Walking Club, (410) 296-1707

Carroll: Piedmont Pacers, (410) 876-1108

Howard: Columbia Volksmarch Club, (410) 730-6011

Montgomery: Seneca Valley Sugarloafers, (301) 530-8173

Multi-county:

Free-State Happy Wanderers, (301) 937-6124

Chesapeake Bay Country Wanderers, (410) 969-8661

Prince George's: Greater Greenbelt Volksmarchers, (301) 937-3549

Volksmarches you can do (almost) anytime:

In addition to 50-plus weekend walks each year, Maryland's volksmarch clubs also operate "year-round" or "seasonal" trails that you can hike almost any time. You go to the start point (typically a restaurant or store), pick up printed directions for the walk and complete the trail. For 1997, more than 30 such walks will be in operation in Maryland. Here's a sampling, plus phone numbers to call for details:

Annapolis (410) 757-2155; Downtown Baltimore (410) 282-4953; Elsewhere in Baltimore (410) 592-3171;

HIKING | equipment

Brandywine (301) 449-6325; Cambridge (301) 937-6124.

Cockeysville (410) 828-0834; College Park (301) 937-3549; Columbia (410) 381-1837; Easton (410) 544-2243; Frederick (410) 848-4469.

Gaithersburg (301) 340-9418; Greenbelt (301) 937-3549; Havre de Grace (410) 679-3594; Laurel (410) 674-5518; Monkton (410) 357-8611.

Rockville (301) 340-9418; Savage (301) 725-0918; Severna Park (410) 360-7913; Thurmont (301) 271-3106; Westminster (410) 848-2480.

Equipment

- Outerwear: Active walkers learn quickly how to dress for weather. Functionality counts more than style. When the weather's cool, chilly or downright cold, think layers and lightness of weight. It's easy to peel off a layer if you get too warm. Nylon windbreakers do just what their name implies in spring and fall, assuming you have the appropriate layers beneath. Remember, a hat helps retain body heat.

In warm or hot weather, walking shorts (so that's where the term came from, eh?) and a T-shirt will do just fine. Just take sunscreen. When it's sunny, especially if it's hot, wear a hat. Fully brimmed hats shade not only the face, but also the back of the neck — important when you're walking for a couple hours.

For walking in the rain, you'll have to decide between toughing it out, getting by with an umbrella, adding a poncho, or going full out with Gortex and its "breathable" (not to mention costly) cousins. Avoid cheap vinyl

ANDRE F. CHUNG

Hikers who dress in layers can adapt to changing weather.

HIKING | equipment

rainwear; it'll make you sweat bucketfuls.

- **Socks:** For most walks, a pair of decent cotton athletic socks gets the job done just fine, especially if the inner layer is soft and absorbent. Don't worry about wearing the classic two pairs unless you're faced with extended, high degree-of-difficulty hikes in rough terrain — and even then, consider some of the newer multitextured walking socks.

Tip: If your feet are apt to get wet because of rain, heavy dew, snow, puddles or excessive perspiration, many regular walkers like an inexpensive pair of polypropylene sock liners. These comfortable, thin miracles of chemistry wick moisture away from your feet without adding noticeable bulk or weight. They're cheap, too.

- **Shoes:** They're the hottest enduring topic among regular walkers, and the options — not to mention preferences — are multitudinous. Consumer or hiking magazines do occasional rating and testing, so you can perform some library research. Listen to other walkers' experiences and opinions, because good shoes can be expensive but, to a point, worth the money. Many walkers keep pairs designed for the predominant surface to be walked.

For paved surfaces: So-called "walking shoes" are desirable, mainly because of their smoother, somewhat firmer and thicker soles (avoid heavily treaded or cleated shoes for this type of walking). Cross-trainers seem to perform fine, too. All these lightweight shoes are cut normally, although they usually feature more padding than everyday shoes. Leather or nylon uppers — take your pick. If you choose leather, invest in a bottle of waterproofing treatment.

For natural surfaces: Especially if rocks, sticks, long grass and/or hills are apt to be factors, choose well-fitted hiking shoes that have a relatively shallow tread for improved traction. "Light-hikers" do well on virtually any hike of a few hours; most have ankle-high tops that provide comfortable — and desirable — support. Heavy-duty, all-leather (and more expensive) hiking shoes are designed for more strenuous demands of rough trails and longer hikes. Even they tend to be lightweight, though.

Tips: Whatever the surface, a shoe's fit is what counts. When buying, take your time; nothing on a walk is worse than blisters or "hot spots" that ill-fitting shoes cause. Always wear to the shoe store the same socks you'd wear on a walk. Pay attention to width and the support you feel. And be sure to allow plenty of toe room, both in shoe width and height for your toes. A little room for the foot to move is desirable, but too much can cause blisters. Try on the new

HIKING | equipment

GEORGE W. HOLSEY

Hikers span the generations at annual Bay Bridge walk.

shoes and walk around the store. Outdoors stores often let you try your new shoes on inclined surfaces that mimic hillsides; take advantage of the trial.

- Other stuff: Lots of merchandise is out there to tempt regular walkers, some of it more useful than others.

Walking sticks: Unnecessary on paved and mostly grassy surfaces, but if you do a lot of walking on rocky or otherwise uneven surfaces, you'll come to appreciate what a stick can do. The idea is to maintain your balance, a la a ski pole, not to provide leverage or easier propulsion. So a light, sturdy stick is best. Stores sell expensive, collapsible, metal models, but doing what walkers have done ever since mankind has been upright works just as well and for little or no expense: Find a suitable stick in the woods (heck, even an old broomstick works well).

Packs: Fanny packs are nice for long, casual walks of any description, holding odds and ends you might need, from tissues to maps to notebooks, cameras, film, quick snacks, your wallet, your keys, a small first aid kit with Band-Aids or moleskin. Day packs are nice, as well, on longer walks requiring, say, an extra layer of clothing, rain gear, lunch and the like.

Pedometers: A fun idea for tech-heads, but unless you can maintain the same stride throughout your walk,

HIKING

MARK BUGNASKI
Hitting hardwood on boardwalk at Calvert Cliffs State Park.

which is difficult on varied terrain, they're not very useful. Instead, figure out how far you can walk, consistently, in an hour and apply that as a rule of thumb.

Water: Scouts are taught to take canteens, but technology provides lighter, smaller containers if you know you're going to be away from water for a long time. This is much more important in extreme cold or heat. But ask ahead of time if water's available, if you can. Water weighs a lot, so if you don't have to carry it don't.

Some hiking trails to try

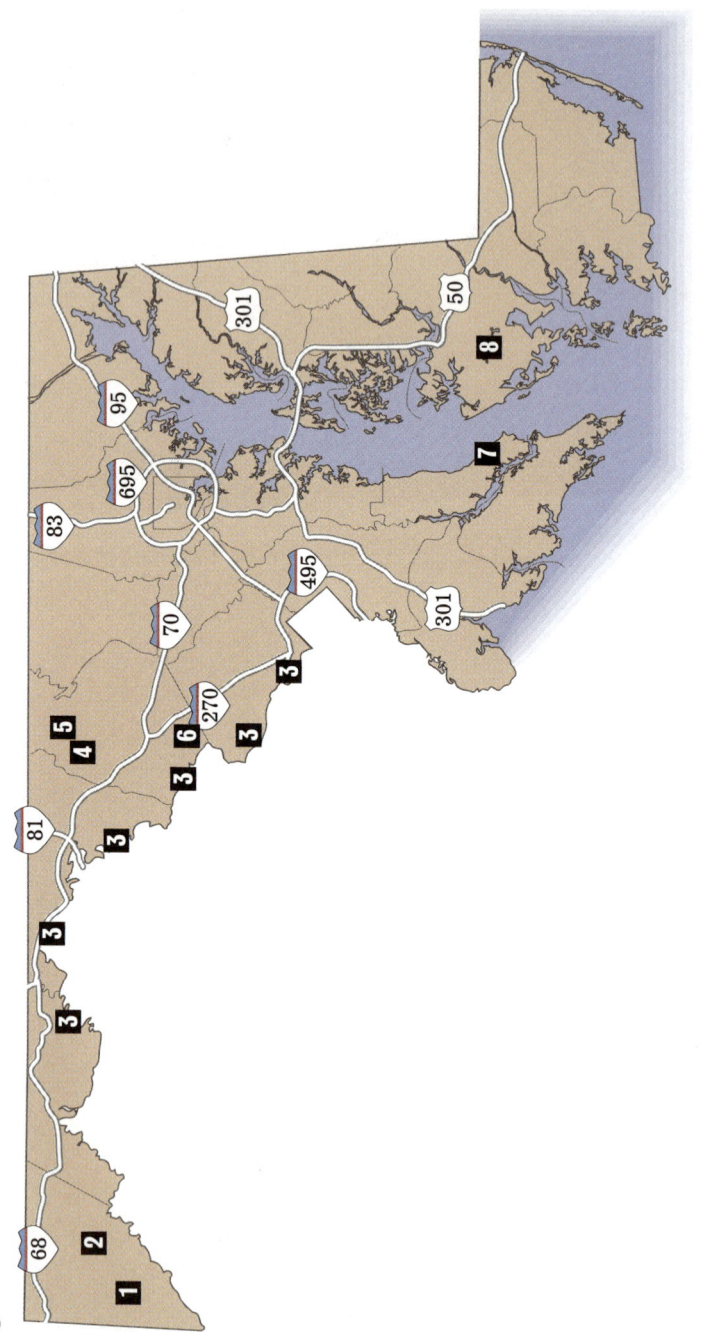

192

Some hiking trails to try

1. Backbone Mountain
2. Savage River State Forest
3. C&O Canal
4. South Mountain
5. Catoctin Mountain Park
6. Sugarloaf Mountain
7. Calvert Cliffs State Park
8. Blackwater National Wildlife Refuge

BIKING

On a roll with nature

BY STEVE MCKERROW

The big rock in the center of the road ahead is moving.

As we pedal nearer and apply the brakes, however, we discover the rock is actually a turtle – perhaps a terrapin, the Maryland state reptile? The plaid-shelled creeper is making its way steadily across the asphalt and seems oblivious to our approach.

My wife and I get off our bikes and squat down, watching as the turtle completes the crossing and disappears into the long grass beside the road. Looking beyond, across a span of marsh water, we suddenly notice that several rocks in the water also hold fat turtles, basking in the late October sun.

Not far along the creek, a great blue heron stalks the shallows, and we study its patient fishing technique – until our attention is drawn overhead by the raucous honks of Canada geese. A dozen or more circle in a ragged "V," preparing for a landing in a denuded cornfield.

Then, even higher up and soaring in circles, we spy a bald eagle.

This is bicycling in Maryland. Our self-guided ride through the Blackwater National Wildlife Refuge, a 314,000-acre wetlands preserve south of Cambridge, covers an easily pedaled loop of about eight miles.

Bicycling magazine in 1993 named the Blackwater tour among the nation's top 10 destinations for bicycling tourists. (For information, call the refuge: [410] 228-2677.)

And only from a bicycle can you sense so intimate a feeling of oneness with

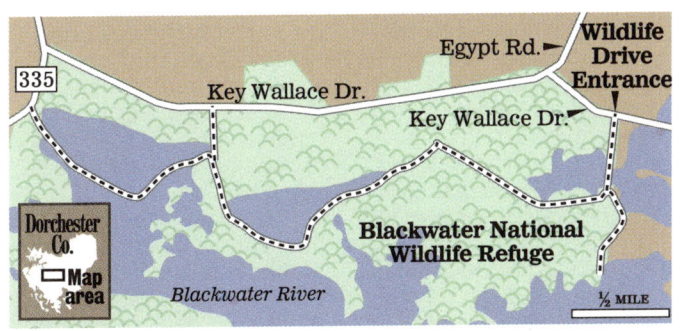

Bikers and bird-watchers alike flock to the eight-mile trail at Blackwater.

BIKING

PERRY THORSVIK

A tired biker rests at a Cycle Across America stop.

nature – hiking and canoeing work, too, but a bike can take you farther, faster.

Is a nature ride too tame? Try this:

You straddle your bike shoulder to shoulder with perhaps 1,000 other cyclists in front of Havre de Grace High School. Suddenly, everybody's clipping into his pedals and starting to move. Soon, this colorfully attired mass hums through the Susquehanna River town, starting the 1996 Cycle Across Maryland bicycling vacation.

For the next six days, you pedal some 350 miles, looping west to Carroll County, south through Howard and Montgomery counties and back north to Bel Air. You camp in tents on high school athletic fields and share communal meals. You get stiff and sore and, at the end, wildly exhilarated for having accomplished a significant physical feat.

That's bicycling in Maryland, too.

Still too tame? Then picture this:

You stand near the 3,100-foot summit of Marsh Hill in McHenry, near Deep Creek Lake. Down below, the Wisp Ski Resort looks about the size of a model railroad building. You snug the strap of your helmet, take a deep breath and get your mountain bike going. You move slowly at first, but the terrain steepens and soon you're bombing down the ski trails, traversing the face of rocky slopes or negotiating narrow "single-track" trails through the trees.

That's also bicycling in Maryland.

"Maryland's just a beautiful state to ride in," says Harvey J. Muller, bicycle/pedestrian coordinator for the Maryland State Highway Administration.

"In a short time span, you can go from the mountains to the sea, from hilly terrain to flat and easy riding," says Pat Bernstein, the executive director and founder of Cycle Across Maryland.

Muller's job proves the state's cycle-ability. The federal Inter-Modal Surface Transportation Efficiency Act of 1991 required each state to create a bicycle/pedestrian coordinator post, but Maryland's job dates to the early 1970s. The state followed the lead of Washington and Oregon to become the third in the nation to integrate bicycle planning into the tranportation system.

Muller says his office responds daily to information requests about cycling, and not only from Marylanders. The office sends out 400,000 to 500,000 packets of cycling literature a year – much of it safety information, but also including resources to plan riding in Maryland – to callers across the nation and even from abroad.

"Maryland got some nice magazine articles recently in Europe," says Muller.

The bicycle coordinator took his position in 1994, after earlier working on State Highway Administration plans for the BWI Bike Trail. That loop around Baltimore-Washington International Airport, due completion in 1998, connects to the 14-mile Baltimore & Annapolis Railroad Trail, a popular asphalt-paved track along a former railroad right-of-way, which connects Annapolis and Glen Burnie.

And that Anne Arundel County system is merely representative of a handful of other such bike-trail systems in the state.

Equipment

Bike riders tend to divide into two distinct camps: "roadies" and "off roaders." Their choice of mount determines their category: a road bike – the traditional thin-tire, drop-handlebar bike still known generically as a 10-speed (although now boasting up to 24 gears); or a mountain bike – the sturdy, fat-tire machine with a more upright seating position and wide gear range, which conquers rougher terrain.

Quality entry-level bikes of each variety start in the $300-$400 range and head on up to the stratosphere of titanium-framed

197

BIKING | best sites

PERRY THORSVIK

Gloves hang out to dry after a sweaty ride.

custom machines costing $3,000 and more.

In both camps, riding can range from casual weekend outings to serious fitness training and racing. In addition, many riders commute to and from work on either style of bike – or aboard a category known as "hybrids" or "city bikes," built to combine the advantage of road and mountain styles. (Commuting is enhanced in the Baltimore region by the 1996 adoption of a policy that allows bikes aboard the Mass Transit Administration's Light Rail system.)

Best sites: Road biking

The big event in Maryland for recreational roadies – although many mountain bikers also participate – is the annual Cycle Across Maryland. In 1997, it is scheduled July 26 to 31, beginning at Bowie State University and covering a 300-mile circular route through Central Maryland. (Overnight stops include LaPlata, Lusby, Harwood, Clarksville and Largo.) A preparation rally is also scheduled May 3 at the

National Wildlife Visitors Center in Prince George's County. For information on both events, call (888) 226-7433.

Many road riders also take part in charitable rides sponsored through the year and across the state. Riders collect pledges to participate in these supported tours, and principal sponsors include:

- The American Lung Association of Maryland, whose annual Chesapeake Bay Bike Tour is usually scheduled the first week of June. Call (800) 642-1184 for details on this and other rides.
- The National Multiple Sclerosis Society Maryland Chapter, whose annual MS 150 ride is usually scheduled on Memorial Day weekend from Washington College in Chestertown. Call (800) 344-4867 for details and dates for at least three other rides later in the year.

Most truly committed roadies will also do at least one "century" ride a year, a supported route of 100 miles covered in 12 hours or less. Many of these events are supported by local bicycling clubs. Three good ones :

- The Annapolis Spring Century of the Annapolis Bicycle Club, scheduled in mid-May. Call (410) 721-9151.
- The Hunt Valley Hundred of the Baltimore Bicycling Club, the first Saturday of October in Baltimore County. Call (410) 484-0306.
- The Seagull Century, an Eastern Shore tour sponsored by Salisbury State University that was voted in 1995 among *Bicycling* magazine's top 10 centuries in the country. It's held in early fall. Call (410) 548-2530.

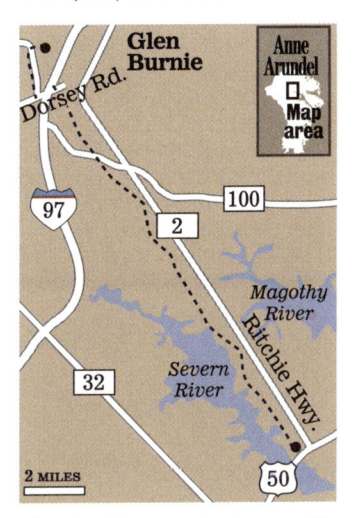

The Baltimore & Annapolis Trail runs 13.3 miles.

Most clubs also offer weekly or more frequent rides of various distances and for riders of varying ability. Check the state's "Bicycling in Maryland" publication for a comprehensive list of clubs.

Best sites: Mountain biking

The state Department of Natural Resources and the State Highway Administration jointly publish a pamphlet, "Bike Trails Through Maryland," that lists more than 50 state parks and other preserves that offer

BIKING | best sites

biking opportunities. (Contact Muller's office, [800] 252-8776.)

Among the most popular:

- The Northern Central Railroad Trail, which reaches from Hunt Valley (beginning off Paper Mill Road, east of York Road in Baltimore County) north into Pennsylvania. The hard dirt track follows the Gunpowder Falls. Call Gunpowder State Park, (410) 592-2897.
- The Baltimore & Annapolis Trail in Anne Arundel County. Call Anne Arundel County Parks, (410) 222-6244.
- The Anacostia Tributaries Trail System, in Prince George's County. Call the Maryland National Capital Park and Planning Commission, (301) 952-3522.
- The Chesapeake and Ohio Canal, along the Potomac River from Cumberland to Washington. To get information (and check on damage from floods in 1996), call (301) 739-4200.

For other mountain-bike opportunities, a pair of prominent organizations are:

- The Maryland Association of Mountain Bike Operators, based in Towson. Call (410) 337-2453.
- The CAPYBARA Mountain Bike Club, in Prince George's and Anne Arundel counties. Call (301) 805-1649.

In the summer months, the Wisp Ski Resort in Garrett County promotes mountain biking on its trails, including rental of bikes and helmets. Call (301) 387-4911. The Whitetail Ski Area in Pennsylvania, north of Hagerstown, also promotes mountain biking. Call (717) 328-9400.

Etiquette

Because mountain bikers must often share trails in nature areas with other users, such as hikers and horseback riders, follow a code of conduct:

1. Yield the right of way to all other trail users.

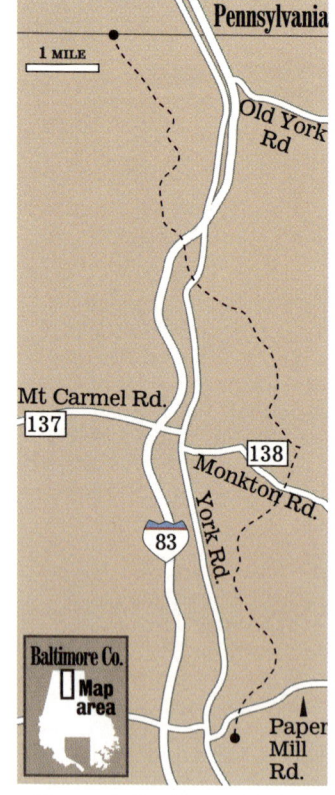

The 19.7-mile Northern Central Trail follows the Gunpowder Falls.

BIKING | etiquette

AMY DAVIS

Certain trails at Loch Raven Reservoir are open to mountain bikers.

2. Slow down and use caution when approaching or overtaking another trail user.

3. Maintain control of your speed at all times.

4. Stay on designated trails to avoid trampling native vegetation and to minimize potential erosion.

5. Do not disturb wildlife or livestock.

6. Do not litter.

7. Respect private and public property.

8. Be self-sufficient.

9. Practice minimum impact bicycling by "taking only pictures and leaving only waffle prints (tire tracks)."

10. Always wear a helmet.

BIKING | safety

Safety

Since October 1995, Maryland has had a law requiring all bicycle riders under the age of 16 to wear helmets.

But cycling authorities universally recommend that all riders wear helmets while riding, always. Costs range from about $30 upward for adult models. And information from the office of the state bicycling/pedestrian coordinator offers three tips for checking for correct fit.

1. The shake test. The helmet should not move around significantly when you shake your head back and forth. If it does, get a smaller size or adjust the pads inside.

2. The open-mouth test. When you buckle your chin strap, open your mouth widely. You should feel the helmet press firmly against the top of your head.

3. The peel-off test. If you can "peel" the helmet off your head from front or rear, without unfastening the chin strap, the straps need adjustment.

Many experts also recommend these safety accessories:

- Cycling gloves. They help you grip the handlebars, provide padding against road vibration and also offer palm protection if you fall.

- Cycling shoes. Many feature reinforced soles, with cleats that clip into pedals. Others have tread patterns that help grip pedal surfaces. With these, you should have toe straps and clips to keep your foot on the pedal.

- A rear-view mirror. Fitting on handlebar, helmet or

JERRY JACKSON
Family rides are popular on the Northern Central Trail.

eyeglasses, these little devices offer riders a chance to see what the awful noise is coming up behind.

- A pump and at least a minimal tool kit. The ability to cope with flat tires and other problems on the road or trail can save riders much frustration.

Resources

If you are a cycling newcomer to Maryland, a relative cycling beginner or even an experienced rider, you will benefit from one telephone call to the state's bicycle hot line at (800) 252-8776. (Or write: Bicycle and Pedestrian Coordinator, Maryland State Highway Administration, 707 N. Calvert St. - C-502, Baltimore, Md 21202.)

The office will send a free packet of "everything-you-need-to-know" cycling information, including the comprehensive "Bicycling in Maryland: A Bicycle Information Guide." The pamphlet offers county-by-county lists of cycling clubs, sources for numerous cycling maps published by the state and counties and a variety of other useful information, from helmet and safety advice to information on how to get your bike across the state's toll bridges.

Another good information resource in Maryland is the League of American Bicyclists, the nation's oldest riders group, which has headquarters in Baltimore. It publishes a magazine and a variety of other material, and membership brings planning resources for tours as ambitious as coast-to-coast crossing, as well as an annual guide to bicycle tour operators around the world. Call the LAB at (410) 539-3399.

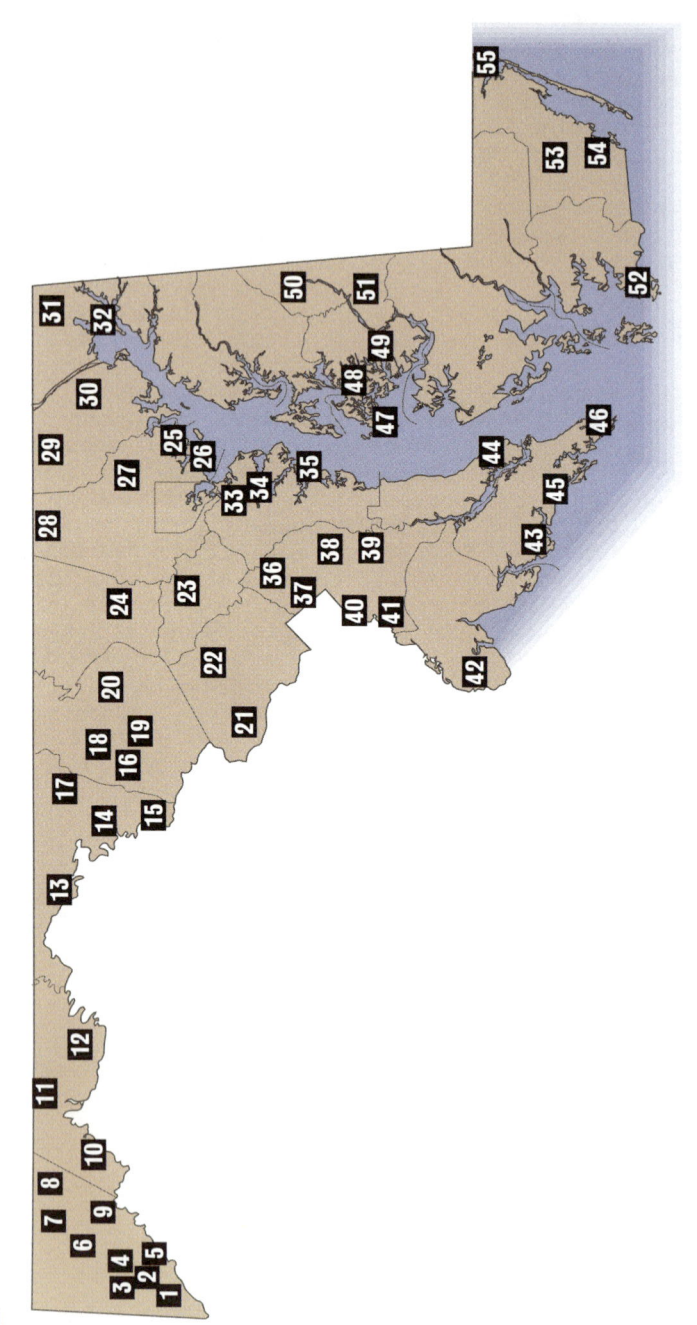

State cycling trails

204

State cycling trails

1. Herrington Manor State Park
2. Swallow Falls State Park
3. Garrett State Forest
4. Deep Creek Lake State Park
5. Potomac State Forest
6. Savage River State Forest
7. New Germany State Park
8. Casselman River Bridge State Park
9. Big Run State Park
10. Dans Mountain State Park
11. Rocky Gap State Park
12. Green Ridge State Park
13. Fort Frederick State Park
14. C&O Canal
15. Gathland State Park
16. South Mountain State Park
17. Washington Monument State Park
18. Greenbrier State Park
19. Gambrill State Park
20. Cunningham Falls State Park
21. Seneca Creek State Park
22. Patuxent River State Park
23. Patapsco Valley State Park
24. Morgan Run Natural Environmental Area
25. Hart-Miller Island State Park
26. North Point State Park
27. Gunpowder Falls State Park
28. Northern Central Railroad Trail
29. Rocks State Park
30. Susquehanna State Park
31. Fair Hill Natural Resources Management Area
32. Elk Neck State Park
33. BWI Trail
34. Baltimore & Annapolis Trail
35. Sandy Point State Park
36. Anacostia Tributaries Trail System
37. Lake Artemesia Trail
38. Rosaryville State Park
39. Merkle Wildlife Sanctuary
40. Henson Creek Stream Valley Park
41. Cedarville State Forest
42. Smallwood State Park
43. St. Clements Island State Park
44. Calvert Cliffs State Park
45. St. Mary's River State Park
46. Point Lookout State Park
47. Black Walnut Point
48. Wye Island Natural Resources Management Area
49. Wye Oak State Park
50. Tuckahoe State Park
51. Martinak State Park
52. Janes Island State Park
53. Pocomoke State Forest
54. Pocomoke River State Park
55. Assateague State Park

SKIING

Having a hill of a time

By Sandra McKee

Up here, among the low, floating clouds on Marsh Mountain, the trees are dressed in their winter coats of frosty ice and the sun takes on the appearance of a silver bulb high above the shimmering slopes.

This is Garrett County, Maryland's ski country. The Wisp Ski Area on this 3,080-foot mountain is the state's only alpine resort.

"I spend most of my free time here," says Lee Railey, who has been skiing at Wisp for the past 14 years. "This is definitely one of the best places to ski in the region.

"I began as a 2-year-old, skiing with my dad, and I still ski with my dad," says Railey, 16, who has skied throughout the East and in Aspen in the West. "What I love about it is the sense of freedom you get while being in control and the feeling that you and the snow form a sort of bond as you're coming down the side of a mountain."

Bonding with the snow, getting exercise and enjoying an exhilarating day outdoors are what skiing is about whether you chose downhill, cross country or snowboarding.

And these days, ski manufacturers are seeking to build ease of learning, safety and excitement into new equipment. There are parabolic-shaped skis, snowboards and something called snowrunners, which are the equivalent of in-line skates on snow. All of them are enticing new skiers and encouraging veterans to expand their repertoires. Railey, an avid snowboarder, says his father, 34, is experimenting with snowboarding.

Ski areas also are becoming more user-friendly. Wisp, for example, has a World Wide Web site (http://www.gcnet.net/wisp), an all-day day-care center affiliated with the national Ski Wee program and is adding the Rossignol Adventure Center, which offers alternatives to traditional Alpine skiing.

JOHN MAKELY
Resorts like Wisp are catering to families.

SKIING

SKIING | downhill

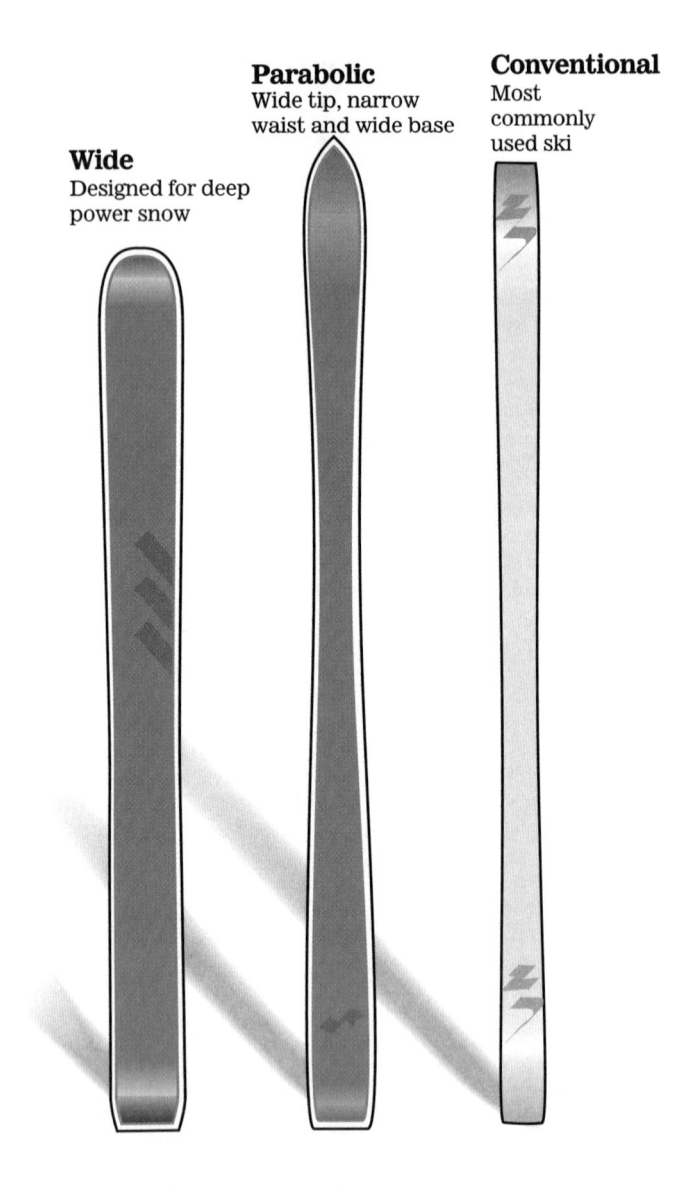

Wide
Designed for deep power snow

Parabolic
Wide tip, narrow waist and wide base

Conventional
Most commonly used ski

Different types of downhill skis.

"It's like an amusement park," said Derek Versteegen, who acts as Wisp's group sales manager, Web master, marketing assistant and ski patrol member. "Every year, we're adding a new ride."

The adventure center offers rentals and instruction in the use of the parabolic "cut ski," snowboards and snowrunners. Railey has signed on as one of six apprentice instructors under the direction of Bill Cox, who at 40 has been skiing for 25 years and instructing for 14.

"I had a passion for skiing," says Cox. "Now, I have a passion for sharing what I know."

There is a lot to know about the sport, but there are also a lot of good resources and ski instructors out there ready to help someone get started or improve on what he already knows.

Here is a look at the three major types of skiing activities.

Downhill

You picture beautiful, sun-filled days, schussing down the slopes with the wind in your face. And it can be that way for almost anyone who has a willingness to learn. New ski shapes are making it easier to stand up, be balanced and learn. New bindings with quick releases have nearly eliminated leg and ankle injuries.

"For most people, the hard part is getting started," said Mary Jo Tarallo, public relations director for the Ski Industries Association. "If they walk into a ski shop, they're intimidated, or they view getting in their car and driving to a ski resort as a major effort. That's not the case with us. People can call us, and we'll send them a basic information snow sport kit that can be your guide to getting started."

Tarallo says the kit (available by calling [703] 506-4232) tells the novice skier how to choose equipment, dress for the sport and even save money.

Maryland's only in-state ski resort is Wisp, but also within an easy ride are three Pennsylvania resorts: Whitetail, Ski Liberty and Ski Roundtop.

WISP: In McHenry in Garrett County. Three hours

JOHN MAKELY

The lifts at Wisps begin running as early as Nov. 2.

SKIING | downhill

Ski resorts in and around Maryland

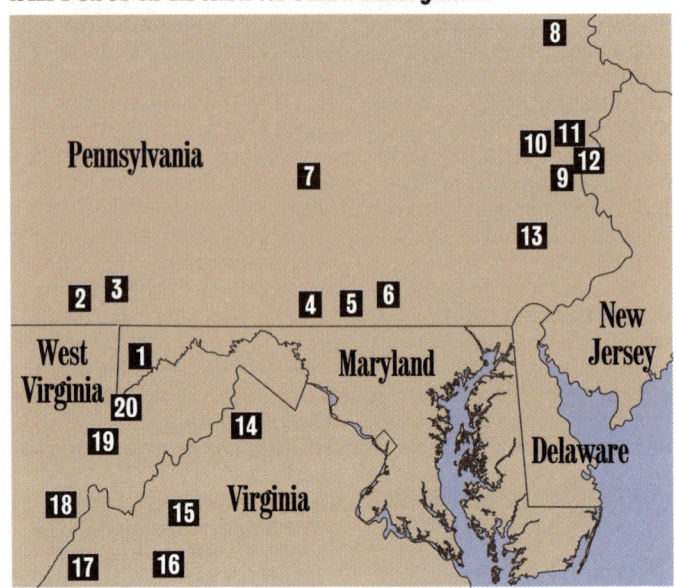

1. Wisp
2. Seven Springs
3. Hidden Valley
4. Whitetail
5. Ski Liberty
6. Ski Roundtop
7. Tussey Mountain
8. Elk Mountain
9. Camelback
10. Blue Mountain
11. Big Boulder
12. Jack Frost
13. Doe Mountain
14. Bryce Mountain
15. Massanutten
16. Wintergreen
17. The Homestead
18. Snowshoe/Silvercreek
19. Ski Timberline
20. Canaan Valley

from Baltimore. Half-day programs for $45, full-day programs for $59; Ski-Wee child-care program, $5 to $6.50 or $25 to $32 daily for Wisp Resort Hotel guests and $36 daily for non-hotel guests; Adventure Center programs to familiarize skiers with new equipment; lift tickets, $32 to $40; rental equipment, $19 to $38. Night skiing. Call (301) 387-4911.

Ski Liberty: Near Gettysburg in Carroll Valley, Pa. About 90 minutes northwest of Baltimore. Half-day programs, $50 to $60; full-day programs, $60 to $74; play care, ages 1-10, $5 per hour; daily adult lift tickets, $29-$37; rental equipment, $20 to $26. Night skiing. Call (717) 642-8282.

Ski Roundtop: In Lewisberry, Pa. About 90 minutes north of Baltimore. Half-day programs, $45 to $55; Full-day programs, $59 to $69; play care, ages 18 months to 10 years, $5 an hour; daily adult lift tickets, $29 to $36;

210

rental equipment, $19 to $25. Night skiing. Call (717) 432-9631.

Whitetail: In Mercersburg, Pa. About 90 minutes northwest of Baltimore. Half-day programs, $50 to $75; full-day programs, $60 to $75; child care, $4 to $6 an hour or $28 to $38 for a full day that includes lunch and snacks. Daily adult lift tickets, $30 to $42; rental equipment, $20 to $25. Night skiing. Call (717) 328-9400.

Snowboarding

The snowboard is about as close to skiing as the surfboard is to swimming. As one snowboard enthusiast has said: "About the only thing you'll find to be the same in both sports is that you slide on the snow."

Once the exclusive domain of kids and thrill seekers, the sport is attracting older adults, like Lee Railey's father and Joey Kramer's mom and dad from Annapolis.

"When I first got into it," says Kramer, who at 17 has been snowboarding for five years, "you'd only see teenagers. Now, it's anyone from 5 to 50 and 60. My dad and sisters started snowboarding after I did and then my mom started, because they all saw how much more fun it can be than skiing."

The average age of the snowboarder has risen to 25 during the past five years – 70 percent men and 30 percent women. And its credibility

Snowboard

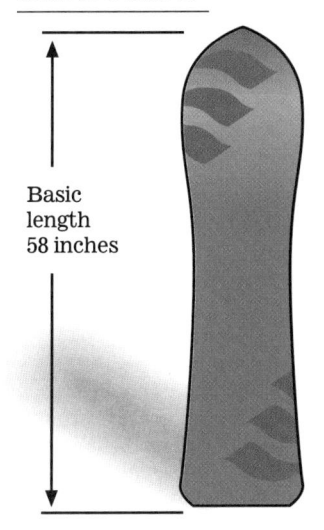

Basic length 58 inches

You can rent snowboards to find a style that fits you.

has been helped by being designated an Olympic sport.

"People tend to think snowboarders make the slopes dangerous," said Railey. "And freestylers really do need a snowboard park to do all the acrobatic things they want to do. But from my experiences on the slopes, the real danger comes from [any] skier who attempts to ski or snowboard on a trail that's beyond their experience level. I've been run over at least three times."

But there are commonsense rules on the slopes and most people follow them.

Wisp's adventure center is ready to instruct snowboarders on the use of equipment, Ski Liberty offers a snow-

SKIING | cross country

boarding park, Ski Roundtop has doubled its snowboarding equipment and Whitetail is offering a new program called "Quick-Carve" designed to teach snowboarding basics to intermediate and advanced skiers.

Cross country skiing

This is where it all began. In Scandinavia, people slapped a couple of boards on the bottom of their shoes and invented one of the earliest forms of transportation, 4,500 years ago.

Now we do it for fun. And it can be many different things to many people – invigorating, relaxing, challenging. It can be solitary or a way to enjoy the outdoors with a group of friends.

It can be done in your own back yard, if it's big enough. Or it can be done at a number of Maryland state parks.

"I can remember a few years ago during one of our big snowstorms skiing up Route 7 when the traffic was bumper-to-bumper with people trying to get to work," said Roger Lohr, director of education for the Ski Industries Association, who lives in Eldersburg. "Cross country offers so much diversity. And on the Nordic skis, nature is so much more affecting. You can take your time, be out in it and see it all around you. You can't go Nordic skiing without being affected by nature."

JOHN MAKELY
Hitting the trails at New Germany State Park.

Cross country skiing hit its peak in the late 1970s and early 1980s, but, according to a National Sporting Goods Association survey, about 3.5 million people participate in the sport annually. The recent creation of shorter cross country skis, which provide as much stability as the longer ones, has made the sport more accessible and is again attracting more participants.

Among the cross country trails available in Maryland are: Oregon Ridge Park, Cockeysville; Cunningham Falls State Park, Thurmont; and New Germany State Park, Herrington Manor State Park and Swallow Falls State Park in Garrett County.

JOHN MAKELY

Snowboarders are becoming a common sight at Wisp.

Equipment

Downhill and cross country skiers should determine how often they are going skiing before rushing out to buy. And both should rent first to determine the right equipment for individual needs. These days, with shaped skis, there are a number of options. In general, a downhill or cross country skier will need skis, boots, bindings and poles. A local ski shop can help. Downhill skiers can rent at the ski resort. Cross country skiers

SKIING | equipment

JOHN MAKELY

Safe skiing starts with a class in fundamentals.

should determine whether there are rental shops near trails before going.

Snowboarders should go first to a local snowboard shop. Generally, if you rent from your local shop, a portion of the rental fee can be applied toward the purchase of equipment. As downhill and cross country skiers have choices, so do snowboarders, so explore your options among freestyle, freeride and freecarve (also known as alpine) boards.

Dress in layers. First, the wicking layer: This is the one next to the skin, usually consisting of long underwear. Look for synthetics that have "wicking" power, which means fibers that will move (wick) moisture away from your skin and pass it through the fabric so it will evaporate. Some brand-name materials to look for: ThermaStat, Thermax, CoolMax and Comfortel. Silk also works.

Next, the insulating layer: This layer includes shirts, sweaters, vests and pull-overs. The layer's purpose is to keep heat in and cold out. Wool is effective, but synthetic fibers, such as fleece, are popular and dry faster. Do not wear jeans. Denim is not waterproof, so water will soak through, making you wet and miserable.

Finally, the weather protection layer: The outer wear or shell serves as a guard against the elements. The shell's purpose is to repel water from snow, sleet or rain and block the wind, while letting perspiration evaporate. Choose a lightweight, versatile garment made of waterproof and breathable material.

Snowboarders are advised to consult a local snowboard shop as a source for proper clothing and apparel, because it differs in style (more loose fitting) from normal ski wear.

Hats are a must – 80 percent of your body heat escapes through your head.

Wear gloves – in cold weather, your hands and feet are the first to get cold. Look for a glove that has a waterproof, breathable shell. Check the amount of insulation: 200 grams of Thinsulate will keep your hands warmer and drier than 75 grams will. Mittens, in general, keep hands warmer.

Socks can be made from the same material as long underwear, so moisture is wicked away and feet stay dry. Other sock materials, silk, wool, nylon and combinations of those fibers, also work. A light to medium weight sock works best.

Safety

No matter what kind of skiing or snowboarding you're doing, you should follow the Responsibility Code endorsed by the National Ski Areas Association, the National Ski Patrol and Professional Ski Instructors of America.

1. Always ski in a manner that does not endanger others. Always stay in control and be able to stop or avoid other people or objects. Never put anyone else at risk.

2. Ski within yourself and adapt your skiing to your ability as well as the weather and terrain conditions.

3. People ahead of you have the right of way. It is your responsibility to avoid them. Remember, skiers are focusing on what's in front of them. Skiers and snowboarders have blind spots. It's like driving a car; you're the one responsible if you hit someone from behind.

4. When making a pass, make sure to give another skier plenty of room, so if either of you turn or fall unexpectedly, you won't hit each other.

5. You must not stop where you obstruct a trail or are not visible from above. If you want or need a break, move to the side - and if you fall, get out of the way as quickly as possible.

6. Don't cross or enter a trail or restart after stopping without making sure no other skiers are nearby. Always remember to look uphill and yield to others.

7. If you are climbing uphill, use the side of the trail. If you lose a piece of equipment, don't just stop and climb back to get it. Again, it's like driving. This time, you're on a one-way street. You don't want to be going the wrong way. Go to the side of trail and walk back.

8. Observe all posted signs and warnings. Don't ski closed trails and stay out of closed areas and don't ski fast on trails marked for slow skiing.

9. If you see an accident, stop to determine if you can help. If it's serious, contact the ski patrol. If your skiing

ability is limited, flag down another skier to go for help.

10. Before using any lift, you must have the knowledge and ability to load, ride and unload safely.

Resources

- Ski Industries America, P.O. Box 3470, McLean, Va. 22103. SIA's Winter Active Sports Kit is designed to arm you with basic knowledge to get started, and in winter, call (703) 506-4232. Also, try SnowLink on the World Wide Web at www.snowlink.com.
- Baltimore Ski Club. Plans ski trips and meets the second Tuesday of each month at the American Legion Hall in Parkville. For information, call (410) 825-7669.
- Potomac Appalachian Trail Club, 118 Park St., Vienna, Va., has a division called Ski Touring Section, which puts out a newsletter called Upslope with a calendar of events. Membership information: Douglas Lesar at (301) 926-5831 before 9 p.m.
- Deep Creek Lake-Garrett County Promotion Council for information on activities and lodging: (301) 334-1948; e-mail at GC-Tourism@gcc.cc.md.us; Web site at www.gcnet.net/gctourism/gct.html.

Books

"Skiing America '97" (includes snowboarding), by Charles A. Leocha, World Leisure Corporation, 177 Paris St., Boston, Mass. 02128. Telephone: (617) 569-

JOHN MAKELY

Skis of all shapes and sizes are available.

1966, fax: (617) 561-7654.
E-mail wleisure@aol.com.

"Skiing on a Budget," by Claire Walter, Betterway Books, 1507 Dana Avenue, Cincinnati, Ohio 45207. Telephone: (800) 289-0963.

"I Know Absolutely Nothing About Skiing," by Steve Eubanks and Robert LaMarche, Rutledge Hill Press, 211 Seventh Avenue North, Nashville, Tenn. 37219.

Magazines

Cross Country Skier 1823 Fremont Ave. S., Minneapolis, Minn. 55403. Telephone/fax: (612) 377-0312.

Eastern Edge Snowboard P.O. Box 350, Bondville, Vermont 05340. Telephone: (802) 297-3432.

Ski Magazine 2 Park Avenue, NY, NY. 10016. Telephone: (212) 779-5113.

Skier Magazine P.O. Box 305, Stowe, Vermont 05672. Telephone: (802) 253-8282.

Skiing Magazine 2 Park Avenue, Fifth Floor, New York, N.Y. 10016. Telephone: (212) 779-5016.

Appendix

Playing it safe in the outdoors

Keep all medicines and toxic substances securely sealed in unbreakable containers.

Test all electrical equipment before departure.

Pack knives, axes and any sharp objects in secure covers. Always wear shoes that are appropriate to the planned itinerary.

A basic first-aid kit inventory:

Sterile gauze pads in a variety of two-by-two and four-by-four-inch pads
Roller gauze: Kling or Kerlix
Dressing: Telfa pads (coat with antibacterial ointment or petroleum)
One-inch adhesive tape
Butterfly bandages or Steristrips assortment
Ace Wrap, 3 inches wide
Large compress: Use feminine hygiene pads
Moleskin (for the prevention and treatment of friction and blisters). SecondSkin (When the blister forms, it will provide soothing protection in most instances.)
Triangular bandage (for holding dressings in place, attaching splints and creating slings)
Cotton swabs
Cotton balls
Antiseptic cleansing pads
Absorbent cotton
Antiseptic soap
Aspirin or acetaminophen
Thermometer
Hydrogen peroxide
Rubbing alcohol
Sunscreen
Insect repellent
Cortisone cream
Calamine lotion
Antihistamine
Water-purification tablets
Salt tablets Benadryl
Diarrhea medicine
Snakebite kit
Betadine

Equipment and accessories

Tweezers
Needle
Single-sided razor blade
Bandage scissors
Safety pins
Low-reading thermometer
Space blanket
Flashlight with extra batteries and bulbs

Treating common injuries

Bruises

Do not rub or massage the bruised area. If the bruise is on the leg, rest it horizontally with the feet propped up. Apply an ice pack to the affected area for 10 minutes.

Bites

If the skin is broken from a bite, sterilize the area and wrap the wound to stop any bleeding. Animal bites require immediate medical attention to prevent infection, tetanus or rabies.

Insect stings

Scrape any stinger out of the skin. Do not squeeze or pull the stinger with fingers or tweezers as this will force the release of more venom into the wound. Wash the affected area with soap and water. Apply hydrocortisone or anti-inflammatory salve, and ice the affected area to reduce swelling. Watch for the symptoms of an allergic reaction, such as a drop in blood pressure or trouble in breathing. If these symptoms occur, seek immediate medical attention.

Ticks

To protect yourself from ticks, proper coverage is important. Wear light-colored long pants and long-sleeve shirts; tuck pant bottoms into your socks. Treat all clothing with DEET. Carefully remove any ticks embedded in the skin. Gently pull the tick out with tweezers. Grasp close to the tick's head with the tweezers and pull firmly and steadily. Do not twist. Check to see that the head has remained attached to its body. If the head remains embedded in the skin, the area may become infected. Once the tick is removed, cleanse the area thoroughly and check for any signs of a rash. A rash, headache, muscle stiffness or unusual fatigue after a tick bite may indicate Lyme disease. A rash accompanied by a fever may indicate a case of Rocky Mountain spotted fever. If you have any of these symptoms, contact a doctor immediately.

Sprains

The most commonly sprained joint is the ankle. Sprains usually result from rolling over on the outside of the foot, causing the ligaments supporting the joint to stretch or tear. A sprain is characterized by painful swelling of the affected joint, and the inability to move the joint without increasing the pain. The symptoms of a severe sprain are similar to those of a fracture. If there is any doubt as to the type of injury suffered, treat it as a fracture.

First aid for a sprained ankle: Put the patient into a comfortable position and apply a cold compress for 30 minutes. Cover the joint with a pad, securing it with a bandage wrapped twice around the foot. Wrap the bandage across the top of the foot and up around the ankle. Wrap the bandage in a sequence of figures of eight overlapping the previous turn by three-quarters of its width. Bandage the area until the foot, ankle and lower leg are covered. Secure the loose end. Seek medical aid.

APPENDIX | first aid

Slivers and splinters

Use tweezers to gently pull any small slivers that project from the skin. To remove slivers that are embedded under the skin, sterilize the sharp end of a needle and gently slit the skin over the sliver and lift the flaps with the needlepoint. With the area exposed, grasp the sliver and pull it from the skin. If there is any resistance from the sliver, seek medical attention.

Poisonous plants

If you come into contact with a poisonous plant, wash the affected area with soap and water, rub with alcohol and apply calamine lotion. Wash all clothing that has come in contact with poisonous plants. Seek medical attention if a severe reaction occurs.

Knocked-out tooth

Clean the tooth with a rinse of water or saliva. Rinse the mouth with an antibacterial. If bacteria enter the tooth, they can cause infection and loss of the tooth. Gently place the tooth back into its socket. Hold the tooth in place with a finger or by biting down on a clean cloth. To reduce the pain, take aspirin. Do not place the aspirin directly onto the affected area. Seek medical attention immediately. The tooth may reattach itself to the bone if properly splinted within two hours.

Fractures and dislocations

It is not possible to diagnose a fracture without an X-ray. If you think a bone is fractured, treat as such. A fracture is characterized by severe pain, the inability to place weight onto or move the affected area, or the area is obviously misshapen. Never try to reset a dislocated joint yourself. Splint the dislocated limb in the position in which you found it. If the injury is a shoulder dislocation, apply a sling to hold the joint in place.

Broken leg

Place padding between the two legs, gently lift the uninjured leg and move it close to the fractured leg. Wrap a bandage in figures of eight around the ankles and tie it as securely as possible. Gently tie both legs together in several places. Do not tie the legs at the site of the fracture.

Broken lower arm

Gently bend the arm and splint it across the chest. Splint the arm in a bent position across the chest. Tie the splint in at least two places near (not on) the site of injury. Any rigid item can be used as a splint. Place the arm in a splint, making sure the fingers are slightly higher than the elbow.

Head injuries

Dressing a head wound: If the wound is not serious, cover the affected area with a sterile pad and apply steady pressure. More serious head injuries require immediate medical attention. Cover the wound with a clean pad and gently hold the pad in place. Do not press hard as this may force foreign particles or pieces of the skull into the brain. Roll a bandage two or three times around the head, securing the bandage with a safety pin. Watch for signs of clear fluid drainage. If fluid flows from the ear, place a pad on the ear and position the victim down on the draining side to ensure complete drainage. If fluid is draining from the nose, place the victim on his side.

APPENDIX | first aid

APPENDIX | food safety

Eating out the safe way

Packing and transporting food

Call ahead and confirm the availability of sanitary water facilities. Pack bottled water or jugs of safe water. Drinking or hand washing in open water is not safe for food-handling purposes.

Plan simple menus with foods that do not require refrigeration, such as peanut butter, fruits and dried meats.

Take only the amount of food you will use. Pack the smallest available sized jars of condiments.

Pack food directly from the refrigerator. Meat and poultry can be packed while frozen. It will thaw during the trip, extending its safety and shelf-life.

Securely wrap all food in waterproof plastic. Bag foods that may drip or leak, particularly raw meat, poultry or fish. Pack mayonnaise, lettuce and tomato separately and add at mealtime.

Cooler rules

First-in, last-out is the rule for packing a cooler.

Pack two coolers, one for perishables, one for beverages and plain water. Do not repeatedly open the cooler containing perishables. A full cooler will stay colder longer than one that is only partially packed. Pack the remaining space with more ice or with fruit and non-perishable foods.

Use a sturdy plastic, steel or fiberglass cooler, and make sure it's insulated. These are more durable and secure than foam chests. Keep the temperature in the cooler lower than 40 degrees. To that end, remember that large ice blocks keep longer than ice cubes.

Always transport coolers in the passenger area of the car, not the trunk. Keep your cooler insulated at the picnic or camp site with a blanket, tarp, poncho or by partially burying in the sand.

The meat department

Cook all meats thoroughly (no visible pink in the middle, and juices run clear) to reduce the risk of contracting food poisoning or salmonella. Cook red meats to 160 degrees Fahrenheit, ground poultry to 165 degrees and poultry parts to 180. Do not partially grill meats for later use.

Marinate raw meat at home in your refrigerator. If you plan to marinate at the picnic or camp site, use fresh marinade, or boil for five minutes any marinade that has had contact with raw meat, fish and poultry.

Do not precook meats before transport. Precooking is safe only as part of a continuous process - food should go directly from the microwave or range to the grill.

Coals should be very hot before cooking food. After

lighting, wait 30 minutes or longer before cooking. Coals should show a light gray ash coating.

Put all cooked foods on clean plates. Never place cooked food on dishes that held raw meat, fish or poultry. Serve grilled foods immediately while still hot.

To prevent food contamination:

Discard any foods that warm above refrigerator temperature (40 degrees). Food poisoning bacteria grow rapidly at warm temperatures. At the end of the day, if the ice has melted and the food feels warm, discard any meat or poultry left.

Be alert for cross-contamination. Produce, shelf foods and salads can be contaminated with drippings from meat, poultry or fish. Non-perishables, like fruits, vegetables, breads and drinks, do not require refrigeration and should be OK.

Never eat snow or use it for any food-related purpose. Snow can contain organisms that are common in birds' fecal matter and can cause a severe form of food-borne illness.

Keep food as far from trash containers as possible, to avoid flies and bees. Keep foods under fine netting to keep them bug-free. Keep pets, birds and other animals away from the cooking site. When cooking, an awning or tarp will prevent contamination from bird droppings.

Never leave food sitting out in the open, even for short periods. Rodents and insects are common in picnic and camping areas.

Finfish

Clean, scale and gut fish when they are caught. Immediately wrap the fish in plastic and place in a cooler with three to four inches of ice on the bottom, alternating layers of fish and ice. Store the cooler out of the sun and cover with a blanket. Keep live fish on stringers or in live wells where they have enough water for movement and breathing. Fresh fish should be eaten in one to two days or stored frozen. For top quality, use frozen fish in three to six months.

Shellfish

Crabs, lobsters and other shellfish must be kept alive until cooked. Store in live wells or out of water in a bushel or laundry basket under wet burlap. Crabs and lobsters should be eaten the day they're caught. Live oysters can be kept for seven to 10 days; mussels and clams for four to five days. People with liver disorders or weakened immune systems should not eat raw shellfish.

Backpacking food safety

Plan menus with safety, portability and disposal in mind. Pack foods that do not require refrigeration or extensive cooking, or the use of many utensils, such

APPENDIX | food safety

as dried meats, fruits, and nuts; dried noodles and soups; breads and crackers; powdered milk.

When carrying foods that require refrigeration, wrap the food in plastic with a large block of ice and pack these in a sleeping bag. Do not pack too much. Leftovers are prone to spoilage and can weigh you down while hiking.

Pack bottled water, for drinking and washing.

Always assume that fresh water is unsafe for drinking and dish washing. Pack water purification tablets, or a stove for boiling water, in case you have to drink fresh water.

Do not discard food along trails. This encourages infestation by rodents and insects. Burn leftovers in a campfire, or carry plastic bags for garbage. Dump dirty water on dry ground away from fresh water.

Outdoors organizations

The Maryland Department of Natural Resources is usually the first place to turn for information on outdoors activities in the state. The main offices are in the Tawes State Office Building, 580 Taylor Ave., Annapolis, Md. 21401. For general information, call (410) 974-3987 or TTY for the hearing impaired (410) 974-3683.

Some specific numbers to keep on hand:

Department of Natural Resources: Coastal and Watershed Resources Division, (410) 974-5780

Department of Natural Resources: Fisheries, (410) 974-8480

Department of Natural Resources: Heritage And Wildlife Administration, (410) 974-3195

Department of Natural Resources: Forest Service, (410) 974-3776

In a Natural Resources Emergency, 800-628-9944

Natural Resources Police- Communications Office, (410) 974-3181

Parking-reserved/permitted, (410) 974-3496

To report violations in state forests and parks, 1-800-825-PARK

To report poaching, (800) 635-6124

To report fish kills, (410) 974-3238

To report sediment problems, (410) 631-3000

To report forest fires, 911 or 1-800-825-PARK or (410) 461-0050

Natural Resources Police: (Regional offices are open Monday-Saturday, 8 a.m-4 p.m.)

Western Regional Office - Flintstone, (301) 777-7771

Central Regional Office - Owings Mills, (410) 356-7060

Southern Regional Office - Cedarville, (301) 888-1601

Eastern Regional Office - Easton, (410) 822-7551

Johnson Sub-Station - Salisbury, (410) 548-7070

DNR's Becoming an Outdoors- Woman

DNR also offers a program worth checking out: Becoming on Outdoors-Woman. A three-day workshop focusing on hunting and fishing skills, it is designed primarily for women 18 or older. It is held at Catoctin Mountain National Park, where participants stay in dormitories at Camp Round Meadow. For information on dates and to receive a registration form,

APPENDIX — organizations

call Alice Harrison at (410) 974-3545 or write: Becoming an Outdoors-Woman, Department of Natural Resources, Tawes State Office Building D-4, 580 Taylor Ave., Annapolis, Md. 21401.

Women interested in fishing can also contact the Female Anglers Network (FAN) at (888) FISHFAN or (614) 384-5432.

Other organizations to check out

Audubon Naturalist Society of the Central Atlantic States, 8940 Jones Mill Road Chevy Chase, Md. 20815
(301) 652-9188
Fax: (301) 951-7179

C & O Canal Association
P.O. Box 366
Glen Echo, Md. 20812-0366

Chesapeake Bay Foundation
162 Prince George Street
Annapolis, Md. 21401
(410) 268-8816
Fax: (410) 268-6687

Chesapeake Bay Regional Information Service (CRIS)
(800) 662-2747)
Information database; lists agencies involved with Chesapeake region cleanup, education materials and publications available.

Chesapeake Wildlife Heritage, P.O. Box 1745
Easton, Md. 21601
(410) 822-5100
Fax: (410) 822-4016

Ducks Unlimited Inc.
1709 New York Ave, Suite 202
Washington, D.C. 20006
(202) 347-1530

Maryland Conservation Council, 6310 Swords Way
Bethesda, Md. 20817

Maryland Forests Association
6907 Avondale Rd.
Baltimore, Md. 21212
Fax: (410) 823-7215

Maryland Recreation and Parks Association, Inc.
201 Gun Road
Baltimore, Md. 21227
(410) 942-7203

Maryland Wetlands Committee
11194 Douglas Avenue
Marriottsville, Md. 21104
(410) 442-5639

National Audubon Society, Mid-Atlantic Regional Office
1104 Fernwood Avenue, No. 300
Camp Hill, Pa. 17011
(717) 763-4985

National Wildlife Federation
Mid-Atlantic Office
1400 16th Street N.W.
Washington, D.C. 20036
(202) 797-6693

Nature Conservancy
2 Wisconsin Circle, Suite 300
Chevy Chase, Md. 20815
(301) 656-8673

Potomac Appalachian Trail Club , 118 Park St., SE
Vienna, Va. 22180
(703) 242-0315

APPENDIX | organizations

Potomac River Association
P.O. Box 76
Valley Lee, Md. 20692
(301) 475-8366

Potomac River Greenways
Commission
6110 Executive Blvd.,
Suite 300
Rockville, Md. 20852-3903
(301) 984-1908

Sierra Club - Appalachian
Regional Office
Contact: Joy Oakes, Regional Staff Director
69 Franklin St., 2nd floor
Annapolis, Md. 21401
(410) 268-7411

Sierra Club - Western
Maryland
Contact: Louis Bernstein,
Program Chair
Route 8, Box 169
Cumberland, Md. 21502
(301) 777-3212

Sierra Club - Catoctin Group
(Encompassing Carroll,
Frederick and Washington
counties)
P.O. Box 534
Frederick, Md. 21705-0534
Newsletter - Eric Whitenton,
(301) 695-6624
Conservation/outings -
Dan Huebner, (301) 663-0479
Membership - Deanna
Hofmann, (301) 831-7606

Trout Unlimited
1500 Wilson Blvd, Suite 310
Arlington. Va. 22209-2310
(703) 522-0200

Wilderness Society
900 17th Street N.W.
Washington, D.C. 20006
(202) 833-2300

Wildlife Society
5410 Grosvenor Lane
Bethesda, Md. 20814
(301) 897-9770

Further reading

Adventuring in the Chesapeake Bay Area. John Bowen. Sierra Club Books, San Francisco, 1990.

Bay Country. Tom Horton. Johns Hopkins University Press, Baltimore 1987.

Beautiful Swimmers. William W. Warner. Little, Brown and Co. Boston 1976.

Chesapeake Almanac: Following the bay through the seasons. John Page Williams. Tidewater Publishers, Centreville, Md. 1993.

Chesapeake Bay: Nature of the Estuary, A Field Guide. Christopher P. White. Cornell Maritime, Ithaca, N.Y. 1989.

Chesapeake Reflections: A Journey on a Boat and a Bike. Ken Carter. Amantha Publishing Company, Marathon, Fla. 1991.

Fishes of the Chesapeake Bay. Edward O. Murdy, et al. Smithsonian Books, Washington, D.C. 1997.

Five Fair Rivers: Sailing the James, York, Rappahannock and Patuxent. Robert de Gast. Johns Hopkins University Press, Baltimore 1995.

From Blue Ridge to Barrier Islands: An Audobon Naturalist Reader. Edited by Kent Minichiello and Anthony White. Johns Hopkins University Press, Baltimore 1996.

Hiking, Cycling, and Canoeing in Maryland: A Family Guide. Bryan MacKay. Johns Hopkins University Press, Baltimore 1995.

Leaning Sycamores: Natural Worlds of the Upper Potomac. Jack Wennerstrom. Johns Hopkins University Press, Baltimore 1996.

Life in the Chesapeake Bay. Alice Jane & Robert L. Lippson. Johns Hopkins University Press, Baltimore 1984.

Lodgings Along the Appalachian Trail. (3 volumes: the Mid-Atlantic region; the South; New England). Appalachian Trail Conference, Harpers Ferry, W.Va. 1995.

Maryland Seafood Cookbook (Vols. 1,2,3). Department of Economic and Community Development, Annapolis undated.

Sports Afield Outdoor Skills. Frank S. Golad. Hearst Books, New York, N.Y. 1991.

Susquehanna, River of Dreams. Susan Q. Stranahan. Johns Hopkins University Press, Baltimore 1993.

APPENDIX | further reading

The Amateur Naturalist. Gerald Durrell. Alfred A. Knopf, New York, N.Y. 1986.

The Chesapeake Bay Book: A Complete Guide. Alison Blake. Berkshire House Publishers, Lee, Maine 1996.

The Chesapeake Bay in Maryland: An Atlas of Natural Resources. Alice Jane Lippson. Johns Hopkins University Press, Baltimore 1973.

The L.L. Bean Game and Fish Cookbook. Agnus Cameron & Judith Jones. Random House, New York 1983.

The Lighthouses of the Chesapeake. Robert DeGast. Johns Hopkins University Press, Baltimore 1993.

The National Parks Fishing Guide. Robert Gartner. Globe Pequot, Old Saybrook, Conn. 1995.

The Oyster. William K. Brooks. Johns Hopkins University Press, Baltimore 1996.

The Visual Encyclopedia of Nautical Terms Under Sail. Basil W. Bathe. Crown Publishers, New York 1978.

Wilderness With Children: A Parent's Guide to Fun Family Outings. Michael Hodgson. Stackpole Books, Mechanicsburg, Pa. 1992.

Index

A

American kestrel, 55
Appalachian Mountains, 22—23
Appalachian Trail, 1—2
Assateague Island National Seashore, 2, 52, 103
Assateague State Park, 10
Atlantic Flyway, 51, 147

B

Bald eagle, 54
Baltimore oriole, 58
Bass fishing, 120—125
    fly-fishing for, 123—124
    sites, 122—123
Battle Creek Cypress Swamp Sanctuary, 43
Bears, 1, 64—65
Belted kingfisher, 56
Big Run State Park, 3
Big Spring Quarry, 28
Biking, 195—203
    bicycle hot line, 203
    equipment, 197—198
    map, 204
    resources, 203
    safety, 202—203
    sites, 198—200
Bird-watching, 51—62
    books, 62
    equipment, 61
    etiquette, 62
    field guide, 54—58
    hot line, 53
    map, 60
    organizations, 62
    resources, 62
    sites, 59—61
    snakes, 62—64
Bites, 219
Black bear, 1
Blackwater National Wildlife Refuge, 2, 52, 195
Blue jay, 57
Board sailing, 91
Boating, 67—103
    books, 74
    charts, 68
    Chesapeake Bay cruises, 74—81
    Department of Natural Resources, 67, 68
    equipment, 86—90
    lighthouses, 84
    operations, 88—90
    powerboats, 85—86
    preparation, 73—74
    resources, 74
    safety, 69, 73, 86—90
    sailing, 68—74
    sound signals, 88
    Whitbread Round the World Race, 82—85
Bows, 161
Broken bones, 220
Brownie's Beach, 26
Bruises, 218

C

Calvert Cliffs, 9, 24, 26—27, 183
Calvert Marine Museum, 24—25
Camping, 169
    children, 169—174
    Department of Natural Resources, 175
    equipment, 170—175
    etiquette, 175
    map, 176—177
    Maryland Association of Campgrounds, 175
    preparation, 170
    resources, 175
    safety, 175
    sleeping bags, 171—172
    tents, 171
    U.S. Park Service, 175

INDEX

Canada goose hunting, 147, 151—152, 159
Canoeing, 92—103
   equipment, 97—98
   etiquette, 98
   field guide, 98—103
   resources, 98
   safety, 95—97
Casselman River, 99
Casselman River Bridge State Park, 3
Catoctin Mountain Park, 2, 42, 182—183
Cedar Island Wildlife Management Area, 10—11
Cedar waxwing, 58
Cedarville State Forest, 9
Chesapeake & Ohio Canal, 2—3
Chesapeake & Ohio Canal National Historical Park, 42—43
Chesapeake & Ohio Canal Trail, 182
Chesapeake Bay, 25, 71—73
   cruises, 74—81
   fishing, 129—134
   lighthouses, 84
Children, v—vi
   camping, 169—174
   crabbing, 139—140
   freshwater fishing, 124—125
   saltwater fishing, 138—139
Chimney swift, 56
Choptank River Fishing Pier, 11
Coast Guard Auxiliary, 68
Common nighthawk, 55
Crabbing, 139—140
Cranesville Swamp, 42
Cross country skiing, 212
   books and magazines, 216—217
   equipment, 213—215
   resources, 216—217
   safety, 215—216
   sites, 212
Crystal Grottoes, 21
Cunningham Falls State Park, 3
Cycle Across Maryland, 196, 198—199
Cylburn Arboretum, 43

D

Dans Mountain State Park, 3
Deal Island Wildlife Management Area, 11
Deep Creek Lake State Park, 3
Deer, 64
Deer hunting, 147, 148—150
   limits, 157
   season, 157—158
Delmarva Birding Weekend, 53
Dental emergency, 220
Department of Natural Resources, 1, 225
   camping, 175
   fishing, 106
   hunting, 148
Dierssen Wildlife Management Area, 6
Dinosaurs, 23—24, 30
Dislocations, 220
Downhill skiing, 209—211
   books and magazines, 216—217
   equipment, 213—215
   resources, 216—217
   safety, 215—216
Downy woodpecker, 56
Duck hunting, 147, 152
   limits, 159
   season, 159

E

Eastern bluebird, 57
Eastern Continental Divide, 36—38
Eastern Neck Island National Wildlife Refuge, 3, 101—102
Eastern screech owl, 55
Elk Neck State Forest, 6
Emergency first aid, 218—221

INDEX

F

Fair Hill Natural Resources Management Area, 6
Federal parks, 1—3
First-aid kit, 218
Fishing, 105—145
    Chesapeake Bay, 129—134
    Department of Natural Resources, 106
    free tidal fishing areas, 134
    map, 108
Fishing Bay Wildlife Management Area, 11
Flag Ponds Nature Park, 43
Flora, 35—45
    best sites, 42—43
    equipment, 44
    etiquette, 44
    field guide, 39
    maps, 46
    organizations, 45
    resources, 44—45
Food
    backpacking food safety, 223—224
    cooler rules, 222
    drinking water, 224
    finfish, 223
    food contamination, 223
    meat, 222—223
    packing and transporting, 222
    safety, 222—224
    shellfish, 223
Forest game, 154—155, 160—161
Fort Frederick State Park, 3—4
Fossils, 22, 23, 24—25
    best sites, 26—29
    books and guides, 30—31
    equipment, 30
    etiquette, 29
    field guide, 25—31
    organizations, 31
    resources, 30—31
Foxes, 64
Fractures, 220
Freshwater fishing, 124—127
    with children, 124—125
Fringed gentian, 38, 43

G

Gambrill State Park, 4
Garrett State Park, 4
Gathland State Park, 4—5
Geology, 19—31
    maps, 20, 32
    minerals, 33
Great blue heron, 54
Great Falls, 36
Great Falls Tavern Visitors Center, 42—43
Green Ridge State Forest, 5, 42
Greenbelt Park, 3
Greenbriar, 5
Greenwell State Park, 9
Groundhogs, 65
Gunpowder Falls, 7, 100—101
Gwynnbrook Wildlife Management Area, 7

H

Hart-Miller Island State Park, 7—8
Head injuries, 221
Henson Creek, 29
Herrington Manor State Park, 5
Hiking, 179—192, 180—183, 193. See also Volksmarch parks, 1
    resources, 184
    safety, 183
Hoye Crest on Backbone Mountain, 181
Hunting, 147—167
    books, 165
    Department of Natural Resources, 148
    equipment, 162—164
    hunting permits, 165
    licenses, 155—156
    limits, 157—161

resources, 164—165
rules, 155—156
safety, 156, 161
seasons, 157—161

I

Indian Springs Wildlife
  Management Area, 5
Insect stings, 219
Irvine Natural Science
  Center, 43
Isle of Wight Wildlife
  Management Area,
  11—12

J

Janes Island State Park, 12
Jet Skis, 91, 92
Jug Bay Wetlands Sanctuary,
  36, 43

K

Kayaking, 92—103
  equipment, 97—98
  etiquette, 98
  field guide, 98—103
  resources, 98
  safety, 95—97

L

Lighthouses
  of Chesapeake Bay, 84
Limestone, 21

M

Martinak State Park, 12
Maryland Association of
  Campgrounds, 175
Matoaka cottages, 26

Merkle Wildlife Sanctuary,
  9—10
Metamorphic rock, 19
Millington Wildlife Manage
  ment Area, 12
Morgan Run Wildlife
  Management Area, 8
Mountain biking, 196—197
  bicycle hot line, 203
  etiquette, 200—201
  resources, 203
  safety, 202—203
  sites, 199—200
Mt. Nebo Wildlife Manage
  ment Area, 5
Muskrats, 65
Muzzleloader hunting, 150,
  162—163, 165
  safety, 161
  season, 157—158

N

Nassawango Creek,
  Pocomoke River, 102—103
National Park Service, 1
Native plants, 35—45
  best sites, 42—43
  equipment, 44
  etiquette, 44
  field guide, 39
  maps, 46
  organizations, 45
  resources, 44—45
New Germany State Park,
  5, 42
Nodding trillium, 38
North Point State Park, 8
Northern cardinal, 58

O

Opossums, 65
Osprey, 54
Outdoors organizations,
  225-227

INDEX

233

INDEX

P

Parks, 1—13. See also
 Specific park
 amenities charts, 14—15
 maps, 16—17
 trash-free policy, 13
Patapsco State Park, 8, 38
Patuxent River, 100
Patuxent River State Park, 8
Personal watercraft, 91—92
Piscataway Creek, 28—29
Pocomoke River State
 Forest and Park, 12—13, 43
Point Lookout State Park, 10
Poisonous plants, 220
Potomac River, 99—100
Potomac State Forest, 5
Purce State Park, 28

R

Raccoons, 65
Rifle, 162
 safety, 161
Rock climbing, sites, 184
Rockfish, 129—130
Rocks State Park, 8
Rocky Gap State Forest, 5
Rosaryville State Park, 10
Ruby-throated humming
 bird, 56

S

Safety, 218—221
 food, 222—224
Salamanders, 65
Saltwater fish, 135—137
Saltwater fishing, 140—145
 books, 144—145
 with children, 138—139
 equipment, 144
 resources, 144
Sassafras River, 101
Savage River State Forest,
 5—6, 181—182
Scarlet tanager, 58
Seneca Creek State
 Park, 8
Shotgun, 162
 safety, 161
Sideling Hill, 22—23
Sideling Hill Wildlife
 Management Area, 6
Ski Liberty, 210
Ski Roundtop, 210—211
Skiing, 207—217
 books and magazines,
 216—217
 equipment, 213—215
 resources, 216—217
 safety, 215—216
 sites, 209—211
Smallwood State Park, 10
Snakes, 62—64
Snowboarding, 211—212
 books and magazines,
 216—217
 equipment, 214—215
 resources, 216—217
 safety, 215—216
Snyders Landing, 42
Soldier's Delight Natural
 Environment Area, 8, 38, 43
South Mountain, 180—181
South Mountain State
 Park, 6
Splinters, 220
Sprains, 219
Squirrels, 64
St. Clement's Island
 State Park, 10
St. Mary's River State
 Park, 10
State Forest and Park
 Service, 1
State parks, 3—13
 central parks, 6—9
 eastern parks, 10—13
 southern parks, 9—10
 western parks, 3—6
Sugarloaf Mountain, 180
Susquehanna State Park,
 8—9, 43
Swallow Falls State
 Park, 6

T

Taylor's Island Wildlife Management Area, 13
Ticks, 219
Trout fishing, 106—119
    equipment, 110—112
    matching fly hatches, 113—119
    resources, 113
    seasons, 106—107
    sites, 109—110
Tuckahoe State Park, 13
Tufted titmouse, 57
Turtles, 65

U

Upland hunting, 155
    limit, 159—160
    season, 159—160
U.S. Park Service, camping, 175
U.S. Power Squadron, 68

V

Volksmarch, 86—188

W

Walking, 184—186. See also Hiking; Volksmarch
    equipment, 188—191
Warrior Mountain Wildlife Management Area, 6
Washington Monument State Park, 6
Water skiing, 90—91
Waterfowl hunting, 151—153
    limit, 159
    season, 159
Webless migratory bird hunting, 155, 160
Wheeler Road, 29
White-breasted nuthatch, 57
Whitetail, 211
Wild turkey, 55
Wild turkey hunting, 154—155, 160—161
Wildflowers, 35—45
    best sites, 42—43
    equipment, 44
    etiquette, 44
    field guide, 39
    maps, 46
    organizations, 45
    resources, 44—45
Wildlife, 62—65. See also Bird-watching
    endangered species, 65
Wisp Ski Area, 207—210
Wood duck, 54
Wye Oak State Park, 13
Wye River, 102

Y

Youghiogheny River, 98—99

STATE OF MARYLAND